PRAYER

BOOKS BY PHILIP ZALESKI AND CAROL ZALESKI

Philip Zaleski

THE BEST AMERICAN SPIRITUAL WRITING 2004–2005

THE BEST SPIRITUAL WRITING 1998–2002

THE RECOLLECTED HEART

THE BOOK OF HEAVEN [WITH CAROL ZALESKI]

Carol Zaleski

OTHERWORLD JOURNEYS

THE LIFE OF THE WORLD TO COME

THE BOOK OF HEAVEN [WITH PHILIP ZALESKI]

PRAYER

A HISTORY

Philip Zaleski & Carol Zaleski

HOUGHTON MIFFLIN COMPANY
BOSTON · NEW YORK
2005

Visit our Web site: www.houghtonmifflinbooks.com.

Library of Congress Cataloging-in-Publication Data
Zaleski, Philip.
Prayer : a history / Philip Zaleski and Carol Zaleski.
p. cm.
Includes bibliographical references and index.
ISBN-13: 978-0-618-15288-9
ISBN-10: 0-618-15288-1
1. Prayer. I. Zaleski, Carol. II. Title.
BL560.Z35 2005 204'.3'09—dc22 2005012990

PRINTED IN THE UNITED STATES OF AMERICA

Book design by Robert Overholtzer

EB 10 9 8 7 6 5 4 3 2 1

TO OUR CHILDREN

— More things are wrought by prayer
Than this world dreams of.

—ALFRED, LORD TENNYSON
Idylls of the King

As Iron at a Distance is drawn by the Loadstone, there being some Invisible Communications between them: So is there in us a World of Lov to somwhat, tho we know not what in the World that should be. There are Invisible Ways of Conveyance by which some Great Thing doth touch our souls, and by which we tend to it. Do you not feel yourself Drawn with the Expectation and Desire of som Great Thing?

—THOMAS TRAHERNE
Centuries

Pray as you can, not as you can't.

—JOHN CHAPMAN

Acknowledgments

WE ARE GRATEFUL first of all to Anton Mueller of Houghton Mifflin, who suggested this project, provided counsel and support along the way, and improved the text with his splendid editing, and to Erica Avery and everyone else at Houghton Mifflin. In addition, we would like to express our thanks for help rendered by the Right Reverend Anselm Atkinson, O.S.B.; Christopher Bamford; Jeremy Black; Léonie and Stratford Caldecott; John Champoux; the Very Reverend Giles Conacher, O.S.B.; Bruce Dahlberg; Andrew and Susan DeLisle; Karl Donfried; Lois Dubin; Daniel Gardner; the Right Reverend Hugh Gilbert, O.S.B.; Peter Gregory; Jamie Hubbard; Dennis Hudson; Will Johnston; Joel Kaminsky; the Reverend Bede Kierney, O.S.B.; Lorraine Kisly; Dechen and Eileen Latshang; the Reverend Daniel P. Liston; Richard Millington; Claire Renkin; Andy Rotman; Vera Shevzov; Jean Sulzberger; Ptolemy Tompkins; and the Very Reverend Mother Mary Clare Vincent, O.S.B. A special thanks to the circulation, interlibrary loan, and reference staff at Neilson Library, Smith College, for their kind attention and selfless assistance, and to our research assistants Donna Ingalls, Mary Helen Kennerly, and John Zaleski for their superb endeavors. Many thanks, too, to Kim Witherspoon, David Forrer, and everyone at InkWell Management for being such wonderful agents. Finally, as always, our deepest thanks to John and Andy.

Contents

Illustrations

PAGE

PART I

God's Breath

CHAPTER 1

The Foundations of Prayer

THE STORY OF PRAYER is the story of the impossible: of how we creatures of flesh and blood lay siege to heaven, speak to the Maker of all things, and await, with confidence or hopeful skepticism, a response. The story of prayer, like that of all treasure sought through the centuries, is rich in myth and dream, revelation and tragedy, secret maps and elusive clues. Here the absurd and the sublime sit side by side, while the fantastic and the banal merge. Consider the following:

A dear friend of ours, a native Tibetan, returned last month from a visit to his homeland in the high plateau region of Gelok, far east of Lhasa. Dechen arrived in Massachusetts haggard but smiling, red Tibetan mud still clinging to his yellow Gore-Tex jacket, bearing with him harrowing tales of vicious customs officials, of torrential rains and deadly mudslides, of uncharted mountain passes and hidden valleys thick with wildflowers. At a welcome-home dinner, he and his wife set up a projector, and we spent the next few hours poring over his slides. Everyone marveled at the herds of Tibetan yaks, their shaggy coats and gracile horns so reminiscent of the prehistoric beasts in the Lascaux caves; at the crowds of Buddhist monks lighting bonfires or blowing impossibly long horns, looking for all the world like Lascaux shepherds transported to a Himalayan castle in the clouds. This was the Tibet of legend, far from the tourist hotels of Dharamsala, an area until recently forbidden to outsiders and still unvisited by television, pollution, and indoor plumbing. Bringing out an atlas, we asked Dechen to trace his journey. His finger landed on a bare white area as large as Massachusetts, a true terra incognita at the dawn of the third millennium. It reminded us of Victorian maps of sub-Saharan Africa, of ancient mariners sailing off the edge of the world. "No one goes there," Dechen said. "Too difficult. Too far." No one, that is, except a handful of Chinese soldiers and bureaucrats, who have done their best over the past quarter of a century to suppress one of the world's great religions. Only in the past few years have the monasteries been rebuilt in a curious Sino-Tibetan architectural idiom whose bright pastels and wedding-cake façades threaten to create a new form of Buddhist kitsch.

One photograph in particular caught our fancy, for it seemed to capture best the spirit of these eastern Tibetans. It depicted a wooden framework, looming above the tallest monk (and the Tibetans are a tall people), and consisting of two massive uprights of rough-hewn lumber supporting four long crossbars. Upon each crossbar stood nine or ten prayer wheels, each containing a bit of paper inscribed with the traditional Buddhist prayer *oṃ maṇi padme hūm* (Hail to the Jewel in the Lotus). As the wind blows down the mountainside, each wheel spins madly, and the mantra is flung into the universe like a message in a bottle, drifting on celestial currents until it reaches its heavenly destination. Of what, we asked, were these glistening wheels made? At a glance they seemed carved from crystal or jade, or were they globes of delicate blown glass? "Oh, no," Dechen explained, refocusing the slide projector for a better look: the wheels were nothing more than cast-off plastic Pepsi-Cola bottles.

This Tibetan fantasia is a portal into a number of truths about the world of prayer: that wherever one finds humans, one finds humans at prayer; that in times of persecution, prayer goes underground, where it continues to wend its course into the depths of the soul; and that any and all objects — Pepsi-Cola bottles as surely as enameled statues, jeweled rosaries, or silvered icons — can be a means of prayer. These jerry-built praying devices demonstrate, too, that technology and prayer — that is to say, applied science and applied religion — need not war with one another. The same evening, Dechen's wife brought out for our inspection an array of homemade prayer wheels: one turned by hand, a second by wind, and a third — a particularly cunning device in the form of a lampshade — spun in convection currents emitted by the heat of a hundred-watt light bulb. The Dalai Lama is on record as approving an even more technically advanced method for making a prayer wheel: download the *oṃ maṇi padme hūm* mantra to your computer's hard drive, where it will spin at a rate of some fifty-four hundred rotations per minute, calling forth the blessings of Avalokiteśvara, the bodhisattva of compassion, as effectively as do the older technologies of prayer.

Dechen's videotapes, which we watched after the slides, demonstrated a yet larger truth about prayer: that it alters the face of the world, revealing unnoticed harmonies and symmetries and knitting together the natural and social dimensions of our existence. As the souvenir footage unreeled, we saw prayer wheels spinning in the sun, bees looping and swirling around those wheels, the sun melting into night as the monks' voices faded into the mountains, all seemingly one motion, one symphony, one grand universal gesture of prayer. Viewed from a perspective that we may call religious but that in truth seems synonymous with human consciousness, it appeared, for just a moment, as if the entire world was collaborating in prayer.

There is, as Dechen's adventure suggests, nothing strange about prayer erupting in the oddest of circumstances. We might even say that it thrives on paradox. Consider this: that prayer deals in eternal truth and yet has its fads and fashions: a hundred years ago, revival tents sprang up from coast to coast to house the inspired preaching of Christian witnesses who passed the torch of the Second Great Awakening to twentieth-century evangelicalism; fifty years ago, FDR led the nation in prayer through the static-charged speakers of a million Sylvania radios; twenty-five years ago, school days often began with a silent meditation; now, at the beginning of the third millennium, football fields and corporate boardrooms have been favored arenas of prayer. Or this: that we pray for worldly goods but also pray for freedom from the desire for worldly goods. Or this: that we seldom pray for prayer itself. Who but a saint prays for better prayer or, God forbid, for more time to pray?

What, then, is this paradoxical action that we call prayer? Ask a team of scholars that question and expect a confusion of tongues in response. You may even hear a curse, for what is "God damn it!" but a perverse petition to the Almighty? But sooner or later our learned company will arrive at something like this: *prayer is action that communicates between human and divine realms.*

That is to say: Prayer is speech, but much richer than speech alone. It is a peculiar kind of speech that acts, and a peculiar kind of action that speaks to the depths and heights of being. Much of the time, prayer seems to be nothing but talk: praising, cajoling, or pleading with God; sending messages to guardian angels or tutelary spirits; appealing to benevolent cosmic powers. But to pray is also to act. Think of what happens when a child recites her nighttime prayer:

> Now I lay me down to sleep,
> I pray the Lord my soul to keep.

If I should die before I wake,
I pray the Lord my soul to take.

This prayer constitutes more than a sweet set of words. It sets events in motion; it puts God and the angels on alert. It affects the child, too, body and soul; anyone who has recited bedtime prayers as a child knows their value as a guarantor of a night's sound sleep.

Prayer is at once spiritual and visceral: it stems from heart and gut as well as head. Prayer is a state of being — when we pray, we are "in prayer," and when we communicate with spiritual beings, we are "in communion" with them — but prayer is also emphatically a state of becoming, a dynamic movement, an incursion into spiritual realms: in the Trappist monk Thomas Merton's words, "a raid on the unspeakable." Prayer has been compared to a siege, a storm, a conflagration, a nosegay, a picnic in paradise. We may also liken it to an athletic event, such as the hurling of a javelin: a shaft of praise, petition, or penance aimed at a higher power. Like the javelin thrower, those who pray must be fit: "Whoso will pray, he must fast and be clean / And fat his soul, and make his body lean" (Geoffrey Chaucer, "The Somnour's Tale"). And those who pray must try their hardest, so that prayer can make them fit: "That prayer has great power which a person makes with all his might. It makes a sour heart sweet, a sad heart merry, a poor heart rich, a foolish heart wise, a timid heart brave, a sick heart well, a blind heart full of sight, a cold heart ardent" (Mechtild of Magdeburg, *Revelations*).[1]

Conventional wisdom divides prayer into a number of categories: petition, confession, adoration, sacrifice, intercession, contemplation, thanksgiving, vows, and so on. But these classifications disguise the complexity of the world of prayer. Consider an archetypal prayer of petition, one so commonplace that it has been lampooned in countless cartoons and comic strips: a plea to God to change the weather. What could be more simple and straightforward? But let us examine the evidence:

Among the Papago (Tohono O'odham) of the American Southwest, rainmaking lies at the heart of ritual life. These Indians inhabit a landscape of sagebrush and lava rock, dry mesas and desert valleys; without the downpours of the rainy season, crops would wither and famine ensue. To ensure an annual harvest, each year the people gather to "sing down the rain." Much of what scholars know about this seemingly quixotic practice comes from Ruth Murray Underhill (1884–1984), an anthropologist from Columbia University who lived among the Papago in the 1930s and later wrote a number of classic studies of American Indians, including *Papago Woman*, the first published life of a Southwestern Indian woman. Underhill was a special kind of researcher, more passionate participant than dispassionate observer: "I met these hard-working but poetic Papagos," she writes, "and fell permanently in love with them."[2] Her description of the Papago as poetic is more than anthropological romanticism; poetry for these Indians is a matter of life or death because through their verse they bring down the rain. Each year in an act of communal supplication they sing:

Come together!

You shall see this thing which we have always done
And what must truly happen.
Because we have planned it thus and thus have done.
Right soon, indeed, it will happen.
It will rain.
The fields will be watered.
Therein we shall drop the seed.
Seed which bears corn of all colors;
Seed which grows big.
Thus we shall do.
Thereby we shall feed ourselves;
Thereby our stomachs shall grow big;
Thereby we shall live.[3]

Such prayer songs bring the Papago into union with I'itoi, First Brother, who prepared the world for people at the beginning of time and who is instrumental in bringing the rain. But chant alone is insufficient. Each year Papago women also collect the red, pear-shaped fruit of the giant cactus *Cereus giganteus* and ferment it into a jellylike wine (Underhill says that it tastes "like spoiled raspberry jam"), which is consumed in a community *tahiwua k-ii* (Sit-and-drink) that along with singing ensures the coming of the rain. This is action by analogy: as the people are filled with liquor, so will the earth fill with rain. An elder calls:

Hurry! Hither bring, each of you, his syrup.
Soon we shall make liquor!
Soon it will ferment,
Soon we shall drink,
Soon it will rain.[4]

The people sing:

Now here you have assembled;
Now thus we shall do!
With our singing we shall pull down the rain.[5]

Sure enough: within a few days of the Sit-and-drink witnessed by Underhill, the skies opened and the drenching rains of July descended. "The clouds come because we call them," explained a Papago, "and we call them with the drinking." The rainmaking ritual ensures not only the watering of crops but also the stability of the world. Ofelia Zepeda, a Papago linguist, recalls her mother's belief that if the ceremony were to be neglected or the prayers forgotten, the world "will ruin itself." Alas, in these amnesiac times aspects of the rite have been discarded or lost, but the prayers, at least for the moment, remain. "As a result," Zepeda comments dryly, "the world is somewhat intact today."[6]

Let us contrast this example of traditional rainmaking with a more urbane tale of weather manipulation set in the waning months of World War II. It is December 1944: the U.S. Third Army surges toward the Rhine. But General George S. Patton Jr. is troubled, for a drenching rain, with no sign of letup, threatens his brilliant advance. On December 14, he summons to his office deputy chief of staff Colonel Paul D. Hawkins and Chaplain O'Neill of the Third Army. The following conversation ensues:

General Patton: Chaplain, I want you to publish a prayer for good weather. I'm tired of these soldiers having to fight mud and floods as well as Germans. See if we can't get God to work on our side.

Chaplain O'Neill: Sir, it's going to take a pretty thick rug for that kind of praying.

General Patton: I don't care if it takes the flying carpet. I want the praying done.

Chaplain O'Neill: Yes, sir. May I say, General, that it usually isn't a customary thing among men of my profession to pray for clear weather to kill fellow men.

General Patton: Chaplain, are you teaching me theology or are you the Chaplain of the Third Army? I want a prayer.

Chaplain O'Neill: Yes, sir.[7]

According to Hawkins, who annotated Patton's blustery 1947 memoir, *War as I Knew It,* the general got his wish. The following prayer was printed and distributed to every soldier in the U.S. Third Army:

> Almighty and most merciful Father, we humbly beseech Thee, of Thy great goodness, to restrain these immoderate rains with which we have had to contend. Grant us fair weather for Battle. Graciously hearken to us as soldiers who call upon Thee that, armed with Thy power, we may advance from victory to victory, and crush the oppression and wickedness of our enemies, and establish Thy justice among men and nations. Amen.[8]

The skies cleared within twenty-four hours. A week of perfect weather ensued, allowing the Allies to advance toward the Rhine. Patton was ecstatic. Summoning Hawkins to his office, he declared, "God damn! Look at the weather. That O'Neill sure did some potent praying. Get him up here. I want to pin a medal on him." The next day, the somewhat abashed Chaplain O'Neill received the Bronze Star.[9]

Both Patton and the Papago prayed to change the weather, but there the similarities end. Patton made his prayer to the biblical God, while the Papago, in Underhill's words, "call upon the powers of Nature." Patton's prayer was composed on the spot by a harassed army chaplain, whereas Papago prayers originate with I'itoi, a supernatural being. Patton's was a prayer for victory and thus indirectly for death to the opposition ("to crush the . . . wickedness of our enemies"), whereas the Papago sing for the life of the corn and thus of the people. Most important, Papago prayer unfolds within a traditional culture steeped in daily intercourse between natural and supernatural realms, one that affirms, beyond any doubt, that "singing down the rain" accomplishes just what it claims to do. Patton, by contrast, issued his prayer amidst the crumbling monuments of Christendom. His petition swims with irony. The general was a devout Christian, and there seems no reason to doubt that he believed God could and perhaps would stop the rain. He was, however, also a canny man, surely aware that in modern times the notion of altering the weather through prayer has about it a touch of the absurd. One suspects that Patton relished this chance to prove his cultural recidivism; this tension between his action and the prevailing skepticism of the age gives the anecdote its humor. Hawkins confesses as much, writing of Patton's spiritual coup that "whether it was the help of the Divine guidance asked for in the prayer or just the normal course of human events, we never knew."[10]

Nor do the complexities of weather making cease here. For while the Papago know beyond all doubt that their prayers work, this knowledge may be rather more subtle than it at first seems. Ludwig Wittgenstein writes in *Remarks on Frazer's Golden Bough* that "I read . . . of a rain-king in Africa to whom the people appeal for rain *when the rainy season comes.* But surely this means that they do not actually think he can make rain, otherwise they would do it in the dry periods when the land is 'a parched and arid desert.'"[11] In light of this observation, it is instructive to ponder the following conversation reported by Underhill:

> "My kinsmen, the wine has fermented," the *makai* said. "Go home. Prepare the feast, for in four days the rain will come."

> I asked later about that prophecy and whether it was always fulfilled.
>
> "Oh yes, yes," was the usual answer and Old Salt made me understand: "The medicine man, he is wise. Maybe the rain come soon and he says, 'yes, but I counted from when the wagons arrived,' or it come late and then, 'I meant four days *after* the wine had fermented.'"[12]

As the above meteorological invocations suggest, prayer entails a multitude of forms and a multiplicity of aims. A recovering alcoholic reciting the Serenity Prayer, a Catholic nun telling her beads, a child crossing himself before a meal, a quaking Shaker, a meditating yogini, a Huichol Indian chewing a peyote button, a Zen monk in satori, a Lubavitcher dancing with the Torah, Saint Francis receiving the stigmata, a bookie crossing his fingers before the final race, Ebenezer Scrooge pleading for just one more chance, dear God, just one more chance: all this is the world of prayer. In this world one may sit, stand, run, kneel, fall prostrate, dance, faint, or whirl in imitation of the cosmic spheres. One may chant, sing, shout, mutter, groan, or keep silent. One may make use of nuts, beads, books, flags, wheels, shells, stones, drums, idols, icons, jewels, incense, flowers, blood, and fruit, for all these belong to the armamentarium of prayer.

Prayer craves ritual expression, and ritual practice virtually always includes prayer; for ritual is the sacred theater in which unfold crucial events, such as blessing of the harvest and initiation into new stages of life from birth to death, whose successful outcome depends on an appeal to divine powers. If prayer is, as the nineteenth-century Russian mystic John of Cronstadt puts it, "the breath of the soul, our spiritual food and drink," then it is ritual that provides the body language and sets the table for the feast. Even the psalmist's spontaneous cri de coeur "Out of the depths, I cry to thee, O Lord" (Psalm 130:1, KJV) avails itself of formulaic words and ritualistic gestures such as kneeling, prostration, and beating of the breast. This intimate kinship between prayer and ritual leads to the inevitable chicken-and-egg question, "Which came first?" Did humans discover prayer and then develop ritual as a means to tame its energies, creating well-worn furrows for the masses to follow? Or did ritual come first and give birth to prayer, in the way that speech gives birth to thought? We have no final answer to these conundrums, although throughout this book we describe various ways in which people have tried to resolve them. This much is clear: *to participate in ritual is to enter the world of prayer, and to make a habit of prayer is to open the door to ritual.*

Prayer encompasses heaven and earth; it tangles angels, paramecia, and humans in its cosmic web. Prayer can be brief — "short prayers penetrate heaven," says the anonymous author of the mystical classic *The Cloud of Unknowing,* who recommends the one-syllable exclamation "God!" as the ideal prayer. Or prayers can be long, stretching for months on end, interrupted only by essential needs of the body, as in the lives of some religious ascetics. Prayer can take place alone or in a vast fellowship, on the deathbed, or in the wedding chamber. Prayer's scope extends from the private ceremonies of the morning toilet to the public arenas of politics and war. Prayer can be a matter of high aesthetics, as in T. S. Eliot's *Four Quartets,* or of low humor, as in Apuleius's brayings in *The Golden Ass.* Prayer can also be a matter of spiritual surrender, as French philosopher Simone Weil reveals in one of her letters to Father Perrin: "In 1937 I had two marvelous days at Assisi. There, alone in the little twelfth-century Romanesque chapel of Santa Maria degli Angeli, an incomparable marvel of purity where Saint Francis often used to pray, something stronger than I was compelled me for the first time in my life to go down on my knees."[13]

One may be seized by prayer, as happened to the apostles on Pentecost, or one may lust after prayer, like some of the Vīraśaiva saints of medieval India, or one may resist prayer with all one's might and yet pray nonetheless with all one's might, as famously happens to the atheist in the foxhole. Prayer may lead one to God, or it may convince one of God's absence. Prayer can bless or prayer can bite ("When the gods wish to punish us they answer our prayers," says Oscar Wilde). Prayer may help one to quit alcohol, stay off drugs, or become a better parent. Prayer may cure an incurable illness or save an unsalvageable marriage. Prayer works miracles, not least in the one who prays (Søren Kierkegaard: "Prayer does not change God but it changes him who prays"). For those who have contemplated the subject, prayer is a cosmos whose center is everywhere, in every human heart, and whose circumference is nowhere, in the infinity of God. Something of the limitless universe of prayer shines brightly through a Christian lens in the following celebrated poem by George Herbert (1593–1633):

Prayer

Prayer the church's banquet, angel's age,
God's breath in man returning to his birth,
The soul in paraphrase, heart in pilgrimage,
The Christian plummet sounding heav'n and earth
Engine against th' Almighty, sinner's tow'r,
Reversed thunder, Christ-side-piercing spear,

The six-days world transposing in an hour,
A kind of tune, which all things hear and fear;
Softness, and peace, and joy, and love, and bliss,
Exalted manna, gladness of the best,
Heaven in ordinary, man well drest,
The milky way, the bird of Paradise,
Church-bells beyond the stars heard, the soul's blood,
The land of spices; something understood.

Banquet, age, breath, soul, plummet, engine, thunder, spear, world, tune, manna, heaven, man, milky way, bird of Paradise, church-bells, blood, land of spices: this torrent of concrete nouns reveals prayer's depth and breadth. Herbert's litany contains images of feasting, warfare, art, religion, agriculture, and industry, which leads to another important truth about our subject: *prayer lies at the heart of culture.* In traditional societies, every significant action begins with prayer. A devout Muslim says *bismillāh* ("In the Name of Allāh"), or more completely, *bismi-Llāhi-r-Raḥmāni-r-Raḥīm* ("In the Name of Allah, Most Gracious, Most Merciful," the opening words of the Qur'ān), before baking bread, negotiating a contract, or starting out on a journey. A Christian may cross himself before eating, swimming, or retiring for the night. In parts of Europe, the Angelus bell still rings from church towers at dawn, noon, and dusk, punctuating the day as decisively as the call of the muezzin in any Muslim village, and the faithful stop in their tracks to recite the angel's greeting to the Virgin Mary and echo her glad response.

The world's oldest urban cultures grew up around buildings that were essentially cultic centers dedicated to sacrifice, propitiation, and prayer: thus Uruk, the ancient city of Gilgamesh, whose brick ramparts were built for the goddess Ishtar and whose center was her sanctuary; Angkor Wat in Cambodia and Borobuḍur in Java, sites of colossal Buddhist stupas that were hubs of temporal and spiritual power; and Jerusalem, whose Temple once seemed the very navel of the earth and whose destruction was the exile of God. Look at any major ancient ruin, and you will see the remains of a people at prayer and the signs of an economy that traded in prayer. All art was originally sacred art — in effect, visual prayer; all drama was originally sacred drama, telling the deeds of the gods in order to win their assistance. Much of the productive work of the world has been instigated and hallowed by prayer. Even today, prayers may accompany as well as initiate our labors: thus the workers' chants given a secular gloss in the "Heigh Ho" of Walt Disney's seven dwarves but still sung in more authentic manner in India, as historian of religion

A priest in prayer before Marduk, chief god of Babylon, and Nabu, god of wisdom and writing. Neo-Babylonian round seal, blue clay, seventh to sixth centuries B.C.E.

Wilfred Cantwell Smith reported in a national radio talk on the Canadian Broadcasting Corporation in 1962:

> I remember a scene in India some years ago when my wife and I were one summer at a mountain resort in the Himalayas, and were out for a hike in the hills; we came upon a work-gang busy in the construction of a rude mountain road. It was, of course, all hand labor; they had crushed the stones with hammers, and were now rolling them with a large and very heavy roller. Rather in the fashion of sailors working to a sea shanty, they were rhythmically pulling this heavy roller in spurts of concerted effort: the foreman would sing out *La ilaha illa 'llah* [There is no God but God], and the rest of the gang, then, would put their shoulders to the

> ropes and with a heave would respond *Muhammadur rasulu 'llah* [Muhammad is the Prophet of God]. This went on and on, as they continued to work, with a will and with good strong heaves. *La ilaha illa 'llah* he would chant; *Muhammadur rasulu 'llah* would come the vigorous response. Such a scene represents, of course, a kind of living in which a split into religious and secular had not come — or had not yet come — to segment life.[14]

If prayer lies at the heart of culture, then it stands to reason that the dominant prayers of a society will reveal to us its preeminent values. Consider, for example, the way that the ethos of Zen meditation permeates Japanese culture, giving rise to characteristic forms of architecture, landscape, interior design, poetry, calligraphy, martial arts, and rules of social etiquette.

> Old pond
> A frog leaps in
> Plash!

With these three lines, the seventeenth-century poet Matsuo Bashō created a new style of *haiku,* indeed a complete aesthetic, that cannot be understood without an appreciation of Buddhist meditative prayer. The special genius of Bashō's verse lies in its ability to fuse Buddhist teachings on transience and "suchness" with the indigenous Japanese love of nature, finding material for prayerful contemplation in the leap of a frog, the fall of a cherry blossom, or the sound of a horse urinating against a rock.

We can detect similarly rich cultural meaning in the ritual prayer *(ṣalāt)* of Islam. Five times a day, all Muslims are expected to turn their faces in prayer toward the shrine of the holy Kaʿbah in Mecca. What better way to express the belief that the only secure foundation for human community is reverent submission to the oneness of God? When prayer is performed congregationally in the mosque, the sense of unanimity in adoration is palpable, as worshipers line up to perform the intricately choreographed series of *rạkʿahs* (prostrations and Qur'ānic recitations) under the direction of the Imām. In the context of the annual pilgrimage to the holy city of Mecca, the centripetal force of this prayer can be overpowering. So Malcolm X discovered when he made his first pilgrimage to Mecca, as he testifies in this letter to his followers back in Harlem:

> Never have I witnessed such sincere hospitality and overwhelming spirit of true brotherhood as is practiced by people of all colors and races here

> in this ancient Holy Land, the home of Abraham, Muhammad and all the other Prophets of the Holy Scriptures. For the past week, I have been utterly speechless and spellbound by the graciousness I see displayed all around me by people of all colors.
>
> I have been blessed to visit the Holy City of Mecca, I have made my seven circuits around the Ka'ba, led by a young Mutawaf named Muhammed, I drank water from the well of the Zam Zam, I ran seven times back and forth between the hills of Mt. Al-Safa and Al Marwah. I have prayed in the ancient city of Mina, and I have prayed on Mt. Arafat.
>
> During the past eleven days here in the Muslim world, I have eaten from the same plate, drunk from the same glass, and slept on the same rug — while praying to the same God — with fellow Muslims, whose eyes were the bluest of blue, whose hair was the blondest of blond, and whose skin was the whitest of white. . . . We were truly all the same (brothers) — because their belief in one God had removed the white from their minds, the white from their behavior, and the white from their attitude.[15]

Prayers have this diagnostic value: they present in microcosm the longings, beliefs, ideals, and assumptions that drive the inner life of individuals and the corporate life of human cultures. In prayer, the dreams of a civilization take lucid and articulate form. The evidence cannot tell us whether there is an instinct to pray inscribed in our biological nature, but there are grounds for suspecting that prayer is as universal as language and as old as any other cultural artifact. To investigate this possibility, let us trace prayer to its prehistoric roots.

The Prehistoric Origins of Prayer

Who was the first human being to pray? Perhaps he or she was a member of *Homo habilis,* the first truly human species, who roamed the gorges and plains of sub-Saharan Africa about two million years ago, or perhaps a member of *Homo erectus* (1.6 million–300,000 B.C.E.), *Homo habilis*'s immediate descendants, who spread across half the globe, from the eastern plains of Asia to the valleys of northern Europe. It seems quite possible that one of these species discovered prayer, with the odds favoring *Homo erectus,* who boasted an average cranial capacity of a thousand cubic centimeters, almost certainly large enough to accommodate the symbolic thought that prayer requires. The archaeological record remains far too sketchy, however, for anthropologists to draw reliable conclusions. For the first tangible, if circumstantial, evidence of prayer, we must turn to our burly cousins, the Neanderthals of the Middle Paleolithic (200,000–30,000 B.C.E.).

The image of the Neanderthal has changed dramatically since 1856, when the first cache of fossils — part of a skull, ribs, assorted limb bones — was unearthed in the Neander Valley of Germany. At the time, physical anthropology was in its infancy. Scholars of the day, reacting to the long, low braincase, heavy brow ridge, and thick, squat thighbones of the remains, described the Neanderthal as brutish, hulking, and almost subhuman. During the past century and a half, however, the scientific consensus has shifted. We now know that despite its flattened cranium, the Neanderthal braincase was in fact impressively large, averaging 1,450–1,500 cubic centimeters, or about 10 percent larger than that of a typical modern human being. Hence, there seems no reason to question Neanderthals' capacity for symbolic thought and, although it remains possible that their stubby pharynx and elevated larynx may have impeded the development of a complete spoken language, few anthropologists doubt that Neanderthals possessed a sophisticated communication system compounded of vocalization, facial expressions, arm gestures, and manual signs.

We know that Neanderthals mastered fire, wore furs, and lived in a variety of encampments, including caves. Neanderthal sites from western Europe to central Asia abound with artifacts, including scrapers, choppers, hand axes, and knives. One such tool, a chopper carved from milky brown jasper, sits atop a bookcase in our dining room at home. We wouldn't want to perform brain surgery with it, but it will crack an egg. Look at it long enough, and its chiseled surfaces begin to morph into everything that has followed, from the slicing blades of the Upper Paleolithic to the silicon chips of today. The tool shines with intelligence, an eloquent if silent witness to a rich cultural life. Might that life have included prayer? The answer may lie in prehistoric clues for Neanderthal religious ritual, for as we explained earlier, wherever one finds ritual, one is almost certain to find prayer.

The most compelling case for Neanderthal ritual practice remains the celebrated burial at Shanidar in Iraq. Here stands a cave that has been inhabited sporadically for almost 100,000 years. When Ralph Solecki, a young archaeologist from Columbia University, excavated the site from 1953 to 1957, he found it packed with living occupants, including seven families and a menagerie of horses, goats, cows, and other animals. It also contained, as he soon discovered, spectacular Neanderthal remains (most of which, incidentally, found their way to Baghdad, where four decades later they endured heavy bombing — and perhaps obliteration — during Operation Desert Storm). Solecki uncovered nine skeletons. Five had been deliberately buried. The most stunning was "Shanidar 4," the remains of an elderly man who had been interred — to this day it snatches the breath away — beneath a blanket of multicolored flowering herbs. Palynologist Arlette Leroi-Gourhan, analyzing soil from the site in the late 1960s, identified pollen of Saint Barnaby's thistle, groundsel, yarrow, woody horsetail, hollyhocks, and other plants thickly distributed around the bones. Solecki, exultant, could hardly contain himself: "We already know that Neanderthal man seems to have had a spiritual concept, since he evidently practiced funerary rites over his dead. . . . With the finding of flowers in association with Neanderthals, we are brought suddenly to the realization that the universality of mankind and the love of beauty go beyond the boundary of our own species."[16] With a nod to the flower-power generation, he titled his book, published in 1971, *Shanidar: The First Flower People.*

Skeptics have suggested that burrowing animals or water seepage deposited the pollen found at Shanidar 4. Such explanations seem flimsy, however, in light of the vast quantity of pollen found on the body and its absence elsewhere. Shanidar remains the only known Neanderthal flower burial, but evidence of other similar, if nonfloral, entombments abound. Some include grave goods or red ocher, a sure sign of ritual activity. At Teshik-Tash in Uzbekistan, archaeologists unearthed a Neanderthal child whose bones had been placed within a ring of goat horns; a burial at La Chapelle aux Saints in France contained the carefully arranged remains of an arthritic male. Its codiscoverers provide this account of the La Chapelle find:

> The man that we have found was *intentionally buried.* He was deposited at the bottom of a trench dug into the marly soil of the cave; this soil, white-colored and hard to dig, is distinctly different from that of the archaeological layer. The body was oriented in it approximately east-west, lying on its back, the head to the west. . . . Over the head [were] placed three or four large fragments of long bone . . . with [the] meat on — perhaps as nourishment for the dead person.[17]

La Chapelle aux Saints and additional Neanderthal sites at least suggest a Neanderthal concept of the afterlife (contemporaneous *Homo sapiens sapiens* burials also show evidence of grave goods; perhaps belief in an afterlife was universal by 50,000 B.C.E.). Not only do we have reason to suspect that Neanderthals enjoyed a rich prayer life, but we have a strong inkling about the content of their prayer: they prayed for the well-being of the dead.

Evidence for prayer grows yet more pronounced when we turn to our immediate ancestors, early modern humans of the Upper Paleolithic.

With delightful appositeness, the systematic evidence emerged largely through the spadework of a modern man of prayer, the Abbé Henri Édouard Prosper Breuil (1877–1961). A person of fierce opinions, high self-regard, and enormous energies, Breuil discovered his passion for prehistory while still a child. By the age of ten, he knew enough about Neolithic graves to write a paper on the subject, and during sixty years of active research he spent, by his own estimate, seven hundred days in underground caves, a record almost certainly unequaled by any other archaeologist before or since. Trained in prehistory at the Sorbonne, Breuil was ordained a Roman Catholic priest as the new century dawned. By all accounts, he enjoyed wearing his twin hats as scientist and prelate and, in keeping with his dual vocations, found a place in his research for a prayerful approach to scientific puzzles:

> To succeed in this [archaeological research] you must have the *spirit of meditation,* both active and passive in turn. As bodily health requires a happy balance of endocrine secretions giving opposite results, so you must sometimes definitely concentrate your thought, chewing the cud, if I may say so, of accumulated observations and, on occasion, leaving the reins to Nature who is extraordinarily clever at handling them. During expeditions, hours spent in the garden, in fishing, shooting or other human diversions, you must *let yourself think.* Thought then travels in the subconscious and returns more complete, sometimes rich in new suggestions and inspirations which should be seized at once.[18]

Breuil's first significant dig took place at Altamira in northern Spain, where the first major cache of Upper Paleolithic art came to light. He describes the scene with a characteristic eye for his own Herculean labors:

> On the 1st of October 1902 . . . we entered the cavern discovered by Sautuola. To light us, we only had candles; acetylene lamps were not yet in current use. What we saw plunged us in deep amazement. . . . There was no question of tracing the big figures on the roof of Altamira. The paint was like a paste and therefore stuck to the paper, and tracing would have meant destroying the paintings. . . . It was only possible to make geometrical copy and this I did, working for eight hours a day on my back, lying on sacks stuffed with ferns; this took me about three weeks.[19]

In the years to come, the indefatigable prelate would neglect his clerical duties — he never ran a parish, heard regular confession, or undertook an ecclesiastical post — in favor of revolutionizing the study of Pleistocene life, an achievement that earned him the nickname "the pope of prehistory." His drawings of cave beasts — prancing horses, snorting aurochs, lowing rhinoceros — reflect a keen sense of drama and beauty. He devised the standard chronology for prehistoric art and proposed a comprehensive explanation for this aesthetic explosion, elaborating the first empirically grounded theory of prehistoric religion and thus of prehistoric prayer. Many cave paintings depict beasts attacked by darts or spears; some appear to be at the brink of death. To Breuil, all this spoke of "hunting magic," a form of proto-prayer in which the cave artists symbolically slaughtered animals in paint and charcoal to ensure the successful bagging of their flesh-and-blood counterparts.

This notion of prehistoric magic, as we will see, plays a crucial role in modern theories about the origin and meaning of prayer. For Breuil, the magical hunt was the key that opened up the Paleolithic mind; and this hunt was presided over by a "God" whom the cave dwellers supplicated with prayer. Breuil advanced his beliefs most completely when discussing the most famous of all cave images, the "Sorcerer" of the sanctuary of Les Trois Frères in the foothills of the French Pyrenees. Painted on a high wall deep within the cave, the Sorcerer mysteriously blends human and animal features, with his horse's tail, deerlike ears, heavy branching antlers, and human torso, feet, and phallus. The face, a charcoal blur, contains round owl-like eyes that stare implacably at the viewer. Breuil insists on the divinity of the famous man-beast: "We have wrongly named him the 'Sorcerer' but like Cernunnos of the Gauls who thousands of years later resembled him, the 'God,' as the Reindeer hunters imagined him, presided here — as in Nature — over all animals."[20]

How did the cave inhabitants relate to this "God"? Giving free play to his beloved "spirit of meditation," Breuil discerns a parallel between this 10,000- to 40,000-year-old scene and modern Eskimo religious practice. In so doing he makes explicit his case for prehistoric prayer:

> It was almost certainly in winter, therefore, when the intense frost and thick snow made hunting difficult or completely impossible, that the caves were most inhabited. Conditions were, in fact, similar to those now obtaining with the Eskimos. This is the season when the latter hold their tribal reunions to initiate the young people in their new obligations as adults and instruct them in the traditions of the tribe. On such occasions magico-religious ceremonies are also performed, including masked dances and invocations to celestial beings or spirits designed to ensure the multiplication of game, the destruction of wild beasts and good fortune in forthcoming hunting expeditions during the summer. The communicating underground system of deep corridors cut out in the limestone [of Les Trois Frères] . . . certainly witnessed such ceremonies for many thousands of years.[21]

The "Sorcerer" from the cave of Les Trois Frères,
Ariege, Pyrenees, France, c. 20,000 B.C.E.

Breuil's equation of Upper Paleolithic humans with twentieth-century Eskimos, his identification of the Sorcerer as a "God" rather than a pelt-clad shaman, and his eagerness to hatch bold new scientific theories all give pause today. His notion of hunting magic has fallen on hard times, too, in part because it doesn't seem to match the fossil record. The famous cave of Lascaux, for example, is scattered with the bones of reindeer *(Rangifer tarandus),* the epoch's most widely hunted beast, and yet contains only one reindeer image; instead, the walls teem with aurochs, ibex, and horse, although these animals were hunted infrequently or never.

Since Breuil's day, explanations for cave art ranging from fertility rites to art for art's sake have risen, flourished, and passed away. Many contemporary anthropologists believe that all these motives, and Breuil's hunting magic as well, may have played a part in the aesthetic revolution of the Upper Paleolithic. What remains beyond dispute is the numinous, otherworldly nature of the cave art that Breuil so fiercely championed. Few can dispel the sense, when visiting a site such as Lascaux, that they are treading on sacred ground. It is not difficult to imagine an ancient priest clad in skins, with an engraved bone for breviary, filling these ancient limestone caverns with, in the Abbé's words, "invocations to celestial beings or spirits." That Upper Paleolithic humans prayed seems, on the evidence, impossible to deny.

Nonetheless, the clues remain circumstantial, a stew of bones, bits of red ocher, and ethnographic observations vigorously stirred by the "spirit of meditation." Anthropologist Alexander Marshack, an independent scholar whose 1989 McDonald Lecture at Cambridge University helped launch the science of cognitive archaeology (the study of the prehistoric mind) offers us something more: cave images that he interprets as overt pictures of people in prayer. A fragment of engraved bone unearthed from Laugerie Basse in the Dordogne depicts a bird-headed man reaching upward toward a giant fish; a second figure and a disembodied arm repeat the action. Is this bird-man a shaman, a mythological figure, or a figment of dream? Does his gesture indicate attack, supplication, or worship? Marshack comments: "The full image of the man and fish as reconstructed recalls a gesture of adoration more than the gesture of killing in a hunt, particularly since there are *two* additional arms added to the composition, each perhaps made at a later date and by a different point, but no added weapon. The fish is above the man, as would be proper for an object in adoration but awkward for a fish in water."[22]

Here and elsewhere, Marshack tends to tilt the scant evidence this way and that to get new perspectives. He does this literally with a second image from the Laugerie Basse site, a chunk of engraved reindeer bone that shows a pregnant woman, arm raised, lying on her back beneath the hind legs and phallus of an enormous bull. The beast, Marshack believes, may be a real animal or perhaps a "sky symbol"; the female may be a human being or a goddess. At first glance, the engraving seems to depict sexual intercourse, but Marshack argues that the woman is too advanced in her pregnancy for this to be an image of copulation. Noting that prehistoric art often can be read both vertically and horizontally, he proposes instead that we rotate the image ninety degrees. We then arrive at a pregnant woman standing before a bull, her arm lifted in what Marshack boldly calls prayer:

> She has her hand raised as though in worship or adoration, recalling the gesture we saw earlier in relation to a huge fish above a man. . . . The attitude of prayer, the subsidiary position of the woman in relation to the animal, the stage of the pregnancy, the realistic decoration she wears, and the relation of this image to other Magdelenian images of men around animals in ceremonial attitudes or positions seem to imply that this is a "real" woman and not the goddess. If this is a representation of a pregnant woman in storied relation to a male animal, then whether it has to do with a prayer for safe delivery or is the depiction of a myth in which the goddess is also involved with the stag or bull is not really important. The prayer by a real woman, depicted on a composition for "magical" purposes, is the telling of a mythical story in which animal and woman are related.[23]

Marshack marshals other impressive finds, such as a bone fragment excavated by a French farmer that depicts two hands with spread fingers reaching for what looks like giant raindrops "as though in adoration or reverence." (Could this be a prehistoric adumbration of the Papago's Sit-and-drink?) In any case, these splinters of darkened bone look more like relics than remains. Marshack, following on Breuil, has begun to limn the very womb of prayer, from which so many millennia of confession and petition, thanksgiving and praise will spring.

The Mythological Origins of Prayer

The Abbé Breuil and Alexander Marshack give us hints about the anthropological roots of prayer. But of course there are other origin accounts, and the peoples who have adhered to them vastly outnumber those who have looked to archaeology and anthropology for an explanation. When we ask men and women from traditional cultures, those endowed with a lively mythic consciousness, about the origin of prayer, their answers send us back to the beginning of time. Prayer, they tell us, is written into our world's primordial charter; it echoes the creator's speech, the animal's lament, the angels' chant.

According to one strand of the mythology of ancient India, the universe began with a primordial fire sacrifice. Heaven and earth were cooked into being by the ardor of prayer, smelted into being on the smithy of prayer, spoken into being by the sacred sounds and syllables of prayer. When the sages sought a name for the infinite spirit behind all shifting forms, they called it *brahman*, a term for the power that resides in sacred speech. God *is* prayer, they seemed to think. So, too, the priest who performs the crucial sacrifice of the fire altar is called *brāhman,* wielder of the power that resides in the words of ritual prayer. Prayer began the world and will sustain the world until it reaches its appointed dissolution. If correctly performed, even the everyday prayers and mantras of Hindu householders, seekers, and saints enjoy this privilege. For the Vedic mantra — from *oṃ* to *śānti* — is believed to be a pure distillation of the absolute and imperishable reality that made the world and to which the world must periodically repair for restoration.

To find similar accounts of the origin and prestige of prayer, one can draw almost at random from the bottomless well of world mythologies. According to anthropologist Robin Ridington, the Beaver Indians of southwestern Canada pray, like the Papago, by means of songs whose mysterious power links the inner life of all people:

> The thread of a Beaver's song is the path his mind can take into the deepest realms of his subjectivity and out to reach the subjectivities of others. It is frustrating to have to use words to describe what must essentially be heard and experienced. . . . As you follow the turns of the song and learn them you are learning the inner paths of the mind. The Beavers translate *songs* into English as prayer because they reach simultaneously inward and outward.[24]

These songs come from many sources. A shaman may visit heaven and return with a God song, *ahata yine,* or an ordinary man may learn his medicine song, *ma yine,* from a mythical animal. Such prayer transmissions usually take place while dreaming, a complex action that seems to include what we might call trance states as well as the everyday dreams of sleep. Always, prayer originates in a sacred world from which our well-being derives, yet where humans tread sparingly and at great personal risk. The human dreamer does not invent the prayer; he receives it in a spirit of humility and thanks and then passes it on to others or keeps it in his heart.

When we turn to the biblical origins of prayer, the landscape alters: the authors of the Hebrew scriptures, imbued with a strong sense of history, begin to cultivate the fields of myth in orderly rows. Time now has beginning, direction, and end. Accordingly, we can point to an episode in the biblical narrative as the decisive moment when prayer came into being. Prayer became possible from the moment when God first spoke to his human creatures, blessing them, commanding them, and establishing the ground rules for all future communication, as described in Genesis 1:28: "And God blessed them, and God said unto them, Be fruitful, and multiply, and replenish the earth and subdue it: and have dominion over the fish of the sea, and over the fowl of the air, and over every living thing that moveth upon the earth."

Optimists and bon vivants take heart: God began the long, thorny discourse with human beings with a blessing and followed it up with a prescription for conjugal bliss. No play without work, however: we must also enlist opposable thumbs and broad frontal lobes in order to reign — benignly, one hopes — over all living things. For a while, at least, Adam and Eve took God's counsel to heart; one might say that while in Eden they lived in a state of constant prayer, with no sin to interrupt their happiness. Adam's naming of the beasts, his joyful song at beholding Eve, the pervasive harmony of man and woman, human and animal, earth and heaven, all unfolded in perfect prayerful openness and ready exchange between Creator and created. Like the Beaver Indians, Adam and Eve experienced prayer as divine gift, and the rest of their history would recount the use or squandering of this gift.

Theories of Prayer

The origins of prayer, historical or mythological, have intrinsic significance, for in the seed lies the tree. As such, origins play a critical role in many influential modern theories about prayer. Among those who have sought the origins of prayer and speculated about the prayer life of prehistoric beings are the founders of all the "soft sciences" — anthropology, sociology, cultural history, and psychology — that have so shaken the structure of our self-understanding. These figures include Sir Edward Burnett Tylor, father of cultural anthropology, Sir James Frazer, father of comparative mythology, and Sigmund Freud, father of psychoanalysis. Each of these architects of modern self-consciousness — none of whom, it should be noted, engaged in prayer as an adult — set out to explain prayer; each based his explanation on what he believed to be prayer's prehistoric roots; and each, in a delicious triumph of irony, advanced a scientific explanation that soon bent under the weight of its creator's obsessions and assumed the shape of myth.

Sir Edward Burnett Tylor (1832–1917), the first significant modern theoretician of prayer, was the son of a wealthy Quaker brass manufacturer. His formal education ceased at the age of sixteen (Quakers were not allowed to attend British universities at the time), and he joined the family business as a clerk. Seven years later, stricken with tuberculosis, he set sail for North America in search of a cure. By 1856 he found himself in Mexico, where he spent six months exploring the mysteries of Toltec religion and settled upon his life's work: to create a science of culture that would explain the genesis of religious belief and practice in the same way that the science of evolution, just then coming into its own, promised to explain the genesis of life forms. The evolutionary principle, which to Tylor meant progression from baser to nobler forms, was paramount. "Savagery and civilization," he declares, "are connected as lower and higher stages of one formation."[25] Just as Darwin scrutinized nineteenth-century animal life for clues to biological evolution, so Tylor scoured present-day religion for survivals of earlier evolutionary stages. Prayer, he came to believe, was one such survival, and in it traces of humankind's primordial religion could be discerned. Tylor calls this religion animism, the belief that the world teems with spiritual beings, and he explains it as the consequence of a simple error in reasoning:

> It seems as though thinking men, as yet at a low level of culture, were deeply impressed by two groups of biological problems. In the first place, what is it that makes a difference between a living body and a dead one; what causes waking, sleep, trance, disease, death? In the second place, what are those human shapes which appear in dreams and visions? Looking at these two groups of phenomena, the ancient savage philosophers probably made their first step by the obvious inference that every man has two things belonging to him, namely, a life and a phantom as being its image or second self; both, also, are perceived to be things separable from the body. . . . The second step would seem also easy for savages to make, seeing how extremely difficult civilized men have found it to unmake. It is merely to combine the life and the phantom. . . . the result is that well-known conception . . . the personal soul or spirit.[26]

Belief in ghost-souls survives, Tylor admits, but rather like the survival of the useless appendix in the otherwise functionally well ordered human digestive system. Prayer, which is the attempt to communicate with these ghost-souls, is therefore only a compulsive behavior carried on because it has always been done. Tylor's conclusions on the origin of religion and of prayer soon became the reigning scientific dogma of the age, receiving the imprimatur of Darwin himself.

The principal heir of Tylor's evolutionist views was Sir James George Frazer (1854–1941), a Scot, scholar, and religious skeptic who enjoyed a brilliant career as a classicist and anthropologist at Trinity College, Cambridge. Frazer fell under the spell of Tylor's theories while still an undergraduate and spent the rest of his life expanding them into his own grand vision of the history of religion. He is best known today for *The Golden*

Bough (1890–1915), a masterpiece of elegant prose that originally appeared in two volumes but that ballooned, by its final version, into twelve books containing well over one million words.

In this massive work, Frazer set out to unravel the ancient Roman tale of Rex Nemorensis (the King of the Wood), a shadowy priest-king who stood guard over a sacred tree, bearing a golden bough, that grew in a glade near the temple of Diana, goddess of fertility and childbirth. Frazer's conclusion about the King of the Wood — that he constitutes a mythological echo of a real prehistoric tribal king — remains a matter for debate. In any case, this proved secondary to his main accomplishment, a majestic three-tiered canvas of human cultural evolution that wielded tremendous influence in its time and continues to inform popular thinking about prayer to the present day.

Frazer's triptych begins in the age of magic, progresses through the age of religion, and culminates in the age of science — which he, and we, are lucky enough to inhabit. Magic, according to Frazer, was a sort of crude proto-science, a primitive attempt to explain and control the forces of nature. When this attempt failed, as it was bound to do, the age of religion dawned. Now humankind began to appeal to superhuman beings who ruled the world, seeking through prayer and sacrifice to win their favor, protection, and largesse. Yet religion, too, was doomed, for such prayers were bound to go unanswered. Therefore religion yielded to science, the only reliable means of mastering the powers of the cosmos. What remains of magic and religion — or of magic mixed with religion, as one finds in folk piety — is purely vestigial, Tylor's appendix preserved in fancier formaldehyde.

The Golden Bough took the Edwardian intellectual world by storm and became required reading for generations of artists, philosophers, theologians, and scientists. It was not, however, the final word in the evolutionary analysis of prayer, for in 1913 Sigmund Freud published *Totem and Taboo,* adding his own twist to the tale. Freud's life story is perhaps too well known to bear repeating here; it is worth mentioning, however, that although his Jewish childhood brought him into contact with the Hebrew Bible, Freud apparently never enjoyed the slightest frisson of religious belief. According to his chief biographer, Ernest Jones, "he went through life from beginning to end a natural atheist."[27]

At the center of Freud's thesis about the origins of religion lay his conviction that the history of culture precisely mirrors human psychosexual development. The emergence of religion in society corresponds to the emergence in the individual of the Oedipus complex, through which a boy develops sexual desire for his mother and hostility toward his father. Drawing from Frazer's account of incest taboos among Australian aborigines and from biblical scholar W. Robertson Smith's writings about ancient sacrifice, Freud postulated that prehistoric humans lived in "primal hordes" ruled by an autocratic patriarch. One day the young males of the horde, jealous of the Father-Ruler's power, and in particular of his sexual prerogatives, took matters into their own violent hands and killed the Father, ate his flesh, and bedded his wives, their mothers. Stricken with guilt, they then selected a totemic animal as surrogate patriarch and worshiped it — and therefore the Father — as divine. Thus did all religion, including prayer, come into being.

This masterpiece of Grand Guignol forms the basis for all of Freud's subsequent writings on religious subjects, culminating in *The Future of an Illusion,* where he asserts that formal prayer is a neurotic practice no different from the repeated hand washing of an obsessive-compulsive and that religion is "the universal obsessional neurosis of humanity" deriving from the primal Oedipal drama. Freud accounts for the well-being that individuals derive from prayer by reasoning that participation in a collective neurosis has spared them the need to construct a private one. Placing civilization itself on the couch, he used the psychoanalytic method to free humanity from its dependence upon these "neurotic relics" of the past.[28]

For all their differences, Tylor, Frazer, and Freud share a number of common assumptions:

1. That in order to discover the essence of prayer, one must find its most primitive, undeveloped, and earliest forms.
2. That the most primitive, undeveloped, and earliest forms of prayer are to be found in tribal societies, and that from these cultures we can glean an understanding of prehistoric culture.
3. That the primitive mentality is essentially similar to the mentality of the child and the neurotic, the chief trait of which is infantile magical thinking.
4. That from its primitive magical beginnings, prayer has evolved to higher forms, rendering its primitive forms obsolete.
5. That religion and magic are misguided prescientific efforts to do what science now does with much greater success: to explain the unknown and control the forces of nature. Once science emerges in all its fullness and wisdom, religion — and consequently the rationale for prayer — will wither away.

These five precepts lead inevitably to:

6. That scientists who decipher human behavior (psychologists, sociologists, anthropologists) are better equipped to explain that behavior than are the human beings they study, for these specialists possess a key to human experience that the general populace lacks.

Unfortunately for the evolutionist viewpoint, these axioms carried considerably more force in the years immediately following the 1859 publication of Darwin's *On the Origin of Species* than they do today. The equation of primitive and prehistoric cultures has long been questioned by anthropologists, for it ignores the historical development and remarkable complexity of so-called primitive cultures. Nonetheless, this view remains very much alive and has infected most studies of prayer, both academic and popular. Equally questionable is the idea that a social scientist is better equipped to explain, say, the satori of a Buddhist nun than is the Buddhist nun herself. Biologists offer biological explanations for prayer, neurologists diagnose it as a misfiring of neurons, philologists trace it to linguistic origins, and economists measure its market value. But a chart of word origins or nerve pathways no more explains prayer than a drawing of an elephant explains an elephant. In this book, we proceed in the belief that science can do much to illuminate religious matters, but that equally valuable lessons can be drawn from the witness of those who have immersed themselves in the vocabulary, grammar, and syntax of belief. Only an empathetic study of prayer, we believe, can reveal prayer's secret life.

One of the first thinkers to put forth this view was the amiable American philosopher and psychologist William James (1842–1910), the great defender of religious experience. James was a man of huge sympathies, a genius at friendship toward all species of people and idea — his fondness for eccentrics, which included lavish financial support from his less-than-bottomless pockets, was legendary — and he possessed too much sturdy common sense to believe that either biology or psychology could provide an exhaustive explanation of human behavior. In James's day, it was fashionable to describe religious experience as a form of auto-intoxication brought on by disordered digestion or nerves (as Dickens's Ebenezer Scrooge tells the ghost of Jacob Marley, "There's more of gravy than of grave in you"). James was one of the first to rebut this "medical materialism," most notably in his Gifford Lectures on Natural Religion, published in 1902 as *The Varieties of Religious Experience,* where he insists that the full meaning and value of an experience must be sought in its "fruits for life."

In the first years of the twentieth century, shortly before his death, James filled out a questionnaire about his own religious beliefs at the request of a former student, James Pratt. To the question "Do you pray?" James writes, "I can't possibly pray, I feel foolish and artificial." Nonetheless, in *Varieties* James calls prayer "the very soul and essence of religion" and prizes its transforming effects on human beings. Prayer, he says, opens a doorway to the "wider self," that extramarginal or subconscious region beyond our normal waking consciousness, through which dreams, visions, and revelations find entrance. If there is a God, James suggests, he may well work upon us through natural channels such as the subconscious mind, producing the exotic effects that sometimes accompany prayer, such as trance states, shuddering ecstasies, or speaking in tongues.[29] But the main thing, for James, is that prayer is a force for positive change:

> Through prayer, religion insists, things which cannot be realized in any other manner come about: energy which but for prayer would be bound is by prayer set free and operates in some part, be it objective or subjective, of the world of facts. When we pray, it is like the difference between looking on a person without love, or upon the same person with love. . . . We meet a new world when we meet the old world in the spirit which this kind of prayer infuses.[30]

James stands as a landmark in the empathetic approach to prayer. Yet too often even this approach fails to do prayer justice, for it frequently drags in confining assumptions about which kinds of prayer are intelligible, effective, or appropriate for a mature human being. Such is the case with one of the most influential scholarly books about prayer, Friedrich Heiler's *Prayer: A Study in the History and Psychology of Religion* (1918). Unlike that of the armchair anthropologists, Heiler's approach to prayer is deeply sympathetic. This comes as no surprise, for he ranks as a pioneer in the phenomenology of religion, which we might describe as the nonreductionist description of religious consciousness. Heiler goes so far as to extol prayer, in a perhaps unwitting echo of James, as "the heart and center of all religion." But he then binds this heart in an evolutionary straitjacket, reversing the classical Darwinian schema with equally devastating results:

> Prayer is at first a spontaneous emotional discharge, a free outpouring of the heart. In the course of development it becomes a fixed formula which people recite without feeling or mood of devotion, untouched both in heart and mind. At first prayer is an intimate intercourse with God, but gradually it becomes hard, impersonal, ceremonial, a rite con-

> secrated by ancestral custom. Originally it springs directly out of the soul's deepest need or highest bliss; later its use is limited to definite, regularly recurring occasions. Originally it is the informal utterance of a depressed or happy soul, accompanied at the most by a simple gift; later it becomes an inseparable part of a complicated ritual of purifications, sacrifices, processions, dances, and consecrations. Originally it is the personal utterance of an individual or of the chief of a group; later it becomes the impersonal, professional business of the priests. Even among primitive peoples this process of petrification and mechanization takes place which transforms free prayer into precise and rigid formulas.[31]

Tylor, Frazer, and Freud tell a story of the evolution of culture from magic to religion to science; Heiler tells a story of the devolution of culture from a hypothetical beginning when humankind conversed freely with God to a degenerate time of priestcraft, in which prayer reverts to mechanical formulas, indulgences sold in the marketplace, and rosary beads clacking mindlessly. Embracing a strict Lutheran standard, Heiler writes that "it is precisely in prayer that we have revealed to us the *essential* element of all religion . . . the 'prevenience and givenness' of the grace of God. Prayer is not man's work, or discovery or achievement, but God's work in man."[32]

Heiler thus disparages prayer that is highly ritualistic, tinged with magic or folk piety, or laden with strong penitential, intercessory, or sacrificial themes. Needless to say, this excludes a significant percentage of the world's repertoire of prayer. At the time he wrote *Prayer,* Heiler was in the process of converting from Catholicism to Lutheranism; one senses here the zeal of the convert overwhelming the catholicity of the scholar. He thus devalues not only the prayers of his former pew mates but also those of Jews, Muslims, Hindus, and Buddhists — indeed, of all people whose prayer life unfolds within rites and ceremonies transmitted from generation to generation, learned by rote and assimilated through practice. Like many polemical works, Heiler's *Prayer* obscures as much as it illumines: it throws light on the immediacy of prayer as a "living communion of man with God" but distorts the relationship between this communion and the living religious traditions — the spiritual practices, ritual behaviors, and cultural forms — within which it grows and takes shape.

For Heiler and the anthropologists, the problem is blinkered vision. Almost to a man (and they are almost all men), theorists have ignored the evidence, or they have developed a theory of prayer and then imposed it upon the evidence. The solution to such ideological straitjacketing could not be more obvious: let us listen to those who pray. This approach yields the insight that prayer in its fullness includes the total spectrum of human experience and draws unstintingly from the vast repertoire of traditional practices. Storming heaven, no less than sitting quietly in one's boudoir, is part of the mature life of prayer. Contemplative prayer is not higher than petitionary prayer; wordless prayer is not superior to prayer with words; spontaneous prayer is not superior to formal prayer. All are essential aspects of the religious life, and all may coexist in a single person: thus the scientist who spills salt during breakfast and immediately throws some over her shoulder and makes a wish, who works in her laboratory following the purest protocols of the scientific method, and who retires for the night by saying the Lord's Prayer. Is she a creature of rank inconsistency or of multiple levels of understanding?

Theorists often contend that the prayers of primitive people are founded on naive conceptual error; on the contrary, we are inclined to think that the instinct for prayer is primary, running ahead of any conceptual notions. Or perhaps it is better to say that the instinct for prayer and the sense of the divine arise simultaneously as immediate facts of consciousness, only later to be articulated as systems of belief. All human beings long for the beautiful, the true, and the good, and every desire — for better crops or greater wisdom, for world peace or a good-night kiss — participates in this longing. We are constituted, by nature or divine gift, in such a way that this longing carries with it, as if its necessary companion, the impulse to pray, the indwelling conviction that prayer, addressed in word, movement, or silence toward God, the saints, heavenly powers, earthly spirits, or the divine spark within, will allay this longing by transporting us to the threshold of our heart's desire. This is a primordial and universal event in the history of human consciousness and the life of every human being. Prayer lies in the ground of our being and connects us to its source, and every creative act bears, manifest or hidden, its imprint. Theories of prayer that fail to recognize its fundamental and perennial character are therefore bound to fall short.

This is not to say that prayer and theorizing about prayer are incompatible, but rather that each must inform — and in the lives of those who pray, usually does inform — the other. Let us consider, by way of illustration, what Mr. Sherlock Holmes has to say on the subject, when, during the course of investigating the theft of a document vitally important to the British Empire, he takes a moment to draw together his thoughts:

> "The authorities are excellent at amassing facts, though they do not always use them to advantage. What a lovely thing a rose is!"

He walked past the couch to the open window and held the drooping stalk of a moss-rose, looking down at the dainty blend of crimson and green. It was a new phase of his character to me, for I had never before seen him show any keen interest in natural objects.

"There is nothing in which deduction is so necessary as in religion," said he, leaning with his back against the shutters. "It can be built up as an exact science by the reasoner. Our highest assurance of the goodness of Providence seems to me to rest in the flowers. All other things, our powers, our desires, our food, are all really necessary for our existence in the first instance. But this rose is an extra. Its smells and its color are an embellishment of life, not a condition of it. It is only goodness which gives extras, and so I say again that we have much to hope from the flowers."

Percy Phelps and his nurse looked at Holmes during this demonstration with surprise and a good deal of disappointment written upon their faces. He had fallen into a reverie, with the moss-rose between his fingers. It had lasted some minutes before the young lady broke in upon it.

"Do you see any prospect of solving this mystery, Mr. Holmes?" she asked with a touch of asperity in her voice.[33]

Many Holmes scholars maintain that the great detective's reverie is a state of prayer. Or perhaps it is a trance, helped along by the 7 percent solution, or perhaps nothing more than a momentary fit of intellectual abstraction. We like to think that all these factors may be at work, for good theories cannot be built of single elements. One is unlikely to come up with deductions about prayer while in the act of praying, just as one is unlikely to pray while caught up in a deductive process. Yet prayer and theory need not be at odds; one can easily imagine someone — a prayerful master of deduction like Holmes or a deductive master of prayer like the Abbé Breuil — shuttling freely and easily between devotion and logic and enjoying the best of both worlds. And in this way, one may prayerfully reason one's way toward a theory of prayer that uses to advantage the realities of prayer as manifested in the lives of individual human beings and human cultures. This, at least, is our aim in this book. Why do we pray, and what do we pray for? How do we pray, and how does it change us? What does prayer say about us, as separate cultures and as a species? These questions, and the answers offered by those who pray, as well as by those who study prayer, will occupy us in the chapters ahead.

CHAPTER 2

Magic

TWO FIGURES STAND GUARD at the threshold of prayer: the magician and the priest. The magician commands; the priest offers. The prayer of the magician is an incantation, a charm, a chanted or inscribed word of power used to achieve a particular end: to heal the sick, revive the dead, send rain, open the womb, defeat the enemy, and so on. The prayer of the priest is an invocation, the spoken or sung portion of a sacrifice, which by honoring the gods attains both temporal and eternal goods. Magical prayer draws down power from the heavens; priestly prayer pours itself out on the altar stone and ascends to the heavens in fragrant smoke. These are archetypal actions. They belong not only to prayer's ancestral past but also to its present and future. We believe that the echo of magical speech and the lingering aura of burnt offerings will always accompany living prayer, however far we may distance ourselves from our archaic beginnings.

In saying this, we know we tread on slippery ground. For the sophisticated believer, anxious to improve prayer's credentials, often the first order of business is to distinguish between magic and prayer, between sacrifice and prayer. In the previous chapter, we saw that early anthropologists of religion (Sir Edward Burnett Tylor, Sir James George Frazer) differentiated these realms all too neatly and that the leading modern authority on prayer, Friedrich Heiler, attempted to sever their connection completely. Magic and sacrifice belong to the childhood of our race, they argue; mature prayer demands that, like Saint Paul, we put away childish things. And yet fascination with such seemingly childish things persists, growing all the stronger for being banished to the margins of our culture. In this chapter and the next, we consider the role of magic and sacrifice as enduring dimensions of a fully realized life of prayer.

Greco-Roman Magical Prayers

The Greek Magical Papyri, the definitive collection of Greco-Roman magical prayers dating from the second century B.C.E. to the fifth century C.E., is almost always checked out of the college libraries in our area.[1] The last time we managed to borrow it, we found that a large chunk of the volume had been torn out, perhaps stolen by an apprentice magician. We had to buy the book ourselves to discover what had been so irresistibly tempting. What we found was an astonishing collection of love charms, healing recipes, petitions, curses, and binding spells, some quite practical in intent ("To keep bugs out of the house: Mix goat bile with water and sprinkle it"; "Lord Sabaoth, repel the pain from me, the headache pain, I pray, take") together with exalted hymns of praise and adoration. Palindromes, anagrams, word pyramids, alphabetical runes, hands and eyes, suns and moons, headless men, and animal-headed gods dance across the page. A heartfelt plea for protection calls upon the improbably named god "KMĒPHIS CHPHYRIS IAEŌ IAŌ AEĒ IAŌ OŌ AIŌN IAEŌBAPHRENE / MOUNOTHILARIKRIPHIAE Y EAIPHIRKIRALITHANYOMENERPHABŌEAI" to fend off illness and demons. A prayer for health forms a triangular shield, to be placed directly on the body of a sick child:

[IA]RBATH AGRAMMĒ PHIBLŌ CHŌĒMEŌ
[A E]E ĒĒĒ IIII OOOOO YYYYYY ŌŌŌŌŌŌ[Ō]
Lord gods, heal Helene, whom [NN] bore, from every
illness and every fit of shivering [fever].
/ daily, daylong, tertian, quartan.
IARBATH AGRAMMĒ PHIBLŌ CHNĒMEŌ
AEĒIOYŌŌYOIĒEA
EĒIOYŌŌYOIĒE
ĒIOYŌŌYOIĒ ⁎☽
YYY IOYŌŌYOI
OYŌŌYO
YŌŌY YYYYY
ŌŌ[2]

But the most impressive portion of this stolen treasure was a complete sequence of magical prayers known colloquially (though not quite accurately) as the Mithras Liturgy.[3] Perhaps some campus pagan group has incorporated this rite into its celebrations. If so, they are aiming high, for the rite makes an intoxicating promise: yoke your speech and breath to these prayers, and you can ascend to heaven and become immortal.

The instructions for the Mithras Liturgy are explicit. The magician begins humbly, begging for protection from the god who is "first origin of my origin." The god's peculiar name, AEĒIOYŌ, is a signal that something unusual is about to transpire. Lacking consonants, the name is pure breath, composed of the seven Greek vowels, which are also the notes of the Greek musical scale. Here is a divine name only a classical diva could pronounce, in which the voice of the ether and the music of the spheres resound. Whoever speaks, breathes, or sings such a name undertakes a process of transformation that, if completed, would make the person divine.

Now the magician recites an elaborate litany of divine invocations, with many long strings of vowels; he must be fairly winded by the end of it. He renews his strength by turning toward the sun and inhaling deeply: "Draw in breath from the rays, drawing up 3 times as much as you can, and you will see yourself being lifted up . . ." Inflated by the sun's warm breath, the magician rises up like a hot-air balloon, ascending past planets and stars to deposit his petitions at the throne of the high solar god. But heaven is a dangerous place for mortals, even hyperventilating ones, to visit. When the magician arrives, the presiding gods rush forth to repel him. The text instructs him to stand his ground and cry out,

> Silence! Silence! Silence!
> Symbol of the living, incorruptible god!
> Guard me, Silence, NECHTHEIR THANMELOU!

Finally, the magician utters a long hissing and popping sound to achieve the desired result: "You will see the gods looking graciously upon you and no longer rushing at you, but rather going about in their own order of affairs."

Hissing and popping? Our pet tortoise makes similar sounds when frightened or annoyed, but this hardly seems a fitting way to greet the gods. Classical antiquity offered any number of graceful alternatives, such as the reverent "Hymn to Zeus" by the Stoic philosopher Cleanthes:

> Most glorious of the Immortals, many named, Almighty for ever.
> Zeus, ruler of Nature, that governest all things with law,
> Hail![4]

Why should gods accustomed to such fine tributes look favorably upon a prayer filled with random noise and static?

The answer is that hissing, popping, clicking, groaning, and other seemingly inarticulate noises are characteristic forms of magical speech. The German historian of religion Rudolf Otto called such noises "original numinous sounds." Roman writers called them *voces magicae* (magical sounds). Neither human speech nor bestial grunt, the *voces magicae* provided a way of praying that could lay claim to the supernatural to a degree that ordinary language cannot. Making bizarre noises disengages the intellect, eliciting an altered state of awareness, more potent than, though perhaps not different in kind from, the hypnotic effect of ordinary chanting or singing.

Freud gives us a ready-made explanation: if magical spells betray a neurotic belief in the "omnipotence of thoughts," then magical noises would seem to be symptoms of a civilization in full retreat, rejecting even primitive rational consciousness in favor of the chaotic sensuality of infancy. But such an explanation overlooks the most impressive feature of these prayers. Far from mindless babble, the *voces magicae* comprise a highly developed magical language popular throughout the multicultural Mediterranean world of late antiquity, from the time of Alexander the Great (fourth century B.C.E.) until the final collapse of Roman civilization in the sixth century. The same *voces magicae*, the same impossibly long vowel sequences, the same palindromes (*Ablanathanalba* was a favorite) and jumbled bits of Egyptian, Hebrew, Greek, and Aramaic, recur in esoteric prayer and magic texts almost as if it were the trade jargon of a far-flung cosmopolitan guild. There was nothing arbitrary about it. Prayer performances such as the Mithras Liturgy were intricately crafted and stage managed; every element had meaning.

A magical treatise from the same period as the Mithras Liturgy — the "Eighth Book of Moses" — offers a partial interpretation of the hissing and popping noises. Popping is the sound made by the sacred crocodile when it rises from the Nile to take a breath; this is how the crocodile (who is a form of the god Horus) salutes the high god. Hissing is the sound made by the sacred snake that devours its own tail, emblem of the endless cycle of regeneration. Popping, moreover, is the first element of the high god's secret name, and hissing the second; and popping and hissing, together with breathing, speaking, and laughing, are among the sounds the high god made when he called the world into being. If we fail to comprehend these sounds, it is because they are of a higher order than human speech, not a lower one. They echo divine speech; they are recovered fragments of the language of paradise. One of the magical papyri relates that the mere sound of them delights the gods.

Magical prayer is not an affair of the mind and voice alone, however, but of the stomach and bowels as well. Magic is a close relative of cooking, and many prayers of the *Greek Magical Papyri* require a well-stocked pantry. A typical prayer recipe, in the "Eighth Book of Moses," calls for the following ingredients: mashed incense and flowers, a square of natron (soap made from native sesquicarbonate of soda, a salt drawn from the Nile — essentially, washing soda), and a mixture of milk and wine. Using the incense-and-flower paste for ink, the magician inscribes petitions on the natron together with pictograms for the divine names, licks the inscription off one side of the natron, washes the other side with the milk and wine, and consumes the solution. Quite literally, the magician eats his prayer.

We can't be sure whether the neopagans in our neighborhood are writing their prayers on soap and eating them, but we do come away from the *Greek Magical Papyri* with a host of questions. How did prayer get mixed up with so much that seems unspiritual and strange? Is the search for concrete benefits such as prosperity, health, success in love, conquest in business, and victory in war a misuse of prayer? If not, then what of overtly aggressive magical prayers that bind a lover's affections or curse an adversary? What of prayers that have the temerity to attempt to force God's hand? Are there virtuosos of prayer — saints, wonderworkers, mystics — who possess exceptional influence over the heavens? What does God think of magical prayer?

These are not new questions. Greek and Roman writers did not separate magic from religion as many moderns have attempted to do, but they did see a difference between good magic and bad magic, between the folk magic of village wise women and the learned magic of the esoteric elite, and between the public religion of the polis and the private religion of the mystery cults. They did find something unwholesome and "un-Greek" about private ceremonies conducted in secret and at night, in which individuals made petitions or cast spells on behalf of individual wants and needs. The official cult was civic and respectable; it took place in daylight, and its prayers were spoken aloud before many witnesses. The characteristic prayer posture — standing tall with one or both arms raised toward heaven — was a gesture of dignity and expansiveness, in keeping with the classical athletic and civic ideal. Aristotle takes this posture for granted when he says, "All of us human beings stretch out our hands to the sky when praying." Prostration was considered a barbarian custom, and kneeling was reserved for prayer under conditions of extreme distress, when throwing oneself on the mercy of a ruler or a god. Similarly, one would pray silently or sotto voce only in the direst circumstances or if one had something shameful to hide.[5]

As the classics scholar Simon Pulleyn puts it, "Nice people at religious festivals did not usually strangle a small menagerie of birds, eat a dead chick, and make sure that all this was done *alone*."[6] And yet nice people did conduct small family sacrifices; nice people did use magic for its practical benefits; public ritual prayer did have its elements of magical strangeness (including eerie sounds such as female ululation), and many of the prayers used in private magical ceremonies are identical to those used in public. The line between public and private and between prayer and magic was always shifting.

The Greek and Roman ambivalence about magic is reflected in their terminology. The Greek *mageia* (Latin *magia*), from which our English *magic* derives, refers to the practices of the *magoi* (Latin *magi*), members of the hereditary Persian priestly class who were admired for their wisdom but feared for their foreignness. Plato had warned against "begging priests and soothsayers" who trafficked in "spells and enchantments that constrain the gods to serve their ends," but the consensus of the ancient world held that such spells do work, and not even Plato's disciples were entirely immune to the charms of magical prayer.[7] Plotinus, the greatest of the Neoplatonic philosophers (who made a mystical system of salvation out of Plato's idealism), writes that "prayer and its answer, magic and its success depend upon the sympathy of enchained forces."[8] The cosmos is tuned like a lyre, Plotinus explains, so that the vibration created by a prayer or spell in one quarter causes an answering vibration in another. Magic is based on the idea that the world is coherent: underlying its apparent diversity lies an intricate system of hidden harmonies and correspondences, whose vivifying and enlightening power can be harnessed by magical prayer. Though Plotinus believed that philosophers should be above casting spells, the evident efficacy of magical prayer points toward this axiomatic truth: as above, so below.

Developing the idea further, some Neoplatonists devised elaborate systems of magic called theurgy (the Greek *theourgia* means something like "god-work"), which were closer in spirit to the Mithras Liturgy than to the spells of a village sorcerer. This was magic for the elite, for philosophers and rulers rather than the masses. But it was controversial: Porphyry, the third-century Neoplatonist and friend of Plotinus, debated the issue fiercely with his own disciple Iamblichus, a leading theurgist. You cannot coerce the gods to come down to you, Porphyry argued; you cannot manipulate them; nor is it dignified to use breathing tricks to climb up to heaven like a fakir ascending a rope. For his part, Iamblichus insisted that theurgy is a spiritual art derived from Plato himself. When the theurgist invokes the gods by their secret names, employs daimonic intermediaries, or practices mystical ascent, he is seeking only to be purified of his passions and raised to a state of communion with the One.

If the extraordinary variety of magical prayer in the Greco-Roman world is any indication, magical prayer means a hundred different things, encompassing love charms and amulets at one end of the spectrum and mystical philosophy at the other. It is not a simple matter to define it. When Apuleius, the second-century philosopher who wrote the satire *The Golden Ass* (in which the hero, changed into a donkey by magic, is saved by the higher magic of the goddess Isis), was accused of being a magician himself, he made this ambiguity a key point in his defense:

> If what I read in a large number of authors be true, namely that "magician" is the Persian word for priest, what is there criminal in being a priest and having due knowledge, science and skill? . . . But, if you, accusers of mine, after the fashions of the common herd, define a magician as one who, by communion or speech with the immortal gods, has the power to do all the marvels he will through a strange power of incantation, I really wonder that they are not afraid to attack one whom they readily acknowledge to be so powerful.[9]

Things haven't changed much. Like the Greeks, we moderns tend to label as magical religious practices that seem foreign, marginal, dangerous, and alluring. Like Tylor, Frazer, and Heiler, we are inclined to view magic as pseudoscience (impersonal, coercive, material, and mechanical) and to separate it absolutely from prayer (personal, spontaneous, spiritual, and vital). One speaks of vestiges of magic in prayer as one might speak of vestiges of primitive thought in the modern world, of Canaanite myths in Israelite religion, of Celtic myths in British Christianity. One speaks of popular prayer degenerating into magic, as one might speak of a good neighborhood turning into a slum.

Yet the boundaries between prayer and magic cannot be so sharply drawn, and this is for the best. Imagine a prayer without any hint of magic in it, without any sense that there is power residing in its words and actions. Such a prayer would be a sterile and lifeless thing. Imagine, on the other hand, a prayer solely concerned with achieving desired ends. It would be nothing more than mechanical technique, lacking the vital spirit of humility and dependency on divine grace.

Prayer must have a magical dimension, or it falls flat; but prayer must keep the magical dimension in check. As long as human beings are torn between selfish and self-transcending impulses, this balance will be difficult to achieve, and prayer will always run the risk of collapsing into magic; but to deny that magic is a factor in prayer is no adequate solution. In prayer, the magical world of "enchained sympathies" still operates, but under the benevolent rule of the divine being who created it. In prayer, what was once a conjuror's spell becomes an act of homage and blessing. Where prayer and magic thus intertwine, the result is pure poetry:

> Eastward I stand, for good gifts I pray.
> I pray the great Lord, I pray the mighty king.
>
> I pray the holy ward of heaven's kingdom.
> Earth I pray and sky above,
> And the true holy Mary,
> And heaven's might and high-built hall,
> that I may open my mouth and make this spell,
> by the grace of the Lord,
> by my thought firmly fixed;
> Wake up these crops for our worldly weal,
> fill this earth-field by my fast belief,
> shed beauty on the meadow-turf; for the prophet says
> that he reaped good gifts on earth
> who, by the grace of the Lord, worthily gave alms.[10]

This early-eleventh-century Anglo-Saxon field prayer *(æcerbot),* addressed at sundown to Christ the rising sun, to earth and sky, and to Mary, Queen of Heaven, would be none the better, none the purer, none the more prayerful for being shorn of magical and pagan associations.

Magic is religion in the subjunctive mood, the French sociologist Marcel Mauss once observed. While religion prays "let it be," magic prays "would that it were" or, to develop the idea further, "would that it were thus changed." The primary concern of magical prayer is transformation — changing arid land to fertile, disease to health, poverty to abundance, death to life; its secondary concern is worship and adoration. The magician possesses special knowledge and power; he discerns hidden correspondences and can tap them to bring about desired effects; thus magic is at once an art, a craft, and a technique. Yet magical prayer is more than this, for it is animated by a sense of dependence on a higher power. While not all magic is prayerful, all lively prayer has a magical dimension.

How can you tell when a prayer is magical? Certain traits recur across cultures. Look for repetition, secret names, and abundant use of ritual materials such as incense, candles, and wine. Look for use of bodily matter such as blood or spittle. Look for extraordinary handling given to prayer texts: kissing, perfuming, or consuming them. Look for unusual modes of speech: crying, ululating, whispering, sighing, and using foreign words or nonsense words. Magical prayer may be shouted, stammered, or uttered sotto voce, as long as it is not spoken in an ordinary voice. Magical prayer may borrow the language of birds, animals, angels, or ancestors — anything but the language of the butcher or baker down the street.

Above all, prayer is magical when employed as a concrete object, when it is oriented to the solution of a concrete problem, when the ritual that accompanies prayer is treated like a recipe for achieving a certain outcome (making rain, healing sickness, hastening redemption), when the emphasis is on the objective efficacy of the prayer rite, and when the prayer includes dramatic reenactment of the desired outcome. The Anglo-Saxon field prayer previously cited was part of a day-long ceremony, which included anointing sod with holy water, oil, honey, and yeast; burying crosses at the four directions; placing incense, fennel, hallowed soap, and hallowed salt into the plough tail; laying fresh-baked bread under the first furrow; turning round thrice in sunwise circles; lying on the ground and chanting litanies; and repeating a growth spell, part Latin and part Old English, nine times: *Crescite, wexe, et multiplicamini, and gemaenigfealda, et replete and gefylle, terram, Þas eorðan. In nomine patris et filii et spiritus sancti sitis benedicti* (Grow, and multiply, and fill the earth. In the name of the Father and the Son and the Holy Spirit be blessed). There is no denying that prayer, in this context, is an overtly magical performance.

But not only in popular piety and folk tradition does prayer take on magical characteristics. Solemn liturgical prayer often has magical features. No one who has attended a pre–Vatican II Roman Catholic Mass can avoid the impression that a hint of magic exists in the whispered *secretum* of the Eucharistic rite: the archaic language, the repetitive litanies invoking angels and saints, the clouds of incense, and the kissing of books and altar stones, all culminating in the offering of body and blood on the altar. Here, too, objective efficacy is emphasized: the grace conferred by the sacrament is *ex opere operato* (from the work done), rather than contingent on the virtue or sincerity of the celebrant. No wonder that the Communion host and wine acquired overtly magical significance in Christian folk traditions, despite the exertions of authorities against this.

Many of the post–Vatican II changes in the Roman Catholic liturgy had the effect of suppressing its magical overtones. Zealous liturgical reformers stripped churches of statues, candles, censors, bells, and beads; they turned up the electric lights and replaced ancient hymns extolling the sacrifice on the altar with upbeat didactic tunes celebrating the togetherness and table fellowship of the congregation. The altar was moved to a central table, the priest turned his face to the people, the *secretum* became audible, and vernacular translations emphasized an almost pedestrian comprehensibility, discarding long litanies and downplaying initiatory, penitential, and otherworldly motifs. Yet modernity is a strange beast: the sense of the magical may be suppressed in one sector of society, only to emerge more powerful than ever in another. The antimagical renovation of Christian liturgies had its heyday during the 1970s, the same era that saw a revival of magic in popular and literary culture; witness the success of *The Lord of the Rings* and *The Chronicles of Narnia,* as well as the proliferation of neopagan and New Age magical groups. Ever since then, the town common has been abuzz with herbalists, astrologers, tarot card readers, and rune writers. Our culture seems split into two opposite camps: to some, magic shimmers with delightful connotations, promising enchantment, empowerment, and freedom from coercive authorities; to others, magic is a manipulative and sinister art, a medley of prescientific thinking and lust for power, a recipe for Faustian bondage.

Few people in either camp realize, however, that for better or for worse, magic is intertwined not only with the exotic prayers of antiquity but also with the heritage of Judaism and Christianity, and not merely as an accidental vestige. Magic colors some of our oldest and most familiar prayers, and many Jewish and Christian heroes, sages, and saints engaged in what looks very much like magical prayer.

Jewish Magic

Let us consider the case of Ḥoni Ha-Me'aggel (Ḥoni the Circle-Drawer), a celebrated Jewish holy man and wonder-worker who lived during the Second Temple period, in the first century B.C.E. The following story about him appears in several rabbinic sources:

> Once it happened that the greater part of the month of Adar had gone and yet no rain had fallen. The people sent a message to Ḥoni the Circle Drawer, "Pray that rain may fall." He prayed and no rain fell. He thereupon drew a circle and stood within it . . . He exclaimed [before God], "Master of the Universe, Thy children have turned to me because [they believe] me to be a member of Thy house. I swear by Thy great name that I will not move from here until Thou hast mercy upon Thy children." Rain began to drip.[11]

Ḥoni's first effort, however, produced only a slight drizzle, and the people complained, "We look to you to save us from death; we believe that the rain came down merely to release you from your oath." Again

Ḥoni Ha-Me'aggel called upon God: "It is not for this that I have prayed, but for a rain [to fill] cisterns, ditches, and caves." Then the rain came down ferociously, in drops the size of barrel openings, and the people complained, "Master, we look to you to save us from death; we believe that the rain has come down to destroy the world." Again Ḥoni exclaimed before God, "It is not for this that I have prayed, but for a rain of benevolence, blessing, and bounty." This time the raindrops were normal, but they fell for so long that the people had to seek shelter at the Temple Mount. They said to Ḥoni, "Master, in the same way as you have prayed for the rain to fall, pray for the rain to cease." But Ḥoni refused: "I have it as a tradition that we may not pray on account of an excess of good." Instead, he asked for a bullock to sacrifice, and laying his hands upon it cried out, "Master of the Universe, Thy people Israel whom Thou hast brought out from Egypt cannot endure an excess of good nor an excess of punishment; when Thou wast angry with them, they could not endure it; when Thou didst shower upon them an excess of good they could not endure it; may it be Thy will that the rain may cease and that there be relief for the world." This final prayer succeeds: "Immediately the wind began to blow and the clouds were dispersed and the sun shone and the people went out into the fields and gathered for themselves mushrooms and truffles."[12]

Was this prayer or magic? Evidently both. The circle Ḥoni inscribed on the ground, likened by some rabbis to the watchtower of the prophet Habakkuk, has obvious affinities to a magical device. The moment Ḥoni stepped within, he grew bolder, as if he were now protected from malevolent forces and empowered to work wonders. Yet the story makes it clear that Ḥoni's wonderworking was not a matter of technical skill so much as deep intimacy with God. He was no mere conjuror. The sage Shim'on ben Shetah, who had been on the point of condemning Ḥoni for his effrontery to God, acknowledged this: "Were it not that you are Ḥoni I would have placed you under the ban. . . . But what shall I do unto you who actest petulantly before the Omnipresent . . . as a son who acts petulantly before his father and he grants his desires."[13]

Unfortunately for Ḥoni, his reputation as a wonderworker eventually did cost him dearly. Asked to use his powers to put a curse on someone, he refused and was stoned. He appeared to die but instead fell asleep for seventy years (a symbolic figure equal to the number of the gentile nations and the years of the Babylonian exile). When he awoke, no one believed that he was truly Ḥoni. He said his last prayer, a plea for death, and it was granted.

Ḥoni Ha-Me'aggel is just the tip of the iceberg. No religion has a more elaborate tradition of magical prayer than Judaism, and no religion has been more anxious to rein in magical prayer when it threatened to send ordinary piety off track.

In the ancient world, Jews had a reputation for being expert in the magical arts. They were learned, but their social position was marginal; they were devout, but their rituals were opaque to outsiders. Hence, they had that special mystique of being foreign yet strangely wise, a status to which the label of magician frequently attaches. Among the hero magicians of Greco-Roman magical lore are patriarchs, prophets, kings, and priests of the Hebrew Bible: Noah, Moses, Aaron, Solomon, Daniel, and so on. In the Bible itself, Daniel is called "chief of the magicians, enchanters, Chalde'ans, and astrologers" (Daniel 5:11 RSV) and Moses the supreme good magus whose wonderworking trumps that of the pharaoh's magicians. Although sorcery and trafficking with spirits are absolutely condemned ("Thou shalt not suffer a witch to live," Exodus 22:18), dream interpretation, casting lots, ritual utterance of blessings and curses, and various forms of folk magic abound. The paraphernalia of Jewish prayer includes amulets and sacred scripts — the tefillin and the mezuzah. The 150 psalms that formed the prayerbook of the Second Temple had magical as well as cultic uses. For instance, during times of mortal danger one could recite the verses of Psalm 91 over oil and anoint oneself with the solution; this was a palpable way of putting on God's name as "shield and buckler" against demonic attack. "I will protect him," God says, "because he knows my name" (Psalm 91:14 RSV).

As this suggests, the divine name is the key ingredient in Jewish magical prayer, as it is in all Jewish prayer. A decisive turning point for Jewish prayer arrived when God revealed his secret name to Moses: "I AM WHO I AM. . . . Say this to the people of Israel, 'I AM has sent me to you'" (Exodus 3:13–15 RSV). I AM is *the* name of God, the gnomic four-letter YHVH, which encodes the idea of a God who was, is, forever will be, and causes all things to be. When the Temple was standing, it was the high priest's privilege to say the name once a year, on Yom Kippur, in the Holy of Holies; but from the time of the destruction of the Second Temple in 70 C.E., the divine name must never be said aloud, and even the substitute expression ADONAI (LORD) has acquired a numinous and forbidden aura. Though ADONAI may be uttered in solemn prayer, observant Orthodox Jews use the more circumspect HASHEM (the Name) in everyday speech and writing. It is an Orthodox practice to recite the angelic doxology "Holy, holy, holy is HASHEM [ADONAI], Master of Legions"[14] in a deep state of concentration, standing on tiptoe. It is an astonishing privi-

Jewish amulet used to protect mothers and newborn infants from evil spirits.

lege to possess the name of God, and to call upon it entails a magic far stranger and wilder than calling a genie out of a lamp.

That a religion staunchly opposed to idolatry should excel in magical prayer may strike some as surprising. But the concerns of Judaism have never been exclusively spiritual. Judaism insists that God created the material world, saw that it was good, gave it to us to tend, and gave us the means to tend it. All created things therefore have God-given qualities that may be harnessed for curing whatever has gone awry; nature's kitchen is full of remedies, and the book of nature is full of spells. Behind all spells is the original spell, the word of God, which calls life into being and calls beings back from death. Jewish magical prayer attempts to harmonize with the original spell and thus to play a part in the redemption of the world God made. Jewish magical prayer works — if it does work — because God wills it. The sympathy of enchained forces is entirely under God's sovereignty and reflects God's sympathy with the world he has made and governs. Whenever Jews pray, it is said, the Divine Presence *(shekhinah)* prays with them; and whenever the Divine Presence prays on earth, all the powers of heaven are mobilized to respond:

> When [a man] opens his mouth to utter the evening prayer an eagle comes down on the weekdays to take up on its wings the evening prayer. . . . For the morning prayer . . . a lion comes down to receive it in his winged arms: this is Michael. For the afternoon prayer an ox comes down to take it with his arms and horns: this is Gabriel. On Sabbath God himself comes down with the three patriarchs to welcome his only daughter. At that moment the celestial beings . . . exclaim "Lift up your heads, O ye gates, and be exalted, ye everlasting doors," and straightway the doors of seven palaces fly open.[15]

This exalted understanding of Jewish prayer is more widespread than we moderns are likely to suspect. It profoundly influenced the Jewish Daily Prayerbook (Siddur), scattering hints of celestial mysteries throughout the most ordinary Jewish prayers. Distinctive schools of Jewish magical prayer emerged: the first-century Merkavah mystics who sought through ecstatic meditation to relive the prophet Ezekiel's vision of the divine throne, the twelfth-century German pietists (Ḥasidei Ashkenaz) who composed sublime liturgical hymns, the thirteenth-century Spanish Kabbalists who studied the ten divine emanations *(sefirot)*, and the sixteenth-century followers of Isaac Luria, living in Palestine, whose prayer was pure theurgy, or (as the scholar of Jewish mysticism Moshe Idel puts it) "redemptive magic."

Pray slowly, advises the twelfth-century Jewish pietist Yehudah ben Shemu'el He-Ḥasid, or Judah the Ḥasid, so that you can contemplate the theosophical mysteries contained in the numerical values of the prayer's words and letters. In contemplating these mysteries, you will acquire both magical powers and mystical graces. You may ascend to the vision of God or cure a disease here below, you may exorcise a tormented spirit or create a golem. As in the Bible, so in the prayerbook — there is nothing accidental in the words, letters, or even punctuation; all is freighted with meaning and filled with power as a living channel of communication between humanity and God. Why look for the magical and miraculous beyond the prayerbook, Judah asks, when the whole world, and worlds above worlds, are contained within its well-worn pages? From Judah comes the "Shir ha-Kavod" ("Song of Glory"), a hymn so holy and mysterious that it is recited at the opening of the Ark only on Sabbath and festivals (or by some congregations only on the high holy days), when the splendor of God is most immediately present to the congregation. The glory *(kavod)* to which this hymn attests is more than just the honor and majesty of God: it is the very radiance of the divine essence, which the soul longs to see, but which images are too opaque to represent truly.

More magical still is the school of prayer founded by Isaac Luria in the sixteenth century, in the final flowering of the medieval Jewish esoteric movement called Kabbalah (tradition). The Lurianic Kabbalists believed that if enough Jews dedicated themselves to theurgic mystical prayer, they would free the sparks of divine light trapped in matter and thus hasten redemption, or *tiqqun ʿolam* (repair of the world). By meditating on the letters of the divine names and recombining them in prayer, the Lurianic Kabbalists sought to bring the Divine Presence back from its exile in the lower realms and achieve a bridal union *(yiḥud)* of the scattered divine powers.

In all these Jewish worlds of prayer, the magical and the mystical intertwine. But in one Jewish movement — a modern one, at that — daily prayer, folk magic, and esoteric redemptive magic converge to form a complete way of life: the Hasidic movement of eastern Europe.

The Baʿal Shem Tov

Mention Hasidism, and you call up the image of men in curling side locks and uncut beards, dressed in the finery of eighteenth-century Polish nobility, with fur-trimmed hats and long black coats. Mention Hasidic prayer, and you call up the image of whole communities of such men worshiping in their prayer shawls, with tefillin (phylacteries) strapped to arms and foreheads, swaying as they intone the words of prayer, singing, clapping, shouting, and on occasions of solemn festivity, dancing with the Torah scroll. The accompanying images of women are less visible to the outside world but no less essential to the faith and culture of the family: braiding challah, lighting the candles for the Sabbath, visiting the ritual bath, caring for children and for neighbors in need, and upholding an environment of purity and prayer. The Hasidim seem to belong to another era, a sort of urban counterpart to the Amish, doggedly holding on to their traditions in separatist enclaves and offering to an uncomprehending secular world the image of a counterculture dedicated entirely to piety and prayer.

In the early days of the movement, however, the Hasidim were seen as heretical innovators, drunk on ecstatic prayer. "They conduct themselves like madmen," complained a widely circulated anti-Hasidic broadside from the 1770s, "and explain their behavior by saying that in their thoughts they soar in the most far-off worlds. . . . When they pray . . . they raise such a din that the walls quake. . . . And they turn over like wheels, with the head below and the legs above."[16]

The "madness," if such it was, can be traced in large measure to a charismatic teacher, Rabbi Yisra'el Ben Eli'ezer, the Ba'al Shem Tov ("Master of the Good Name," known by the acronym *Besht*), born in 1700 in the small shtetl of Okopy in Podolia, southeast Poland. According to tradition, his parents were elderly and impoverished, and they left him orphaned as a young boy. The region in which they lived had survived the wars, hardships, persecution, and internal strife accompanying the breakup of the Polish-Lithuanian commonwealth, from the Chmielnicki massacres of 1648–49 to the Haidamack pogroms. The area had also witnessed the rise and fall of the false messiah Shabbetai Tsevi (1626–1676). Jewish culture, one of the glories of the Polish-Lithuanian commonwealth, was under siege. Torah learning, the heart of Jewish culture, had become the preserve of a privileged few with the means to devote themselves to full-time study; later Hasidic sources would depict these scholars as turning from a proper delight in the Talmud's treasury of law and lore to a pompous pride in showing off their mastery of the intricacies of *pilpul* (dialectical argument).

Young Yisra'el received some education at an elementary Hebrew school *(cheder)* but is remembered as a chronic runaway from lessons. He supported himself as a young man by working at odd jobs and as a teacher's assistant in the synagogue. His charismatic wisdom manifested itself at an early age; children followed him, singing, to *cheder* as if charmed by a pied piper, and villagers began to seek him out for advice and arbitration of petty quarrels. The eminent Rabbi Ephraim of Kuty admired Yisra'el so much that he gave him his daughter in marriage. After his marriage, the Besht began to focus more intensely on mystical prayer. He retired to the Carpathian Mountains, where he labored as a lime digger. It is said that during this time of seclusion the Besht received supernatural instruction directly from the teacher of Elijah and learned his Kabbalah from the secret manuscript of a mysterious figure called Rabbi Adam. Under this mystical tutelage, Yisra'el became a *ba'al shem* (master of the Name), with the power to heal, exorcise evil spirits, and write protective amulets.

The Besht believed he was under a divine obligation to keep his gifts private until he reached the age of thirty-six. During the 1730s, he settled in the town of Miedzyboz and, when the time was right, revealed himself to the community and began to work and teach publicly.[17] His responsibilities included overseeing marriage settlements, resolving property disputes, making kosher rulings, exorcising dybbuks, and negotiating with Christian neighbors. Above all, he was a teacher of Kabbalah who gathered his innermost circle of disciples for instruction every week after the third Sabbath meal; from this informal spiritual court the modern Hasidic hereditary dynasties claim descent, although the Besht does not appear to have established a dynasty in his own lifetime.

The teachings of the Ba'al Shem Tov revolved around prayer. Conservative in his fidelity to the Torah and the rabbinic tradition, he was at the same time radical in popularizing a way of esoteric magical prayer that had formerly been the exclusive privilege of learned elites and virtuosos of Kabbalah. Redemptive magical prayer was, according to the Besht, the prerogative of every Jew, even the unlettered. He encouraged his followers to pray spontaneously, exceeding the bounds of the established prayer times. Don't mope about the prayer house mortifying the flesh, the Besht commanded, but rejoice and be glad; for the divine presence rests on one who prays with ecstatic joy *(hitlahavut)*, and it brings messianic redemption near.

The story is told in the *Shivhei ha-Besht (Praises of the Besht)*, the earliest collection of legends about the Ba'al Shem Tov, of the turmoil in heaven that resulted when the Besht failed to be joyful in prayer. During preparations for the Sabbath, the Besht received a letter telling him of a blood libel in which twelve Jews had been tortured and killed. He went to the mikveh weeping bitterly and recited the afternoon prayer with such great bitterness that his followers, greatly disturbed, consoled themselves by saying, "Perhaps when he will begin welcoming the Sabbath, he will do it joyfully." But the Besht wept as he prayed the Reception of the Sabbath prayer and continued to weep as he sanctified the wine. Finally he retired to his room and lay prostrate on the floor. At midnight, a brilliant light shone through the cracks of the door, and a disciple overheard him saying:

> "Welcome, Rabbi Akiva." And he also welcomed the martyrs whose names no one knows. . . . The Besht said to the martyrs, "I decree that you go and take revenge on the enemy, the persecutor." The martyrs answered, "Do not let these words pass from your lips again, and let what you have said be nullified. You, sir, are not aware of your power. When you, sir, upset the Sabbath, there was a great tumult in paradise and we fled from the palaces as though we were running before the sword. Even when we reached an upper palace we found that all had to flee from

> there as well, though they knew not why. Finally, we came to an upper palace where they understood the cause, and they shouted at us: 'Hurry and go to quiet the Besht's tears.'"[18]

Had the Besht's cries been heeded, the martyrs might have been reincarnated and thus missed their chance of sanctification: "We might commit sins, God forbid, from which we would not have any redemption." Hence, the martyrs explained, it would be better for the Ba'al Shem Tov to fulfill his obligation to honor the Sabbath with joyful prayer. Joyful prayer, in other words, is a discipline that overrides other concerns, even grief and desire for revenge. This discipline requires solemn preparation and must be yoked to deep interior concentration *(kavvanah)* in order to bear fruit. One Hasidic rebbe explains, "I anticipate prayer for eight days. The same is true of the Sabbath. By Wednesday, I can recognize if the coming Sabbath will be an exciting one."[19]

As he prayed, the Besht's deep state of *kavvanah* would cause him to sway and shiver. Swaying in prayer and Torah study, a norm for traditional Jews and a familiar sight in synagogues and houses of study around the world, can induce mild trembling; pressed further, it becomes the "fear and trembling" with which a mortal approaches the divine throne. The prophet Daniel fainted when the angel appeared before him; when he stood up, he trembled from head to toe (Daniel 10:9–11). This became a model for Hasidic prayer: "Serve the LORD with fear, and with trembling kiss his feet" (Psalm 2:11 RSV). The Besht was such a virtuoso of prayer that the fringes of his prayer shawl would sway and tremble of their own accord.[20] In prayer raptures he ascended to heaven to intercede for his community and bring their petitions to the divine throne; when persecution loomed, he often managed to avert the divine decree by which such trials were permitted to occur. He plummeted, while in prayer, into the depths of hell to rescue imprisoned souls. His prayers could elevate any soul that retained even the smallest spark of holiness. The sheer intensity of his ecstatic communion with God endowed even the most routine prayers of the Besht with magical power and esoteric significance.

Once, it is said, the Besht prayed so deeply that he lost track of his surroundings and walked for three days and three nights until he found himself in a deserted region far from home. A large frog appeared and revealed that in a former life he had been a Torah scholar but had fallen under Satan's influence through neglecting the obligatory ritual of hand washing. The punishment for this transgression was to spend five hundred years as a frog, far from the paths of Jews who might inadvertently bless him by thinking good thoughts as they passed by. The Besht prayed over the frog-man until his soul went up to heaven, leaving only a wrinkled amphibian shell behind.[21]

The Besht's power to bless was matched by his power to curse. The false messiah Shabbetai Tsevi appealed from the grave to the Besht, begging him to redeem his soul. The Besht took pity on him at first and began to pray but then thought better of it, reversed his intention, and cast the apostate down to hell.[22]

The magical power of Hasidic prayer was not restricted to the Ba'al Shem Tov but extended to his disciples as well. As *tsaddiqim* (righteous men), the great Hasidic rebbes had sweeping authority to intercede with God for their communities, and even the lowliest Hasid could storm heaven through prayer:

> The Rebbe Levi Isaac of Berditchev asked an illiterate tailor what he did on Yom Kippur since he could not read the prescribed prayers. The Jew reluctantly replied: "I spoke to God and told Him that the sins for which I am expected to repent are minor ones. I also said to Him: 'My sins are inconsequential; I may have kept leftover cloth or occasionally forgotten to recite some prayers. But You have committed really grave sins. You have removed mothers from their children and children from their mothers. So let's reach an agreement. If You'll pardon me, I'm ready to pardon You."
>
> The Berditchever rabbi angrily rebuked the unlettered Jew: "You are not only illiterate but also foolish. You were too lenient with God. You should have insisted that He bring redemption to the entire Jewish people."[23]

One wishes the tailor had persisted and that the magic of Hasidic prayer had averted the Holocaust that was to come. But Hasidic prayer did, in a sense, subdue the Holocaust by bringing hope to more than a few Holocaust survivors and providing a focus and inspiration for the post-annihilation reconstruction of Jewish life. After the Holocaust, the influence of Hasidic prayer spread beyond the boundaries of the Old World Hasidic courts (Bobova, Satu Mare, Lubavitch, Belz) into New World Hasidic enclaves (Williamsburg, Crown Heights, Boro Park in Brooklyn; Fairfax in Los Angeles) and even beyond the established Hasidic communities.

Many Jewish intellectuals of liberal and secular sympathies pine for the intact Jewish cultures of the pre-Holocaust past, the folklore and folkways of Hasidic eastern Europe, and the fervor and immediacy of

Hasidic prayer. One thinks of Martin Buber, the Jewish existentialist philosopher in whose affectionate portrayal the Hasidic masters appear as playful bohemians of the spirit; Elie Wiesel, whose chronicles of Hasidic communities annihilated by the Holocaust stress the more sober aspects of their spirituality; Isaac Bashevis Singer, S. Y. Agnon, Scholem Aleichem, Scholem Asch, and Chaim Potok, whose stories enshrine both the magical and the mundane aspects of Hasidic life, from golems to market gossip; or Abraham Joshua Heschel, a scion of Polish Hasidim who ended his days as a prominent spiritual leader and social activist in New York. Heschel speaks movingly of what it felt like, during his student days in Berlin, to be cut adrift from his childhood experience of Hasidic prayer:

> . . . In those months in Berlin I went through moments of profound bitterness. I walked alone in the evenings through the magnificent streets of Berlin. I admired the solidity of its architecture, the overwhelming drive and power of a dynamic civilization. There were concerts, theaters, and lectures by famous scholars about the latest theories and inventions and I was pondering whether to go to the new Max Reinhardt play or to a lecture about the theory of relativity.
>
> Suddenly I noticed the sun had gone down, evening had arrived. . . . I had forgotten God — I had forgotten Sinai — I had forgotten that sunset is my business — that my task is "to restore the world to the kingship of the Lord."
>
> So I began to utter the words of the evening prayer. Blessed art thou, Lord our God, King of the Universe, who by His word brings on the evening twilight.[24]

Sunset is my business. Heschel recognized that by praying as a faithful Jew, he would perform his essential task: to collaborate in the work of *tiqqun 'olam,* the repair of the world by redemptive magic. The magic inherent in Jewish prayer comes from God as a gift and returns to God as a thank-offering; there is nothing mechanical or coercive about it. As the Hasidic master Rabbi Pinḥas of Korets writes, "It is stated in the *Zohar* that he who slays the dragon is given in marriage the king's daughter, which is prayer. Consequently, a man must wait to see whether or not prayer has been given to him. . . . if prayer is not given to a man from Heaven and he wishes to take the hand of the king's daughter without permission . . . it is sheer effrontery in the face of Heaven."[25] Prayer, in other words, can be magical without being manipulative, aggressive, self-centered, or Faustian; it all depends on whether one acknowledges, with humility, awe, and gratitude, the sovereignty of the divine Creator and King.

Christian Magic

Christian prayer, similarly, is steeped in a magic that honors, rather than subverts, the power of God. A remarkable ninth-century Old Saxon alliterative poem called the *Heliand (Song of the Savior)* illustrates this in high dramatic fashion. Recasting the gospel in language comprehensible to Saxon warrior culture, the *Heliand* tells of four heroes who inscribe in a "bright-shining book" the spells by which the Creator made and redeemed the world. The heroes sing of a Great One born in a humble hill fort, who in infancy narrowly escapes death at the hands of a "slime-hearted" king, flees into exile, and then returns to be proclaimed son of the Chieftain and lord of the middle world. Immersed in sacred waters by a soothsayer, he emerges in shining strength to do single combat with a supernatural enemy. He gathers twelve thanes, warrior companions, with whom he travels the countryside, healing the sick, turning water into apple wine, magically increasing bread to feed a hungry crowd, and performing other miracles. As his enemies draw near, he bestows upon his thanes a gift of bread and wine transformed: "'Believe me clearly,' He said, 'that this is My body and also My blood. . . . This body and blood is a thing which possesses power [*mahtig*]: with it you will give honor to your Chieftain.'"[26] The next day, the son of the Chieftain is captured, tortured, and hanged from a criminal tree. But in the morning his holy breath returns to his body, the doors of the underworld burst open, the road to heaven shines forth in brilliant sunlight, and he rises from the dead.

To see Jesus and his disciples transported to a feudal world of thanes and soothsayers, where magic and holiness coincide, is extraordinary enough. Yet more remarkable is how little of the essential Christian message is lost in the process. The *Heliand*'s version of the Lord's Prayer, for example, while saturated with magic, remains faithful to the New Testament account. It begins with one of the twelve asking Jesus to teach them how to pray: "'Our good Lord,' he said, 'we need Your gracious help in order to carry out Your will and we also need Your own words, Best of all born, to teach us, Your followers, how to pray—just as John, the good baptist, teaches his people with words every day how they are to speak to the ruling God. Do this for Your own followers—teach us the secret runes.'"[27] And so he teaches them this prayer:

> Father of us, the sons of men,
> You are in the high heavenly kingdom,
> blessed be Your name in every word.

May Your mighty kingdom come.
May Your will be done over all this world —
just the same on earth as it is up there
in the high heavenly kingdom.
Give us support each day, good Chieftain,
Your holy help, and pardon us, Protector of Heaven,
our many crimes, just as we do to other human beings.
Do not let evil little creatures lead us off
to do their will, as we deserve,
but help us against all evil deeds.[28]

No prayer is more familiar, yet a mere twist of poetic diction makes it strange again, and in this strangeness a magical potency stands revealed. The secret runes sought by the thanes are primordial words of power, at once cryptic writing and sacred speech, which echo the runes by which God created heaven and earth. The petitions of the Lord's Prayer, to those accustomed to the more abstract English version, are here surprisingly concrete, with "deliver us from evil" recast as "do not let evil little creatures lead us off." The Old Saxon here is *leđa uuihti* (literally "loathsome wights," evil beings who attack the human race, according to G. Ronald Murphy, the *Heliand* translator and scholar of Germanic languages and mythology).[29] Yet the same solidity and specificity are found in the Greek New Testament, where "deliver us from evil" (*tou ponhrou*, genitive singular, masculine or neuter) may be rendered "deliver us from the evil one," namely, from Satan and his servants, from the glamour of evil, the lies of hell, the craft and power of our ancient enemy, and all the present and final tribulations they bring.

To turn from the *Heliand* to a fresh reading of the New Testament is to have the scales fall from our eyes. Instantly we recognize that the early Christian community must have seen Jesus, in part, as a warrior engaged in mortal combat with satanic powers, using as his weapon prayer infused with divine magic. It was Jesus' custom, according to Mark, to recharge himself for the combat by praying in solitude: "And in the morning, rising up a great while before day, he went out, and departed into a solitary place, and there prayed. And Simon and they that were with him followed after him. And when they had found him, they said unto him, 'All men seek for thee'" (Mark 1:37).[30] From such intervals of secluded prayer, Jesus would emerge with the power to cast out demons, heal the sick, teach with authority, and forgive sins.

Modern readers may view driving out evil spirits as stage hypnosis rather than prayer, but Jesus unequivocally called it prayer. When his disciples ask why they had been unable to free a young boy of an evil spirit that produced intractable seizures, Jesus explains, "This kind cannot be driven out by anything but prayer" (Mark 9:29 RSV). Yet it is prayer in the imperative mood. To a demon Jesus commands, "Be silent, and come out of him"; to a leper, "Be clean"; and to a dead child, "*Talitha cum*" (Aramaic for "Little girl, get up!"; Mark 1:25, 1:41, 5:41 RSV). This is prayer as spiritual warfare, with the forces of darkness arrayed against the forces of light and the fate of human lives in the balance. In such a context, prayer is bound to have magical characteristics, as it plainly does in this account:

> And they bring unto him one that was deaf, and had an impediment in his speech; and they beseech him to put his hand upon him. And he took him aside from the multitude, and put his fingers into his ears, and he spit, and touched his tongue; And looking up to heaven, he sighed, and saith unto him, "Ephphatha," that is, "Be opened." And straightway his ears were opened, and the string of his tongue was loosed, and he spake plain. And he charged them that they should tell no man: but the more he charged them, so much the more a great deal they published it; And were beyond measure astonished, saying, "He hath done all things well: he maketh both the deaf to hear, and the dumb to speak." (Mark 7:32–37)

Looking up to heaven and sighing are classical gestures of prayer; spitting, touching, and crying out in an archaic tongue are classical forms of magic, mixing strange speech with bodily fluids to effect a transformation. In a similar episode in the Gospel of John, Jesus heals a man blind from birth by anointing his eyes with clay made of Jesus' own spittle mixed with dirt (John 9:1–11).

From a Christian perspective, the magical works of Jesus are eschatological signs announcing the reign of God, signs whose full meaning would be revealed only with the death and resurrection of the divine-human Christ. Those hostile to Jesus call him a common sorcerer: "He casts out demons by Be-el'zebul, the prince of demons" (Luke 11:15 RSV), but Jesus answers, "If it is by the finger of God that I cast out demons, then the kingdom of God has come upon you" (Luke 11:20 RSV). "This is the finger of God" was what the pharaoh's magicians declared when they realized that their magic was no match for that of Moses. Jesus is in this respect the second Moses, the definitive wielder of redemptive magic.

Yet the burning of the magic books in Acts 19 shows that the early Christian community inherited the Jewish and Greco-Roman ambivalence toward magic and was anxious to distinguish miracles and redemptive magic from the magic of common amulets and spells. Saint Paul fought against a magical understanding of the sacraments of baptism and the Eucharist,[31] and the story of Simon Magus in Acts 8 (impressed by the disciples' magic, Simon attempts to buy his way into their guild) is an object lesson in the difference between the higher magic of the gospel and the lower magic of a self-aggrandizing wizard.

Christian antimagical polemic crested in the Protestant Reformation, leading to a wholesale rejection of sacraments, devotions, and doctrines suggestive of magic in any way: purgatory and indulgences, scapulars and novenas, veneration of relics, the whole kit bag of Catholic and folk religion. Biblical scholars influenced by this polemic have been reluctant to acknowledge the magical elements in the New Testament and the early Christian world. For example, one prominent New Testament scholar insists that the import of Jesus' use of spittle was to challenge the purity laws, and he dismisses its family resemblance to the healing practices of magicians throughout the ancient world.[32] At the other extreme, maverick scholars flaunt their radicalism by exaggerating the magical elements; thus Morton Smith, in his controversial *Jesus the Magician,* interprets Jesus as an itinerant wonderworker whose teachings on private and persistent prayer, cryptic references to the keys to heaven, episodes of ritualized anger and shamanistic frenzy, employment of standard exorcistic techniques, and grandiose claims of divine sonship make him no different from the sorcerers who populate the Greek magical papyri.[33]

The truth is not well served by either of these positions. The early Christian portrayal of Jesus and the sacraments draws upon a tradition of magical language and practice to convey a deeper, redemptive magic that Christians believe to be the core mystery of faith. Deeper magic it may be, but recognizably magic nonetheless. It was necessary and inevitable, and not a matter for Christians to regret, that the magic of the gospel would partake of the magic of the ancient world and would commingle with the folk magic of the many cultures to which Christianity spread. The relics, rosary beads, statues, icons, medals, and votive offerings that line the old highways of Europe, and especially the great pilgrimage routes; the magical uses of familiar prayers; the vigils, pilgrimages, processions, novenas, and litanies of the faithful — all these are signs not of atavism or degeneration, but rather of a fully realized culture of prayer.

Christians have always looked to the divine for guidance and protection and have employed every means — moral, ascetic, mystical, magical — to reinforce the appeal. But the magic of Christian prayer is personal and vital, not mechanical; its source is a relationship to living persons: the three Persons of the Trinity, the incarnate Redeemer, the Mother of God, the heavenly companies of saints. These holy beings enclose the

Madonna of the Misericordia, *by Lippo Memmi (c. 1285–1361).*

supplicant in a mantle of safety, expressed most vividly by the "Madonna of Mercy" images (by Piero della Francesca, Domenico Ghirlandaio, and many others), in which the faithful crowd together to pray under the Blessed Virgin's generously overarching cloak. "Remember, O most gracious Virgin Mary," pleads the Catholic Memorare prayer, "that never was it known that anyone who fled to your protection, implored your help, or sought your intercession, was left unaided."[34]

Exuberant, unstinting, all-encompassing, all-forgiving reassurance is such an insistent theme of Christian devotion that it produced a special genre: the all-encircling, 360-degree prayer for divine protection, suggesting a magical shield. Such prayers can be lyrical, like this meditation from the Anglican divine Lancelot Andrewes: "Be, Lord, within me to strengthen me, without me to preserve, over me to shelter, beneath to support, before me to direct, behind me to bring back, round about me to fortify." They can also be visceral, like the tenth-century prayer that begins, "Christ's cross over this face, and thus over my ear. Christ's cross over this eye. Christ's cross over this nose," and then proceeds to name all the limbs and organs and to mark each step in every direction with the seal of the cross.[35] The most striking examples of this genre are Celtic "breastplate" prayers, which are inspired by Ephesians 6 ("take unto you the whole armour of God, that ye may be able to withstand in the evil day. . . . having on the breastplate of righteousness"). A breastplate prayer, according to legend, protected Saint Patrick when passing through an ambush set by the pagan king Loeguire:

> Christ to shield me today
> Against poison, against burning,
> Against drowning, against wounding,
> So that there may come to me abundance of reward.
> Christ with me, Christ before me, Christ behind me,
> Christ in me, Christ beneath me, Christ above me,
> Christ on my right, Christ on my left,
> Christ when I lie down, Christ when I sit down, Christ when I arise,
> Christ in the heart of every man who thinks of me,
> Christ in the mouth of every one who speaks of me.[36]

Having sung these words, Patrick and his companions were changed into the likeness of deer and escaped unseen. In this mythic guise, the 360-degree prayer is an invisibility spell, but in all its forms it speaks to a legitimate need for comprehensive grace and guidance. Since this need is well-nigh universal, every tradition has its own version of the 360-degree prayer. Consider this particularly fine Muslim example:

> O God appoint for me light in my heart and light in my tomb and light before me and light behind me; light on my right hand and light on my left; light above me and light below me; light in my sight and light in my perception; light in my countenance and light in my flesh; light in my blood and light in my bones. Increase to me light, and give me light, and appoint for me light, and give me more light, give me more light, give me more light![37]

In cultures where ordinary acts of devotion are part of the daily routine, prayer and magic happily unite. The baseball player crosses himself before he raises his bat; ordinary Christians cross themselves before eating. The sign of the cross, the quintessential Christian prayer made flesh, is at once a means of grace and a magical protective charm. Inscribed on the forehead like a brand, the cross recalls the mark traced on the foreheads of those spared from the destruction of Jerusalem (Ezekiel 9:4). Traced from head to breast and from shoulder to shoulder, the sign of the cross resembles a 360-degree prayer. Girded with the breastplate of the cross, the knight of faith prepares to go to battle. Sheltered under the mantle of the cross, the child of faith takes refuge in divine protection. Imprinted at baptism and confirmation with the seal of the cross, the pilgrim of faith sets forth in the power of the divine name, Father, Son, and Holy Spirit.

Writing at the beginning of the third century, the North African theologian Tertullian describes this gestural prayer as a defining mark of Christians: "At every step, at every movement, at every coming in and going out, in dressing and putting on our shoes, in the bath, at the table, at the lighting of the candles, lying down or sitting down, whatever affair concerns us, we mark our foreheads with the sign of the cross."[38] Examples abound of both its efficacy and the perils of neglecting it. In his celebrated dialogues on saints and miracles, Pope Gregory the Great recounts many instances in which the sign of the cross vanquished temptation, deadly peril, and demonic attack. When Saint Benedict made the sign of the cross over a poisoned drink given to him by mutinous monks, the cup shattered as if struck by a stone. When Satan manufactured an illusion that a monastery was on fire, the sign of the cross quenched the imaginary flames. When a woman failed to cross herself before eating her lettuce, she paid for her neglect by swallowing a demon.

The cross is a universal symbol as well. In various world cultures it appears as a symbol of the sun, a world tree, a ladder to heaven, a map of the four winds, a royal scepter, and a compass rose — all tokens of life and order. The Egyptian ankh and the Indian svastika are in this sense close cousins to the Christian cross. Justin Martyr, the second-century apologist, saw in all cross-shaped things a foreshadowing of the sacred cross: you cannot cross the sea without a cross to hold your sail, he pointed out; you cannot dig the earth without a cross-shaped shovel; you cannot consecrate emperors, bury the dead, or engage the enemy without insignia and banners in the shape of the cross. Moreover, Justin observed, cruciformity separates human beings from animals: when we stand erect with arms outstretched in prayer, we form a cross; and in the right angles that set off the eyes, nose, and mouth, by which our spirit breathes and our soul utters its thoughts, we are forever making the sign of the cross.[39] No wonder that the cross (often in the form of an anchor or ship's mast) figures so widely as a motif of magical amulets within Christianity and beyond; for Justin, it is humanity's native dress.

Magic all this may be, but it hints at something more, for overshadowing the cross — and eclipsing its solar symbolism — is the figure of the crucified one whose sacrifice it represents. While the sign of the cross steels the knight of faith against danger, it also makes an extraordinary demand: we must be willing to pour out our life for the sake of others. The message is clear: While there is no prayer without some element of magic, there is no fully realized prayer without some element of sacrifice. That the universe is a magical "sympathy of enchained forces" is implicit in prayer, and where magic is absolutely ruled out, prayer must suffer. But as we will see in the next chapter, magic is only one side of the story of prayer. The other side is the mysterious encounter between divine sovereignty and human freedom in which prayer, unchaining the enchained forces, freely sacrifices self-interest to the divine will.

CHAPTER 3

Deeper Magic

A HALF MILE NORTH of the center of Oxford, on St. Giles Street just before it becomes the old Woodstock Road, sits an unremarkable English public house whose sign depicts a child riding an eagle as a pictogram for the pub's name: The Eagle and Child. Locals call it The Bird and Baby. Here the Inklings (C. S. Lewis and his brother, as well as J. R. R. Tolkien, Charles Williams, Owen Barfield, and others) met to drink, eat, smoke, and argue during the middle decades of the twentieth century. Over pints and pipes they discussed their common goal: to awaken modern culture from its imaginative slumber. They mined the folklore and mythology of northern Europe and the poetry and philosophy of the Romantic tradition, searching for alternatives to a world bedeviled by industrialization, dehumanizing ideologies, and world war. The magic of Faërie attracted them, but not the magic of Faust. Above all, they were drawn to the magic of Christian redemption, through which sacrifice runs like a crimson thread.

In his first fantasy work about the land of Narnia, Lewis speaks of "a magic deeper still" in the willingness of the lion Aslan to die in place of the child Edmund, who had forfeited his life through an act of betrayal:

> "It means," said Aslan, "that though the Witch knew the Deep Magic, there is a magic deeper still which she did not know. Her knowledge goes back only to the dawn of time. But if she could have looked a little further back, into the stillness and the darkness before Time dawned, she would have read there a different incantation. She would have known that when a willing victim who had committed no treachery was killed in a traitor's stead, the Table would crack and Death itself would start working backward."[1]

Similarly, Tolkien's works suggest that the deeper magic of sacrifice is the antidote to the intoxicating glamour of evil. In the hobbit Frodo's words, "It must often be so, Sam, when things are in danger: someone has to give them up, lose them, so that others may keep them."[2] Sacrifice — both mortal and divine — is written into the constitution of the world, Tolkien believed, as the means of its recovery from ruin. Yet humans and hobbits placed in "sacrificial situations," as Tolkien called them, inevitably reach the limits of their moral and physical strength and must appeal to grace for help ("O Elbereth! Gilthoniel!"). Tolkien knew intimately from his own experiences in the Great War that prayer runs deepest when its theme is sacrifice and surrender rather than self-power: *not my will but Thy will be done.*

Such prayer was the daily stuff of Tolkien's own life. He regularly prayed, in Latin, the Our Father, the Hail Mary, the Litany of Loreto, and the Divine Praises — and made several attempts to render these beloved prayers into his Elvish languages. Every morning Tolkien could be seen in his pew attending "the holy sacrifice of the Mass," as it was then called, and praying before the consecrated host. In a 1941 letter to his son Michael, Tolkien commended Eucharistic adoration as the consummate sacrificial prayer:

> Out of the darkness of my life, so much frustrated, I put before you the one great thing to love on earth: the Blessed Sacrament. . . . There you will find romance, glory, honour, fidelity, and the true way of all your loves upon earth, and more than that: Death: by the divine paradox, that which ends life, and demands the surrender of all, and yet by the taste (or foretaste) of which alone can what you seek in your earthly relationships (love, faithfulness, joy) be maintained, or take on that complexion of reality, of eternal endurance, which every man's heart desires.[3]

If prayer is to be something more than pleading for favors, it must acquire this sacrificial note, this willingness to surrender all into God's hands. Sacrifice of self-will is the distinctively religious element in prayer, as William James observes in *The Varieties of Religious Experience:* "There is a state of mind, known to religious men, but to no others, in which the will to assert ourselves and hold our own has been displaced by a willingness to close our mouths and be as nothing in the floods and waterspouts of God. In this state of mind, what we most dreaded has become the habitation of our safety, and the hour of our mortal death has turned into our spiritual birthday."[4]

But what does sacrifice of the ritual sort — the burnt offering, the blood-sprinkled stone — have to do with prayer? Is it only metaphorical sacrifice that should interest us? Many would argue, surveying the long history of religions, that ritual sacrifice is an atavism: materialistic, crude, and amoral; atrocious when it involves killing human beings, cruel when the victim is an animal, profligate when it consumes food and valuables that could be put to better use, regressive in imagining that God thirsts for libations, and damaging in the notions of victim and scapegoat that it perpetuates. The age of sacrifice is long over, it would seem, and happily enough, for it was all along a misunderstanding of the true service of God: "For I desired mercy, and not sacrifice, and the knowledge of God more than burnt offerings" (Hosea 6:6). What need does prayer, communicating heart to heart, have for such external observances? "Only two things will I seek to know," says Saint Augustine of Hippo, "God and the soul, the soul and God." The spirit of prayer, according to the great philosopher of modernity, Immanuel Kant, is nothing other than the "heart-felt wish to be well-pleasing to God." What could be more antithetical to prayer than labyrinthine rules for selecting the spotless victim, consecrating ground and vessels, purifying participants, and preparing the acceptable oblation?

Nonetheless, early anthropologists such as Sir Edward Tylor have seen ritual sacrifice as closely akin to prayer, as if sacrifice were prayer's half-witted cousin:

> Sacrifice has its apparent origin in the same early period of culture and its place in the same animistic scheme as prayer, with which through so long a range of history it has been carried on in the closest connexion. As prayer is a request made to a deity as if he were a man, so sacrifice is a gift to a deity as if he were a man. The human types of both may be studied unchanged in social life to this day. The suppliant who bows before his chief, laying a gift at his feet and making his humble petition, displays the anthropomorphic model and origin at once of sacrifice and prayer.[5]

According to Tylor, sacrifice at its earliest stage was a matter of preserving and maintaining the human world by keeping the gods or spirits satisfied with food and drink; at a later stage, sacrifice became an act of homage and finally an act of abnegation. Gift, homage, and abnegation: these were for Tylor the three phases in the evolution of sacrifice, each one giving way to the next until a higher attainment of civilization made the whole system of sacrifice obsolete, leaving prayer to undergo further moral refinement on its own.

An attractive sequence to be sure — but it bears little resemblance to the realities of history. Far from just a primitive phenomenon, ritual sacrifice can be a highly civilized activity involving domesticated animals or agricultural produce, elaborate legal codes, rich mythologies, and fine arts. The Greek sacrificial arena was the world's first theater. Jewish prayer is full of reminiscences of the sacrifices performed when the Jerusalem Temple was still standing. The annual Islamic pilgrimage to Mecca culminates in a great festival of sacrifice ('Īd al-Aḍḥā), celebrated in honor of Abraham's obedience. The Christian Eucharist is sacrificial in form. Sacrifice is a fundamental religious act, arguably *the* fundamental religious act. Although our modern assumptions may lead us to overlook it, the affinity between prayer and sacrifice is a permanent religious fact.

In everyday conversation we use *sacrifice* to mean something like a tradeoff: a parent sacrifices time and energy to care for a child, a family sacrifices its vacation to pay for college tuition, a batter bunts into a deliberate out to allow his teammate to advance a base. But in its original meaning, sacrifice is an offering made holy (Latin *sacer* plus *facere*) by donation to a higher power, gods or God, spirits or venerated ancestors. How do you send the gods a gift? You must transform the material offering into a substance that can travel from human to divine realms, by killing, dismembering, or dematerializing it; by pouring it onto hallowed ground, burning it to let the smoke rise to heaven, dissolving it into the ocean, or offering a substitute that is symbolic and therefore already free enough from materiality to release its essence to a higher world. Chief among such symbolic substitutes, as we shall see, is prayer itself, which is a gift to the gods in word and spirit.

Sacrifice repays the debt of life to the source of life by offering the poured-out blood in which life energy resides or the first fruits of the harvest on which life depends. We have our life on loan, and sacrifice is a way of making the loan secure. In return for offering life, the sacrificer receives abundant life; the good willingly sacrificed redounds a hundredfold. *Do ut des* is the Latin formula for the most basic kind of sacrifice, "I give, so that you might give," in a reciprocal exchange. Prayer is the essential nonmaterial cargo in this exchange, for every sacrificial gift carries with it a particular prayer intention: a request for health or well-being, a confession of sin, a thank-offering, the fulfillment of a vow, or a simple hospitable greeting to the higher powers.

Sacrifice is prayer made flesh; it communicates with the gods, discharges guilt, binds together the community, and forges communion between heaven and earth. As in all things, *corruptio optima pessima* (the corruption of the best is the worst), and sacrifice can also be a horrific and degrading act of socially sanctioned violence and victimization. Human sacrifice still goes on, it is sobering to realize, in some pockets of the world, and it occurred to varying degrees in most ancient cultures—

Apollo (with lyre) and Artemis sacrificing over a fire burning on an altar. Red figure Attic hydria, 490–480 B.C.E.

Mesopotamia, Egypt, ancient Israel and its Middle Eastern neighbors, India, China, archaic Greece, and the Americas. Few civilizations have managed to escape this horror, perhaps because the logic of human sacrifice is universal and self-evident: human life is the most precious gift one can offer.

But the logic of human sacrifice is also suicidal, and the great religious traditions have come to reject it. That we owe God nothing less is the lesson of the biblical story in which Abraham consents to sacrifice his beloved son. That God has no need for human sacrifice is the lesson of the ram offered in Isaac's place. Substitution saves the day, and substitution is possible because sacrifice, like magic, relies on a system of symbolic correspondences, a great chain of being in which the lower things recapitulate the higher. A domestic animal may stand in for a human or a god (like the ram substituted for Isaac), or a food offering may stand in for a human, god, or animal (like the bread and wine substituted for the body and blood of Christ). The substitute victim stands in for its exemplar by resemblance, mystical participation, or simple fiat, and the efficacy of the rite is guaranteed as long as the prayers and ceremonies retain their sacrificial form. Prayer is the one indispensable ingredient.

Sacrifice speaks to the gods, pleading, cajoling, praising, bribing, binding, or bargaining. What is implicit in the deeds and gestures of sacrifice becomes explicit in prayer. And since the law of sacrifice is substitution, there is a built-in mechanism by which prayer can stand in, as if by synecdoche, to represent the whole. In a pinch, an entire sacrifice may be condensed into prayer: the holy syllable *Om,* for example, is said to contain the essence of the Vedic sacrifice, and the Jewish 'Amidah (Standing Prayer) is the equivalent of the daily and Sabbath sacrifices of the Temple cult. When prayer takes the place of sacrifice, the process of dematerialization is nearly complete, as the smoke of incense yields to the even more incorporeal "sacrifice of praise."[6] We might put it this way: if sacrifice is prayer made flesh, then prayer is sacrifice made spirit. Two traditions of sacrificial prayer, East and West, will illustrate this idea.

The Fire Sacrifice

In the beginning was the fire sacrifice. This at least is the conviction of the world's oldest living scripture, the Rgveda, a compilation of 1,028 hymns composed in around 1500 B.C.E. by Indo-Aryan poet-priests and faithfully recited for the past three millennia. The text carries such authority that Hindus believe that it sprang from eternity itself without an author.

The first hymn of the Rgveda is an appeal to Agni, the fire god, messenger of the gods and master of sacrifice: "I pray to Agni, the household priest who is the god of the sacrifice, the one who chants and invokes and brings most treasure. . . . Now get dressed in your robes, lord of powers and master of the sacrificial food, and offer this sacrifice for us. Young Agni, take your place as our favourite priest with inspirations and shining speech."[7] The hymn grows ever more complex, asking Agni to come down from heaven, emerge from his hiding places on earth (in water, plants, and stones); make his dwelling in the sacrificial altar pit; consume the offerings of nectar, flesh, or grain with his brilliant razor-sharp teeth; grant "shining speech" to the celebrants; and transmit prayers to the gods. If Agni accepts this manifold commission, the fire will be pleasing; if the fire is pleasing, then the prayers of the sacrificer will be granted, "for when the gods have a good fire, they bring us what we wish for."[8] Hastening to heaven with his flaming body robed in prayers, leaving behind him a trail of smoke, Agni carries the sacrificial tribute to the gods; and he returns from the gods as lightning, bearing divine gifts.

One prays, it seems, not just with words but also with the quintessential elements of the material world, which are gods in their own right — Agni's fire, first of all, but also the liquid Soma (from the hallucinogenic mushroom *Amanita muscaria,* some believe) pressed into bowls and poured into the sacred fire as a libation. King Soma is the poet and sage of the fire sacrifice; his intoxicating liquor, like "butter and milk milked from the living clouds," infuses tongues with skill and prayer with ecstatic joy. Under the influence of Soma, the words of prayer become perfected speech, the language of paradise. "I have tasted the sweet drink of life, knowing that it inspires good thoughts and joyous expansiveness," sings the Soma drinker. When the fire sacrifice is good, gods and humans drink the Soma together and sing prayers one to the other. "Let these intoxicants intoxicate you," a Vedic hymn prays to the warrior god Indra. "Enjoy yourself, hero, at this drinking fest of ours." Prayer becomes so sweet and exalted that one can hardly tell whether it is a god or a mortal who utters it: "The prayer has come to me as a lowing cow comes to her beloved son. Have I not drunk Soma? I turn the prayer around in my heart, as a wheelwright turns a chariot seat. Have I not drunk Soma? . . . In my vastness, I surpassed the sky and this vast earth. Have I not drunk Soma?"[9]

The best-known hymn of the Ṛgveda sings of the creation of life by a fire sacrifice. The victim was Puruṣa, a colossal god-man with a thousand heads, a thousand eyes, and a thousand feet. Submitting to a sacred law older than time itself, Puruṣa agreed to be bound and immolated in Agni's fire. From his rendered fat came animals, and from his mouth and dismembered limbs came the four classes of society: priest, warrior, merchant, and laborer. Henceforth every sacrifice, from the humble domestic hearth offering to the pageantry of the royal horse sacrifice, would be a reenactment of this sacred drama. The sacrifice of Puruṣa was the foundation of the world's order and the means of its repair. "With the sacrifice, the gods sacrificed to the sacrifice, these were the first ritual laws,"[10] and all subsequent acts of worship are built upon this divine model.

During the first millennium B.C.E., the Brāhmaṇ poet-priests reached the height of their powers and made the primordial sacrifice of Puruṣa the decoding key to reality. Sacrifice provided a "theory of everything" — not unlike evolutionary theory in our own day. All natural phenomena could be understood as the material result of the sacrifice of Soma's divine juices into Agni's dry heat. The sacrificial fire flamed forth again and again in sexual union, birth and death, cremation and rebirth, the cycle of the seasons, the waxing and waning of the moon, and the revolution of the days and months of the year. Sacrifice was the foundation of social order and also the paradigm for prayer.

"What was the metre, what was the invocation, and the chant, when all the gods sacrificed the god?" the Ṛgveda asks — in other words, how should we pray?[11] The answer lay with the Brāhmaṇ priests. Without their specialized knowledge of rites and lore, their purity and unique power to utter the holiest mantras, the sacrifices could not be performed properly and the world would fall back into chaos and darkness. No other civilization has placed such power in the hands of priests or developed such a vast mythology, technology, and spiritual theology of ritual sacrifice and sacrificial prayer.

Prayer, in this context, was the libretto for sacrifice. And so it remains to some degree for South Asians who revere the Vedic canon as their mother and source. Even in these days of Bollywood and MTVIndia, Vedic ritual practices have not entirely died out. In many ways the fire sacrifice still burns at the heart of the prayer traditions of modern Hinduism.

For a case in point we can consider the celebrated performance of a major Vedic fire sacrifice in 1975, made possible by an unprecedented alliance of village Hinduism and international academic punditry. The principal in the matter was the Indologist Frits Staal, who in 1955, while in his twenties, came upon a group of Vaidikas (Vedic ritualists) in the remote region of Kerala, an area on the southwestern tip of India cut off from the rest of the subcontinent by the Western Ghats. Here among the Brāhmaṇs of the Nambudiri caste, Staal discovered a lost world, where Vedic ritual lore and practices long believed extinct survived, "preserved in their pristine purity, uninterrupted, unaffected by what went on elsewhere."

> I have long stood in awe of this unique survival, so archaic yet so sophisticated, so close to the early history of man, and so lovingly preserved through millennia that elsewhere saw the birth and death of entire civilizations. While pyramids, cathedrals, and skyscrapers were built and fell into decay, languages and religions came and went, and innumerable wars were fought, the Vedas and their ritual continued to be transmitted by word of mouth, from teacher to pupil, and from father to son. What a triumph of the human spirit over the limitations of matter and the physical body![12]

But it was a precarious triumph. The Nambudiri families no longer had the resources to support full-time Vaidikas, and though their sons were continuing to receive Vedic instruction, they also attended secular schools, seeking careers as teachers, engineers, and entrepreneurs. After three thousand years of unbroken transmission, the tradition was in jeopardy, and the Nambudiris were ready to turn to an outside scholar for help in preserving it. To Staal it seemed like destiny. He invited the Finnish Indologist Asko Parpola from the University of Helsinki to join him; together they persuaded Staal's Nambudiri friends to perform the greatest and most elaborate of Vedic rites, the twelve-day fire sacrifice called Agnicayana (the piling up of Agni).

The preparations were daunting: house and support the sacrificer *(yajamāna)* and his wife, as well as forty priests and assistants, for two and a half months of rehearsals; make the offering spoons and bowls out of wood and clay (no metal, no plastic); prepare the pressing stones for extracting Soma juice; collect sacred grass to strew around the fire pits; build the multichambered sacrificial hall out of bamboo poles and palm-leaf thatching; and clean and consecrate every implement, every inch of the sacrificial hall, and every person who would enter it. The budget submitted on grant applications included fourteen goats for sacrifice, two white horses, the skin of a black deer, stipends for the priests and assistants, lodging for guests, rice, lentils, coconut, ghee, salt, spices, coffee powder, gourds, fruits, washing soap, firewood, and lamp oil. Also needed were salaries for cooks, servers, watchmen, maids, and much more, with costs approaching $200,000.

"Kerala Yajna [sacrifice] with Foreign Participation" ran the cover story of the *Illustrated Weekly of India.* Local Communists called it an instance of the "penetration of Dollar Imperialism into India." A group of Jain monks from South Canara arrived to plead against animal sacrifice. A young activist announced that "he would immolate himself in the sacrificial fire if the goats were to meet with that fate." The day before the ritual, the Nambudiri priests met with Staal and a few other scholars and pandits and decided that "for the first time in the history of the Nambudiri tradition, the animals would be represented by rice flour folded in banana leaf in the same manner in which this is done at the śrāddha or funeral ceremonies." To Staal this felt like a setback: "It is not easy to kill rice cakes by strangulation and cut them open to take out particular organs." But the ritual experts agreed that as long as the prayers were performed properly, the replacement of goats by rice cakes would not invalidate the rite. The law of sacrificial substitution prevailed.[13]

The rite itself, which took place from April 12 to 24, 1975, was an immensely complex undertaking. To build the eagle-shaped fire altar required piling up a thousand bricks of ten different kinds, in five layers, at a rate of two hundred bricks a day for five days, first consecrating each brick to a Vedic god by "sprinkling" it with prayers. New fire had to be captured from heaven through friction, Stone Age style, by drilling the *arani,* a carved wooden cylinder, into the hole of a wooden platform and stoking the flames with ghee. No matter that there were Bic lighters on hand; they could not be used, for archaism in such matters is essential.

To what purpose, one may ask, was all this trouble and expense? Did the sacrificer receive the desired fruits (well-being, longevity, prosperity, the promise of a happy afterlife) that an Agnicayana performance is supposed to obtain? Nowhere in the two-volume, 1,600-page book *Agni: The Vedic Ritual of the Fire Altar,* in which Staal and his team of scholars meticulously describe, measure, transcribe, chart and analyze every aspect of the sacrifice, is this question answered. But getting results is not the main point. For in addition to being a petitionary prayer of monumental proportions, the Agnicayana is intended to be a spiritual journey for the participants, a rite of passage from death to eternal life.

The sacrificer is identified with Puruṣa, the sacrificed god; his own body is the unit of measurement for the immense altar; and at the beginning of the ceremony, he chants an oath of relinquishment *(tyāga),* surrendering his claim to the fruits of the sacrifice. He will get what he prays for only if he freely gives up all that he requests.

This sacrifice within a sacrifice exerted a charismatic appeal. Pilgrims flocked to the site, numbering ten thousand by the last day, not merely to gawk at the foreigners with their cameras but also to pray and partake of the overflowing spiritual power and grace. Approaching the ritual enclosure, they bowed in homage, as they might have done at the shrine of a god or saint: "Among these outsiders there was a strong tendency to conceive of the ritual enclosure as a kind of temple or place of pilgrimage, where devotees could receive 'darshan' (a glimpse of a presiding deity), make a donation, perform a circumambulation, and return home with freshly acquired religious merit."[14]

On the last day of the sacrifice a large eagle flew directly over the eagle-shaped altar, and the pilgrims shouted, "It is Garuḍa!" (the mythical celestial bird). Then the monsoon rains began, another sign of the gods' good pleasure. The main parties took a final ceremonial bath, and the entire sacrificial enclosure was set ablaze, sending pilgrims scattering in all directions. "There was a widespread rumor," Staal notes in an oblique description of his own elation, "that the chairman of the International Committee danced in the rains 'with the innocent pleasure and satisfaction of a child.'"[15]

What impresses most about this event is that a reenacted Vedic sacrifice — which might have amounted to little more than a recondite exercise in time travel — elicited an outpouring of devotion from modern, post-Vedic Hindu pilgrims. The pilgrims who visited Frits Staal's sacrifice had no hope of actively participating in it, and few of them understood its lore; yet at the perimeter of the sacrificial enclosure, they took part in the rite by offering up their prayers. In this strange and memorable scene, modern and ancient devotions commingled; contemplating it, we seem to see, as if through a reversed telescope, the long road by which Hindu prayer descended from Vedic sacrifice. It shows that sacrifice is not just an archaic practice preserved here and there in aspic, or fossilized in the depths of Indian culture, but a way of life to which nonsacrificing Hindus continue to feel drawn and to which prayer gives privileged access. Prayer is the essence of the sacrifice; therefore it can take the place of literal sacrifice much as rice cakes take the place of sacrificial goats. To this day not only the forms but also the ideals and lore of Hindu prayer bear the indelible mark of the old sacrificial system.

Sacrifice into Prayer

The transmutation of sacrifice into prayer took a glacially slow path; in India (or more broadly, South Asia) the process began during the period some call the Axial Age (midway through the first millennium B.C.E.), when the Brāhmaṇs saw their hegemony begin to decline, and it crested during the medieval centuries, the golden age of devotional Hinduism. The first stage of this process belongs to the *sannyāsi* (renunciant), a new kind of religious specialist who appeared in the civilization of the Indus and Ganges plains during a period of intense social upheaval (approximately 800–500 B.C.E.). *Sannyāsis* were a loosely affiliated group of wandering mendicants, beatniks of the spirit, who dropped out of the caste-structured social order and sought through yogic meditation and austerities to acquire saving knowledge. Among them were Mahāvīra (the founder of Jainism), the Buddha Śākyamuni, and the sages whose oral teachings are collected in the Upaniṣads and the later Brāhmaṇas.

The *sannyāsis* questioned whether ritual sacrifice was sufficient to ensure a blessed afterlife in the "world of the fathers." Eventually, they reasoned, sacrifices would fail, the memory of ancestors fade, and the souls of the departed fall back down to earth, to be trapped in the cycle of birth and death. To invest one's wealth, time, and substance in performing rites for the sake of world maintenance began to seem a mere vanity. Better to seek union with *brahman* through spiritual sacrifice than to sacrifice a thousand goats.

Brahman is a mysterious word; impersonal in gender, it connotes the sound of the Vedic mantra, the soul of the fire sacrifice, the hidden meaning of its prayers, the power of the sacrificial priest, and the ultimate reality from which all things derive their being. Whoever possesses *brahman,* or is possessed by it, tastes infinite bliss beyond time, change, and death. The wisest Brāhmaṇs, therefore, were those who knew how to build an "internal sacrifice" on the altar of the heart, seeking only union with *brahman.* Prayers began to take on a lofty, world-transcending tone: "From the unreal lead me to the real! From darkness lead me to light! From death lead me to immortality!"[16]

The path to immortality went by way of meditation, self-mastery, and mortification of the flesh. "Sky-clad" (naked), celibate, fasting, sleepless, immobile, adorned with ash and dust, the *sannyāsis* internalized the fire sacrifice, generating through their austerities an ardent physical and spiritual heat *(tapas)* capable of burning off sensory attachments. Their prayers were those of the fire sacrifice, especially the "tranquil, soundless, fearless, sorrowless, blissful, satisfied, steadfast, immovable, immortal, unshaken, enduring" Vedic syllable *Om* that radiates from the altar at the center of the universe. They sacrificed possessions, comforts, the desires of the ego-self in order to unite with the higher self; for "the knowing self is never born; nor does he die at any time. He sprang from nothing and nothing sprang from him. He is unborn, eternal, abiding and primeval. He is not slain when the body is slain."[17]

But how many are willing to give up everything for a higher self? The Hindu tradition recognizes that most people are obliged to carry on the work of the world and strive for the good things of life, according to their station. For householders, the task of world maintenance is inescapable. They must act in the world, and what they sow in life, the fruits of karma *(karmaphala),* they reap in future lives; thus they remain bound to the endlessly turning wheel of birth and death, from which no escape is possible without divine assistance.

Here, according to Hinduism, is the great problem for ordinary worldlings like us. With every action, good or ill, we ensnare ourselves further in *saṁsāra,* the cycle of birth and death. Prayers, offerings, and meritorious works can improve our circumstances somewhat, bringing about a favorable rebirth, but they cannot release us from the net. True freedom comes only when we surrender self-interest, praying and acting in such a way that we make a willing sacrifice of our own longings.

This is the theme of the greatest philosophical poem of world literature, the Bhagavad Gītā (Song of the Lord), which belongs to India's glorious epic, the Mahābhārata. The Gītā is a timeless dialogue set on the battlefield of a catastrophic war between the forces of good and evil. The action begins when the hero Arjuna, a prince of the warrior caste, refuses to act. To fight would mean to kill his own kinsmen; not to fight would mean to allow chaos to overtake the world. As Arjuna collapses in dejection on the field, the deity Kṛṣṇa (Krishna), who has assumed the form of his charioteer, steps into the fray, urging Arjuna not to abstain from the action that his sacred duty *(dharma)* prescribes. Arjuna has a job to do, a role to which he is bound by his divinely ordained station in life. Yet freedom can be found within these bounds if he acts in a spirit of selfless obedience, offering his actions as a sacrifice without attachment to the results: "Action imprisons the world unless it is done as a sacrifice; freed from attachment, Arjuna, perform action as sacrifice!"[18] Like the Vedic sacrificer, Arjuna must relinquish the fruits of his action.

Needless to say, this is an extremely difficult discipline. It is easier to stop acting altogether than to act without concern for results. The path of disciplined action *(karmayoga)* is as narrow as a razor's edge. Fortunately, Kṛṣṇa provides an alternative, directing Arjuna to the broad highway along which members of all classes and castes may travel to salvation: the path of *bhaktiyoga,* devotion to a personal god. "Keep your mind on me, be my devotee, sacrificing, bow to me — you will come to me, I promise, for you are dear to me."[19] To those who take refuge in him, Kṛṣṇa extends his promise of unconditional protection.

Kṛṣṇa has no need to be fed by sacrificial oblations, for he embodies in his own divine being the fire sacrifice that sustains the world ("Of words, I am the eternal syllable OM, the prayer of sacrifices. . . . I stand sustaining the entire world with a fragment of my being").[20] Nonetheless he accepts oblations for his devotees' sake and freely dispenses grace to all who seek it. More remarkable still, Kṛṣṇa accepts prayer directed to any god, counting it as a sacrifice performed in his service. Thus by stages Kṛṣṇa leads Arjuna from discipline to devotion, from sacrifice to trusting prayer. By the end of the Bhagavad Gītā, Arjuna has learned how to pray with pure, self-donating sacrificial devotion. The sacrifice of prayer has become the Vedic fire sacrifice perfected.

During the Hindu Middle Ages, the alchemy of theistic devotion transformed the rites of Vedic sacrifice into acts of worship called *pūjā* — a kinder, gentler form of sacrifice. Today *pūjā* is the predominant religious act, the universal though ever variegated way in which Hindus pray. In temples and at home shrines, devotees lovingly bathe consecrated statues and images of their gods with holy water; anoint them with fragrant sandalwood and spices; adorn them with bright clothing, jewels, and flower garlands; and present them with honor offerings *(upacāra)* of fire, water, incense, coconuts, bananas, lotus blossoms, hibiscus, sugar, and sweet confections, gifts that also characterized the hospitality Frits Staal enjoyed in the home of his Nambudiri friends. In place of the fire altar is the fire offering *(āratī),* in which the householder or priest (not necessarily a Brāhmaṇ) waves a camphor or butter lamp in clockwise circles before the deity. Agni, it seems, can be a gentle fire as well as a searing conflagration, a delicate camphor flame cool enough to permit devotees to immerse their hands in it for a blessing. Soma lives on — if not in hallucinogenic libations milked from the clouds, then at least in the clarified butter with which the devotee regales his or her god. Each offering of fire, flowers, or fruit comes back to the giver transformed into a divine gift. The devotee receives *darśan,* the auspicious vision of the deity, as well as a portion of the food oblation, returned as grace *(prasād),* divine leftovers to share with the family. Thus prayer comes full circle in communion, when the gods share their feast with humans, much as they did in Vedic sacrifice.

"With the sacrifice, the gods sacrificed to the sacrifice," the Rg̣veda says, speaking of the primordial Puruṣa sacrifice; and in the devotional forms of Hinduism the principle holds good, for the gods are said to sacrifice themselves by their willing descent into visible and tangible forms:

> This is the greatest grace of the Lord, that being free He becomes bound, being independent He becomes dependent for all His service on His devotee. . . . In other forms the man belonged to God but behold the supreme sacrifice of Isvara, here the Almighty becomes the property of the devotee. . . . He carries Him about, fans Him, feeds Him, plays with Him — yea, the Infinite has become finite, that the child soul may grasp, understand and love Him.[21]

Divine courtesy, gracious descent, reciprocal sacrifice, the Infinite becoming finite: this is the warrant for prayer in nearly all theistic traditions, and it is a powerful corrective to manipulative magic. Magical prayer asks for results, but sacrificial prayer asks for grace, relinquishing the fruits. Kṛṣṇa teaches Arjuna that sacrificial prayer is the most acceptable offering, and it returns to the devotee as grace *(prasād).*

Mahatma Gandhi, the activist mystic, learned from his beloved Gītā (which he first read in the English translation of Sir Edwin Arnold and came to revere as "the universal Mother") to perform "the internal fire sacrifice" through works of asceticism, prayer, and disinterested service. Purification, a goal that grew in significance for Gandhi over the course of his life, was the deeper meaning of the fire sacrifice, he believed, and service formed the quintessence of prayer. The spinning wheel, he often said, was his preferred rosary:

> If I am strong enough to turn the wheel, and I have to make a choice between counting beads or turning the wheel, I would certainly decide in favor of the wheel, making it my rosary, so long as I found poverty and starvation stalking the land. I do look forward to a time when even repeating the name of Rama will become a hindrance. When I have realized that Rama transcends even speech, I shall have no need to repeat the name. The spinning wheel, the rosary and the Ramanama are all the same to me. They serve the same end, they teach me the religion of service.[22]

Gandhi was in some respects a child of the European Enlightenment, a spiritualizer of prayer not entirely sympathetic to the magically tinged piety of most Hindus. But he never gave up repeating the name of Rāma. Struck by an assassin's bullet on January 30, 1948, while on his way to the evening prayer service, Gandhi met his death just as he had vowed to do, with "Rām, Rām" on his lips.

In a similar vein, Gandhi's beloved disciple, the "walking saint" Vinoba Bhave, spent thirteen years crisscrossing the Indian subcontinent on foot, seeking to persuade landowners to make a "Sacrifice Land Offering" (Bhoodan Yajna) in response to the Gītā's call for self-donation. Each day began with prayer, and each step was measured by prayer and hymns. He covered thirty-six thousand miles and accepted the offering of four million acres for redistribution to poor and Untouchable families. Eventually the movement unraveled, as utopian ventures generally do, but the Gītā was Vinoba's guide in failure as well as success. Perform action as a sacrifice, the sacred text told him, without attachment to the results. Place yourself on the fire altar by prayer and selfless service to others, and leave the rest to God. In *Talks on the Gita,* composed in jail, Vinoba explained what the life of sacrificial prayer entails: "'I' and 'mine' are swept away and then whatever remains is for the sake of the Lord. Life is lived entirely for the good of others. There is nothing else. This is what the Gita teaches again and again."[23]

Sacrificial prayer assumes that God's will is in harmony with our deepest wish, whether we realize it or not. Human beings are ambivalent creatures, and our immediate wishes are often at war with our deepest wish. When we pray sacrificially and perform actions as a sacrifice, we gain freedom, self-mastery, and joy — being, consciousness, and bliss *(sat-chit-ananda),* in the Hindu formula — even if our immediate wish is denied. Sacrificial prayer never ceases to ask for assistance, protection, and all good things; but it asks in a spirit of self-donation. By relinquishing all, one gains all; one passes through death to life. While not all sacrifice is prayerful, all fully realized prayer has something of this sacrificial character.

Consider again, in this regard, the story of Ḥoni the Circle-Drawer in Chapter 2. His three rainmaking prayers, like the three wishes in a fairy tale, were granted literally, to a comical effect: first too little rain, then too much, and then excessively prolonged. The danger of magical prayer, evidently, is that you may get what you pray for. Ḥoni's fourth prayer, on the other hand, and his only completely successful one, was sacrificial. Sacrificial prayer, with its dimension of willing surrender, works a deeper and more lasting kind of magic.

But sacrificial prayer also entails a peculiar vulnerability, unknown to purely magical prayer. Any gift one brings to the gods may be rejected as unworthy. No offering can be spotless enough; each is a shadow substitute for something higher and more whole. The very logic of sacrifice leads to an anti-sacrificial critique; possibly even to the abolition of sacrifice as a ritual act. For every priest who offers fruits or flesh at the altar, there is a prophet waiting to pounce with this challenge: What does God really want? Not your inadequate gifts, but you! — an upright spirit and a clean heart, works of mercy, radical obedience, and radical freedom. Among the *bhakti* saints of India are many who spurn sacrificial ritualism and formal worship of all kinds, claiming that their own body has become the temple where the god most truly dwells. Sacrificial traditions East and West press toward the same conclusion: the transformation of sacrifice into a life of prayer and the transformation of prayer into a path of self-transcendence.

The Sacrifice of Abraham

Once we begin looking for sacrifice, or stop looking away from it, we seem to find it everywhere. In the Bible, sacrifice is the obligatory donation to God of the precious things that come from God and rightfully belong to God. As for the Vedas, so for the scriptures of the West: sacrifice is a fundamental human act — if not necessary to survival, then at least to civilization and culture. In the book of Genesis, the first human society is formed and deformed by the contrasting sacrifices of Abel and Cain. Cain, whose sacrifice God rejects, becomes the first murderer. Abel, whose sacrifice God accepts, becomes the first victim. No explanation is given for God's preference; but then, the God of Israel rarely gives reasons for his choices. He sets down the rules for acceptable worship, and those whom God favors follow his instructions. To obey is to sacrifice, and to sacrifice is to obey; therefore the biblical imagination associates sacrifice not only with appeasement and petition but also with righteousness and justice.

The first world-age ends with the flood, and the first act of Noah after the flood is to begin a new civilization by making a burnt offering "of every clean beast, and of every clean fowl," feasting God with the "sweet savor" of the cooked meat (Genesis 8:20–21). Pleased with the aroma of the sacrifice (for it is redolent with the sweetness of Noah's righteousness), God pledges under the sign of the rainbow never again to revoke the blessings of creation.

The second world-age belongs to Abraham, whose steadfast faith is manifest in his willingness to sacrifice his beloved son at God's command: "'Take now thy son, thine only son Isaac, whom thou lovest, and get thee into the land of Moriah; and offer him there for a burnt offering upon one of the mountains which I will tell thee of'" (Genesis 22:2). We read this story retrospectively, keeping in mind the ram that was waiting in the wings. The Hebrew Bible scholar Jon D. Levenson has established, however, that a precedent and a rationale for child sacrifice existed in ancient Israel.[24] Although the Bible condemns child sacrifice ("thou shalt not let any of thy seed pass through the fire to Molech," Leviticus 18:21) as something that false gods demand, the Genesis account implies that child sacrifice is a reasonable privilege to which the sovereign God of Israel mercifully renounces his claim. God has the right to demand sacrifice — even the sacrifice of the beloved son — and it is a most laudable act of fidelity to obey. Having passed this crucial test, Abraham receives the reward of the covenant promises: "in blessing I will bless thee, and in multiplying I will multiply thy seed as the stars of the heaven, and as the sand which is upon the sea shore; and thy seed shall possess the gate of his enemies; And in thy seed shall all the nations of the earth be blessed; because thou hast obeyed my voice" (Genesis 22:17–18).

Modern readers find this rather shocking and look for ways to explain it away, but it cannot be done, for the text is fairly plain. Child sacrifice is a rejected possibility, not a rejected impossibility, and sacrifice remains at center stage. It is no accident that the instructions for animal and grain sacrifice, down to the minutest detail, sit cheek by jowl with the ethical teachings revealed to Moses on Mount Sinai. Today such rubrics seem more appropriate for appendixes or technical users' guides; but for biblical religion, sacrifice is front and center, the very essence of spirituality and ethics. The covenant between God and Israel under Moses is sealed in the blood of sacrifice (Exodus 24:3–8). The most direct way to communicate with God is to slay the fatted calf and entertain God as an honored guest. Sacrifice is the divinely ordained means of worship, thanksgiving, confession, expiation, and communion with God. Like a safety valve, sacrifice discharges the guilt and defilement that inevitably build up in human societies and human hearts over time; the blood sprinkled on the altar makes atonement for blood spilled on the ground (Leviticus 17:1–6).

But sacrifice does not work automatically. The prophets stress importance of the disposition of the sacrificer and the intent behind the gift: "Hath the LORD as great delight in burnt offerings and sacrifices, as in obeying the voice of the LORD? Behold, to obey is better than sacrifice, and to hearken than the fat of rams" (1 Samuel 15:22). They depict God as rejecting sacrifices offered by the unjust:

> I hate, I despise your feast days, and I will not smell in your solemn assemblies. Though ye offer me burnt offerings and your meat offerings, I will not accept them: neither will I regard the peace offerings of your fat beasts. Take thou away from me the noise of thy songs; for I will not hear the melody of thy viols. But let judgment run down as waters, and righteousness as a mighty stream. (Amos 5:21–24; see also Isaiah 1:11–17)

Yet such jeremiads against unworthy sacrifice are part and parcel of the sacrificial system. For the prophets, lawgivers, mystics, sages, and priests of Zion, sacrifice steadfastly remained the central act of worship. Obedience, justice, purity, care for the needy and oppressed, all these virtues derived from the sacrifice of the altar and returned to the sacrifice of the altar as to a touchstone.

Sacrifice is an affair of calendar and compass; time and place matter. Biblical prayer, because of its intimate connection to sacrifice, also has its special places and seasons. There are hot spots for prayer, places where God has been known to appear, often in the former dwelling grounds of Middle Eastern gods whose star is setting. Wherever God or his angelic envoy touches down is an outpost of heaven, a locale where prayers are answered. When Jacob awoke from his dream of the heavenly ladder, he cried out in astonishment, "How dreadful is this place! This is none other but the house of God, and this is the gate of heaven," and he set up his stone pillow for an altar, pouring oil upon it in tribute (Genesis 28:17). Thus Bethel joined the list of open-air prayer fields and enclosed prayer fortresses whose names crowd the Bible: Shechem, Shiloh, Mizpah, Gilgal, Nob, Hebron, Beersheba, Dan, Penuel, Gibeon, Ophra, the Mount of Olives, and so on.

The Jerusalem Temple, when it was standing, was the locus of sacrificial prayer par excellence, for here God dwelt on earth not as a casual visitor but as an enduring presence. The priests who served there also shaped much of the Hebrew scriptures, so that the biblical account of sacred history — the founding of Israel and the establishment of its worship — is in many respects a priestly reconstruction, a view from the Temple porch.

It did not escape the prophets, priests, and kings of Israel that there is something strange about expecting the high God to hold court and receive supplicants in an earthly sanctuary, however gorgeously decked out with hewn stone, cedar pillars, golden vessels, colossal cherubim, and carved images of lions, oxen, and palms. Solomon's prayer at the dedication of the First Temple (1 Kings 8:27–53) begins on this note of wonderment: ". . . will God indeed dwell on the earth? Behold, heaven and the highest heaven cannot contain thee; how much less this house which I have built!" But there is confidence in Solomon's supplication "that thy eyes may be open night and day toward this house," and he does not hesitate to present a detailed list of the favors he wants God to dispense to those who seek him there: forgive sins, vindicate the innocent, vanquish invaders, bring rain, overcome famine "or pestilence or blight or mildew or locust or caterpillar" or illness of any kind, and grant "whatever prayer, whatever supplication is made by any man or by all thy people Israel."

As 2 Chronicles relates it, God answered Solomon's prayer with a powerful sign of approval: "When Solomon had made an end of praying, the fire came down from heaven, and consumed the burnt offering and the sacrifices; and the glory of the LORD filled the house. And the priests could not enter into the house of the LORD, because the glory of the LORD filled the house" (2 Chronicles 7:1–2). Seeing this, the children of Israel "bowed themselves with their faces to the ground upon the pavement, and worshipped, and praised the LORD," and Solomon made a thanksgiving sacrifice of "twenty and two thousand oxen, and a hundred and twenty thousand sheep" (2 Chronicles 7:3, 5). After seven days of feasting on the remains, Solomon dismissed the praying crowds, who returned joyfully to their homes. That night, God appeared to Solomon, saying,

> "I have heard thy prayer, and have chosen this place to myself for a house of sacrifice. If I shut up heaven that there be no rain, or command the locusts to devour the land, or if I send pestilence among my people; if my people who are called by my name shall humble themselves, and pray,

Solomon's prayer at the consecration of the Jerusalem Temple. Oleograph, c. 1870.

> and seek my face, and turn from their wicked ways; then will I hear from heaven, and will forgive their sin and will heal their land. Now mine eyes shall be open and my ears attent unto the prayer that is made in this place." (2 Chronicles 7:12–15)

Solomon's prayer tells us much about the cultic purpose of the Temple. It is not a house of congregational worship so much as a holy mountain touching heaven, a footstool for God in the midst of his people, and a royal city where consecrated priests wait upon God with sacrifice and solemn service. Prayers sent like arrows by the scattered children of Israel find their mark here; foreigners, too, will be drawn to pray toward the Temple, Solomon says, attracted by the powerful name of the LORD. Solomon begs God to grant their prayers as well, "that all people of the earth may know thy name, and fear thee, as doth thy people Israel, and may know that this house which I have built is called by thy name" (2 Chronicles 6:33).

Though surely not the only place of prayer, the Jerusalem Temple was, according to those with priestly and royal interests, its main engine room. Yet unlike its heavenly exemplar, the Temple was vulnerable to the wrecking ball; during the decades of desolation under Babylonian rule (587–520 B.C.E.) it fell to rubble, to be rebuilt twice during the Second Temple period (515 B.C.E.–70 C.E.). Finally, on the day marked by Jewish calendars as the ninth/tenth day of Av (Tish'ah Be-'Av) in the year 3828 (70 C.E.), the Second Temple was utterly destroyed by Roman authorities seeking to put down the rebellion led by Bar Kokhba'. Only the western wall remained standing, to become the bitterly contested site of Jewish prayer (the "Wailing Wall") that it is today.

Judaism as we know it was born from the rabbis' inspired response to this catastrophe. Tradition has it that the first-century Palestinian sage Yoḥanan ben Zakk'ai, smuggled out of Jerusalem in a coffin, saved the day by teaching that Israel might be "a kingdom of priests and a holy nation" (Exodus 19:6) even in exile, that good deeds atone for sin as effectively as a blood offering does, that Torah study allows one to meet God outside the sanctuary, and that prayer *('avodah)* is the true and original divine service. Yoḥanan was undoubtedly not alone in thinking thus; for the promise proclaimed by Isaiah, "mine house shall be called an house of prayer for all people" (Isaiah 56:7), hints at this idea. Might not every house of prayer, or synagogue, or Jewish home for that matter, be a small sanctuary *(miqdash me'at),* a spiritual substitute for the Temple? Might not sacrifice, whose law is substitution, be sublimated into prayer, the "sacrifice of the mouth"? Once again, as in Vedic India, sacrifice was transformed into prayer. From the destruction of the altar, from the desolation of the shrine, from the ruins of the Temple, prayer made itself an edifice as large as the universe itself.

Even when the Temple was still standing, Jews living far from Jerusalem had been obliged to substitute prayer for sacrifice. The Jewish Platonist Philo of Alexandria (30 B.C.E.–40 C.E.) valued sacrifice for its allegorical symbolism rather than its substance, and the sectarian mystics at Qumran, who had an exalted view of their own spiritual attainments, esteemed prayer above what they regarded as the impure material offerings of the Temple cult. After 70 C.E., however, the substitution of prayer for sacrifice became a permanent feature of mainstream Jewish life. The Temple was destroyed; now the Temple would be rebuilt, as the rabbis put it, not on pillars of stone but on the three pillars — Torah, prayer, and deeds of loving-kindness — that support the world.

According to the Talmud, Abraham foresaw the catastrophe of 70 C.E. and extracted from God the promise that he would count prayer, good deeds, and Torah study as an acceptable offering in place of sacrifice. God assured him, "I have already fixed for them [in the Torah] the order of sacrifices. Whenever they will read the section dealing with them, I will reckon it as if they were bringing Me an offering, and forgive all their iniquities."[25] To this day, the Jewish morning prayer service recalls God's promise to Abraham:

> Lord of the universe, thou hast commanded us to sacrifice the daily offering at its proper time. . . . Now, through our sins the Temple is destroyed, the daily offering is abolished, and we have neither priest officiating, nor Levite [singing] on the platform, nor Israelite attending the Temple service. However, thou hast declared that we may substitute the prayer of our lips for the sacrifice of bullocks. Therefore, may it be thy will, LORD our God and God of our fathers, that the prayer of our lips be favorably regarded and accepted by thee as if we offered the daily offering at its proper time and attended at its service.[26]

After proclaiming the Shema' ("Hear, O Israel: the LORD is our God, the LORD, the One and Only . . ."), the morning service embarks on a lengthy account of the daily Temple sacrifice, describing in precise and loving detail the copper laver for purification, the ashes and incense, the priestly vestments, the yearling lambs, bulls and rams for slaughter, the fine flour, olive oil, and wine libations, the bowls of frankincense and showbread, the primary and secondary fires, the incense of eleven spices, and all the ingredients required to render to God a sweet savor. Only after this verbal reenactment of the sacrifice does the service proceed to the magnificent Qaddish ("May His great Name grow exalted and sanctified in the world that He created as He willed . . ."); the Pesuqei de-Zimra', praising God's glory in creation ("Blessed is He Who spoke, and the world came into being. . . ."); the exuberant litany of prayers and hymns recounting God's acts of deliverance and sounding the depths of the Shema'; and finally the great crescendo of the 'Amidah (Standing Prayer, also known as the Eighteen Benedictions), which proceeds from praise and confession to petition and gratitude for answered prayers.

This three-stage progression from praise and confession to petition to thanksgiving suggests the image of a supplicant who approaches the sanctuary from a distance. The pattern is set down by the book of Psalms, the main prayerbook of the Second Temple. First the supplicant calls out in praise: "O send out thy light and thy truth: let them lead me; let them bring me unto thy holy hill, and to thy tabernacles. Then will I go unto the altar of God, unto God my exceeding joy: yea, upon the harp will I praise thee, O God my God" (Psalm 43:3–4). Then the supplicant enters the porch of the Temple, approaching with a humble and contrite heart, lays down his gifts, and offers his petitions and lamentations before the divine throne. Finally, the supplicant exits, keeping his face Godward, with words of gratitude, as in the glorious thanksgiving prayer of Psalm 116:

> I love the LORD, because he hath heard my voice and my supplications.
> Because he hath inclined his ear unto me, therefore will I call upon him as long as I live.
> The sorrows of death compassed me, and the pains of hell gat hold upon me: I found trouble and sorrow.
> Then called I upon the name of the LORD; O LORD, I beseech thee, deliver my soul.
> Gracious is the LORD, and righteous; yea, our God is merciful.
> The LORD preserveth the simple: I was brought low, and he helped me.
> Return unto thy rest, O my soul; for the LORD hath dealt bountifully with thee.
> For thou hast delivered my soul from death, mine eyes from tears, and my feet from falling. . . .
> . . . .
> I will offer to thee the sacrifice of thanksgiving, and will call upon the name of the LORD.
> I will pay my vows unto the LORD now in the presence of all his people,
> In the courts of the LORD's house, in the midst of thee, O Jerusalem. Praise ye the LORD. (Psalm 116:1–8, 17–19)

If we think of prayer in this way, as a journey to the courts of the Most High and to the very altar of God, it seems a solemn and dangerous business. God is not a tame lion. Isaiah trembles when he sees God in the heavenly sanctuary, "Woe is me! for I am undone; because I am a man of unclean lips, and I dwell in the midst of a people of unclean lips: for mine eyes have seen the King, the LORD of hosts." There is nothing Isaiah can do to deserve an audience with God, and it is death to look upon God unworthily. But God, who has his own reasons for choosing Isaiah as a prophet, sends a seraph to him, bearing a live coal from the altar. Touching the coal to Isaiah's lips, the seraph burns away all iniquity and mortal corruption (Isaiah 6:5–7).

The implication is that God alone can restore to the confused of tongue that pure, singular, universal language that can address God worthily: "For then will I turn to the people a pure language [in Hebrew, "pure lip"], that they may all call upon the name of the LORD, to serve him with one consent" (Zephaniah 3:9). The words of prayer, the ability to pray them, and the promise that the prayer will hit its mark — all these are divine gifts. Sacrificial prayer is a human act undertaken by divine initiative, which succeeds only by divine consent.

Not all Jewish prayer is a spiritualization of the sacrifice; no single idea can embrace the entire spectrum of liturgical and domestic, public and private, formal and spontaneous prayers. But a sacrificial note can be heard whenever Jewish people remember their obligation and privilege to pray to the Author, Master, and Redeemer of the universe. Indeed, it is a chief duty of the angels, according to Jewish tradition, to receive the prayers of humankind, carry them up to heaven, and place them before the divine throne as sacrificial offerings.

The Sacrifice of Christ

The Gospels portray Jesus as the consummate practitioner and teacher of sacrificial prayer. He prays in the Temple, in synagogues and homes, in crowds and solitary places. He prays at the outset of each new stage of his work, addressing God in the Jewish fashion as Father and King, offering in prayer the sacrifice of his own will, and praying in such a way that even ordinary petitions take on a sacrificial meaning.

The Lord's Prayer, which is a profoundly Jewish prayer comparable to the Qaddish and at the same time a Christian Gospel in miniature, is saturated with sacrificial connotations. It begins, like the psalms of ascent to the sacrificial altar, by glorifying the unspeakable divine name and acknowledging that God alone is holy. The first three petitions, which address God in the second person, express adoration, praise, hope for the advent of the kingdom, and — most significant — the sacrifice of human interests to divine: "Thy will be done." The four remaining petitions (sometimes counted as three), spoken in the first person, concern human needs: daily bread for sustenance now and in the age to come, forgiveness of debts and repair of fractured relationships, protection from persecution as the age nears its end, and deliverance from the power of evil or the devil himself. Yet a sacrificial dimension is present as well, for the concrete blessings requested are exactly what is needed to create the conditions for personal sacrifice. No one who receives daily provisions from God, experiences forgiveness of sins, reconciliation with enemies, and liberation from demonic obsessions can harbor the illusion of being self-made. If the petitions are granted, they entail the remaking of the petitioner.

"Thy will be done" also brings to mind the prayer of Jesus in agony before his arrest: "Father, if thou be willing, remove this cup from me: nevertheless not my will, but thine, be done" (Luke 22:42). Jesus does not dilute his petition for deliverance or rescind it in a stoic act of resignation, but rather he transforms it, by the alchemy of sacrifice, into willing consent. The sacrifice on the cross is the final movement of this sacrificial prayer in the garden, and it is the interpretive key to Christian prayer.

After the destruction of the Jerusalem Temple in 70 C.E., the early Christians developed a new understanding of Christ's sacrifice. All the ancient sacrifices of Israel seemed, to the followers of Jesus, to converge in the self-offering of Christ, who was both high priest and sacrificial victim, prophet and king. The Temple was destroyed, yet raised on the third day when Christ rose from the dead; the new Temple would be the church, the body of those who in baptism unite themselves with the death and resurrection of Christ and in communion partake of the deeper magic of redemption.

The ancient Eucharistic prayers convey a vivid sense of participating in a true sacrifice: "We offer to your excellent majesty from your gifts and bounty a pure victim, a holy victim, an unspotted victim, the holy bread of eternal life and the cup of everlasting salvation," declaims the priest in the classic Roman Catholic formula for Eucharistic consecration.[27] The liturgy recalls the Temple cult, redolent with incense and adoration; it is a solemn drama crowded with heavenly actors. Christ is present "wherever two or three are gathered in my name," the Holy Spirit presides and consecrates, the Queen of Heaven and all the saints play their supporting roles, while the angels busy themselves with carrying the prayers of the faithful up to the throne of the Most High. And the prayers of the mortals in attendance are marked by that peculiar combination of deep abasement and cosmic optimism (or "holy audacity" as the fourth-century bishop Saint Gregory of Nyssa calls it) that marks sacrificial prayer in all traditions.

Yet not even the traditional Roman Catholic Mass is a sacrifice in the most literal sense. No new offering is made, for Christ's sacrifice, which was "once for all" (Hebrews 7:27), cannot be repeated. It remains only to accept the divine gift, to submerge oneself in it, and to appropriate it in sacrificial prayer, self-giving service, and the whole gestalt of Christian life. Saint Paul tells the Christians in Rome how this is done: "present your bodies a living sacrifice, holy, acceptable unto God" (Romans 12:1).[28] Christian prayer is not an ethereal substitute for the sacrifice of Calvary, but a way of connecting to it and thus opening oneself to God's will. That is why it is sometimes said that all Christian prayer ideally is Eucharistic, sacrificial, and cruciform.

Intercession

Sacrificial prayer is inherently intercessory. "I pray for them," Jesus says in the Gospel according to John, "that they all may be one; as thou, Father, art in me, and I in thee, that they also may be one in us: that the world may believe that thou hast sent me. And the glory which thou gavest me I have given them; that they may be one, even as we are one." Christians have seen this prayer as continuous with the sacrifice of Christ, pouring out his life to glorify God and redeem humankind.

But the idea of intercessory prayer is not unique to Christianity. It is a universal idea. The great religions take as a given what John Donne teaches in his famous sermon: that "all mankind is of one author, and is one volume," that "no man is an island, entire of itself, every man is a piece of the continent, a part of the main." Intercessory prayer assumes that one individual can take up the burdens of another without increasing the total sum of misery and that one person's merits can be transferred to another's account without decreasing the total sum of grace, for all beings are in some fashion connected. For Mahāyāna Buddhism, dedicating one's merit to other beings is the heart of saintliness; thus the bodhisattva (who embodies heroic compassion) prays, "May I be the medicine and the physician for the sick. May I be their nurse until their illness never recurs. . . . For the sake of accomplishing the welfare of all sentient beings, I freely give up my body, enjoyments, and all my virtues."[29]

The Anglican writer and Inkling Charles Williams believed that intercessory prayer was the sovereign remedy for the sinful will to power. He loved to meditate on the mystery of human creatures bearing one another's burdens in prayer, "dying in each other's life, living in each other's death." "Co-inherence" he called this mystery, borrowing the word used in Christian dogma for the mutual indwelling of the three Persons of the Trinity. Human beings are social animals, Williams observed, and in bearing one another's burdens in prayer we foreshadow the ideal commonwealth, the new Jerusalem. There "we shall be graced by one and by all, only never by ourselves," Williams writes; "the only thing that can be ours is the fiery blush of the laughter of humility when the shame of the Adam has become the shyness of the saints."[30]

Intercessory prayer binds the living and the dead and also keeps the dead from untimely return. The Chinese matron whose daily housekeeping tasks include lighting incense and bowing before the family altar is a stalwart of intercessory prayer. She knows (though it may be more a matter of tradition than of articulate conviction) that her dead kin must be sustained by sacrifice and prayer through the perilous forty-nine days of judgment and beyond, lest they return, famished and desperate, to haunt and possess the living. Heaven, in most traditions, is sociability perfected; and it is the everlasting labor and amusement of saints, angels, prophets, and divine beings to spend their eternity interceding in prayer for those who still struggle here below. Islamic prayer acknowledges Muḥammad as the "giver of graces" to his community, who intercedes for every believer at the hour of judgment. Catholics ask the Blessed Virgin and all the saints to pray for the living and for the souls in purgatory; ligaments of prayer connect heaven, purgatory, and earth. In Dante's *Divine Comedy*, intercessory prayer is the native language of purgatory. The once-proud penitents who have reached the first terrace of Mount Purgatory offer a unique rendition of the Lord's Prayer, which concludes with an act of intercession:

> Our virtue, which faints at the lightest touch,
> put not to the trial of our ancient foe, but
> deliver us from the one who incites to evil.
>
> This last petition, dear Lord,
> we make not for ourselves, who have no need,
> but only for those who remain behind us.[31]

While the living pray for the dead to hasten their passage through purgatory, the dead, who are no longer subject to temptation, pray that the living will persevere. Dante's own ascent is made possible by the intercession of his beloved Beatrice, who commends him to the intercession of the angels and saints. Such is the economy of co-inherence, the great interlocking chain of intercessory prayer.

Among the living, intercessory prayer can be a way to dissolve ancient enmities and create new forms of solidarity. The French Islamicist Louis Massignon (1883–1962) took this path when he cofounded, with Arab Melkite Christian Mary Kahil, the sodality of the Badaliya (Arabic for "substitution"), a group of Christians dedicated to praying for and with Muslims under fire in Algeria and Palestine. Inspiration for the group came in part from Massignon's beloved Sufi martyr al-Ḥallāj and in part from the Catholic hermit and explorer Charles de Foucauld (1858–1916), who died in a remote region of Morocco as a victim of tribal violence and a martyr to hospitality.[32] If prayer is a battle, then intercessory prayer is its elite unit. Intercessory prayer "stands in the breach" like Abraham and Moses (Psalm 106:23; Exodus 32:31–34) to avert God's wrath, repel enemies, and comfort the afflicted. Thus the military cast of modern intercessory prayer groups, which are legion, filling the Internet, church bulletins, and inspirational magazines with talk of prayer warriors, prayer shields, and gap-standing promise-keepers.

Intercessory prayer is also magical prayer, predicated on the belief that human creatures are caught in a web of mutual influence, members of that vast "sympathy of enchained forces," which the right words and gestures can tap, channeling power for healing and salvation. Even the Lord's Prayer has a magical dimension. One need only consider the magical uses to which it has been put over the centuries or the tradition that the "Back-Paternoster" is the surest way to call up the devil: "Thus best things may be turn'd to greatest harm, / As saying th'Lord's Prayer backward proves a charm."[33] The version recorded in the *Heliand*, which we considered in Chapter 2, is but one instance of a rich Germanic and Old English tradition associating the Lord's Prayer with runes of power and healing, and placing it in a setting both martial and magical. Then there is the mysterious word square, inscribed on walls and used as a protective charm, which appears in all the far-flung territories of the late Roman Empire:

S A T O R
A R E P O
T E N E T
O P E R A
R O T A S

By anagrammatic conversion it becomes a paternoster cross, with only the letters *A* and *O* (for alpha and omega) remaining:[34]

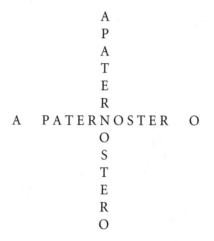

A
P
A
T
E
R
A PATERNOSTER O
O
S
T
E
R
O

With this curious emblem we come full circle to the prototypes of the magician and the priest. How close are they to each other, and how close is their affinity to prayer? The magician calls forth the virtue in created things. To the extent that he does so by calling on powers that transcend his own ego, he is engaged in prayer; and in his self-discipline he may even approach sacrificial prayer. Yet if magic is only a conjuring act, it falls short of prayer. The priest has something of the magician in him; but the magical power of sacrifice derives paradoxically from surrender of power. Ideally, at least all prayer has a dimension of self-transcendence, reaching beyond the ego to a power deeper and higher.

Magical prayer may be either personal or impersonal, private or public; but sacrificial prayer is of necessity both personal and corporate. One may pray with magical intentions to abstract powers ("May the Force be with you"), but sacrifice can be offered only to personal beings. With sacrificial prayer a world of reciprocal giving opens up, in which the first gift, the gift of prayer itself, comes from God.

In this discussion of magic and sacrifice, we do not claim to have explained the ultimate origin of prayer or exhaustively traced its evolution from some imagined missing link. The impulse to pray may well be more primal than the impulse to perform magic or offer sacrifice; on one level it is simply the will to communicate, to make contact with something — anything — beyond oneself. The history of prayer is hidden too deep or too high to be reconstructed directly. But this much we do know: prayer travels through history in the company of the magician and the priest. If at times the three part ways and prayer takes the road alone, it still carries tokens of its comrades. In other words, prayer partakes of magic and sacrifice yet reserves to itself something altogether more mysterious, more difficult to define. To explore that mystery as it plays out in human lives is our task for the rest of this book.

PART II

Heart in Pilgrimage

Part II explores, through four archetypal figures, the fundamental modes of prayer.

Earlier writers on prayer typically divided their subject into abstract categories: petition, confession, ecstasy, adoration, healing, and so on. This is a useful but limited approach, one that fails to acknowledge that every prayer requires a person who prays, that prayer in the abstract — prayer as a generic category, prayer that molders in an unread book, all prayer that fails to engage a living soul — leads a ghostly, ersatz existence. Here, then, is our alternative: four portrait galleries of prayer in life, filled with images of men and women of prayer, arranged according to four presiding archetypes: the refugee, the devotee, the ecstatic, and the contemplative.

Whenever possible, we let people speak for themselves, believing that those who have explored the near spaces and far ranges know best how to describe them. Through their testimony, we see universal truths about prayer brought to life, for each person prays in a way that incorporates, to varying degrees, elements of magic, sacrifice, or ritual; each participates, through prayer, in the shaping and transmission of society and its offspring, culture; each seeks God, higher truth, ultimate reality — terms differ from one person or path to the next — to find the pearl of great price, the sweetness of salvation, that which "turns us to gold," in Ramakrishna's memorable formulation. This much each person in Part II shares, and yet each has his or her own approach to prayer. Together these figures make up the fellowship of prayer, a company whose lineaments, if studied with sufficient care, may disclose something of the mystery of our being and its eternal longing for the divine.

CHAPTER 4

The Refugee

"READ NOT THE TIMES, read the Eternities," famously enjoined Henry David Thoreau. It isn't often that these two realms intersect, but they did in the late spring of 2001, not only on the *New York Times* bestseller list but in news media across America, with the astonishing publishing success of Bruce Wilkinson's *The Prayer of Jabez: Breaking Through to the Blessed Life.* This slender book, only ninety-three pages long, describes the blessings that flow from an obscure prayer buried in a dense genealogical litany in 1 Chronicles, the driest book in the Bible. The pertinent text, in the New King James Version favored by Wilkinson, reads: "Now Jabez was more honorable than his brothers; and his mother called his name Jabez, saying, 'Because I bore him in pain.' And Jabez called on the God of Israel, saying, 'Oh, that You would bless me indeed, and enlarge my territory, that Your hand would be with me, and that You would keep me from evil, that I may not cause pain!' So God granted him what he requested" (1 Chronicles 4:9–10).

Wilkinson first recited the prayer of Jabez as a young seminary student uncertain about his future. The results, he writes, "revolutionized my life," launching him on a thirty-year career as minister and writer and spawning a mini-industry of audiotapes, gift items, spinoff books, and websites teeming with accounts of "miracles" posted by those rescued or revitalized by the prayer (one correspondent tells how the prayer foiled a plane hijacking, another of how it comforted a child scared by a mouse).

The Prayer of Jabez is, if nothing else, an astute blend of literary archaeology, evangelical cheerleading, and attractive packaging. That Wilkinson brought Jabez's entreaty to public attention is in itself commendable; like Poe's purloined letter, it has been in plain sight for centuries, translated into hundreds of languages as a portion of the most widely read book in the world, yet has remained utterly invisible. Even the church fathers, exegetical argonauts who explored the vast seas of the Old Testament inch by inch, managed to overlook it; the prayer receives nary a mention in the standard thirty-eight-volume Edinburgh edition of the Ante-Nicene, Nicene, and Post-Nicene Fathers. In bringing it to the public eye, Wilkinson maintained that he had no interest in scholarly analysis. Instead, each of the prayer's five petitions became the springboard for an affable, upbeat sermon explaining that God wishes to "release his miraculous power in your life now. And for all eternity, He will lavish on you His honor and delight." The public rushed to embrace this divine largesse with open arms and wallets, purchasing nearly five million copies of the book in its first year of publication alone.

The response of the news media and the intelligentsia, including the professional theological community, was another matter entirely. Some objected to Wilkinson's literary style, with some justification, as his prose can read like a roadside billboard ("Friends, have you ever seen the Holy Spirit break through emotional and spiritual barriers right before your eyes?"). Others, embarrassed by the book's populist and evangelical roots, settled for a condescending, tongue-in-cheek response (the *Washington Post* began its front page story on the prayer by asking readers to "Please bow your heads"). The bulk of the attacks, however, zeroed in on the second clause in Jabez's prayer, "enlarge my territory." This petition, especially in light of Wilkinson's declaration that "if Jabez had worked on Wall Street, he might have prayed, 'Lord, increase the value of my investment portfolios,'" raised for many the specter of Reverend Ike and other mammon-friendly evangelicals; thus the *London Times* headline of May 10, 2001: "Please, Lord, make me rich." The prayer of Jabez, these critics asserted, is crude, self-serving, and narcissistic. And so it may be, although in defense of Wilkinson's proselytizing, one might note his insistence that those who say the Jabez prayer must desire "nothing more and nothing less than what God wants for us" as well as the nature of the "answered prayers" cited in the book, which have little to do with self-aggrandizement and a great deal to do with spreading peace and goodwill—typical is the worried mother for whom Jabez's plea to "enlarge my territory" means that her children will now accompany her to Sunday School.

One may reasonably conclude, from all this Sturm und Drang, that the prayer of Jabez serves a variety of purposes: to some, a means to succor family and friends; to others, a ticket to wealth and success. But both

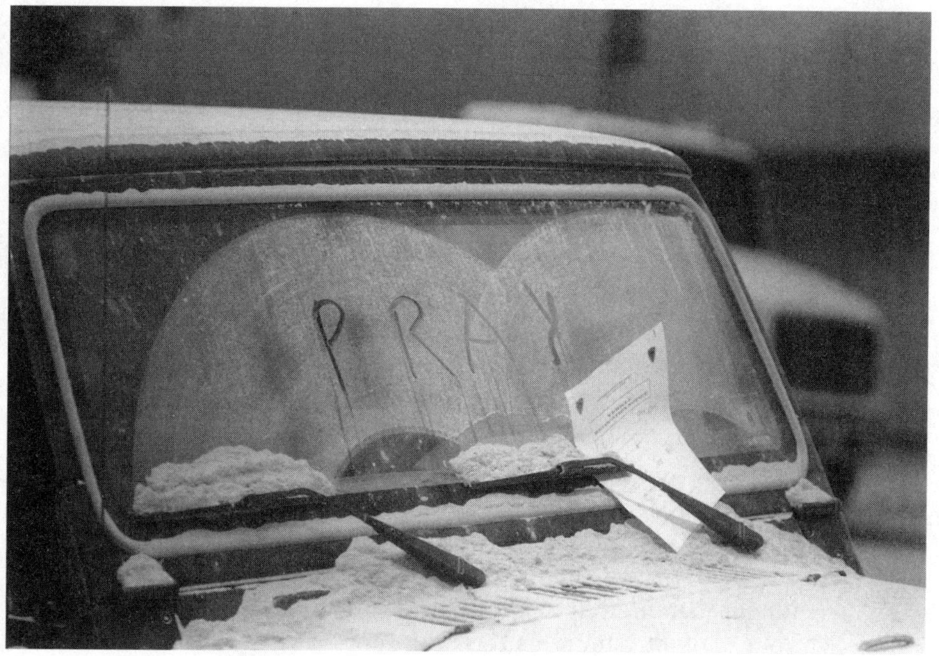

"PRAY," inscribed on an ash-coated windshield near the World Trade Center, September 11, 2001.

camps overlook the very ordinariness of the five petitions of Jabez. They are in no way exceptional. On the contrary, they are about as normative as prayer can get. The Jabez prayer is a quintessential example of the *prayer of the refugee*, the prayer of those who seek shelter in God, flying to him for assistance, succor, or salvation. The prayer of the refugee is the most common form of prayer, probably engaged in more frequently than all other varieties combined. It addresses the raw fundamentals of life — sin and illness, suffering and death, fear of evil and the longing for redemption. As such, men and women (and children) of every age, class, and faith embrace it. Its myriad forms encompass every emotion, every circumstance of life, and every possible relationship between humankind and God. Those who see it as an aberration, symptomatic of a self-centered, consumerist culture, have missed sight of its universality: the prayer of the refugee flourishes wherever people pray.

Nothing is more basic than a call for help. It seems likely that the very word *help* — perhaps the first word coined by our hominid ancestors — appears in more prayers than any other, outpacing *save* and *bless*. This is a truth of long standing; thus the anonymous thirteenth-century author of *The Cloud of Unknowing* advises readers to "cry ceaselessly in your spirit this one thing: 'Sin! Sin! Sin! Help! Help! Help!'"[1] When the disciples ask Jesus, "Lord, how shall we pray," he does not counsel them in advanced meditative techniques; instead, he instructs them in adoration ("hallowed be thy name") and obedience ("thy will be done"), but above all in petition ("Give us this day our daily bread," "forgive us our trespasses," "lead us not into temptation," "deliver us from evil"). A well-known *ḥadīth* (traditional saying) of the Prophet Muḥammad insists that "nothing is more honorable in God's eyes than petition," while another Islamic story reports that when Adam arrived on earth, his first act was a prayer and his first prayer was a supplication: "The Apostle of God said: When Adam was sent down to earth he circumambulated the *Ka'ba* for a week and performed a prayer of two prostrations behind the prayer-platform. Then he said, 'O God Thou knowest my secret and my outward life, receive then my apology. Thou knowest my need, then grant my request. Thou knowest how I stand, then forgive all my sins for there is none that forgiveth sins but Thee.'"[2]

The prayer of the refugee appears at the very dawn of world literature on the cuneiform tablets that recount the *Epic of Gilgamesh* of ancient Babylon (c. 2750 B.C.E.). On tablet 1, the women of Uruk, an ancient city-state of Sumer, beg the goddesses to deliver them from their tyrannical king, who demands his droit du seigneur:

> Gilgamesh leaveth no maid to her mother, nor daughter to hero,
> Nay, nor a spouse to a husband
> (And so), to (the appeal of) their wailing
> Gave ear the Immortals.[3]

In the *Iliad,* the Achaian elder Nestor, "stretching his hand towards the starry heaven," begs for the safety of his troops, hard-pressed by the Trojan army, in an entreaty filled with images of sacrifice: "O father Zeus, if ever any one of us in wheat-bearing Argos did burn to thee fat thighs of bull or sheep, and prayed that he might return, and thou didst promise and assent thereto, of these things be thou mindful, and avert, Olympian, the pitiless day, nor suffer the Trojans thus to overcome the Achaians."[4]

This ancient Greek plea is distantly mirrored in our day, for example in the traditional Buddhist vow: "I take refuge in the Buddha, I take refuge in the Dharma, I take refuge in the Sangha." Patrul Rinpoche, a prominent nineteenth-century Tibetan teacher, calls this prayer "the foundation stone of all paths."[5] The same note sounds, too, in primordial traditions of Africa and the Americas whose prayers have come down to us without dates of origin but with beauty intact, as in this Inca plea with its curious echoes of Jabez's request "that Your hand would be with me":

> Creator! You who dwell at the ends of the earth unrivaled, you who gave being and power to men, saying: let this be man, and to women, saying, let this be woman! So saying, you made them, shaped them, gave them being. These you created; watch over them! Let them be safe and well, unharmed, living in peace. Where are you? Up in the sky? Or down below? In clouds? In storms? Hear me, answer me, acknowledge me, give us perpetual life, hold us forever within your hand. Receive this offering wherever you are. Creator![6]

The prayer of the refugee varies dramatically in subject, tone, intent, and form. It may be brief and tinged with humor, like the supplication of the youthful Saint Augustine, "Make me chaste and continent, but not just yet"; it may be baldly comical, like this prayer widely distributed on the Internet: "Lord, help me to avoid the sin of perfectionism (did I spell that right?). Amen!" It may deliver a simple, poignant plea, as in the following example composed and read by Robert Louis Stevenson to his family on the night before his death: "Go with each of us to rest; if any awake, temper to them the dark hours of watching; and when the day returns, return to us, our sun and comforter, and call us up with morning faces and with morning hearts, eager to labour, eager to be happy, if happiness should be our portion, and if the day be marked for sorrow, strong to endure it."[7]

Whatever its form, the prayer of the refugee not only deals with the basics of life but harbors a philosophical conundrum about the nature of prayer and the nature of God. *Why is petition necessary?* Doesn't an omniscient God already know our most intimate needs and desires? Wouldn't an all-loving God provide whatever we truly require? Isn't petitionary prayer redundant, a form of sanctified nagging? These questions were familiar to Saint Augustine, who contended, in "On the Lord's Sermon on the Mount," that the purpose of prayer must be to transform the one who prays (anticipating Kierkegaard's maxim "Prayer does not change God, but it changes him who prays"), softening resistance to God's will and opening us to divine influence:

> The very effort involved in prayer calms and purifies our heart, and makes it more capacious for receiving the divine gifts, which are poured

> into us spiritually. . . . there is brought about in prayer a turning of the heart to Him, who is ever ready to give, if we will but take what he has given; and in the very act of turning there is effected a purging of the inner eye, inasmuch as those things of a temporal kind which were desired are excluded, so that the vision of the pure heart may be able to bear the pure light, divinely shining, without any setting or change: and not only to bear it, but also to remain in it; not merely without annoyance, but also with ineffable joy, in which a life truly and sincerely blessed is perfected.[8]

Eight centuries later, Saint Thomas Aquinas bent his cool, rational mind toward the problem and, as was his wont, both complicated and clarified matters, on the one hand by perceiving issues that had eluded or failed to interest Augustine, and, on the other hand, by discovering answers that have stood for centuries. Thomas begins by listing three objections to petitionary prayer: (1) God already knows our needs; (2) petitions are designed to change God's mind, but God is eternally unchanging; and (3) since it is more generous to give to those who don't ask than to those who do, and since God is supremely generous, one would do better not to ask God for anything. Laying a foundation to respond to these objections, Thomas notes that divine providence — God's love as manifested through his holy will — determines not only which events will unfold, but how they will unfold. It may be, Thomas suggests, that God has decided that certain events — for example, a miraculous healing — will take place only if prayer is involved. As Thomas puts it, "We do not pray in order to change the decree of divine providence, rather we pray in order to impetrate those things which God has determined would be obtained only through our prayers. In other words, men pray that *by asking they might deserve to receive what Almighty God decreed to give them from all eternity,* as Gregory says."

The key word here is *impetrate* (*impetremus* in the original Latin), an obscure term meaning "to obtain by request or entreaty." We impetrate, or obtain through beseeching, those things that God wishes to grant us *if and only if we pray.* By the very act of praying, we become partners or co-agents (admittedly subordinate) with God in effecting the results of prayer — a far cry from the Augustinian (and, later, Reformation) notion of the human being as a passive recipient of God's grace. With this argument in place, Thomas answers the three objections to petitionary prayer. We pray not to tell God our needs, but to remind ourselves of our need for divine help; we pray not to change God's mind, but to obtain through impetration that which God wishes for us; and, even though God, who is infinitely generous, gives us many things without asking, we pray because God wishes us to do so, in order to "gain confidence in God and acknowledge him as the source of all our blessings." Some theologians liken God's desire for prayer to the love of parent for child; all parents, even if they can easily anticipate a child's needs, rejoice when a child approaches them to ask for help, for this act fosters an atmosphere of mutual love; just so, petitionary prayer engenders reciprocal love between us and God.[9]

Thomas's arguments have proved remarkably resilient and continue to hold considerable sway among philosophers and metaphysicians. Some thinkers, however, approach the problem on a markedly different tack. Immanuel Kant comes close to repeating Augustine's original argument; for this Enlightenment philosopher, supposedly so predictable in his habits that the housewives of Königsberg set their watches by his daily walks, prayer offers little in the way of adventure: "Praying, thought of as an *inner formal* service of God and hence as a means of grace, is a superstitious illusion (a fetish-making), for it is no more than *a stated wish* directed to a Being who needs no such information regarding the inner disposition of the wisher; therefore nothing is accomplished by it."[10]

Well, then, what purpose does prayer serve? It buttresses the moral sense, always Kant's primary aim in the practice of religion: "The purpose of prayer can only be to induce in us a moral disposition; its purpose can never be pragmatic, seeking the satisfaction of our wants. It should fan into flame the cinders of morality in the inner recesses of our heart."[11] This view of prayer marks a severe attenuation even of Augustine's perspective, for Augustine sees prayer as the gateway not only to morality but to something larger and more encompassing, the "blessed life" in which we abide in the "pure light that shines divinely without wavering or setting" — a consummation far beyond Kant's idea of what religion can achieve.

Other critiques of Thomas's defense of petitionary prayer have been proposed. It may be, for example, that God is not omniscient and needs to be informed of our desires through the grapevine of prayer (of course, such a God will also likely prove less than omnipotent, hobbling his ability to answer our petitions). It may be that prayer operates within a universal economy of reciprocal exchange, that one must give — through suffering, love, or prayers — in order to receive God's blessings. Or it may be that God's unfathomable being makes room for prayer in ways that reach beyond human understanding.

New arguments in support of Thomas's point of view continue to proliferate as well. C. S. Lewis forwards a particularly intriguing one, that once you admit God's existence, objections to prayer become objections to any human act:

> The case against prayer . . . is this. The thing you ask for is either good — for you and for the world in general — or else it is not. If it is, then a good and wise God will do it anyway. If it is not, then He won't. In neither case can your prayer make any difference. But if this argument is sound, surely it is an argument not only against praying, but against doing anything whatever? . . . Why wash your hands? If God intends them to be clean, they'll come clean without your washing them. If He doesn't, they'll remain dirty (as Lady Macbeth found) however much soap you use. Why ask for the salt? Why put on your boots? Why do anything?[12]

No doubt further arguments will emerge on both sides, as petition continues to dominate the world of prayer. The impulse to ask for divine assistance seems an indelible part of being human; when we declare that there are no atheists in foxholes, we are saying that petitionary prayer dwells, at least *in potentia,* in us all.

The De Profundis Prayer

Petitionary prayer is complex, controversial, and ubiquitous. To understand it better, we propose to narrow our focus to one variety of petition that in its intensity and profligacy of expression epitomizes the genre as a whole. The prayer *de profundis* — "out of the depths" — erupts whenever a man or woman finds himself or herself trapped in the bowels of despair, bereft of answers or resources. The soul wallows in affliction; nothing remains but utter abandonment to divine mercy. The nethermost pit thus becomes the womb of that most penetrating of prayers, the cri de coeur: Help me, O God! Forgive me, O Lord! Rescue me! Make me whole! Give me back my life!

The *de profundis* prayer derives its name from Psalm 130 (RSV):

> Out of the depths I cry to thee, O Lord!
>   Lord, hear my voice!
> Let thy ears be attentive
>   to the voice of my supplications!
> If thou, O Lord, shouldst mark iniquities,
>   Lord, who could stand?
> But there is forgiveness with thee,
>   that thou mayest be feared.
> I wait for the Lord, my soul waits,
>   and in his word I hope;

my soul waits for the Lord
 more than watchmen for the morning,
 more than watchmen for the morning.
O Israel, hope in the Lord!
 For with the Lord there is a steadfast love,
 and with him is plenteous redemption.
And he will redeem Israel
 from all his iniquities.

Scholars know little about the origins of this song. The anonymous author, who most likely lived during or just after the Babylonian exile (c. 597–538 B.C.E.), may have been of royal blood, although today few accept the traditional ascription to King David. Whatever his status, the psalmist sings from "out of the depths," as if from Sheol, the fathomless watery underground of the dead where social distinctions count for nothing. Through his iniquities he has severed himself from God; he is walled in by anguish like Jonah in the belly of the whale: "Out of the belly of hell cried I. . . . The waters compassed me about, even to the soul: the depth closed me round about, the weeds were wrapped about my head" (Jonah 2:2, 5). In the throes of suffering the psalmist turns to God, confesses his sins, and expresses confidence in the Lord's compassion and mercy, both for himself and his nation. Psalm 130 is surely not the earliest utterance of the prayer *de profundis*, an honor that may belong to the first Neanderthal to see a woolly mammoth bearing down on him in the Pleistocene snows, but it distills, with incomparable eloquence and power, the prayer's irreducible sequence of need, plea, and response. I hit bottom; I call for help; I await a reply. This, as we shall see, is the universal code of the *de profundis* prayer.

Psalm 130 presents this sequence in eighteen lines, offering more of a template than a case history. To see precisely how this prayer works, we need to observe it *in situ*, and we need to find an example that conveys, through its individual twists and turns, universal truths about the prayer. Happily, just such a combination of the unique and the generic lies readily at hand, thanks to the seventeenth-century convict, spy, hoaxer, journalist, and father of the English novel, Daniel Defoe. For in *The Life and Strange Surprizing Adventures of Robinson Crusoe of York, Mariner; Who Lived Eight and Twenty Years, all alone in an uninhabited Island on the Coast of America, near the Mouth of the Great River of Oronoque; Having been cast on Shore by Shipwreck, wherein all the Men perished but himself. With an Account how he was at last as strangely deliver'd by Pirates. Written by Himself*, the intricate workings and saving power of the *de profundis* prayer burst forth with unsurpassed power and beauty.

Robinson Crusoe as the Archetypal Man of Prayer

Robinson Crusoe remains, nearly three centuries after publication, the most widely reprinted of all book-length fictions, appearing in more than twelve hundred editions in English alone, translated into countless tongues (including an 1820 Latin version for schoolboys, *Robinson Crusoeus*), and spawning innumerable pastiches and homages, from the science fiction knockoff *Robinson Crusoe on Mars* to Michel Tournier's postmodernist *Friday.* Robinson's adventures have enriched the lexicon, giving us the handy noun *robinsonade* (the generic term for a tale of castaways), the gawky adjective *Robinson Crusoic,* and the hideous transitive verb *Robinson-crusoe* (to maroon), the usage of which, the *Oxford English Dictionary* mercifully reports, remains "rare." The London Royal Mail regularly receives letters addressed to Robinson Crusoe, a distinction shared, among fictional creations, only by Sherlock Holmes. Defoe's tale has, in effect, become a myth, an essential story conveying essential truths, fully as resonant as anything in James Frazer or Joseph Campbell.

Let us check off what we all know about this myth: a sailor is shipwrecked without resources on a desert island, survives for years by his wits, suffers terribly as a result of his isolation, discovers a footprint in the sand belonging to a native named Friday, and finally is rescued from his exile — all this in the context of a boys' adventure tale. Such is our common store of Robinsoniana — and all of it is wrong. Robinson's island is not a desert in the modern sense of the word. Robinson does not proceed without resources, he does not live solely by his wits, he does not suffer inordinately for his solitude, and that famous footprint, the best-known in the world, does not belong to Friday. Even the word *rescue,* applied to Robinson's escape from the island, turns out to be false. But more significant than these details is that our overall perception of *Robinson Crusoe* is wrong. The most important fact about this boys' adventure book is that it is not a boys' book at all, but a grown-up tale of a man's discovery of prayer and the fruits that prayer may bring.

As Defoe's book begins, Robinson Crusoe, a youth of nineteen, self-willed, arrogant, and mad with wanderlust, commits what he calls his "Original Sin," spurning his father's entreaties to join the family business and instead heading to sea. His maiden voyage ends in shipwreck, presaging the greater disaster to follow. Robinson contemplates a return to the family home in York, especially after the father of a friend interprets this first crisis as "a plain and visible Token that you are not to be a Seafaring man," but following the way of all youth, he scorns this advice and signs on for a voyage to Guinea in western Africa. Many catastrophes ensue — violent storms, tropical disease, enslavement under Turkish pirates, run-ins with lions and leopards — in all of which Robinson acts, as he himself puts it, as "the willful Agent of all my own Miseries," choosing always self-indulgence over duty, a destructive course that culminates in the famous shipwreck on September 30, 1659, off the Atlantic coast of South America.

Washed ashore, Robinson finds himself on a subtropical island that resembles the Pacific islands of the Juan Fernandez group where Robinson's real-life prototype, Alexander Selkirk, was marooned alone for six years, from 1704 to 1709. Robinson manages to retrieve from the sinking vessel a stockpile of supplies that constitute, as soon becomes clear, the building blocks of English Christian culture. The rescued treasures include biscuits, rum, rice, cheeses, sugar, flour, and corn; rifles, pistols, knives, razors, swords, ax, gunpowder, and a dozen hatchets; grindstone, hammock, canvas, forks, spade, scissors, two saws, hammer, nails, and spikes; pen, ink, paper, compasses, navigational charts, mathematical instruments, and last but not least, three English Bibles and "two or three Popish Prayer-Books."

Like any castaway, Robinson rues his fate. "I had great Reason to consider it as a Determination of Heaven, that in this desolate Place and in this desolate Manner I should end my life; the Tears would run plentifully down my Face when I made these Reflections." At the same time, he rejoices in his good fortune in escaping the shipwreck that drowned all his companions. He draws up a ledger of debits and credits, along the lines of "I have not Clothes to cover me . . . But I am in a hot Climate, where if I had Clothes I could hardly wear them"; this moral arithmetic leads him to the platitudinous conclusion that "there was scarce any Condition in the World so miserable, but there was something *Negative* or something *Positive* to be thankful for in it" and provides ample evidence that the suffering occasioned by his calamity has not yet destroyed the willful thinking that led him to sea in the first place.

Soon after, however, a series of events propels Robinson toward a new worldview. He tosses some corn husks, gnawed by rats, on the side of his habitation; a month later, green shoots emerge from the soil, which prove to be English barley. A belief in God's beneficent providence dawns:

> It is impossible to express the Astonishment and Confusion of my Thoughts on this Occasion. I had hitherto acted upon no Religious Foundation at all, indeed I had very few notions of Religion in my Head,

> or had entertain'd any Sense of any Thing that had befallen me, other wise than as a Chance . . . but after I saw Barley grow there, in a Climate which I know was not proper for Corn, and especially that I knew not how it came there, it startl'd me, strangely, and I began to suggest, that God had miraculously caus'd this Grain to grow without any Help of Seed sown, and that it was directed purely for my Sustenance, on that wild miserable Place.

Along with the corn, the seeds of prayer take root, and when an earthquake strikes three months later, Robinson utters, albeit unconsciously, his first request to God: "I had not the least serious religious Thought; nothing but the common, *Lord ha' Mercy upon me,* and when it was over, that went away too." Several weeks later, deathly ill from a flu, he cries out, *"Lord Look upon me, Lord pity me, Lord have Mercy upon me."* This ejaculation, still a matter of instinct rather than conscious entreaty, is followed by a terrifying dream in which a flaming angel descends from a cloud, strides toward Robinson with spear in hand, and exclaims, *"Seeing all these Things have not brought thee to Repentance, now thou shalt die."* "No one," writes Robinson in his diary, "that shall ever read this Account, will expect that I should be able to describe the Horrors of my soul at this terrible Vision." He reproaches himself ruthlessly for his self-love, self-will, and hardness of heart; for two days he weeps, rent by repentance, and finally, in a paroxysm of despair, cries out: "*Lord be my Help, for I am in great Distress.* This was the first Prayer, if I may call it so, that I had made for many years."

This petition proves to be a watershed. As the fever abates, Robinson the mariner becomes Robinson the metaphysician, turning over in his mind those perennial questions: Who am I? Why am I here? Who made me? Insights follow with breathtaking rapidity, encapsulating the catechism of Puritan England: God made me, he knows all, he has appointed all. Why do I suffer? Because of my misspent life. What hope is left me? Robinson turns to his sea chest and hauls out his Bible. Opening it at random, he discovers a definitive call to prayer: *"Call on me in the Day of Trouble, and I will deliver, and thou shalt glorify me"* (Psalm 50:15). And with this, Robinson assumes not only the words but the posture of prayer, doing "what I have never done in all my Life, I kneel'd down and pray'd to God to fulfil the Promise to me, that if I call'd upon him in the Day of Trouble, he would deliver me." From this moment on, Robinson's life becomes inextricably intertwined with prayer. He weaves prayer into his work, his recreation, his rambles and meditations; he feels the urge to pray wherever he goes and whatever he does. He adopts a course of daily Bible study, grows ever "more deeply and sincerely affected with the

Wickedness of my past Life," and undergoes the defining moment of his life:

> With my Heart as well as my Hands lifted up to Heaven, in a Kind of Extasy of Joy, I cry'd out aloud, *Jesus, thou Son of David, Jesus thou exalted Prince and Saviour, give me Repentance!* This was the first time that I could say, in the true Sense of the Words, that I pray'd in all my Life; for now I pray'd with a sense of my Condition, and with a true Scripture View of Hope founded on the Encouragement of the Word of God; and from this Time, I may say, I began to have Hope that God would hear me.

With this prayer, Robinson's comprehension of deliverance changes; before it had meant rescue from this tropical island of despair; now it means rescue from his baleful spiritual condition, from the guilt that torments him, from the horror of his misspent life. "As to my solitary Life it was nothing; [I] did not so much as pray to be deliver'd from it, or think of it; It was all of no Consideration in Comparison to this." Discovering God, he discovers too a world of goodness, truth, and beauty. He surveys his land and finds meadows lush with tobacco, sugar cane, and aloe, valleys resplendent with coca, lemon, orange, lime, citron, melon, and grapes. What had formerly seemed a prison becomes a paradise, as if original sin had been washed away, and he, the new Adam, had returned to Eden: "The Country appear'd so fresh, so green, so flourishing, every thing being in a constant Verdure, or Flourish of Spring, that it looked like a planted Garden." He builds a country house to complement his seacoast cave, declares himself "King and Lord of all this Country," and sets aside the first anniversary of his landing as a day of fasting and prayer, "prostrating my self on the Ground with the most serious Humiliation, confessing my Sins to God, acknowledging his Righteous Judgments upon me, and praying to him to have Mercy on me, through Jesus Christ." In the years that remain before his rescue, Robinson becomes, in effect, a castaway Carthusian, a common-law member of that most austere of monastic orders whose members spend the day in solitary prayer and manual labor.

Robinson Crusoe is, of course, a fiction — or, better, a metafiction, a story that transmits universal truths — in this case, about prayer, conversion, and humankind's tumultuous relations with God. In describing Robinson's wayward path to salvation, Defoe draws upon not only the experiences of Alexander Selkirk but also on his own religious life as a Dissenter, which included scripture study, daily prayer, small martyrdoms (he served a term in Newgate Prison for remaining stalwart in his faith), and fierce adherence to the Pauline heritage of spiritual rebirth. He relied, too, upon his own varied experience of regeneration, for he reinvented himself from decade to decade, become successively a manufacturer, cow trader, secret agent, marriage counselor, journalist — he ran eight newspapers simultaneously, writing the bulk of every issue — and first master of the English novel. This manic enterprise coalesced in the character of Robinson; Defoe was, in a sense, ten or twenty men, and similarly Robinson is not so much a seventeenth-century sailor but rather Everyman, primordial man cast away upon the enchanted shores of the island of prayer. This universal quality, as Samuel Taylor Coleridge points out, is the key to *Robinson Crusoe*'s success: "Nothing is done, thought, or suffered but what every man can imagine himself doing, thinking, feeling, or wishing for . . . Crusoe rises only where all men be made to feel that they might and that they ought to rise — in religion, in resignation, in dependence on, and thankful acknowledgement of the divine mercy and goodness." The overall effect, Coleridge insists, brings more than literary rewards: "You become a man while you read [Defoe]."[13]

You become, too, an expert on the *de profundis* prayer, for there is no better primer on the subject than *Robinson Crusoe*, which presents, directly through Robinson's monologues and indirectly through the tale's dramatic incident, the basic laws that govern this species of prayer. We learn that the *de profundis* prayer arises not when people fall into the depths, but when they realize that they are irrevocably trapped; that the prayer is preceded by mental confusion, intense emotion, and surrender of the personal will to the will of God; and that the prayer itself brings solace, even if the crisis continues. We learn, too, that cries from the depths (and, by extrapolation, all forms of petitionary prayer), no matter how spontaneous they may appear, have always a traceable ancestry and conform to religious tradition, social convention, and individual psychology — even if these conditioning factors remain invisible to the supplicant. Thus Robinson, while insisting that he has had no intercourse with religion, in his moment of crisis shouts, "Lord Ha' Mercy On Me," — a phrase, no doubt absorbed from his father or from a pious sea mate, whose brevity conceals a wealth of assumptions about Jesus Christ, divine mercy, the cosmic hierarchy, and other theological matters. Robinson may not be conscious of this background, but it shapes his perception of the nature and effects of prayer.

Defoe's tale discloses, too, the archetypal pattern of spiritual renewal in which the *de profundis* prayer and other petitionary prayers play such a crucial role. Robinson's journey from degenerate to regenerate passes through five distinct stages:

1. *Innocence:* Early years in York, before the demon of self-will takes possession of his soul
2. *Rebellion:* Decision to go to sea against the advice of father and friends
3. *Fall:* Shipwreck off South America
4. *Struggle to reform:* Battle between despair and hope, between love of self and love of God, as Robinson makes his first halting efforts at prayer and repentance
5. *Transformation:* Immersion in prayer, acknowledgment of sin, surrender to God, return to a Christian way of life, and the subsequent reconstruction of Christendom on Robinson's tiny desert empire

This pattern, with the exception of the desert empire, will ring familiar to many readers, for it reproduces closely the classical "born again" path to salvation of evangelicalism. Robinson's passage through repentance and conversion corresponds, for example, to the well-known tale of John Newton (1725–1807), author of the beloved hymn "Amazing Grace." Newton rebelled as a youth and fled to sea; sank into iniquity; converted under great duress, uttering his first conscious prayer, "Lord have mercy on us!" on May 10, 1748, as his ship foundered during a violent storm; carried within him from childhood the seeds of this prayer, planted through biblical stories his mother had read aloud; followed his initial act of surrender to God by a long period of wavering and backsliding; and eventually immersed himself in religion as a minister and writer of hymns. The parallels with Robinson's tale (composed three decades before Newton's conversion) suggest that in the stories of these two men, one fictional, the other flesh and blood, we can discern typical, if not always universal, manifestations and effects of the *de profundis* prayer.

The Agonies of Samuel Johnson

Not all examples of the *de profundis* prayer conform so neatly to this evangelical pattern. For some, the pattern of fall, supplication, and transformation repeats itself incessantly, until it becomes a habit, a curse, a nervous tic of the soul, a plague from youth to old age. Nowhere does this Sisyphean pattern display itself with greater pathos than in the prayer life of the great English critic, essayist, lexicographer, and spellbinding conversationalist, Samuel Johnson (1709–1784).

Dr. Johnson, as he will ever be known, has become a curiosity: the subject of the most celebrated biography in the English language yet someone whose influence today is very nearly nil. Who reads him, apart from Anglophiles and graduate students? Who searches out old issues of the *Rambler,* the biweekly periodical for which he wrote over two hundred issues? Who pores over his *Dictionary of the English Language,* compiled single-handedly over nine years, that placed our quicksand tongue on solid footing? Who seeks out his edition of Shakespeare, his political pamphlets, his letters to Mrs. Thrale? Our diffidence toward Johnson's writings is not entirely misplaced, for his genius, as Boswell and a horde of other biographers have shown, resided less in his pen than in his person. The fascination of his character shone forth in his scintillating table talk, in his bon mots and biting wit, in his obsession with bunions and boils, in his bumpy but loving marriage, in the prized pocket watch on which he inscribed in Greek as a memento mori "The Night Cometh," in his voracious hugeness of mind and body.

Johnson's omnivorous hunger for life encompassed God, heaven, and the means by which he might please the one and attain the other. Most of our knowledge of his inner life derives from *Prayers and Meditations,* assembled after his death from his private journals by the Reverend George Strahan. Here Johnson bares his soul, disclosing the details of his prayer life and the fears and desires that drove it as few men have before or since. "That he should have wished his friend to publish all that is included in these *Prayers and Meditations* almost passes belief," comments George Birkbeck Hill, the editor of Johnson's letters.[14]

Prayers and Meditations leaves no doubt that Johnson valued his inner life — primarily his relationship with God and the possibility of salvation — above all else. Six months before his death, he wrote to Queeney Thrale, a close friend: "Believe a man whose experience has been long, and who can have no wish to deceive you, and who now tells you that the highest honour, and most constant pleasure this life can afford, must be obtained by passing it with attention fixed upon Eternity." Indifferent to religion as a child, Johnson discovered while at Oxford the Anglican writer William Law's *Serious Call to a Devout and Holy Life* and thereafter became obsessed — no other word will do — with his spiritual state, a fixation he both worried and alleviated through prayer. Mrs. Thrale testifies that "the piety of Dr. Johnson was exemplary and edifying: he was punctiliously exact to perform every public duty enjoined by the church, and his spirit of devotion had an energy that affected all who ever saw him pray in private. The coldest and most languid hearers of the

Samuel Johnson.

word must have felt themselves animated by his manner of reading the holy scriptures."[15]

To the outward observer Johnson must have been an uplifting figure, his pockmarked face a beacon of hope and inspiration as he sang hymns, recited the Creed, received Communion, or read the holy texts. But a glimpse into his mind would have revealed a very different Johnson, seething with self-doubt that sometimes blossomed into self-loathing, convinced of his own moral failure and acutely afraid of damnation, and happy to imagine his friends in heaven but reserving for himself a bed in hell. *Prayers and Meditations* teems with finely drawn accounts of Johnson's self-perceived inadequacies. Indolence reigns supreme. It is the focus of his first entry, inscribed in Latin in October 1729, at the age of twenty: "*Desidiae valedixi; syrenis istius cantibus surdam posthac aurem obversurus* (I bid farewell to Sloth, being resolved henceforth not to listen to her syren strains)"[16] and runs as a leitmotif through all his prayers and meditations, catching other vices in its wake. He composed this prayer on his twenty-ninth birthday:

> O God, the Creatour and Preserver of all Mankind, Father of all mercies, I thine unworthy servant do give Thee most humble thanks, for all thy goodness and lovingkindness to me. I bless Thee for my Creation, Preservation, and Redemption. . . . Create in me a contrite Heart, that I may worthily lament my sins and acknowledge my wickedness, and obtain Remission and forgiveness, through the satisfaction of Jesus Christ. And, O Lord, enable me, by thy Grace, to redeem the time which I have spent in Sloth, Vanity, and wickedness; to make use of thy Gifts to the honour of thy Name; to lead a new life in thy Faith, Fear, and Love; and finally to obtain everlasting Life.[17]

Here Johnson reveals his full repertoire of prayer: thanksgiving, blessing, praise, and hope, couched in phrases drawn often from the Book of Common Prayer, sung to a drumbeat of self-denigration, self-accusation, and commitment to self-reform. Beneath the prayer text Johnson writes, echoing Robinson Crusoe, "this is the first solemn prayer, of which I have a copy. Whether I composed any before this, I question."

It was not to be his last. Regularly, on major days of the year — Good Friday, Easter, New Year's Day, his birthday, and, later, the day of his wife's death — Johnson composed similar prayers, fraught with self-recrimination. On Easter Eve, 1761, he writes:

> Since the Communion of last Easter I have led a life so dissipated and useless, and my terrours and perplexities have so much encreased, that I am under great depression and discouragement, yet I purpose to present myself before God tomorrow with humble hope that he will not break the bruised reed. . . . Almighty and most merciful Father, look down upon my misery with pity, strengthen me that I may overcome all sinful habits, grant that I may with effectual faith commemorate the death of thy Son Jesus Christ, so that all corrupt desires may be extinguished, and all vain thoughts may be dispelled.[18]

Yet three years later, again on Easter Eve, he writes that "my indolence, since my last reception of the Sacrament, has sunk into grosser sluggishness, and my dissipation spread into wilder neglect. . . . A kind of strange oblivion has overspread me, so that I know not what has become of the last year, and perceive that incidents and intelligence pass over me without leaving any impression."[19]

As these yearly petitions indicate, Johnson's remorse crowded and tortured his mind but left little or no impression on his behavior. One of his favorite, but ineffective, weapons against sin was the composition of lists. The first of these extraordinary litanies, appearing on July 13, 1755, addressed strictly religious matters — from now on, Johnson resolves, he will more faithfully read scripture, attend church, meditate, and say his prayers — but by 1760 the net had been cast more widely, enclosing vows to God such as "to rise earlier," "to reclaim imagination," and "to repent and foresake my sins before the miseries of age fall upon me."[20]

That Johnson repented his sins is certain, that he forsook them before old age remains doubtful. The lists appear annually, decade after decade, the content scarcely changed. Desperate prayers accompany the promises; a typical New Year sees him falling to his knees and crying out, "O Lord let me not sink down into total depravity; look down upon me, and rescue me at last from the captivity of Sin" (January 1, 1766). Improbable schemes arise to help win the battle: in 1664 he promises God to study the scriptures in Greek and Hebrew, 640 verses every Sunday, thus completing the Bible within a year. Sometimes, the miscellany of life intrudes: a visit from Boswell; the death of his wife; complaints about flatulence, hunger, and colds; odd scientific experiments ("I shaved the part of my right arm that is next to the wrist and the skin of my chest round the right breast so that it might be seen how long it would take for the hair to grow again"). But always the monotonous round returns: rise early, keep a journal, study scripture; repent, reform, be reborn.[21]

Johnson, who missed very little in himself or others, was aware of his plight. One year he notes that "I have now spent fifty five years in resolving, having from the earliest time almost that I can remember been forming schemes of a better life. I have done nothing, the need of doing therefore is pressing, since the time of doing is short. O God grant me to resolve aright, and to keep my resolutions for Jesus Christ's sake. Amen." This entry appears on his fifty-sixth birthday, leading the editor of *Prayers and Meditations* to note archly that Johnson "began resolving, it seems, from his birth." So it must have seemed to the poor, tortured man. On Good Friday, 1775, he looks back on his history of resolutions, "made and broken, either by negligence, forgetfulness, vicious idleness, casual interruption, or morbid infirmity," and wonders why he should resolve again. He has a ready answer: "reformation is necessary and despair is criminal"; the corollary to this, of course, is that "prayer is necessary and silence before God is criminal."[22]

Prayer, in Johnson's mind, was the prerequisite for transformation. Each of his manifold resolutions was itself a prayer: a pledge addressed to God, solemnly inscribed in his journal and accompanied by heart-rending pleadings for help and mercy. Only through prayer could he escape the horror of his failings, both physical — his illness and infirmities, his pockmarked face — and moral. He saw this activity as "a reposal of myself upon God, and a resignation of all into his holy hand." Writing alone loomed as large in his mind; he "conceive[d] of writing as something very like a Christian sacrament," according to Paul Fussell, and he often sanctified a new writing enterprise with a prayer, as in this entry for April 3, 1753: "I began the second vol. Of my Dictionary. . . . O God, who hast hitherto supported me, enable me to proceed in this labour, and in the whole task of my present state; that when I shall render up, at the last day, an account of the talent committed to me, I may receive pardon, for the sake of Jesus Christ. Amen."[23]

Yet despite his extensive experience with prayer and his acute self-awareness, one senses that Johnson missed something vital when assessing his inner life. An anecdote relayed by his biographer James Boswell is telling: During a breakfast conversation in June 1784, Johnson lets slip that he has considered compiling an anthology of prayer, prefaced by an essay on the subject. The table crowd urges him to tackle the project when something odd occurs:

> He seemed to be a little displeased at the manner of our importunity, and in great agitation called out, "Do not talk thus of what is so aweful. I know not what time God will allow me in this world. There are many things which I wish to do." Some of us persisted, and Dr. Adams said, "I never was more serious about anything in my life." JOHNSON: "Let me alone, let me alone; I am overpowered." And then he put his hands before his face, and reclined for some time upon the table.[24]

What could explain this fainting spell except an unconscious ambivalence about prayer? To bring his thoughts about prayer into the public arena appealed to Johnson and yet terrified him. Could it be that he sensed something amiss in a cri de coeur that lasts a lifetime? He may have glimpsed what, in the hindsight of centuries, has become obvious to many of his readers: that for Johnson, the longing for *metanoia*, with its self-recrimination, resolutions, and tearful pleadings to God, mattered more than reform itself, that only during the *de profundis* petition did he feel fully alive; that he was a Don Juan of prayer, valuing the chase and the first heady moments of conquest; but when faced with the long, steady grind of marriage — the vigilance and sacrifice necessary to maintain his new life — he backslid, eager to enjoy the chase once more. Thus in the confusion of his great heart, attraction to sin and desire for change waltzed together down the decades, to the endless fugue of petitionary prayer.

All this would be terribly sad if it weren't so endearing. Johnson invites love, as much as anyone who has ever picked up a pen. We love his honesty, his boldness, his courage, his golden ear for language. We love his ugliness and ungainliness, his irascibility, his self-doubts, his twinned perceptiveness and blindness toward himself. He is a great man riddled with flaws, above us and yet one of us, and as such claims our admiration and compassion. His magnetism radiates most strongly in his anguished petitionary prayers, in their tenderness, beauty, and intelligence — and in their comic failings. What begins in youth as ordinary pleas becomes, by Johnson's elderly years, the very manner of his presence in the world. Without prayer, there would be no Samuel Johnson.

A World of De Profundis Prayer

Daniel Defoe presented the *de profundis* prayer as a once-and-for-all triumph over self-will and self-destruction, as the gate to *metanoia* and, in the character Robinson Crusoe, as a rapturous return not only to God but to England and all its civilized charms. For Samuel Johnson, the prayer functions as a never-ending apocalypse, the moment of supreme sacrifice and self-surrender arriving again and yet again like a skipping record. Between them, Defoe and Johnson mark the two poles of the evangelical experience; all modalities of Protestant conversion lie between these extremes. But the *de profundis* prayer flourishes far beyond the borders of evangelicalism, as its presence in the Hebrew psalms makes clear. This prayer arises wherever a bereft heart calls for help from on high; it recognizes no boundaries of region or religion. Nor does its evangelical form translate exactly into other traditions. Each religion has its own grammar of prayer and salvation. The prayer can be found in Islam, for example in this plea from the twelfth-century shaykh 'Abd al-Qādir al-Jīlānī: "My breast is oppressed, my thoughts wander, I am bewildered. Lord have mercy on one whose disease is great, whose cure is impossible to him, whose sickness increases while his means of healing decrease, whose strength lessens while his will grows stronger. Thou art his refuge and strength, his help and healing."[25] In traditional societies, by contrast, the *de profundis* prayer may shed its personal character and speak as the voice of a nation, as it does in this example from the Ojibway of Canada:

> Grandfather,
> Look at our brokenness.
>
> We know that in all creation
> Only the human family
> Has strayed from the Sacred Way.
> We know that we are the ones
> who are divided.
> And we are the ones
> Who must come back together
> To walk in the Sacred Way.
>
> Grandfather,
> Sacred One,
> Teach us love, compassion, and honour.
> That we may heal the earth
> And heal each other.[26]

The *de profundis* prayer may even determine the shape of an entire culture, as it did through the revelation of Ganaioda'yo, better known as Handsome Lake (1735–1815), the Seneca prophet who in 1799 brought to his people the Gaiwiio (Good Word), a teaching that survives to this day in the longhouses of eastern woodlands Indians. By the turn of the eighteenth century, the Seneca, along with most of their allies in the Iroquois Confederacy, teetered on the brink of extinction, ravaged by alcoholism and poverty and persecuted by the new American government for having backed the British during the Revolutionary War. Handsome Lake's brother-in-law, Seneca chief Edward Cornplanter, describes the situation in apocalyptic terms: "Now all the men become filled with strong drink [*goniga'nongi*]. They yell and sing like demented people. . . . Now they are beastlike and run about without clothing and all have weapons to injure those who they meet. . . . Now the dogs yelp and cry in all the houses for they are hungry."[27] At the center of this nightmare scene stands Handsome Lake, an elderly man driven half-mad by drink and despair. One day, at the end of his tether, he utters a *de profundis* prayer:

> Now as [Handsome Lake] lies in sickness he meditates and longs that he might rise again and walk upon the earth. So he implores the Great Ruler

> to give him strength that he may walk upon this earth again. And then he thinks how evil and loathsome he is before the Great Ruler. He thinks how he has been evil ever since he had strength in this world and done evil ever since he had been able to work. But notwithstanding, he asks that he may again walk.[28]

Handsome Lake receives a most unexpected answer to his plea: his condition deteriorates, and he dies (or so Cornplanter reports). His family dresses him for burial when suddenly the dead man returns to life and exclaims, "Never have I seen such wondrous visions!" Three angelic beings, he tells his awestruck audience, have appeared to him with a new gospel, a lengthy set of moral and social prescriptions — a ban on whiskey, witchcraft, and abortion; a new economy, replacing hunting-gathering with agriculture; and a new emphasis on care for children, the elderly, and the infirm — that would profoundly alter life for the Seneca and neighboring peoples. Handsome Lake's story may raise some eyebrows — was his death a religious trance, a symptom of disease, or a drunken stupor, and is the Gaiwiio more than transplanted Christianity? Still, his petition in extremis remains a striking nonevangelical example of the *de profundis* prayer, and his teachings, influential to this day in the lives of thousands of Iroquois, offer evidence of its abiding effects.

As the experiences of Shaykh 'Abd al-Qādir al-Jīlānī, Handsome Lake, and others demonstrate, the *de profundis* prayer saturates world religion. Nor has its influence ended there. Sooner or later the abyss opens under us all; everyone stands in need of rescue. The prayer has wielded much influence in the lives of those who, for one reason or another, have strained or severed their relationship with conventional religious life. Even as traditional a Christian as Christina Rossetti (1830–1894), a high church Anglican given to orthodox devotions, detaches the phrase from its biblical origin and uses it to express a more generic longing in her poem "De Profundis":

> Oh why is heaven built so far;
> Oh why is earth set so remote?
> I cannot reach the nearest star
> That hangs afloat.
>
> I would not care to reach the moon,
> One round monotonous of change,
> Yet even she repeats her tune
> Beyond my range.
> I never watch the scatter'd fire
> Of stars, or sun's far-trailing train,

But all my heart is one desire,
And all in vain:

For I am bound with fleshly bands,
Joy, beauty, lie beyond my scope,
I strain my heart, I stretch my hands,
And catch at hope.

Rossetti, unlike Robinson or Johnson, laments not specific sins but our frail, imperfect nature, unable to attain the bright beauties of heaven. Even the moon, for which she cares nothing, remains beyond her grasp. She looks at the heavens from the depths; her isolation is complete. But when she "strains her heart," a movement analogous to prayer, she catches at one of the three great Pauline virtues. Perhaps the other two will soon swim into reach.

For Rossetti, hope remains, but no hint of escape from the depths arises in the bitter world of her contemporary Charles Baudelaire (1821–1867). The most influential of nineteenth-century Continental poets, Baudelaire produced work in which the ubiquity of evil overwhelms any faith in God's saving power. Splenetic anxiety and hallucinatory imagery reign, as in his poem "De profundis clamavi" ("Out of the Depths I Have Cried"):

I beg your pity, You, the only one that I love,
From the bottom of the dark abyss where my heart has fallen.
It is a somber universe, horizoned with lead,
Where horror and blasphemy swim through the night.

A sun without heat rules for six months,
And the other six months night covers the earth,
It is a country more naked than the polar earth,
Neither beasts, nor streams, nor greenery, nor woods!

But there is no horror in the world that surpasses
The cruel cold of this sun of ice
And this immense night, like ancient Chaos;

I envy the most vile of animals
Who can plunge themselves into stupid sleep,
So slowly does the skein of time unwind![29]

Rossetti's heavenly bodies, however remote, retain their natural, fiery beauty and thus remain emblems of hope; but for Baudelaire the universe has turned cold, pitiless, blasphemous. Nature is in revolt: the sun is icy, the horizon leaden, time itself an endless horror. A cry arises from the depths, as it does in Psalm 130, but no God listens and responds; the poem could be addressed to anyone or anything. Who is the "You" whom Baudelaire loves? God? A woman? His fevered imagination? The lack of a sure answer shows how far from its orthodox roots the *de profundis* prayer has traveled. "De profundis clamavi" may be described as an effort to subjectivize the prayer of the refugee, making it, in addition to a plea to God or some other being, an impressionistic painting of a mental and emotional state. This tendency exists in most petitionary prayer, of course — who pleads without a dash of self-explanation? — but as prayer is severed from traditional forms and beliefs its subjectivity increases, until a cry from the depths may come to signal self-absorption rather than abandonment to God, self-justification even in the midst of repentance.

Few works exemplify this approach more fully than Oscar Wilde's confessional self-portrait, *De Profundis.* Who better than Wilde to take up the *de profundis* prayer? Picture the most celebrated wit of the age, a brilliant playwright, essayist, novelist, and aphorist, a bon vivant born for the limelight, cast into the wan gray shadows of Reading Gaol, where he marches with the common prisoners, sharing their bug-infested food, rancid water, cold beds, and vulgar talk. Could there be a more precipitous tumble into the depths? The fault lay with England, for its outmoded sodomy laws, but it lay with Wilde also (as he repeatedly confessed), for the cockiness and artistic insularity that gave him a false sense of invulnerability, of standing above the law. He toppled from the peak of English culture into the pit of English jurisprudence; and yet *De Profundis,* despite its title, betrays barely a hint of the psalmist's tripartite sequence of fall-cry-reply. Wilde cries from the depths, to be sure, but he addresses his cry not to God but to Lord Alfred Douglas, his estranged lover. He offers no conventional prayers, instead imagining a "Confraternity of the Faithless" whose priest will "praise God daily for having hidden Himself from man." As one of the Faithless, Wilde substitutes for prayer a sustained meditation on sorrow, "the supreme emotion of which man is capable" and "the type and test of all great art." In this aesthetic based on suffering, the greatest of artists is Christ, the Man of Sorrows, and Wilde is his faithful disciple, almost an alter Christus. Both shoulder the sins of others, champion the individual, value art over dogma, and "stand in symbolic relations to the art and culture of [the] age." *De Profundis* is a sadly comic vision, with its long, rambling passages of self-justification and its anemic portrait of Christ as a type of nineteenth-century aesthete. Nonetheless, it remains a heart-rending cri de coeur built on the foundations of Psalm 130 and, as such, a valuable, albeit eccentric example of the *de profundis* prayer.[30]

Such irregular readings mark one way in which the *de profundis* prayer has veered from its traditional course. Recent years have witnessed another far more influential variant: a movement of international scope founded by a drunk from Brooklyn and a drunk from Ohio that has brought salvation to millions. Let us turn now to the greatest modern triumph of the *de profundis* prayer, Alcoholics Anonymous.

Bill W. and Deflation at Depth

Everything about Alcoholics Anonymous seems designed to put us at ease. The organization favors the affable acronym AA, its bumper stickers offer sunny slogans such as "Easy Does It" and "Live and Let Live," and its founders never go by their full legal names — historians may know them as William Griffith Wilson and Dr. Robert Holbrook Smith, but in the innumerable meeting rooms of AA, Bill W. and Dr. Bob will do just fine. This coziness is rooted in the camaraderie produced by shared battle against a common enemy; the guiding principle that the cure for alcoholism is intimate and personal, one drunk speaking to another; and perhaps most important, the desire to offer a deliberate contrast to the horrors of addiction and the cold sterility of the hospitals that await all who fail to conquer it. AA deals in life and death and uses whatever tools it can, from a hot cup of java to cold turkey detox, to give life the upper hand; no wonder the *de profundis* prayer, the quintessential prayer of life and death, plays such a large role in its success.

The early story of AA is synonymous with that of its principal founder, William Griffith Wilson (1895–1971), whom Aldous Huxley termed "the greatest social architect of the twentieth century," a man whose turbulent life and intimacy with prayer make him a worthy successor to Crusoe, Johnson, and Wilde. Born and raised in the mountains of Vermont, Wilson as a child received incessant warnings about the siren charms of booze, to which several of his relatives had succumbed. It was not until 1917, while an officer in the armed forces, that he had his first rapturous drink: "One night someone handed me a Bronx cocktail. . . . Ah, what magic! I had found the elixir of life! Down went the strange barrier that had always stood between me and people around me. . . . I could talk easily, I could communicate. Here was the missing link!"[31]

That first night, Wilson got royally plastered. A few drinking sessions later, he suffered a blackout, the first of hundreds. As the years flashed by, he hopped from one occupation to another, working as a doughboy, law student, and stockbroker, each position in turn sabotaged by drink. He completed his courses at Brooklyn Law School but never saw his diploma, for, as his wife, Lois, reports, "He was too drunk to leave the apartment the next day to pick it up." Wilson dazzled people with his manic energy — he was always hatching schemes, brokering deals, working the angles — but repelled them when his hyperkinetic enterprise derailed, as it always did, into brawling, womanizing, and the bottle. By the late 1920s, he was a hopeless "rumhound from New York" (as he called himself), regularly inscribing vows in the family Bible to forswear the bottle, pledges that he would break within the day. He checked repeatedly into New York's Charles B. Towns Hospital, a posh alcoholic recovery center, but every drying-out session was followed by another drunken spree. Madness or death seemed certain. Forty pounds underweight and wallowing in despair, he moved his mattress to the ground floor of his home so he couldn't commit suicide by jumping out a window. "In the night hours, I was filled with horror, for snaky things infested the dark. Sometimes by day, queer images danced on the wall." And so it went, until a dark November morning in 1934, when Wilson encountered the power of prayer.[32]

The turning point was a visit from Wilson's childhood friend, the inveterate alcoholic Ebby Thatcher. When Thatcher appeared that day in Wilson's Brooklyn kitchen, he was sober and beaming with happiness. "What on earth has got into you? What is this all about?" demanded Wilson. "I've got religion," Thatcher replied. As Bill sat sipping gin and pineapple juice cocktails, Thatcher unfurled the horrific tale of his own descent into hell, an unbroken nightmare of solitary drinking, multiple arrests, and commitment to a mental asylum, a headlong plunge reversed by a chance encounter with an old friend, Rhode Island state senator Rowland Hazard. Hazard, too, had spent years battling the demons of alcohol; after guzzling away his family fortune, he had flown, in a last desperate measure, to Switzerland and had thrown himself at the feet of the famous psychiatrist Carl Gustav Jung. A year of futile treatment followed, until finally Jung threw up his hands. What happened next is recounted in a 1961 letter from Wilson to Jung:

> You frankly told him [Hazard] of his hopelessness, so far as any further medical or psychiatric treatment might be concerned. . . . When he then asked you if there was any other hope, you told him that there might be, provided he could become the subject of a spiritual or religious experience — in short, a genuine conversion. You pointed out how such an experience, if brought about, might motivate him where nothing else could. . . . You recommended that he place himself in a religious atmosphere and hope for the best.[33]

Such an experience, as Jung explains elsewhere in his writings, may spark a revolution in the deepest level of one's being:

> Surrender to God is a formidable adventure. . . . He who can risk himself wholly to it finds himself directly in the hands of God, and is therefore confronted with a situation which makes "simple faith" a vital necessity; in other words, the situation becomes so full of risk or overtly dangerous that the deepest instincts are aroused. An experience of this kind is always numinous, for it unites all aspects of totality.[34]

Hazard had placed himself in the hands of God by joining the Oxford Group, a conservative Christian movement founded in Oxford, England, by the American preacher Frank Buchman. It emphasized moral and social renewal through personal surrender to Christ. Hazard soon led Ebby Thatcher to the same healing waters. As Thatcher explained to Wilson on that dreary November morning, he had found salvation by strict adherence to the core teachings of the group — admission of one's helplessness, examination of conscience, confession of defects, restitution to those whom one has wounded — a list that Wilson would later transfer nearly intact into AA. Of all the teachings of the Oxford Group, however, the most important was the saving power of prayer. "I know you are going to gag on this," Thatcher said to Wilson,

> but they taught me that I should try to pray to whatever God I thought there was for the power to carry out these simple precepts. And if I did not believe there was any God, then I had better try the experiment of praying to whatever God there might be. And you know, Bill, it's a queer thing, but even before I had done all this, just as soon as I decided that I would try with an open mind, it seemed to me that my drinking problem was lifted right out of me.[35]

Thatcher's advice haunted Wilson, who pondered it while contemplating the bottom of one empty glass after another. He was swayed by the simplicity and bluntness of Thatcher's story but rebelled at the mention of religion: "I could not, and would not, go along with any God concept. . . . there would be no conversion for me." Meanwhile, the drinking worsened, and on December 11 Wilson reentered Towns Hospital, where he sank into a tremendous depression, feeling as if he were "at the very bottom of the pit." He still "gagged badly" at the notion of God, but in spite of his dearly held atheism he suddenly heard himself shouting, "If there is a God, let Him show Himself. I am willing to do anything, anything!" The results are best described in Wilson's own words:

> Suddenly the room lit up with a great white light. I was caught up into an ecstasy which there are no words to describe. It seemed to me, in the mind's eye, that I was on a mountain and that a wind not of air but of spirit was blowing. And then it burst upon me that I was a free man. . . . All about me and through me there was a wonderful feeling of Presence, and I thought to myself, "So this is the God of the preachers!" A great peace stole over me and I thought, "No matter how wrong things seem to be, they are still all right. Things are all right with God and His world."[36]

Wilson's "hot flash" — as he called this event for the rest of his life — with its imagery of incandescence, its sense of separation from the here and now, its cascading joy and pervasive peace, is a far more dramatic example of the *de profundis* prayer and its aftermath than one finds in the reports of Defoe, Johnson, or Wilde. The character of the vision may be debatable: did it result from delirium tremens or the hospital's pharmaceutical treatments, which included belladonna and hyoscyamus (henbane), both psychoactive drugs? Whatever its source, Wilson's hot flash triggered that miraculous transformation that Samuel Johnson craved and John Newton realized. From December 1934 until his death in January 1971, Wilson never drank again. When Lois entered his hospital room the day after the hot flash, she grasped immediately that everything had changed: "I knew that something overwhelming had happened. His eyes were filled with light. His whole being expressed hope and joy."[37]

To unravel the meaning of his vision, Wilson began to read avidly in the literature of mystical and ecstatic experience, in particular William James's *The Varieties of Religious Experience,* in whose many firsthand accounts of conversion he found his own story repeatedly described. He was not a mental freak or a religious aberration, but a new link in a golden chain of spiritual transformation. How, then, should he forge the chain's next link? Instantly Wilson realized that reforming other alcoholics would be his passion and vocation. It wasn't a question of choice but of survival: to remain sober himself, he had to help others.

At first, dazzled by his own recovery and the spectacular conversions that pepper *Varieties,* Wilson attempted to trigger hot flashes in other drunks, urging on them the program of the Oxford Group and in particular its "four absolutes": absolute honesty, absolute purity, absolute unselfishness, absolute love. His efforts failed miserably. What these people needed, as Wilson's doctor counseled him, was not a hot flash but cold reality. "Give them the medical business," he urged Wilson, "and give it to them hard. Pour it right into them about the obsession that condemns them to drink. . . . maybe that will crack those tough egos deep down. Only then can you begin to try out your other medicine, the ethical principles you have picked up from the Oxford Groups."[38] In other words, make sure that every drunk knows that he has landed in the pit of despond, an experience that AA terms "deflation at depth"; only then will he or she be forced to reach out to God. Wilson took the advice. A few weeks later, on a business trip to Akron, Ohio, he met Dr. Robert Holbrook Smith, a proctologist and inveterate alcoholic. Wilson poured on "the medical business" and then prescribed a spiritual solution. Dr. Bob took his last drink on June 10, 1935, a date henceforth commemorated as the birthday of Alcoholics Anonymous.

Deflation at depth is, of course, the prerequisite to the *de profundis* prayer. It thus appears as the first of the Twelve Steps, AA's famous program for recovery from addiction: "We admitted we were powerless over alcohol — that our lives had become unmanageable." As shaped by Wilson's extensive knowledge of conversion literature, the entire structure of the Twelve Steps closely matches that of the *de profundis* prayer, from the self-evaluation of Step One to the ongoing *metanoia* of Step Twelve ("Having had a spiritual awakening . . . we tried . . . to practice these principles in all our affairs").

Wilson expands on this abbreviated program in the *Big Book* (known formally as *Alcoholics Anonymous*), the key text of the movement, first published in 1939 and a perennial bestseller. The *Big Book* is a curious work, set in a pre–World War II America of harried businessmen, bored housewives, and a tavern on every corner. At its center lies a collection of confessional tales, bound by the common thread of prayer. The task of every drunk, Wilson insists, is to acknowledge God's presence and cry for help:

> Self-reliance was good as far as it went, but it didn't go far enough. . . . Perhaps there is a better way — we think so. For we are now on a different basis; the basis of trusting and relying upon God. We trust infinite God rather than our finite selves. We are in the world to play the role He assigns. Just to the extent that we do as we think He would have us, and humbly rely on Him, does He enable us to match calamity with serenity.[39]

Relying on God, as Wilson knows, is not an easy job; how can one discern God's will, let alone have the strength to carry it out? This underscores the importance of Step Eleven, which establishes a regimen of prayer: "Sought through prayer and meditation to improve our conscious contact with God, as we understood Him, praying only for knowledge of His will for us and the power to carry that out." If the alcoholic trusts all to God's mercy, he or she will not be abandoned. Neglect of Step Eleven, Wilson never tired of saying, was the greatest mistake that an alcoholic could make. In June 1958, in the AA newspaper the *Grapevine,* Wilson comes close to describing Step Eleven's prescription of prayer as a universal panacea, a modern-day nectar of the gods:

> The other Steps can keep most of us sober and somehow functioning. But Step Eleven can keep us growing, if we try hard enough and work at it continually. . . . if [someone] persists [with Step Eleven], he will almost surely find more serenity, more tolerance, less fear, and less anger. He will acquire a quiet courage, the kind that doesn't strain him. He can look at so-called failure and success for what they really are. Problems and calamity will begin to mean instruction, instead of destruction. He will feel freer and saner. . . . His sense of purpose and of direction will increase. His tensions and anxieties will commence to fade. His physical health is likely to improve. Wonderful and unaccountable things will start to happen.[40]

Wilson's own life, it must be admitted, offers but checkered witness to his claims. His marriage survived, despite reports of philandering that continued until his death, but he suffered massive depressions throughout the 1940s and 1950s, and although it seems clear that his "sense of purpose and direction" improved — how else could he have founded and led an international organization that today comprises millions of members? — he wandered far afield in search of cures for his emotional ailments, experimenting with séances, niacin therapy, and, most notorious of all, LSD. Yet through it all he remained sober, and given this, who can doubt that through prayer Wilson grew "freer and saner," that "wonderful and unaccountable things" had come his way?

That these blessings arrived for Wilson and so many other participants in AA may be due to not only tenacity in prayer but also the ingenious, even revolutionary way in which Wilson presented his gospel of deflation and resurrection. He had but one aim: to break the chains of addiction. Nothing could impede this goal, not even God — or rather, a too sharply defined notion of God. Heretofore, the *de profundis* prayer had been uttered within a specific religious context — Protestant evangelicalism for John Newton, a Christian–Native American hybrid for Handsome Lake — freighted with specific understanding of divine nature. Not so with AA. Wilson would offer a definition of God large and loose enough to invite even agnostics into the fold. The Twelve Steps would speak only of "God as we understood Him." There would be no dogma, no doctrine, no elaborated theology at all. Step Two defines God simply as "a Power greater than ourselves," a definition that Wilson insisted "anybody — *anybody at all* — could accept and try."[41]

AA's generic treatment of God has intensified over the years as the organization has expanded to include members of every spiritual stripe. Some, unable to accept even Wilson's broad concept of God as a "creative intelligence" or "spirit of the universe," think of AA itself or their local group as the superintending Power. Others, in an exercise perhaps exhibiting more intellectual dexterity than spiritual insight, proclaim inanimate objects — a rock, a stove, a light bulb — as the Higher Power. Most members, though, remain content with Wilson's big-tent deity. His definition meets admirably the needs of the organization and the cultural predilections of Western liberal democracies, which favor inclusive notions of God, religion, and prayer. To this extent, at least, Wilson qualifies not only as a healer but as a prophet.

Wilson's insistence on generic religion has informed, too, the preferred prayers at most AA meetings. The Lord's Prayer — which, although a Christian prayer, makes no mention of Christ — is ubiquitous. Dick B., a recovering alcoholic and expert on the early history of AA, reports that of the two thousand meetings that he has attended, "almost every one has closed with the Lord's Prayer. At the 1990 International A.A. Conference in Seattle . . . some 50,000 members of Alcoholics Anonymous joined in closing their meetings with the Lord's Prayer."[42] Also commonly recited is the Prayer of Saint Francis, a long petition whose stark oppositions ("that where there is hatred, I may bring love," "that where there is error, I may bring truth," and so on) echo the choice each addict must make between slavery and freedom, death and life, and whose prescriptions for self-forgetting, forgiving others, and so on neatly summarize the Twelve Steps. No wonder it was reportedly Wilson's favorite prayer. Most commonly associated with AA, though, is the appealingly succinct Serenity Prayer:

> God grant us the serenity to accept the things we cannot change,
> Courage to change the things we can,
> And wisdom to know the difference.

Although usually ascribed to American theologian Reinhold Niebuhr, the true source of the Serenity Prayer, as with the Prayer of Saint Francis, remains a mystery. Wilson first encountered it in 1942, in an obituary notice in a New York newspaper. "Never had we seen so much A.A. in so few words," he wrote in *Alcoholics Anonymous Comes of Age*, and "with amazing speed" the Serenity Prayer became a vital part of the alcoholic's petitionary canon. Wilson speculated that the author might have been an ancient Greek, an English poet, an American naval officer, or perhaps Reinhold Niebuhr. Others have traced it back to Cicero, whose *Six Mistakes of Man* includes "the tendency to worry about things that cannot be changed," or to Boethius, Augustine, Marcus Aurelius, or Thomas Aquinas.

Niebuhr, meanwhile, insisted that he was the author and had scribbled the Serenity Prayer for a sermon preached at Heath Evangelical United Church in western Massachusetts. He controlled legal rights to the prayer, granting permission during World War II for the U.S.O. to print and distribute it to American troops. Later he assigned commercial rights to Hallmark Cards, who used the prayer in their 1962 Graduation Line, a move that continues to provide ammunition for those who accuse the prayer of greeting-card blandness. Certainly nothing in it smacks of ideology or sectarianism, and yet its demands, if followed faithfully and to the letter, require Solomonic insight and saintly fortitude. "To change the things we can" is by no means an easy task. The Serenity Prayer aims high, if no higher than the prayer of Jabez, with its pleas for blessing and right action, or the petitions of Robinson Crusoe, Samuel Johnson, Bill Wilson, and their company of fellow spiritual mendicants. The prayer of the refugee, at first glance an ego-driven act of self-preservation or self-aggrandizement, proves to be the bedrock of prayer, a ladder to salvation, humankind's last chance, and God's delight, the one song that the human heart is always singing: Lord, be with me now!

CHAPTER 5

The Devotee

THE MOST CELEBRATED and reproduced image of prayer must surely be Jean-François Millet's *Angelus,* a small nineteenth-century oil painting of two peasants at prayer in a rustic landscape. The original hangs in the Musée d'Orsay in Paris, but its reproduction shows up with astonishing regularity on tea towels, wine bottles, cheese wrappers, calendars, porcelain knickknacks, and a host of other commercial vehicles. There is good reason for this popularity, for the *Angelus* breathes the very atmosphere of prayer. A man and a woman — easily understood as Everyman and Everywoman, for their features grow vague in the twilight — bend over their devotions. A wheelbarrow, a pitchfork, and a basket of potatoes occupy the foreground; a church spire rises in the distance; the lowering sun spills yellow, red, and green across the mottled clouds. Every element of creation is in balance, transfigured by prayer into an intimation of heaven.

At the time he painted the *Angelus,* Millet was beset by poverty, overwork, and illness. According to his close friend Alfred Sensier, he was haunted by dreams of suicide and even produced a sketch in which a painter lies dead beside his easel while a woman throws up her hands in alarm. The *Angelus* was Millet's escape from all this, a return to the purity of the farming life he had known as a child. The canvas radiates the admirable spectrum of nineteenth-century French peasant virtues: simplicity, humility, the serenity of hard work punctuated by prayer. No wonder Van Gogh, describing the painting to his brother Theo, said, "Yes, that picture by Millet, '*The Angelus,*' that is it — that is beauty, that is poetry." The *Angelus* ensured Millet's fame, and on July 1, 1889, fourteen years after his death, the painting sold at auction for the unprecedented sum of 553,000 francs (about $3,000,000 in modern funds). According to press reports, when the *Angelus* was carried into the auction chamber, the audience rose en masse to applaud the great canvas, and when the winning bid was announced, cheers and sobs of joy filled the room.

The publics enthusiasm seems well placed. In its vast receding vistas of earth and sky, its hushed serenity and luminous presence, its humble peasants who subordinate all to God, the *Angelus* is not only a painting about prayer; it is a call to prayer. This is entirely as it should be, for Millet's peasants are offering up more than random petitions and thanksgivings; they are reciting the Angelus, a hymn of praise to the Virgin that until modern times poured out in every Catholic land three times a day, every day of the year, in response to the tolling of the Angelus bell:

> The Angel of the Lord declared unto Mary,
> And she conceived of the Holy Spirit.
> *Hail Mary . . .*
>
> Behold the handmaid of the Lord.
> Be it done unto me according to your word.
> *Hail Mary . . .*
>
> And the Word was made flesh and dwelt among us.
> *Hail Mary . . .*
>
> Pray for us, O holy Mother of God.
> That we may be made worthy of the promises of Christ . . .

The Angelus, with its repetition and affective intensity, exemplifies a species of prayer that we call the *prayer of the devotee.* Devotional prayer is cyclical, regular, and routine, reiterated at set intervals throughout the day, week, or year. It has a sacrificial character, offering the act of faith and the gift of loving attention to the divine beloved, sometimes accompanied by material goods such as incense, water, or food. It not only sets off the parts of the day apportioned to work and rest but also serves a more ambitious aim, the sanctification of time itself. To pray the Angelus is to quit profane time, the domain of labor and other mundane actions, and to enter sacred time, the domain of prayer, worship, and God. Regular repetition of the prayer establishes a rhythm between these two states of being, a contrapuntal flow as vital as inhalation and exhalation or the systole and diastole of the heart. Those who pray the Angelus live with one foot on earth and the other in heaven — or rather, they step from earth to heaven and back again 3 times a day, 27 times a week, and 1,404 times a year. And they return to earth bearing gifts, infusing mundane time with God's grace and blessings, as Benedictine monk David Steindl-

The Angelus, *by Jean-François Millet, 1857.*

Rast suggests: "Bells or no bells, I pray the Angelus. I let the silence drop like a pebble into the middle of my day and send its ripples out over its surface in ever-widening circles. That is the Angelus for me: the now of eternity rippling through time."[1]

Parallels to the Angelus can be found everywhere. Within the Christian world, the preeminent precursor is the Divine Office, also commonly called the *opus Dei* (work of God). The Divine Office intensifies the pattern of the Angelus, for it entails, in keeping with the famous prescription of Psalm 119, "seven times a day I praise you," seven periods of daily prayer devoted to reciting psalms, canticles, and scripture, as well as silent meditation. This octave of prayer has been the centerpiece of monastic life since the fourth century; Saint Benedict of Nursia (c. 480–543), father of Western monasticism, insisted that "on hearing the signal for an hour of the divine office, the monk will immediately set aside what he has in hand. . . . Indeed nothing is to be preferred to the Work of God." High praise indeed, and warranted, Benedict suggests in his Rule, because "the divine presence is everywhere . . . but beyond the least doubt we should believe this to be especially true when we recite the divine office."[2]

What accounts for the Office's ability to inflame the soul? The mix of devotional activities — singing, reading, meditating — that absorbs both body and mind in prayer; the self-effacement needed in order to say prayers in unison with others, a willed anonymity that Thomas Merton describes as "the complete opposite to the logic of the world";[3] the literary and spiritual beauty of the biblical texts being sung, read, and meditated upon; and the serenity of the music, traditionally Gregorian chant, which has a special power to bring one close to God. Merton explains the effect of chant at the Abbey of Gethsemani outside Louisville, Kentucky, where he resided for twenty-seven years:

> The cold stones of the Abbey church ring with a chant that glows with living flame, with clean, profound desire. It is an austere warmth, the warmth of Gregorian chant. It is deep beyond ordinary emotion, and that is one reason why you never get tired of it. It never wears you out by making a lot of cheap demands on your sensibilities. Instead of drawing you out into the open field of feelings where your enemies, the devil and your own imagination and the inherent vulgarity of your own corrupted nature can get at you with their blades and cut you to pieces, it draws you within, where you are lulled in peace and recollection and where you find God.[4]

Benedictine monk Jean Leclercq points out that such encomiums to chant have been rare in monastic literature, for Gregorian melodies have so permeated the daily life of the cloister that a monk would no more comment on them than on the quality of air or sunlight. "The monk's entire life was led under the sign of the liturgy, in rhythm with its hours, its seasons, and its feasts."[5] Here we see in full measure the sacrificial element of prayer, for the monk surrenders time, freedom of movement, and the chance to marry and have children in order to chant the daily round. This cuts against the grain of our hedonistic culture, and the number of monks who sing the office has dwindled in recent years; Merton's remarks may serve as a welcome reminder of what has been lost.

The roots of the Divine Office lie in the tripartite daily prayer of classical Judaism, encountered in Chapter 2. According to tradition, each of the three prayer sessions can be traced to a founding patriarch: *shaḥarit* (morning prayer) to Abraham, who "got up early in the morning to the place where he stood before the Lord" (Genesis 19:27); *minḥah* (afternoon prayer) to Isaac, who went "to meditate in the field at the eventide" (Genesis 24:63); and *ma'ariv* (evening prayer) to Jacob. Together this triad fulfills the promise of Psalm 55:17: "evening and morning and at noon will I pray, and cry aloud, and he shall hear my voice"; it also parallels the sacrifices enacted morning, evening, and night in the Temple of Jerusalem until its destruction in 70 C.E.

Two great prayers dominate the daily prayer sequence. The Shema', recited during *shaḥarit* and *ma'ariv,* is the fundamental Jewish declaration of faith. Its first and most important passage reads as follows:

> Hear, O Israel: the Lord our God is one Lord: And thou shalt love the Lord thy God with all thine heart, and with all thine soul, and with all thine might. And these words, which I command thee this day, shall be in thine heart: and thou shalt teach them diligently unto thy children, and shall talk of them when thou sittest in thine house, and when thou walkest by the way, and when thou liest down, and when thou risest up. And thou shalt bind them for a sign upon thy hand, and they shall be as frontlets between thine eyes. And thou shalt write them upon the posts of thy house, and on thy gates. (Deuteronomy 6:4–9)

It is difficult to imagine a purer expression of monotheism or of humankind's obligation to respond to God with unqualified love. This love must bear fruit in action. God's revealed truths must be kept within the heart, talked about day and night, carried in the hands and before the eyes, written on doors and gates, and passed on to future generations. Devout Jews recite the Shema' during afternoon and evening prayers and before retiring as a prophylactic against nighttime dangers; this bedtime prayer ensures also that the dreaming soul remembers, praises, and loves God.

The 'Amidah, the second major prayer in the daily cycle, blends praise, petition, and thanksgiving, in benedictions that range from praise for God's holiness to affirmation of his omnipotence to a request that he rebuild Jerusalem, location of the once and future Temple. The prayer begins with three steps backward and forward, sufficient to remove oneself from profane surroundings into the presence of God. According to Talmudic scholar Adin Steinsaltz, the worshiper "has . . . ascended from world to world, entering from one room to another until he reaches the innermost sanctum, standing now face-to-face with the Utmost Holiness itself. This is the moment for direct communion — to plead and give thanks, to praise and to make supplication. The *Amidah* is thus the meeting point at which man stands before his Divine Father, Creator, and Ruler."[6] Fittingly, one recites the 'Amidah in a whisper, and one never breaks off in midstream, for who would interrupt a conversation with God?

Similar prayers pervade all the great religions. The threefold structure of Jewish daily devotions and the Angelus reemerges, for example, in the three daily *sandhyas* (devotions) of Hinduism, celebrated by James Joyce in the final chapter of *Finnegans Wake:*

> Sandhyas! Sandhyas! Sandhyas!
> Calling all downs. Calling all downs to dayne. Array! Surrection!
> Eireweeker to the wohld bludyn world.[7]

Closely matching patterns can be found also in the meditations at Buddhist monasteries, the devotions of Sikhs and Jains, and so on across the religious spectrum. Unquestionably, however, cyclical devotion achieves its apotheosis, at least in terms of number of participants, in the *ṣalāt,* the five daily prayer sessions of Islam — taking place at dawn, noon, afternoon, dusk, and night. At these set times, one billion people around the globe unroll their prayer rugs and prostrate themselves before Allāh the Compassionate, the Merciful.

The Ṣalāt

The most impressive — and baffling — aspect of *ṣalāt,* to a non-Muslim observer, is the intricacy of its motions and postures. The sequence begins with ritual ablutions, the laving of face, mouth, hands, and feet to produce a state of *ṭahāra* (ritual purity). This is followed by recitation of the *shahāda* (witness), which states, "There is no God but God and Muḥammad is his Prophet," elaborated through a harmonious interplay of bowing, kneeling, sitting, prostration, and vocal prayers. According to Islamic scholar Annemarie Schimmel, these postures symbolize for some Muslims the hierarchy of creation — standing erect represents human life; kneeling, animal life; prostration, vegetable life. Thus, during *ṣalāt* the complete cosmos worships God. Others discern in the three basic postures a secret alphabet, the erect body mimicking the Arabic *alif,* the bow a *dal,* and the prone position a *mim,* letters that in unison spell the name of Adam, the primordial man. Michael Wolfe, an American convert to Islam, encountered this mystical-somatic alphabet in Marrakesh while preparing to go on pilgrimage to Mecca:

> All at once I was being informed that the words I had learned by rote *were contained in a larger word spelled out with the body,* a word I could read and make sense of: the collective name of Man.

> The implications were astounding to me. If flesh could be formed into writing, did that not make the world a book? And if so, what sort of book was it? Were we sentences in it, as we sat here? And who would read it? Who *could* read it? Who was turning the pages?[8]

To perceive oneself as part of a book authored by God — to learn that one is written, not writer; passive, not active, in relation to the Creator — leads ineluctably to the principal purpose of the various postures: they serve as gestures of submission (*Islām* means "surrender") in this religion of submission to the One True God ("Prostrate thyself and draw nigh [to God]," declares Sūra 96:19 of the Qur'ān). The vocabulary of the body expresses the believer's decision to submit and, through repetition, may induce deeper states of surrender. One cannot draw near to God without emptying oneself; when one is nothing, God is all. The Islamic mystic Kharraz (d. 890) describes the appropriate state:

> When entering on prayer you should come into the Presence of God as you would on the Day of Resurrection. . . . When a man bows in prayer, then it is fitting that he should afterwards raise himself, then bow again to make intercession, until every joint of his body is directed towards the throne of God, and this means that he glorifies God Most High until there is nothing in his heart greater than God Most Glorious and he thinks so little of himself that he feels himself to be less than a mote of dust.[9]

With perseverance, a marvelous transformation may ensue. According to the twentieth-century Algerian Sufi Shaykh Aḥmad al-ʿAlawī, the essential effect of the *ṣalāt* is *ontological shrinkage.* The believer, through regular daily prayer, begins to decrease "like the folding of a written scroll, all on account of nearness to the Truth," until he "descendeth from the stature of existence unto the fold of nothingness. . . . effaced in himself and Eternal in the Lord." The result is a devotional state so perfect that God entirely envelops the believer, who attains *fanā'* (annihilation) in the Beloved: "My slave ceaseth not to draw nigh unto Me with devotions of his free will until I love him; and when I love him, I am the Hearing wherewith he heareth, and the Sight wherewith he seeth, and the Hand wherewith he smiteth, and the Foot whereon he walketh."[10]

The effect of *ṣalāt* can be remarkable indeed. Al-Ḥārith ibn Asad al-Muḥāsibī, a ninth-century contemporary of Kharraz, reports that

> what predominates in the heart of the mystic while he is at prayer is his sense of the mystery of Him in Whose Presence he stands and the might of Him Whom he seeks and the love of Him Who favors him with familiar intercourse with Himself, and he is conscious of that until he has fin-

Muslim women, recently returned from pilgrimage to Mecca, praying together in Cirebon, Java, Indonesia.

ished praying, and he departs with a face so changed that his friends would not recognize him, because of the awe that he feels at the Majesty of God.[11]

This passage calls to mind the shining countenance of Moses when he descended from Mount Sinai (Exodus 34:29). But of course such tales are ancient. We inhabit a different age, rife with skepticism, more immune to the transformative power of prayer. What effect, we may fairly wonder, results from a daily cycle of devotional prayer, such as the practice of the Angelus, the Divine Office, Jewish daily prayer, or the *ṣalāt*? Testimony today is sparse and tepid, compared to that of former epochs, but witnesses still report the deep influence of these prayers. For Kabir Helminski, an American shaykh in the Mevlevi order of Sufis, the *ṣalāt* infuses a sense of wholeness through surrender to the Infinite:

> I prostrate myself, head to the ground, and am grateful for this simple posture, which has guided me to a bodily experience of surrender — as the finite before the Infinite, as the conditioned before the Unconditioned, as the natural before the Supernatural, existence annihilated in Eternity. . . . The flow of the day is punctuated by these intense, wholehearted exercises of devotion and remembrance. The prayer occupies a very short but concentrated period of time, and I find myself longing for these moments in which I find wholeness in surrender.[12]

Thomas Merton took to reciting the Divine Office while traveling between New York City and the Catskills during the years immediately preceding his conversion to Catholicism. Here he recalls the revitalizing effect of this project:

> This business of saying the Office on the Erie train, going up through the Delaware valley, was to become a familiar experience in the year that was ahead. . . . God began to fill my soul with grace in those days, grace that sprung from deep within me, I could not know how or where. But yet I would be able, after not so many months, to realize what was there, in the peace and the strength that was growing in me through my constant immersion in this tremendous, unending cycle of prayer, ever renewing its vitality, its inexhaustible, sweet energies, from hour to hour, from season to season in its returning round. And I, drawn into that atmosphere, into that deep, vast universal movement of vitalizing prayer, which is Christ praying in men to his Father, could not help but begin at last to live, and to know that I was alive.[13]

For Merton and Helminski, daily devotions proved to be a royal road to God. But they were ardent believers. What of the reluctant, the doubting, the fair-weather friends of prayer? What of those for whom even a hint of daily devotion provokes both fascination and dismay? To throw some light on these questions, let us turn to the curious case of Salvador Dali (1904–1989) and the Angelus.

The Surreal Surrender of Salvador Dali

Dali's obsession with the Angelus — more exactly, with Millet's painting *Angelus* — began in 1932, when he was still in his twenties, a rising young star in the surrealist firmament. One June day a vision of the painting burst upon him, and the *Angelus* became for him, "'all of a sudden' the pictorial work that is the most disturbing, the most enigmatic, the most dense and the richest in unconscious thoughts ever to have existed." For Dali, who drew artistic inspiration from what he called his paranoiac-critical method, which involved simulating paranoid states and letting the unconscious overwhelm the conscious to reveal hidden truths, this was high praise indeed. It entailed far more than an aesthetic response; Dali acknowledged that during his childhood Millet's painting had "strangely moved" him, but after encountering Freud and the surrealists, it had come to exemplify "the most discredited and ineffective hierarchies of spiritual activity." He fiercely rejected the image and all it stood for, yet apparently it haunted his subconscious until the 1932 eruption.[14]

From this time on, Dali and the *Angelus* became inseparable. He amassed a vast collection of objects — tea cozies, inkwells, plates — that depicted the work; and he began to paint his own variations on the theme. In most of these canvases, the peasants, farm implements, and landscape of the original shrivel, shatter, or melt into grotesque, decaying forms. In *Les Chants de Maldoror* (1933–34), two hideous figures, one impossibly tall and the other composed of bones and protoplasm, bend their heads in prayer before a setting sun. *Atavism of Twilight* (1933–34) depicts the two peasants in a rocky landscape; the male is a skeleton with a wheelbarrow growing out of his head. Dali painted and repainted the *Angelus* throughout his life. Thirty years after his first efforts, he produced *The Railway Station at Perpignan* (1965), in which the peasants appear multiple times, praying or copulating within a fantastic landscape of clouds and railroad cars, dominated by the central figure of Dali himself, arms and legs comically akimbo like a misfired crucifixion.

The extreme agitation that the *Angelus* provoked in Dali once again erupted in "The Tragic Myth of Millet's *L'Angelus*," a text that he wrote in the 1930s, misplaced for decades, then rediscovered and published in 1963. Here Dali fantasizes apparitions of the *Angelus* in a collection of beach pebbles, among the rocks of northeast Catalonia, and in the hall of insects at the Museum of Natural History in New York City. He imagines plunging the painting into a bucket of lukewarm milk. He discourses on the "symbolic eroticism" of the woman's posture, which reminds him of a female praying mantis preparing to devour its mate. The hat held by the man "betrays [his] state of sexual excitation," while the wheelbarrow represents erection.[15]

Dali's ferocious and sustained reaction to the *Angelus* underscores both his obsessive personality and the painting's profundity. We can laugh at his arch-Freudian interpretations and squirm at his embarrassing iconography. Nonetheless, the disruptive effect, sustained at high pitch for over four decades, of the painting on his psyche cannot be so easily dismissed. Only one explanation seems plausible: that Dali harbored two intense and contradictory impulses — on the one hand, he longed for the piety and peace represented by Millet's *Angelus;* on the other, he reveled in the frenetic, experimental, antireligious world of surrealism, home of his artistic triumphs — and he expressed this conflict in a thirty-year series of canvases that at once celebrate and mock Millet's painting. The religious instinct triumphed, albeit imperfectly, for in his later years Dali became an ardent though wildly eccentric Catholic, painting numerous religious canvases with traditional themes but also achieving notoriety for lavish parties, flamboyant stunts (such as manipulating an octopus to ink a lithograph for a limited edition of *Don Quixote*), and a general air of decadence.

Did Dali pray the Angelus? No evidence suggests that he did, although immersion in Catholic devotions would certainly fit his colorful personality. When he announced his embrace of Catholicism in a private publication, *Mystical Manifesto* (1951), he praised, in typically tortuous prose, a daily practice that might be akin to prayer: "The mystic artist must form for himself, aesthetically, through the fierce daily self-inquisition of a 'mystic reverie' that is the most rigorous, architectonic, Pythagorean and exhausting of them all, a dermo-skeletal soul — bones on the outside, superfine flesh within — like that which Unamuno attributes to Castille, in which the flesh of the soul cannot help but rise up to the sky."[16]

The final direction of Dali's soul has been the subject of much speculation, judging by the number of biographies and critical studies that have alternately lauded and damned both him and his art. Such mysteries are best left to God; in any event, Dali's fixation on Millet's *Angelus* may be most fruitfully viewed as a parable of the inability of the modern mind, even when enmeshed in antireligious doctrines such as those of Freud or Marx, to rid itself of prayer. The call of infinity sounds in infinite ways; rare is the person who evades them all.

Practitioners of daily devotions, as we have seen, avidly heed this call. They share one aim: to spend some portion of every day in communion with God and thus to transform their lives. Some people, however, raise the bar. They desire a harder path, a more unbroken intercourse with God. They seek the way of never-ending prayer, to which we now turn.

The Jesus Prayer

At the heart of J. D. Salinger's 1961 novel *Franny and Zooey* lies the discovery by Franny Glass, a precocious, mimosa-sensitive college student, of an obscure nineteenth-century Russian text known as *The Way of a Pilgrim,* which describes a method of prayer based on continuous repetition of the name of Jesus. The Jesus Prayer, Franny assures her supercilious boyfriend, will allow anyone "to see God." Moreover, she adds, almost the same technique can be found in Buddhism and Hinduism. Her enthusiasm knows no bounds. "I mean the point is, did you ever hear anything so fascinating in your *life,* in a way."[17]

Franny's experiments with this prayer bring mixed results, but her keenness infected the reading public. *Franny and Zooey* became an international bestseller and so too, riding on its coattails, did *The Way of a Pilgrim,* a book nearly unknown outside monastic circles before Salinger lit upon it. Nor has this enthusiasm dampened. *Franny and Zooey* has remained in print for over forty years; *The Way of a Pilgrim,* currently available in five English translations, may be the most widely circulated prayer manual in the Western world; and the Jesus Prayer has become, after the Lord's Prayer and the Hail Mary, perhaps the most popular Christian prayer.

The appeal of *The Way of a Pilgrim* can be easily explained, for it is a manual with a twist. It offers, in lieu of dry textbook exposition, a stirring tale of adventures and marvels, purportedly the authentic memoirs of a homeless peasant in search of the secret of constant prayer. One late autumn in the mid–nineteenth century, on the twenty-fourth Sunday after Pentecost, the charismatic protagonist wanders into church in time to hear the lector read Saint Paul's famous directive to the small Christian community in Thessalonica: "Pray without ceasing." The phrase sets the pilgrim's heart aflame. But how to accomplish such a seemingly impossible task? "I thought and thought, but knew not what to make of it." The pilgrim sets out on foot, carrying only a Bible and some dry husks of bread, in search of wise men who might offer him advice. Eventually he encounters a starets (spiritual elder) who discloses that constant prayer is nothing other than "a constant uninterrupted calling upon the divine name of Jesus with the lips, in the spirit, in the heart, while forming a mental picture of His constant presence, and imploring His grace, during every occupation, at all times, in all places, even during sleep."[18]

The method, the starets explains, could not be simpler: one merely repeats the words "Lord Jesus Christ, have mercy on me." Under the starets's guidance, the pilgrim moves into a little thatched hut and begins to pray with gusto. At first he repeats the formula three thousand times per day, marking each recitation on a rosary. When this becomes "easy and likable," he increases his pace to twelve thousand repetitions per day. No wonder his jaw grows stiff, his tongue numb, and the thumb of his left hand, with which he counts his beads, begins to throb. He persists nonetheless, saying the prayer ceaselessly day after day, at first in his hut and then on foot, as he makes his way east toward Jerusalem. The effects of this discipline surpass all expectations:

> Sometimes my heart would feel as though it were bubbling with joy; such lightness, freedom, and consolation were in it. Sometimes I felt a burning love for Jesus Christ and for all God's creatures. Sometimes my eyes brimmed over with tears of thankfulness to God, who was so merciful to me, a wretched sinner. Sometimes my understanding, which had been so stupid before, was given so much light that I could easily grasp and dwell upon matters of which up to now I had not been able even to think at all. Sometimes that sense of a warm gladness in my heart spread throughout my whole being and I was deeply moved as the fact of the presence of God everywhere was brought home to me.[19]

In time the prayer takes on a life of its own, repeating without conscious volition, even during sleep. "It never stopped even for a single moment," the pilgrim reports. "My soul was always giving thanks to God and my heart melted away with unceasing happiness." Subsequent adventures, including an attack by wolves, a tumble into a frozen lake, floggings, and exile, fail to impinge upon the pilgrim's devotions. The prayer works its miracles, and in time the pilgrim becomes a revered healer and spiritual guide.[20]

The Way of a Pilgrim entrances with its landscapes of barren tundra and onion-domed churches, its spiritual epiphanies, and its delightful protagonist, who elicits our sympathy with his sincerity and our admiration with his steadfast pluck. Franny Glass does not stand alone in being inspired by the tale; millions have taken up the Jesus Prayer in emulation of the pilgrim. What this handicapped and impoverished Russian peasant could accomplish, we, with our freedom and wealth, should also be able to achieve. Alas, the promise of the pilgrim has proved, at least on one level, specious. Historians have long puzzled over how to reconcile the author's polished style with his reported poverty, which would seem to preclude a literary education. In recent years, consensus has been reached that the book is likely a pious fabrication. If so, however, it is fiction born of truth and this in two senses: it conveys spiritual verities with admirable insight; and the origins of the tale may lie in a firsthand narrative written in 1859 by Orthodox priest Mikhail Koslov (1826–1884), to which the prayer experiences of generations of monks have accreted, like layers of nacre on a bit of sand, resulting in the opalescent pearl we have today. In any event, it seems clear that *The Way of a Pilgrim* represents the collective wisdom of the Russian Orthodox Church and the culmination of a long process of evolution worth examining in detail.

The roots of the Jesus Prayer lie in the traditional belief that names contain power (an idea discussed in Chapter 2) and that repetition of a name concentrates and focuses this power. The authority of the divine name of Jesus informs the entire New Testament. The blind beggar Bartimaeus, who hears Jesus preaching on the road to Jericho, shouts, "Jesus, thou son of David, have mercy on me" (Mark 10:47; a partial source of the Jesus Prayer) and finds his sight restored. Elsewhere, Jesus himself declares, "Verily, verily, I say unto you, Whatsoever ye shall ask the Father in my name, he will give it you" (John 16:23). As Paul explains in his second letter to the Philippians, this name wields power in every sphere: "God also hath highly exalted him, and given him a name which is above every name: That at the name of Jesus every knee should bow, of things in heaven, and things on earth, and things under the earth" (Philippians 2:9–10).

Early Christian texts continue this refrain; the second-century *Shepherd* by the freed slave Hermas declares that "no one will enter the kingdom of God unless he receives the name of his Son."[21] Soon after, in the deserts of Egypt and Syria, preliminary forms of the Jesus Prayer began to proliferate. John Cassian (360–435), transmitting the teachings of the Desert Fathers to monks in southern France, writes of a "Blessed Isaac" who recommends the brief exclamation "God come to my assistance; Lord, make haste to help me" (Psalm 69:2), an invocation that later made its way into the Divine Office. Blessed Isaac explains, in words strikingly reminiscent of those of the Russian starets one thousand five hundred years later, that

> the thought of this verse should be turning unceasingly in your heart. Never cease to recite it in whatever task or service or journey you find yourself. Think upon it as you sleep, as you eat, as you submit to the most basic demands of nature. . . . You will write it upon the threshold and gateway of your mouth, you will place it on the walls of your house and in the inner sanctum of your heart. It will be a continuous prayer, an endless refrain when you bow down in prostration and when you rise up to do all the necessary things of life.[22]

The first specific reference to the Jesus Prayer appears in the *Centuries* of Pseudo-Hesychius, a text difficult to date but perhaps from the eighth century: "Truly blessed is he who ceaselessly pronounces in his heart Jesus' name and who in the depths of his thought is tied to the Jesus Prayer as the body is tied to the air around it and as wax is tied to a flame."[23] Those who became wax to the prayer's flame called themselves hesychasts (seekers after *hesychia*, Greek for "quietness"). None was more prominent than Saint Symeon the New Theologian (949–1022), who as a youth prayed a variation of the Jesus Prayer and received in return a mystical revelation, recounted here by his disciple Nicetas Stethato:

> At that time he was filled during prayer with great joy and suffused with burning tears. Not yet initiated into such revelations, in his amazement he cried aloud continually "Lord, have mercy" . . . and so it was that, toward the heights of heaven, there appeared to him a kind of highly luminous cloud, without form or shape, full of the ineffable glory of God. . . . Finally, much later, when this light gradually withdrew, he found himself again in his body and inside his cell, and he felt his heart filled with an indescribable joy, while his mouth cried aloud, as has been said, "Lord, have mercy," and his whole person was suffused with tears sweeter than honey.[24]

Later church leaders, inspired by Saint Symeon's extensive writings on the Jesus Prayer, would incorporate the formula, now in its conventional form — "Lord Jesus Christ, Son of God, have mercy on me, a sinner" — into the everyday life of the monastic church. There it remained until the late eighteenth century, when through the publication of a large collection of hesychast texts known as the *Philokalia* (Greek for "love of the beautiful"), the Jesus Prayer escaped the cloisters and became widely diffused among Christian laity, finally falling into the hands of the pilgrim and Franny Glass.

The immense popularity of this prayer resides, above all, in the potency of the divine name repeatedly invoked; but other reasons contribute to its success. Practitioners customarily recite the Jesus Prayer alone and in silence. These conditions set it apart from other repetitive devotions such as the *ṣalāt* or the *opus Dei,* which are often said in groups; the Jesus Prayer is available to any person under any circumstances. In addition, some people adopt special physical postures while reciting the prayer, thus engaging both body and mind in prayer. Some execute a bow from the waist to conclude each repetition; others favor a more athletic approach, a complete prostration, head and toes to floor; yet others say the prayer with head between knees, in imitation of Elijah on Mount Carmel ("Elijah went up to the top of Carmel; and he cast himself down upon the earth and put his face between his knees," 1 Kings 18:42). Whatever the posture, the use of a prayer rope — a cord with one hundred evenly spaced knots — is nearly de rigueur, to keep count and to stabilize the mind.

Rhythm, too, plays an important part in the Jesus Prayer, as it does in the Angelus and the *ṣalāt.* The prayer shuttles between sound and silence, movement and stillness; many devotees enhance these patterns by breathing in harmony with the words, drawing in breath while saying, "Lord Jesus Christ, Son of God," and releasing it while saying, "have mercy on me, a sinner." In effect, they inhale divinity and exhale sin. The person who prays in this manner inhabits two worlds in rapid alternation: a divine world of stillness and silence, and a human world of sound and movement. In time, it is said, one may learn to inhabit these worlds simultaneously. Repeated recitation also produces psychosomatic effects. Islamicist Constance Padwick suggests that the prayers of the Sufi *dhikr* (remembrance) appeal to laborers because "hypnotized by rhythm of sound and action, they may escape from the immediate pressure of hard lives."[25] Comparable trance states may play a role, unrecognized or at least unacknowledged, in prolonged recitation of the Jesus Prayer.

This prayer, its practitioners believe, initiates an economy of grace: one offers oneself to God, and God responds with an outpouring of grace upon the soul. Actually, the process describes a circle, for grace initiates the sequence, inducing the giving of oneself to God, as Saint John Climacus describes it: "When the fire descends into the heart, it revives prayer. And when prayer has arisen and ascended to heaven, then the descent of the fire takes place in the cenacle of the soul."[26] To what extent, one might wonder, is this reciprocal sequence a free exchange, and to what extent is it a magical operation with a foregone conclusion? Those who recite the Jesus Prayer seem so enamored of its power that at times they seem to treat it as infallible: thus an early Christian theologian declares with finality that "the remembrance of the Name of God utterly destroys all that is evil," and the pilgrim himself seems to treat the prayer as a magical talisman, using it to assuage hunger, cold, and injuries inflicted by others. Yet the New Testament also suggests, with a touch of mordant humor, that the name of Jesus, at least in the wrong mouth, may sometimes fail to work: "Some of the Jewish exorcists who traveled around the country tried to invoke the name of the Lord Jesus on those who were possessed, saying, 'I adjure you by Jesus who Paul preaches . . .' The evil spirit answered, 'Jesus I know and Paul I know, but who are you?'" (Acts 19:13–16 RSV).

One might conclude that calling upon the name of Jesus, like so many other prayer acts, marries magical thinking to a sense of God's grace in a manner theologically suspect but dramatically satisfying; the devout recite the Jesus Prayer with an unshakable conviction of its efficacy because they also hold an unshakable conviction of God's goodness and strength. God could fail to respond, for God is God and can do as he wills; but God will not fail to respond because God is God and loves his creatures.

The magical aura surrounding the Jesus Prayer is manifest also in its startling physical effects. Many have testified that the Jesus Prayer generates in its devotees substantial warmth and light. The warmth, which may be intense, is considered a natural by-product of the prayer. Novices are warned to proceed with caution, for the heat may inflame passions, lead to spiritual pride ("I have attained warmth! My prayer is progressing nicely!"), or even trigger heart failure; some startsy recommend a splash of cold water to douse the inner inferno (and, perhaps not incidentally, to dampen the libido). The production of light, by contrast, is read as a sign of grace. According to the *Philokalia,* the ultimate aim of human life is deification, transformation into the perfect image and likeness of God. One outward sign of this inward glory has always been a dazzling light that surrounds the deified, a supernatural effulgence epitomized in the biblical account of the Transfiguration of Christ upon Mount Tabor: "And after six days Jesus taketh with him Peter, and James, and John, and leadeth them up into a high mountain apart by themselves, and he was transfigured before them. And his raiment became shining, exceedingly white as snow; so as no fuller on earth can white them" (Mark 9:2–3).

This radiance, unlike the warmth also generated by prayer, does not belong to the natural order; it is uncreated, eternal, a shining forth of supernatural holiness. It appears in the haloes encircling the heads of saints, in the colored beams emanating from Jesus' Sacred Heart in certain devotional images, in the preternatural light witnessed at the tombs of holy men and women, and, it is said, in the luminescence that may surround those most proficient in the Jesus Prayer. Given the reportedly transcendent source of this mysterious light, it is perhaps understandable that theologians have encountered difficulty in pinning down its constitution and properties. Saint John Climacus, as early as the seventh century, proposed that the remembrance of Jesus leads to the perception of what he called the "sun of the intelligence," which in turn illuminates with a blinding light the one who prays. Seven centuries later, Saint Gregory of Palamas (c. 1296–1359) improved on this rather unsatisfactory explanation while battling skeptics who derided practitioners of the Jesus Prayer as *omphalopsychoi* (men with their souls in their navels). The uncreated light, Saint Gregory proposed, is the sensory manifestation of God's "divine energies," the aspect of God that can be perceived by human beings, in contradistinction to God's "divine essence," which remains forever unfathomable. When these divine energies shine within or through a person so brightly as to illuminate his or her surroundings, they become a powerful sign of holiness perfected, the ultimate aim of the Jesus Prayer and perhaps of all religious activity.

Litanies and Aspirations

The Jesus Prayer belongs, in provenance if no longer in practice, to the Eastern Orthodox Church. Western Christianity, most notably the Roman Catholic Church, has meanwhile developed its own forms of repetitive devotion based on the divine name. In the fifteenth century, the Franciscan saints John Capistran and Bernardine of Siena traversed Italy, healing the sick and using as medicine a large wooden board, engraved with the monogram of Christ (*IHS*, an abbreviation of the Greek *Iesous*), before which the faithful would prostrate themselves and pray. This device has obvious affinities to a talisman or amulet and demonstrates, despite (or alongside) the orthodox explanation that cures depend entirely upon God's grace, the ever-present fingerprint of magical thinking. To Capistran and Bernardine can also be credited, at least according to tradition, authorship of the immensely popular Litany of the Most Holy Name of Jesus. This prayer, a string of repetitive petitions or invocations, calls upon the divine name under various aspects ("Jesus, most obedient"; "Jesus, author of life"), for various causes ("from everlasting death, Jesus, deliver us"), and through various powers ("through thy joys, Jesus, deliver us").

A century or so later, Richard Whytford, an English monk, composed the complex Jesus Psalter as a means of solace and supernatural protection during the bloody anti-Catholic persecutions of Henry VIII. This psalter includes lengthy petitionary passages along with monotonous repetitions of the name of Jesus which call to mind Padwick's charge of prayer as autohypnosis. The whole brims with devotion but reveals little artistry, only a piling on of traditional motifs and phrases, and it proved a dead end in the evolution of prayers based on the divine name. Almost no one recites the Jesus Psalter today. The true strength of this form of prayer lies in brevity and intensity; at its best (or most helpful) it is handy and portable, instantly available to meet any occasion.

One form of prayer perfectly fits this description: aspirations, or ejaculations, that call upon the name of Jesus in the context of a specific request ("Jesus, be with me now" is a typical example). Aspirations may be described as the most successful Western counterpart to the Jesus Prayer; Saint Ignatius of Loyola ranked them as the best form of prayer, and for Saint Francis de Sales they were "the keystone of devotion and can supply the defects of all your other prayers."[27] Among masters of aspiratory art, the Irish Jesuit William Doyle (1873–1917) dominates the field. Photographs show a clean-shaven man with sad, hooded eyes, a face that seems to gaze beyond the camera into eternity. Perhaps Doyle sensed his early death, for he would fall at the age of forty-four during the dreadful Third Battle of Ypres, one of the bloodiest conflicts of World War I. Today he is most often remembered as an indefatigable army chaplain (several books and websites testify to his heroism during combat), but more impressive may be his Olympian efforts at composing and reciting aspirations. Favorite phrases — most bearing a resemblance, near or far, to the Jesus Prayer — include "Jesus, Thou Saint of saints, make me a saint" and "Blessed be God for all things." For Doyle, these compact prayers inspired self-sacrifice, love of others, and union with Christ. They became a source of power, as he records in his diary for September 1915: "This morning I lay awake powerless to overcome myself and to make my promised visit to the chapel. Then I felt prompted to pray; I said five aspirations and rose without difficulty. How many victories I could win by this easy and powerful weapon!"[28]

Like the Russian pilgrim, his spiritual predecessor, Doyle began slowly, mouthing a few thousand aspirations a day in the early months of 1909. By September 1911 the number had reached ten thousand; by July 1913, he was writing in his diary that he "resolved to bear small pains and make 20,000 aspirations." October saw the number accelerate to sixty thousand per day. By 1916, while he was slogging through the trenches as a member of the Royal Dublin Fusiliers, the figure had climbed considerably higher: "Again a clear interior light that God wants me to aim at the 100,000 aspirations daily. I feel a longing to take up this life of unceasing prayer and at the same time a dread and a loathing of this burden, for I must watch every spare moment of the day to perform my penance. I feel Jesus asks this in reparation for His priests. With the help of the Blessed Lady I have this day begun the big fight." The fight went well. Making a compact with God, he aimed yet higher: "I have made a bargain with our Lord to give me a soul for every 1,000 aspirations over the daily 100,000."[29]

The ever-accelerating process reached its crescendo just before Doyle's death, when this athlete of prayer achieved the staggering figure of 120,000 aspirations per day. The number gives pause. A day contains 86,400 seconds, so how can one perform 120,000 aspirations per diem? Doyle's biographers have done their best to resolve the problem, proposing that he may have considered some of his choice phrases to contain five or ten aspirations at once, or that some aspirations were silent, almost instantaneous recollections of God. One also wonders whether Doyle's ambitions reveal holiness or neurosis, an ecstasy of obsessive-compulsive impulses. Extreme behavior in the service of prayer has always had its place; consider Saint Simeon Stylites's sixty years atop a desert pillar, a feat as bizarre as it is breathtaking and one certainly provoked in part by mental disturbance (long before Simeon ascended his first pillar, his fellow monks judged him incapable of communal life and drove him into exile). Nonetheless, Simeon's asceticism purified him, and he became a revered spiritual teacher to the many disciples assembled at the foot of his outpost. Similarly, Doyle's contemporaries, especially his fellow soldiers, testify to his sweetness, kindness, and charity on behalf of others while performing his 120,000 aspirations a day amid a rain of bombs. Exceptional measures, especially in the life of prayer, may prove to be the path to wisdom.

The Dhikr

Devotional prayers thrive in every religious soil. Franny Glass, enthusing to her boyfriend, Lane, about the Jesus Prayer and its ability to confer "a really tremendous mystical effect . . . an absolutely new conception of what everything's about," says that in "the Nembutsu sects of Buddhism, people keep saying 'Namu Amida Butsu' over and over again — which means 'Praise to the Buddha' or something like that — and the *same thing* happens." So too in medieval Europe: "the same thing happens in 'The Cloud of Unknowing,' too. Just with the word 'God.' I mean you just keep saying the word 'God.'" And again, "In India, they tell you to meditate on the 'Om,' which means the same thing, really, and the exact same result is supposed to happen." Dazzled by this cornucopia, Franny puffs on her cigarette and declares that she keeps "running into that kind of advice — I mean all these really advanced and absolutely unbogus religious persons that keep telling you if you repeat the name of God incessantly, something *happens*."[30] Franny goes overboard in her homogenizing of disparate traditions — few contemporary scholars of religion would agree that reciting the name of Jesus and Buddha are synonymous acts — but her sense that all repetitive prayers involving divine names are, if not identical twins, at least close relations, bears investigation. Let us open our inquiry by turning to an important variety that Franny omitted from her list: the *dhikr* of Islam.

An Arabic term, *dhikr* means "to recollect" or "to remember"; the Islamic *dhikr,* worship based on repetitive recitation of God's name, derives its authority from Qur'ānic passages such as "remembrance of Allāh is the greatest [thing in life]" (Sūra 29:45) and "O you who believe! Recollect God often" (Sūra 33:40, 41). These injunctions and declarations establish a cosmic exchange: we offer prayers, and God offers life itself.

To remember God is to remember his divine name, radiant with his presence. Every chapter, or sūra, of the Qur'ān except the ninth opens with the *basmalah: "bismi–Llāhi–r-Raḥmāni–r-Raḥīm"* (In the Name of Allāh, the Compassionate, the Merciful). The *basmalah* permeates the Islamic world, plastered on walls and fences and printed at the beginning of every book. Constance Padwick reports a welter of proscriptions and prescriptions involving the *basmalah* sent by an Algerian correspondent, indicating the formula's presiding importance and power: "Never tread on a piece of paper, the Name of God may be written upon it"; "Always put your hand before your mouth when you yawn, lest the devil enter in. Should you forget to do this, repeat the *basmalah* and then spit three times."[31] The *basmalah*'s quasi-magical powers, as suggested by these admonitions, receive confirmation in the following tradition regarding Muḥammad:

> The Apostle of God was sitting with a man who was eating and did not name the Name of God Most High until he reached the last mouthful of his food. Then as he raised that to his mouth he said, "In the Name of God, the first of it and the last of it." And the Prophet laughed and said, "A *shaytān* [devil] had been eating with him all the while, and when he made mention of the name of God the food in that *shaytān*'s belly turned to poison."[32]

The divine name is itself the quintessential food. Annemarie Schimmel tells of a Sufi student who, after several days of starvation (presumably as an ascetic discipline), pitifully asks: "O master, what is the food?" The master responds, "The recollection of God the Immortal."[33] Most traditional catalogues recognize ninety-nine divine names, beginning with *Ya Raḥmān ya Raḥīm,* (O Merciful, O Compassionate) and ending with *Ya Ṣabūr* (O Patient); this is why Islamic prayer ropes contain thirty-three or ninety-nine beads. In some systems, names correspond to cosmic attributes or qualities; for example, the Khalwatiyyah Sufi order associates divine names such as *Ya Ḥaqq* (O Truth), *Ya Ḥayy* (O Living), *Ya Qayyūm* (O Eternal), and *Ya Qahhār* (O Subduer) with colors, celestial spheres, and stages of spiritual illumination. Each name has its own proper sphere of action; employing a divine name under the wrong circumstances or for base motives invites disaster. On the other hand, even an inarticulate wail can be a divine name, according to Shaykh al-'Alawī, in an anecdote recalling the blind beggar crying out the name of Jesus: "The question of invocation is of wider scope than you imagine. A sick man lay groaning in the presence of the Prophet and one of the Companions told him to stop and to be patient, whereupon the Prophet said, 'Let him groan, for groaning is one of the Names of God in which the sick man can find relief.'"[34]

All this bears close resemblance to ideas and practices connected with other repetitive prayers, especially the Jesus Prayer. Both the *dhikr* and the Jesus Prayer entail continuous recitation of the divine name; both may be facilitated by use of a prayer rope; both may generate heat, light, or visions (Khalwatiyyah Sufis use such signs to measure spiritual progress in the *dhikr*). Both involve special postures. During *dhikr,* the devotee may sit cross-legged or stand, swaying back and forth, perhaps bowing at regular intervals or directing attention to various limbs in succession until the entire body becomes itself a prayer. He may, in striking parallel to recitation of the Jesus Prayer, inhale while reciting the first part of the divine name and exhale while reciting the second. The Shādhilī *dhikr* begins with the full name of Allāh clearly enunciated and ends by speaking only the final syllable, *ha,* produced by the voiceless expulsion of air through contraction of the diaphragm. "Each of these exhalations," one commentator suggests, "symbolizes the last breath of man, the moment when the individual soul is reintegrated into the cosmic breath."[35]

But the *dhikr* differs from the Jesus Prayer in one crucial regard. The Jesus Prayer, as we have seen, is customarily a solitary activity, but the *dhikr* comes to full flower in group recitation, and in this respect it more closely resembles the Christian *opus Dei.* If, as the French Islamicist Jean-Louis Michon asserts, "the *dhikr* constitutes the very essence of religion" — for it awakens awareness of God — then Sufi orders or brotherhoods (like their Christian counterparts, Benedictine and other monastic orders) constitute the environment in which that essence can be best apprehended.

Sufism emerged near the end of the first millennium C.E., rapidly proliferating into several hundred different *ṭarīqas* (paths or schools), each with its own spiritual lineage, initiatory rituals, and prayer techniques. A typical weekly gathering of the *ṭarīqa* might begin with the *wird,* a recitation of Qur'ānic passages that reestablish the aims and goals of the religious life, followed by a sermon by the shaykh, and lastly, the chanting proper. All members of the *ṭarīqa* participate in these events, a shared experience that fosters an ethic of comradeship and cooperation. The unity of the *ṭarīqa* is so complete — at least in the ideal — that egos dissolve and individuals merge into one.

This union of beings, in which the individual Sufi evanesces into the brotherhood, portends ultimate absorption into God. The final goal of *dhikr* is the extinction *(fanā')* of which we spoke earlier in this chapter. Islamic mystics occasionally call this process deification, but the term carries a different meaning in Islam than it does in Christianity. The deification sought through the Jesus Prayer conforms the soul to the image and likeness of the Trinitarian God, in particular to a personal relationship with Jesus, whereas the deification sought in *dhikr* is better likened, in an image often encountered in Sufi literature, to the immersion of a drop of water in the limitless Ocean of God or the light of a candle held up to the Sun. One is swallowed up in God. This engulfment or extinction leads, some say, to *fanā'–al–fanā'* (the extinction-of-extinction), so that truly nothing is but the Absolute Oneness. Or it may lead to *baqā'* (infinite life) of a nature unknown to us now, within the very being of God. The central note remains the surrender of individual personality, a goal seemingly difficult to square with the Qur'ānic teachings on the resurrection of the dead, but one that, according to Islamicist R. A. Nicholson, "kindles in the Sufi an enthusiasm . . . deep and triumphant." Nicholson cites the following celebrated lyric by Jalāl al-Dīn Rūmī as epitomizing the longing for *fanā':*

> I died as mineral and became a plant,
> I died as plant and rose to animal,
> I died as animal and I was man.
> Why should I fear? When was I less by dying?
> Yet once more I shall die as man, to soar
> With angels blest; but even from angelhood
> I must pass on: all except God doth perish.
> When I have sacrificed my angel soul,
> I shall become what no mind e'er conceived,
> "Oh, let me not exist!" For Non-existence
> Proclaims in organ tones, "To Him we shall return."[36]

To acknowledge that diverse recitations of the divine name tend toward different goals is vitally important; by doing so, we enjoy the unique genius of each religious tradition, its inimitable interweaving of revelation, ritual, theology, mythology, art, science, and the like. It allows us to give each its due. Ignoring differences, by contrast, plunges us into one of the common fallacies that plague the study of prayer and of religion in general, the peculiarly modern assumption that all religions are ultimately alike or contain the same mystical doctrines. A popular metaphor describes truth as a great mountain, and each religion as a path wending toward the summit, where all paths meet. The evidence of most mystics, sages, and saints — those who have actually made the ascent — indicates otherwise: the mountain is shrouded in fog, some paths empty into precipices whereas others spiral aimlessly up and down, and the summit is crowned by a multitude of peaks. Each zenith offers a long, clear view, even to infinity, but each stands alone; the Christian experience of deifying conformity to the Trinitarian God of love is not the same as the Sufi experience of deifying annihilation.

The Secret of Unceasing Prayer

Christianity and Sufism offer different models of ultimate perfection, but they agree that the path to this highest goal may lie not only in repetitive devotional prayer, but also in intensifying this repetition into a state of unceasing prayer. To pray without surcease is prayer's Ultima Thule, seemingly unobtainable yet beckoning always with unimaginable spiritual rewards. Our first reaction, upon hearing of it, is likely to be (as it was for the Russian pilgrim) to ask how such a thing can possibly exist. How can we pray at all times, when we must sleep and eat and work and procreate and love and worship and engage in the countless other necessities and pastimes that enchain our lives? That angels pray without ceasing we can readily accept, for they are bloodless creatures, with little to do but sing God's praises, girdled round his throne day and night. It is different for us mortals, trapped in the web of life and death. Yet traditions from around the globe affirm that ceaseless prayer can indeed be achieved.

Our chief source of information on this subject has been the pilgrim, who testifies that after considerable practice, his recitation of the Jesus Prayer sustained itself without conscious volition, first verbally ("it was as though my lips and my tongue pronounced the words entirely of themselves without any urging from me") and then in his heart, delivering "a foretaste on earth of the bliss of heaven." Although the pilgrim's witness may be a pious fiction, his account finds corroboration not only in the writings of other hesychasts but also in non-Christian sources. For the Buddhist iconoclast Nichiren (1222–1282), whose followers wield wide political and social influence in modern Japan, repetition of the phrase *Namu Myōhōrengekyō* (Homage to the Wonderful Lotus Sūtra) ensures eternal bliss. Nichiren described himself as living the Lotus Sūtra "while walking, sitting, standing, and lying down," so that "even when I am not conscious of thinking of the sūtra, I am reading the sūtra. Even when I am not looking at the sūtra, I am living its words."[37] Sikhism, founded in northern India by Guru Nanak (1469–1539), teaches that

Nam, the name of God, is written on every human heart and that to recite it is happiness, salvation, and freedom from death. "By prayer I live, without it I die," counsels the Sikh scripture, the Ādi Granth. Even as children, Sikhs are taught to recite Nam by repeating the word Waheguru, a blend of *wah*, an exclamation of delight, and *guru*, meaning "Lord." As they mature, they enunciate Nam silently, within the mind, until it sustains itself without volition; eventually this activity fades from consciousness, and only an undifferentiated remembrance of God remains. Similarly, Muslim texts describe an ascension from the "*dhikr* of the tongue," marked by conscious vocal repetition, through the "*dhikr* of the heart," in which prayer has passed to the seat of life and become self-actuating, to the "*dhikr* of the inmost being," the heart within the heart where the devotee achieves *fanā'* so that only the ceaseless *dhikr* remains.

Methods such as these rely upon repetition of a set phrase until the prayer becomes self-actuating. There have been, however, other means to ceaseless prayer. One cannot help but admire that curious religious order known as the Acoemetae (Sleepless Ones), active in Byzantium from the fifth through twelfth centuries, who perfected the clever device of praying by relay — day and night teams of monks would take turns reciting the psalms without pause, each team picking up where the last left off (a modern variant can be found in La Crosse, Wisconsin, where the Franciscan Sisters of Perpetual Adoration have prayed in rotating shifts without pause from August 1, 1878, to the present day). Other ardent souls have simply tried to pray consciously at every waking moment, even at the cost of embarrassing inattention to the world, as in the case of Constantine, father of Saint Gregory of Salonica and tutor of a happily forgiving emperor:

> That amazing Constantine, who, although he was leading a court-life, was called the father and teacher of the emperor Andronicus, and daily was occupied with state affairs, besides his household duties, having a large fortune and a troop of slaves, as well as a wife and children, nevertheless was constantly with God and so attached to unceasing mental prayer that he often forgot that the emperor or the courtiers were talking to him about imperial affairs and frequently asked about one and the same thing twice or even more. This disturbed the other courtiers who, not knowing the cause of it, rebuked him for forgetting a matter so quickly and worrying the emperor by his repeated questions. But the emperor, knowing the cause of it, defended him and said: "Constantine has his own thoughts which sometimes prevent him from paying full attention to our affairs."[38]

In a yet more daring rupture with the mainstream of repetitive devotions, others have dispensed with words altogether. For the Syriac monastic writer Isaac of Nineveh (died c. 700), perpetual prayer is catalyzed by the presence of the Holy Spirit: "When the Spirit dwells in a person . . . prayer never from then on departs from his soul. Whether he is eating or drinking or sleeping or whatever else he is doing, even in deepest sleep, the fragrance of prayer rises without effort in his heart. Prayer never again deserts him."[39]

Theophan the Recluse (1815–1891), who assembled a Russian edition of the *Philokalia,* describes constant prayer as a matter of disposition. Christ's apostles, he writes, achieved prayer without end by living in unbroken devotion to God; for us, too, "constant repetition is not required. What is required is a constant aliveness to God — an aliveness present when you talk, read, watch, or examine something."[40] But how can one attain this state of supernatural quickening? The hesychasts provide numerous programs to this end, almost entirely directed toward cloistered monks, and one can find parallel suggestions in the writings of Sufis and members of other religious orders. Almost always, the proffered advice involves making great sacrifices of time, energy, friends, and family, anything that may obstruct the goal. It seems a path for saints, holy fools, and those with nothing to lose.

Exceptions do arise, however. A few courageous figures have ventured to introduce unceasing prayer into the lives of ordinary men and women, developing methods that require dedication and hard work, yet without exacting the extreme payment demanded by monasteries and brotherhoods. Perhaps the most appealing and readily accessible of these pioneers hails not from Russia or the Middle East but from the suburbs of Philadelphia, in the person of the remarkable Quaker mystic Thomas Kelly (1893–1941).

By all accounts, Kelly led a placid life. His childhood and youth read like vintage Americana: born on an Ohio farm to Quaker parents; raised, after his father's sudden death, by a resourceful mother who made ends meet by marketing butter and eggs; destined, while studying chemistry as an undergraduate at Wilmington College, for a quiet, unassuming middle-class life. His constricted Midwestern horizons widened dramatically when he transferred for a year to Haverford College, where he discovered the treasures of Western spirituality under the influence of the great Quaker scholar Rufus Jones. Jones, in turn, couldn't help but notice Kelly, recalling that one day his young pupil "sat down in front of me, his face lighted up with radiance, and . . . said suddenly, 'I am just going to make my life a miracle!'"[41] Kelly realized his ambition, albeit in the most hidden of ways. Outwardly, the rest of his life excelled only in its ordinariness, as he married, fathered two children, traveled as a missionary to England and Germany, and enjoyed a peripatetic academic career, teaching philosophy at Earlham, Wellesley, the University of Hawaii, and Haverford, with moderate success but no notable scholastic triumphs. He died of a heart attack on June 27, 1941, in his forty-seventh year.

Inwardly, however, Kelly was anything but sedate. A photograph shows a slender man with receding hairline, rimless glasses, and dark tie, perhaps an accountant or a banker; but the impression is belied by the wild, toothy grin and the gleam in the eye. This is a man with a happy secret, struggling to contain his mirth. If the origins of this joy can be located in Kelly's pious, healthy childhood, its apotheosis seems to have arrived soon after a bitter blow that struck in 1937, when he failed his oral examinations before Harvard University examiners for a second doctorate in philosophy (he already possessed one from Hartford Theological Seminary). This defeat devastated Kelly, who for years had longed for academic success. But then, in an event that remains mysterious but, given its proximity to his shattering humiliation, may have some relation to the *de profundis* experiences recounted in Chapter 4, Kelly underwent a mystical episode in which, as he later described it, he was "melted down by the Love of God." For three years afterward his pen flowed with ecstatic prose, collected after his death and published as *A Testament of Devotion.*

Kelly's magnum opus is a slender volume, 124 pages in its original edition, and thus a fitting companion to other terse spiritual classics such as *The Cloud of Unknowing,* the *Tao Te Ching,* and *The Conference of the Birds,* books slim enough to slip into a pocket and nearly brief enough to memorize. Like these works, *A Testament of Devotion* is dense with truth. It is a small, heavy fruitcake of a book, and like a fruitcake it cloys with its overripe prose, *amazing*s and *astounding*s studding the text at every turn. But this gee-whiz enthusiasm has the ring of authenticity, and we are ready to trust and try the results.

Kelly begins by asserting that "deep within us there is an amazing inner sanctuary of the soul, a holy place, a Divine Center, a speaking Voice, to which we may continuously return." His aim is to describe how we may attain that sanctuary, dwell in that center, hear that voice. The secret, of course, is ceaseless prayer. Like all devotions, Kelly's rely on repetition. "Continuously renewed immediacy . . . lies at the base of religious life." This immediacy consists in awareness of what Kelly terms the "Divine Light," the radiant presence of God. This light abides with us always; that we seek it proves that on some subliminal level we already sense its presence. To grow ever more fully aware of God, we must cultivate "secret habits of unceasing orientation" toward the Divine Light. These habits in turn will lead us to be "perpetually bowed in worship, while we are also very busy in the world of daily affairs." Ceaseless prayer, he insists, is not the exclusive domain of monks but belongs to everyone. He proceeds, in an unfortunate display of sectarian allegiance, to explain that Catholics have known these habits in the past but have allowed "the Law" to obscure them; Protestants have known them but have allowed rationalism to obscure them; Quakers, however, know them in abundance, and they know how to make use of them.[42]

Partisanship aside, Kelly has brought us where we want to be: on the brink of a new world, ready to receive the philosopher's stone of prayer, the great jewel that the pilgrim sought on the steppes of Russia and Nichiren on the slopes of Mount Minoru: the secret of unceasing devotion, presented by — who would have guessed? — a hyperbolic American with the open, pale white face of a dairy farmer. Happily, Thomas Kelly delivers the goods. The key to unending prayer, he tells us, is to construct our psychic life in such a way *that we inhabit more than one level of being at a time.* On one plane, we will be conducting our ordinary life, eating, working, going to the movies. Simultaneously, on a deeper plane, we will engage in continuous prayer, including "song and worship and a gentle receptiveness to divine breathings." "It is at this deep level," Kelly says, "that the real business of life is determined." Our particular responsibility is to bring all the ordinary concerns of life from the first level to the second, where these concerns can be bathed in the Divine Light. The result, he suggests in one of his stuttering but heartfelt rhetorical passages, can be revolutionary:

> Much apparent wheat becomes utter chaff, and some chaff becomes wheat. Imposing powers? They are out of the Life, and must crumble. Lost causes? If God be for them, who can be against them? Rationally plausible futures? They are weakened or certified in the dynamic Life and Light. Tragic suffering? Already He is there, and we actively move, in His tenderness, toward the sufferers. Hopeless debauchees? These are children of God. His concern and ours. Inexorable laws of nature? The dependable framework for divine reconstruction. The fall of a sparrow? The Father's love.[43]

One can discern, amidst the tangled prose, some startling promises: that if we live a two-tiered life and lay all before the Almighty, then lost causes will triumph, suffering will diminish, the laws of nature will proclaim the power of God, and love will rule all. Who would not desire these fulfillments with all his heart? To accomplish them, Kelly summons us to, in effect, a perpetual *metanoia.* The key to this conversion is a peculiar psychological practice, which we might describe as the division of attention. We must learn to participate in the outer world while, at the same instant, worshiping God within. Immediate action is required; Kelly urges us to attempt this division of attention even "now, as you read these words." In counsel obviously drawn from *The Cloud of Unknowing,* he proposes that whispered ejaculatory prayers, such as "Thine" or "So panteth my soul after Thee, O God," may help us turn toward the deeper level.[44]

At first, and perhaps for months or years to come, our ability to divide attention will be intermittent, awkward, and painful. Many will find their minds flying uncontrollably between God and the world. But eventually change will come. When we return to God, we will discover that we had not entirely left him; we will experience not "reinstatement of a broken prayer" but reinvigoration of a prayer that never ceased. "The currents of His love have been flowing, but whereas we had been drifting in Him, now we swim." During our months or years of struggle, we will be transformed by the Divine Light, "tutored, purged and disciplined, simplified and made pliant in His holy will." Finally, we will enjoy a steady inner awareness of God's presence. Kelly envisions a great crowd of men and women who have attained this level of ceaseless prayer, "housewives and hand workers, plumbers and teachers, learned and unlettered, black and white, poor and perchance even rich" who can lay claim to sanctity. These holy masses no longer retain command of their prayer, which "pours forth in volumes and originality such as we cannot create" in echo of the self-actuating prayer of the pilgrim and the Sufis. We no longer pray, but God prays within us. "In holy hush we bow in Eternity, and know the Divine Concern tenderly enwrapping us and all things within his persuading love."[45]

In his call to live simultaneously on two levels, Kelly issues a formidable challenge. To grasp its difficulty, try a simple experiment in the division of attention: spend a minute or two thinking of God without pause, while at the same time counting on your fingers from one to ten and back to one again. You will find that you cannot sustain this exercise for more than a few seconds; soon the thought of God flickers and then disappears entirely. As it happens, the division of attention has long been a part of religious practice — reciting the rosary, for example, entails simultaneously counting beads, saying prayers, and contemplating a holy mystery, such as the Nativity or the Resurrection — and almost everyone who prays the rosary will confirm the difficulty of keeping the mind clamped to the task and the corresponding ease with which it wanders into daydream, memory, or random associations.

Precedents exist, too, for using division of attention as a path to ceaseless prayer. In *A Testament of Devotion,* Kelly twice refers to a Brother Lawrence, better known to history as Brother Lawrence of the Resurrection, a seventeenth-century Carmelite monk whose "practice of the presence of God" provides a theoretical basis for much of what Kelly has written. Brother Lawrence was the quintessential monk, the sort depicted in a thousand tales and legends, a humble cook of unprepossessing appearance but with a heart that brimmed with wisdom. His approach to ceaseless prayer consisted of abandoning all devotions not strictly required by the monastic regimen and instead relentlessly directing his attention, while performing daily chores, to God's vivifying presence. As he informs one interlocutor,

> I flip my little omelette in the frying pan for the love of God, and when it's done, if I have nothing to do, I prostrate myself on the floor and adore my God who gave me the grace to do it, after which I get up happier than a king. . . . A multitude of methods makes it more difficult for us to remain in God's presence. Isn't it shorter and more direct to do everything for the love of God, to use all the works of our state in life to manifest our love to him . . . ?[46]

Brother Lawrence emphasizes the difficulty of sustained attention, writing to a nun that "the first steps are very difficult, and we must act purely in faith." In another letter he observes that we "must continually resolve to persevere to death"; stalwart resolve will help overcome the "repugnance" that is sure to arise as we divide our attention, given our natural inclination to focus on only one thing at a time. Steadfast application will win out, however. "I cannot doubt at all that my soul has been with God for more than 30 years," he is reported to have said.[47]

Brother Lawrence's success was, of course, that of a cloistered monk who enjoyed ample opportunity and encouragement for prayer. How many chefs at L'Étoile or the local greasy spoon can fall on the floor in adoration and retain their jobs? Thomas Kelly's great contribution was to take the teachings of the cloister and transport them, in his florid, fustian way, to the workaday world. In doing so he proved that the prayer of the devotee, of regular loving attendance upon the divine, with its parallel gifts of the sanctification of time and the divinization of the human being, is not restricted to traditional cultures or to saints, paranoiacs, and messianic dreamers. It belongs to us all.

CHAPTER 6

The Ecstatic

UNTIL A FEW YEARS AGO, the most intimate moments of life — childbirth, sexual intercourse, the instant of death — had largely eluded the recording eye of the visual artist. Connoisseurs of such images turned not to museums or sumptuous coffee table books, but to the local pornographer or a willing medical professional. But there has always been one exception. The ecstasy of prayer — the moment of shuddering union with the divine — has ever been a favorite subject of painters, East and West. Giotto's *Ecstasy of Saint Francis* (1297–1300), Poussin's *Ecstasy of Saint Peter* (1643), Bertoni's *Ecstasy of Saint Catherine of Siena* (1743), Beardsley's *The Ascension of Saint Rose of Lima* (1896), and the close-ups of the martyr's face in Dreyer's *The Passion of Joan of Arc* (1928) amply demonstrate the importance of this theme across the centuries throughout the Christian West. On these canvases, saints soar or swoon in transports of bliss, their fainting limbs often supported by helpful angels. Similar exuberance characterizes the scrolls and statuary of Asia, where countless gods and humans plunge into *samādhi* or find tantric rapture in one another's arms.

In recent years, the camera has added immensely to this catalogue of exaltation. A Vodun priestess possessed by a *lwa,* a drug taker in a mescaline-induced trance, a Pentecostal speaking in tongues — all these images are now readily available on the Internet or in any well-stocked bookstore. This is astonishing: a spiritual event so profound that it is often likened to a ravishment has been made available, at the click of a button or the flip of a page, for all the world to see.

The most remarkable of such photographic images — not least because it depicts the most remarkable of modern ecstatics — was taken in

India in the last quarter of the nineteenth century. It originally appeared in one of the most extensive accounts on record of the day-to-day sayings and actions of a spiritual master, *The Gospel of Ramakrishna,* published in Bengali in five volumes from 1897 through 1932 and in English in 1942. The photograph, entitled "Ramakrishna in Ecstasy," shows the great Indian sage Sri Ramakrishna (1836–1886) standing amidst his disciples in a room in Calcutta. His nephew Hriday stands beside him, supporting him at elbow and back. The saint is raising his right hand, forefinger and pinky pointing to the sky, middle fingers closed against the thumb. His left hand is open, held chest high, as if receiving gifts. But what draws our attention is the face. Ramakrishna's eyes are closed, and a slight smile plays along the lips. His features radiate . . . What? Light? Glory? Bliss? Happiness? All of these and something more, something mysterious, uncanny, almost supernatural. We can readily understand, even if we hesitate to accept, the assessment of novelist and playwright Christopher Isherwood, a devotee, that "I believe, or am at least strongly inclined to believe, that he was what his disciples declared that he was: an incarnation of God upon earth."[1]

Ecstatics abound in the world of prayer, and not all of them claim divine status. Bill W. was an ecstatic during his hot flash; so at times was the Russian pilgrim, and those anonymous Muslims immersed in the *dhikr,* and the apostles at Pentecost, and the Ba'al Shem Tov while reciting the benedictions of the 'Amidah, and Saint Francis of Assisi receiving the stigmata, and Jalāl al-Dīn Rūmī whirling, and Julian of Norwich beseeching. The list is long and impressive. But however familiar these figures may be, when we turn to their ecstasies we encounter something *unknown.* To study ecstatic prayer is to venture beyond sociology, psychology, biology, anthropology, and all other familiar scholarly disciplines. We enter that mysterious realm within the human being where heaven meets earth. What unfolds in that place is frequently and famously described as ineffable, and not only by religious figures, who for the most part lack literary skill, but even the world's great literary masters. For example, Jorge Luis Borges comments,

> In my life I only had two mystical experiences and I can't tell them because what happened is not to be put into words, since words, after all, stand for a shared experience. . . . It was astonishing, astounding. I was overwhelmed, taken aback. I had the feeling of living not in time but outside time. . . . I did my best to capture it, but it came and went. I wrote poems about it, but they are normal poems and do not tell the experience. I cannot tell it to you, since I cannot retell it to myself, but I had

Ramakrishna in ecstasy.

> that experience, and I had it twice over, and maybe it will be granted me to have it one more time before I die.[2]

And Borges again: "in the case of ecstasies, that can only be told through metaphors, it cannot be told directly."[3]

C. S. Lewis, in his space fantasy *Perelandra,* offers a convincing reason for this literary aphasia. Ransom, an Oxford don who has traveled to Venus, finds himself unable to describe what he has experienced there. The narrator says, "I was questioning [Ransom] on the subject — which he doesn't often allow — and had incautiously said, 'Of course, I realize it's all rather too vague for you to put into words,' when he took me up rather sharply, for such a patient man, by saying, 'On the contrary, it is words that are vague. The reason why the thing can't be expressed is that it's too *definite* for language.'"[4]

Ecstasy is like that. It is sharp, precise, engulfing; it turns one inside out; there is nothing vague about it at all. And for this very reason it remains under descriptive embargo. This places students of ecstasy in an awkward position: we will limn the outward shapes and hope that the inward reality will become visible to our unecstatic eyes. Let us begin by looking more closely at the life and teachings of the most famous ecstatic of our time, Sri Ramakrishna.

Sri Ramakrishna

The modern world has produced more than its share of religious geniuses: for compassion, one thinks of Mother Teresa of Calcutta; for moral leadership, Gandhi; for theological penetration, Karl Barth. In the realm of ecstasy, the enchanting personality of Sri Ramakrishna towers over the rest. According to Albert Schweitzer, Ramakrishna "was inspired . . . by a spirit of warmest love." To Arnold Toynbee, Ramakrishna's "activity and experience were, in fact, comprehensive to a degree that had perhaps never before been attained by any other religious genius, in India or elsewhere"; Toynbee believed that Ramakrishna had attained "an absolute union with absolute spiritual Reality." William Digby, historian of India, commented that "during the last century the finest fruit of British intellectual eminence was, probably, to be found in Robert Browning and John Ruskin. Yet they are mere gropers in the dark compared with the uncultured and illiterate Ramakrishna, of Bengal, who, knowing naught of what we term learning, spake as no other man of his age spoke, and revealed God to weary mortals."[5]

What do we know about this man, who garnered such acclaim yet spoke no tongue but Bengali, never traveled outside India, and left no written teachings? Even at first glance, there was something odd about him. Mahendra Nath Gupta, a schoolmaster from Calcutta who wrote *The Gospel of Ramakrishna* under the pseudonym "M.," recalls his initial meeting with the saint (M. writes in the third person; there is no room for "I" in the presence of the Master):

> It was on a Sunday in spring, a few days after Sri Ramakrishna's birthday, that M. met him the first time. . . .
>
> M., being at leisure on Sundays, had gone with his friend Sidhu to visit several gardens at Baranagore. As they were walking in Prasanna Bannerji's garden, Sidhu said: "There is a charming place on the bank of the Ganges where a paramahamsa ["great swan," that is, great soul] lives. Should you like to go there?" M. assented and they started immediately for the Dakshineswar temple garden. They arrived at the main gate at dusk and went straight to Sri Ramakrishna's room. And there they found him seated on a wooden couch, facing the east. With a smile on his face, he was talking of God. The room was full of people, all seated on the floor, drinking in his words in deep silence . . .
>
> [M. goes for a walk, then returns with Sidhu and meets Ramakrishna alone.] M. with folded hands saluted the Master. Then, at the Master's bidding, he and Sidhu sat on the floor. Sri Ramakrishna asked them: "Where do you live? What is your occupation? Why have you come to Baranagore?" M. answered the questions, but he noticed that now and then the Master seemed to become absent-minded. Later he learnt that this mood is called bhava, ecstasy. It is like the state of the angler who has been sitting with his rod: the fish comes and swallows the bait, and the float begins to tremble; the angler is on the alert; he grips the rod and watches the float steadily and eagerly; he will not speak to anyone. Later M. heard, and himself noticed, that Sri Ramakrishna would often go into this mood after dusk, sometimes becoming totally unconscious of the outer world.[6]

These moods, as it happens, had seized Ramakrishna since his childhood. Born Gadadhar Chatterji, the child of a devout but poor Brahman family, the young Ramakrishna (who was, by the way, not illiterate, as William Digby claims, but able to read and write Bengali, although not Sanskrit or English) experienced his first ecstasy when only six years old:

> One day in June or July, when he was walking along a narrow path between paddy-fields, eating the puffed rice that he carried in a basket, he looked up at the sky and saw a beautiful, dark thunder-cloud. As it

> spread, rapidly enveloping the whole sky, a flight of snow-white cranes passed in front of it. The beauty of the contrast overwhelmed the boy. He fell to the ground, unconscious, and the puffed rice went in all directions. Some villagers found him and carried him home in their arms.[7]

This experience filled Ramakrishna with ineffable joy. He spent hours memorizing devotional hymns, studying traditional religious tales, and serving the wandering *sadhus* (monks). As he matured, he underwent *upanayana* (initiation) and undertook the many religious duties expected of male members of the highest caste. He learned to meditate, and when praying before a stone image of Raghuvir, the family deity, would "lose himself in contemplation," as the *Gospel of Ramakrishna* puts it, and the god would appear to him as the "living Lord of the Universe."[8] Already, ecstasy was the warp and woof of his religious life; his sole desire was to achieve experiential knowledge of God.

At age sixteen, Ramakrishna moved to Calcutta to work as assistant to his elder brother, the director of a Sanskrit academy. He proved a poor student, preferring to spend his hours in devotional practice. "Brother, what shall I do with a mere bread-winning education?" he asked. "I would rather acquire that wisdom which will illumine my heart and give me satisfaction for ever."[9] The door to wisdom opened a few years later, when he accepted the post as priest at a temple in Dakshineswar, four miles north of Calcutta, dedicated to Kālī, the Divine Mother. Kālī is the Hindu deity most feared and misunderstood outside India, thanks largely to her terrifying iconography: the basalt image in the temple at Dakshineswar depicts a four-armed goddess holding a severed human head and a bloody sword, wearing a garland of skulls and a girdle of arms, and standing over the body of her divine consort, Śiva. As these symbolic horrors indicate, Kālī is the Divine Destroyer. But she is also, in other manifestations, the Divine Creator, the Universal Mother, Absolute Consciousness, Reality itself. Ramakrishna threw himself at Kālī's feet, worshiping her around the clock. Every night he entered the jungle beyond the temple, stripped naked, and meditated on her holy presence; every day he would sit before her image, singing hymns, and would beg her to appear before him. He had no time to eat or sleep. Ramakrishna later provided a description of his condition:

> As I was perfectly unmindful of the cleaning of the body at that time, the hairs grew long and got matted of themselves, being smeared with dirt and dust. When I would sit in meditation, the body would become stiff

> and motionless like a stork, through intense concentration of mind, and birds, taking it to be an inert substance, came and freely perched on the head. . . . In meditation, prayer, and other devotional practices, the day used to fly by so quickly that I was not conscious of it. At dusk . . . a frenzy of despair would seize my soul and I would throw myself on the ground and rub my face on it, crying out loudly, "Mother, another day has passed and still you have not appeared before me!"[10]

His anguished prayers sound remarkably modern: "Art Thou real, Mother, or is it all fiction — mere poetry without any reality? If Thou dost exist, why do I not see Thee? Is religion a mere fantasy and art Thou only a figment of man's imagination?"[11] As the prayers intensified, the doubts increased, and Kālī continued to withhold her presence. Finally, in a fit of despair, Ramakrishna spied a sword hanging in the sanctuary and decided to take his own life.

> I jumped up like a madman and seized it, when suddenly the blessed Mother revealed Herself. The buildings with their different parts, the temple, and everything else vanished from my sight, leaving no trace whatsoever, and in their stead I saw a limitless, infinite, effulgent Ocean of Bliss. As far as the eye could see, the shining billows were madly rushing at me from all sides with a terrific noise. . . . within me there was a steady flow of undiluted bliss, altogether new, and I felt the presence of the Divine Mother.[12]

In these oceanic metaphors, with their limitless waters and shining waves, we see a manifestation of Borges's assertion that "in the case of ecstasies . . . it cannot be directly told. It has to be told through metaphors." The experience to which the metaphors point electrified Ramakrishna. Instead of feeling satiated with the presence of the divine mother, he pined for her more than ever. He prayed day and night that she would remain with him forever. He wept uncontrollably and suffered bouts of paralysis; blood oozed from his pores, and he found himself surrounded by flashing lights or swirling mists from which the divine mother appeared at whim, speaking to him, breathing on him. He watched her walk the temple grounds or gaze over the parapet at Calcutta's distant haze. He pranced and sang before her icon. To emphasize his subservience, he assumed the behavior of Hanuman, the mythological monkey-king and prototype of all servants. He leaped and chattered like a monkey and ate only roots and fruit. Some reports describe a stubby one-inch tail emerging from his coccyx. Again fearing for his sanity, he prayed, "I do not know what these things are. I am ignorant of mantras and the scriptures.

Teach me, Mother, how to realize Thee. Who else can help me? Are Thou not my only refuge and guide?"[13]

Not surprisingly, Ramakrishna's friends and acquaintances suspected that he had gone mad. They hatched schemes to cure him, including an arranged marriage with a five-year-old girl, but these interventions led nowhere. The prayers, the physical sufferings, the incomprehensible behavior, the visions continued unabated. What Ramakrishna needed was not domestication but rather the traditional disciplines of the Indian world.

At last this came, through the unexpected offices of two complete strangers. The first was a woman whose name remains unknown. Ramakrishna dubbed her the Bhairavi Brahmani (the Brāhmaṇ nun). She appeared one day at the temple of Kālī, carrying some clothes and holy books; Ramakrishna took to her immediately and poured out to her his long, strange tale. "My son," she declared, "everyone in this world is mad. Some are mad for money, some for creature comforts, some for name and fame; and you are mad for God."[14] She declared Ramakrishna to be a Divine Incarnation. Over the next several months, she initiated him into the esoteric rites of Tantra, which he mastered with extraordinary rapidity. According to the *Gospel of Ramakrishna,*

> Evil ceased to exist for him. The word "carnal" lost its meaning. He went into ecstasy at the sight of a prostitute, of drunkards reveling in a tavern. . . . The barrier between matter and energy broke down for him, and he saw even a grain of sand and a blade of grass vibrating with energy. The universe appeared to him as a lake of mercury or of silver. . . . He saw in a vision the Ultimate Cause of the universe as a huge luminous triangle giving birth every moment to an infinite number of worlds.[15]

The Bhairavi Brahmani continued to educate her ward, following Tantra with a complete course in Vaiṣṇavism, the worship of Viṣṇu, the Supreme God. Perhaps Viṣṇu's most beloved incarnation is Kṛṣṇa, the blue-skinned lover of Rādhā, the milkmaid; their love, widely celebrated in Indian popular legend and literature, symbolizes the union of divine and human. In one of the strangest episodes of a very strange life, Ramakrishna became for a time the embodiment of Rādhā. He adopted woman's dress and jewelry, his flesh lost its roughness, his breasts expanded, and he danced and prayed ardently until Kṛṣṇa appeared before him, approached him, and merged into his own body. "Thus," declares the *Gospel,* "he drank from the fountain of Immortal Bliss. The agony of his heart vanished for ever."[16]

This attainment would be enough for most people, but not for Ramakrishna. He needed yet more rigorous education in traditional Indian thought, and to supply it came a wandering ascetic, clad only in a loincloth, named Totapuri but known to Ramakrishna as Nangta (the naked one). Totapuri introduced Ramakrishna to the philosophical system that would provide the intellectual foundation for his God-intoxicated prayers. Known as Vedānta (literally, "end of the Veda"), it teaches that the ultimate reality is *brahman,* the unconditioned primordial being (Ramakrishna would often refer to brahman as God). *Ātman* (the soul) is itself brahman, but this truth is obscured by *māyā* (illusion) and as a result we are subject to a terrifying cycle of birth, death, and rebirth. Through intense spiritual discipline, we may rip the veil of *māyā,* attain liberation, and escape the cycle of rebirth.

Totapuri initiated Ramakrishna into the mysteries of Vedānta. This required, however, overcoming the allure of Kālī, who was herself a contingent being, not the undifferentiated Absolute. The struggle was white-hot and brief. Whenever Ramakrishna tried to reach ultimate awareness, Kālī blocked his way. Finally Totapuri, enraged, seized a piece of broken glass and pressed it against Ramakrishna's forehead, ordering his pupil to concentrate the mind just there: "With stern determination I again sat to meditate. As soon as the gracious form of the Divine Mother appeared before me, I used my discrimination as a sword and with it clove Her in two. The last barrier fell. My spirit at once soared beyond the relative plane. I lost myself in samadhi!"[17]

This was Ramakrishna's final breakthrough. Totapuri was stunned: "Is it really true? Is it possible that he has attained in a single day what it took me forty years of strenuous practice to achieve?"[18] Indeed, it did seem to be true, and then some. For Ramakrishna not only attained mastery of Vedānta but also proclaimed a new understanding of *māyā* not as an obstacle to God but an expression of God. From now on, *everything* was God; *māyā* was Kālī and *māyā* was brahman.

Totapuri departed, but Ramakrishna remained in a state of *samādhi* for six months — an unparalled achievement in Indian religion, for according to tradition, a human being can sustain this state for only twenty-one days before death intervenes. During this state Ramakrishna lay senseless to the world, force-fed by a disciple.

In time the saint returned to the mundane world. Disciples gathered; his fame spread through India and then around the world. More breathtaking spiritual adventures followed: in 1866 Ramakrishna assumed the practices of a Muslim until Muḥammad appeared to him in a vision and merged with his body, just as Kṛṣṇa had done years before; in 1874, he turned to Christian prayer, triggering an ecstasy that climaxed when one day he saw Jesus approaching him in the street. "It is He, the Master Yogi, who is in eternal union with God," said an inner voice. "It is Jesus, Love Incarnate."[19] This figure, too, entered his own body and became a part of him. The transformation was complete. He, Ramakrishna, the Divine Incarnation, embodied all the great religious teachers of the world; He was They. They were He. All was One.

Ramakrishna continued to teach and to dwell in ecstasy until his death of throat cancer in 1885, at the age of fifty. He left behind a core of disciples whose work continues to this day in the Ramakrishna Mission, with centers throughout the world (including eighteen in the United States at the time of this writing). His influence on intellectuals has been immense; an extravagant but not entirely atypical example of the praise he garners comes from the late writer, teacher, and radio personality Lex Hixon, a self-proclaimed follower of multiple religions including Islam, Christianity, and Hinduism: "Ramakrishna mysteriously provides a master key that opens all cultures and all hearts."[20] The most exact word here may be the adverb, for the biggest challenge in looking at Ramakrishna is grasping exactly what happened to him during his ecstasies.

We can begin by observing that Ramakrishna's raptures varied dramatically over the years. He was Picasso rather than Rembrandt, an experimenter always ready to venture into new spiritual realms. His language, like his ecstasies, remained in flux; he refers to his experiences as visions, raptures, God-intoxications, *samādhi,* and so on, with no apparent consistency of definition or usage. He speaks as a practitioner, not a theoretician. As an exasperated compiler of a concordance to the *Gospel* has pointed out, Ramakrishna might use *see* to refer to ordinary vision, ordinary understanding, or a mystical apprehension of divine truths. The source of this problem seems to lie in the startling fact that, at least during long stretches of his life, ecstasy was Ramakrishna's regular state of consciousness; during rapture he would dance, sing, chant the divine name, pray, drink, eat, and even carry on conversation; what we experience as normal waking consciousness was, for him, the exception rather than the rule.

Given this, the abundance of bewildering revelations is perhaps to be expected. We may note, then, that Ramakrishna enjoyed visions of Śiva, the Divine Mother, and God ("I used to see God directly with these very eyes, just as I see you now"). The universe appeared to him as a chandelier, liquid silver, a lake of mercury, or light; he saw people as flames, peacocks, flowers, or bubbles; he saw Kṛṣṇa and the *gopīs,* Rāma, Jesus, and Muḥammad; he saw his doppelgänger many times and in many guises; he saw his soul emerge from his body and "like a protruding tongue of flame [it] tasted everything"; he turned to stone, to fire; he saw women as if with x-ray eyes ("I could see both their inside & outside; entrails, filth, bone, flesh, & blood. The mind preferred to remain fixed at the Lotus Feet of God"). He saw heaps of human heads, mounds of supernatural food, money, and sweets. He saw his disciples as luminous beings; he saw threatening creatures with tridents, ready to strike him if his mind should wander away from God.[21]

This wild landscape was governed by a single principle: all is one, all is consciousness, all is *brahman.* "I saw food-stuff, dirt, and even excreta," Ramakrishna says. "It was revealed to me that all these are one Substance, the non-dual and indivisible Consciousness." At another time he reports that "I clearly see that God is everything & beyond everything. I come to a state in which my mind & intellect merge in the Indivisible." This monism applies to human beings as well: "When I see a man, I see that it is God Himself who walks on earth, as it were, rocking to & fro, like a pillow floating on the waves." Sinner or saint, it is all one: "Now I see that it is God alone who is moving about in various forms: as a holy man, as a cheat, as a villain." It even applies, in a statement deliberately shocking in its imagery, to animal sexuality: "I have seen with my own eyes that God dwells even in the sexual organ. I saw Him once in the sexual intercourse of a dog & a bitch."[22]

This cornucopia of rapture, Ramakrishna tells us again and again, springs from a life of prayer. Addressing Kālī, he says, "If a man prays to Thee with a yearning heart, he can reach Thee, through Thy grace, by any path." He advises prayer and yet more prayer: "How long should one perform devotions? So long as one's mind does not merge in God while repeating Om." As for the specifics of prayer, he counsels against asking for mundane things such as jobs or money; petitions should focus on requesting divine aid in the struggle for purification of mind and body. He himself has faults that need purging; he begs for freedom from lust and for a favorable rebirth, for the companionship of other sages. At times his requests startle with their normality; he prays for protection, for peace, for love; several times, he begs Kālī, most touchingly, to free him from *samādhi:* "Mother, don't make me unconscious with the Knowledge of Brahman. . . . I want to be merry. I want to play." But to no avail. For Ramakrishna, prayer meant rapture. There was no other way. "The slightest thing," he observes, "awakens God-Consciousness in me." Meditating, chanting hymns, listening to sacred music or scripture readings, reciting the divine name, walking by the sacred Ganges, worshiping statues, even observing the religious practices of others were enough to ignite his mind.[23]

Ramakrishna seemed unable to control his ecstasies; they struck at will, whenever the right catalyst appeared. He describes the process in this way: "something goes up creeping from the feet to the head. Consciousness continues to exist as long as this power does not reach the head; but as soon as it reaches the head all consciousness is completely lost." According to Tantric anthropology, this "something" is *kuṇḍalinī*, (cosmic energy). Coiled at the base of the spine, it may through meditative practices be released to travel up through the six centers (chakras) to the seventh chakra atop the head, where it produces *samādhi*. Ramakrishna's *kuṇḍalinī* ascended with profligate regularity. He describes the movement as a "tingling sensation," varying in intensity and feeling, and he likened it, following scriptural models, to the motion of creeping ants, hopping frogs, slithering snakes, flying birds, or brachiating monkeys. As for what happens at the climax of this experience, Ramakrishna found it impossible to articulate. Whenever he tried to describe *samādhi*, he fell back into it. "Alas," he exclaims, "I have a desire to tell you everything without concealing anything whatsoever, but in spite of all my efforts, Mother did not allow me to speak; She pressed my mouth." The natural bent of his mind, he said, was to stay in *samādhi;* the disciples learned that cow's ghee, smeared upon his spine and legs, would ease his raptures; perhaps the very materiality of the butter — an earthy echo of the spiritual milk of the divine mother — drew him back to the mundane realm. Once there, he said, he needed to nurture some desire — to smoke tobacco, to drink water — in order to stay sober.[24]

During rapture, he would sing, dance, eat, drink, converse. Sometimes he would engage in erratic behavior — slapping devotees on the cheek if they seemed far from God — or even forbidden acts, such as accepting food from a prostitute. Once he broke his teeth during rapture, another time his arm. He would stagger like a drunk or tremble uncontrollably. He would talk like a child. His hair would stand on end. At times he became speechless and motionless. He could not bear the touch of metal ("When I touch a metal cup I feel as if I had been stung by a horned fish. There was excruciating pain all over my arm") — an odd affliction, if all is *brahman*. His flesh would turn red; his disciples reported a divine glow emanating from his body. Sometimes he would fall unconscious. Touchingly, he sometimes expressed doubts about how his *samādhi* appeared to others. To M., he asked once, "Does what I saw in the state of ecstasy attract people? What do they think of me? Do they think anything in particular about me when they see me in that condition?" Sometimes he worried about who would look after him if he became lost in ecstasy permanently. At other times, fully experiencing his divinity, he found peace only when he was being worshiped as a Divine Incarnation.[25]

No doubt many people find Ramakrishna's behavior grotesque, even horrifying, but his disciples saw in it a supernal beauty, as this reminiscence by Swami Saradananda makes clear:

> Before we met the Master, our idea was that people would enjoy the artless dancing and gestures of a child, but that it would be nothing but ludicrous or disgusting to them when a grown-up robust youth performed such antics. Swami Vivekananda used to say, "Does one appreciate a rhinoceros dancing a dancing-girl's dance?" But, coming to the Master, we had to change our opinions. Although he was advanced in age, the Master danced, sang, made various gestures — and ah, how sweet they were! "We never dreamt," said Girish Babu, "that a grown-up robust youth looked so well when dancing." But how beautiful was the posture of his body and limbs under the influence of the infusion of the spirit of Gopala into him today at Balaram Babu's house! We did not understand then why all these looked so beautiful. We only felt that they were beautiful and nothing more. We now understand that, whenever any mood came on him, it came on fully without the admixture of any other mood with it, and with no touch of insincerity or showing off. He was then completely inspired . . . the strong waves of Bhava [ecstasy] within burst out and completely changed his body or made it assume a different form altogether.[26]

These ecstasies were, to Ramakrishna's disciples, proof of his divinity. His experiences were more radical and more continuous than any described in traditional Indian religious literature; only a divine being could live like this.

To those hesitant or unwilling to grant Ramakrishna this status, another question arises: are his raptures as universal as they appear? They incorporate the iconography of the great religions, but do they faithfully reflect their essence? Most scholars of religion would answer no. Ramakrishna's experiences are Hindu in nature — a fact underscored by his primary devotion to Kālī — and present precisely the erasure of borders between faiths that one would expect from a practitioner of Vedānta, for whom all religions are equal and lead to the same truth. It is unlikely that a Christian or Muslim, well-versed in his or her own tradition, would recognize Jesus or Muḥammad in the persons that Ramakrishna encountered; to describe Jesus, for example, as the "Master Yogi" is to see him as a psycho-physical adept in a way foreign to first-century Palestine.

To point out that Ramakrishna is a product of a particular culture and a special religious ethos is to recognize a strength: only in a country like India, and perhaps in a region like Bengal, could an ecstatic like Ramakrishna thrive. As historian of religion June McDaniel puts it, "There is a nostalgia for madness in Bengal. The lovers, poets, and saints are mad, full of intense passion and desire for direct experience. A person may be mad for love or mad for God."[27] This "nostalgia for madness," evidenced in the thousands of sages and saints who have wandered the Bengali countryside for millennia, provided a matrix in which Ramakrishna's intense prayer life could blossom into mature ecstasy, fruitful to himself and others. In a different society, Ramakrishna would likely be regarded as demonic or mad; in nineteenth-century Calcutta, he was revered as both mad and divine.

Saint Teresa of Ávila

If Ramakrishna is the premier spokesperson of religious ecstasy, then the great Spanish Carmelite mystic Saint Teresa of Ávila (1515–1582) is its foremost scribe. In *The Interior Castle* (1588) and in her autobiography *Life of Mother Teresa of Ávila* (published posthumously in 1611), she has given the world its most elaborate and useful accounts of the prayer of ecstasy. She fills the gaps in Ramakrishna's cryptic, sometimes frustratingly brief descriptions, and she does so twice, supplying detailed representations, based on aquatic and architectural imagery respectively, of the stages of prayer, from the first steps of the beginner to the apotheosis of the master. In gritty detail she describes exactly what she experienced — body, mind, heart, and soul — while in the grip of rapture. All this she accomplishes in supple, subtle prose whose literary excellence seems a perfect corollary to her spiritual preeminence. In recognition of her mastery, she was declared, on September 27, 1970, the first female Doctor of the Church.

Teresa's life was, in its own way, as exceptional as Ramakrishna's. Unlike her Indian counterpart, however, she excelled in practical tasks — an attribute to bear in mind when considering her ecstasies. She founded nearly twenty convents; established a vastly influential religious order, the Discalced Carmelites of the Primitive Rule; worked tirelessly for monastic reform, especially a return to the poverty and discipline of earlier years; and provided spiritual guidance to untold numbers of nuns and the occasional monk (including Saint John of the Cross). Alongside these public achievements, she managed an intense life of private prayer. It may be more appropriate to say that her prayers managed her life, for one gets the sense that, as with Ramakrishna, communion with the divine was the driving force to which everything else — family, writings, religious reforms — submitted.

Born to nobility, Teresa spent her early years in Ávila as a pampered child, enjoying perfumes and fine clothes, reading romances about chivalrous knights, and dreaming of martyrdom at the hands of the Moors. At age twenty-one, she entered the Carmelite Convent of the Incarnation in Ávila. She soon fell ill, afflicted by fainting spells, heart pains, inability to eat, and other ailments so severe that, she later remembered, "I was always on the verge of losing consciousness, and sometimes wholly unconscious." On one occasion, after she fell into a catatonic fit, she received last rites and was declared dead; her grave was dug and her body prepared for burial. According to her memoir, when she awoke, "I found wax on my eyes."[28] Despite her illnesses, she learned, during these early monastic years, the rudiments of Catholic prayer, especially the liturgical prayers included in the Mass and Divine Office and the practice known as meditation — not, as it is frequently understood today, silent contemplation or mindfulness practice, but rather the ancient technique of reading a passage of scripture and ruminating on it to draw out its wisdom. The method involves the whole person, as Benedictine scholar Jean Leclercq nicely observes: "To meditate is to read a text and to learn it 'by heart' in the fullest sense of this expression, that is, with one's whole being: with the body, since the mouth pronounced it, with the memory which fixes it, with the intelligence which understands its meaning and with the will which desires to put it into practice."[29]

Meditation lays a sturdy foundation for the interior life by making scriptural wisdom one's own. In Catholic prayer manuals, it is often understood as a prerequisite to contemplative prayer. Teresa balked at exploring these hidden chambers, however, held back by fear and lack of capable instruction. Her illnesses abated, although she never again enjoyed truly good health. But her prayer remained that of simple *meditatio*. Except for a brief time after Holy Communion, she reports,

> I never dared to begin praying without a book. For my soul was as afraid to be without one, as to go into battle against a great horde. With this support, which was like a company and a shield to withstand the blows

> of my many thoughts, I felt consoled. For dryness was not my usual state, but it always troubled me when I was without a book. Then my soul would be cast off and my thoughts run astray.[30]

So it continued for twenty years, which she describes as a time of "great aridities." There was, however, one hint of the great change to come. In about 1539, she experienced her first vision, a chastising visitation by the Lord:

> Christ appeared before me, with a most severe expression, giving me to understand that this was something that grieved him. I saw Him with the eyes of the soul more clearly than I could have seen Him with those of the body, and it left such a deep impression on me that, though more than twenty-six years have passed, it still seems present before me. I remained very astonished and disturbed.[31]

That Teresa recalls this vision as appearing to the "eyes of the soul" is significant. An inveterate systematizer, she developed a three-tiered typology of vision, echoing earlier classifications set out by Augustine and Thomas Aquinas. Some visions are corporeal, seen with the eyes of the body in the same way that we see a tree, a house, or an automobile. Other visions are imaginary — not false, but "seen with the eyes of the soul" as an interior image. These visions may vary in intensity; Teresa, describing apparitions of Christ, writes that "on some occasions it seemed as if what I saw was an image, but on many others, no, it was Christ Himself, in all the clarity with which he was pleased to show Himself to me."[32] Yet others are intellectual, received as a pure idea without accompanying imagery.

All of Teresa's visions, by her own evaluation, were either imaginary or intellectual. Unlike Ramakrishna, she always saw inwardly rather than corporeally. The 1539 apparition of Christ was imaginary. She had no doubt of its authenticity, then or later, but she was aware of the Catholic Church's views on such matters — visions might be the work of God, angels, the devil, or an illusion brought on by natural causes such as fever, dyspepsia, or trompe l'oeil. The vision's supernatural origins would have to be proved by its fruits: a lingering sense of peace, increased piety and virtue, perhaps a deeper understanding of the cloistered life.

In Teresa's case, it took sixteen years for these fruits to ripen. She fell into a kind of spiritual torpor, trudging through the rounds of daily monastic life, fulfilling her duties faithfully but without enthusiasm or inner reward. Her future seemed assured: she would be a decent, unremarkable nun, a foot soldier for Christ, one of the thousands that build the foundation upon which great sanctity can arise. That sanctity would be left for others — or so it seemed.

Then, in about 1555, her transformation began. For reasons that remain unclear — perhaps maturity (she was now entering her fifth decade), divine intervention, or a combination of the two — Teresa's relationship with God began to deepen. "Suddenly a feeling of the presence of God would come upon me, such that I could in no way doubt that He was within me or I totally engulfed in Him."[33] At the same time, visions and locutions returned in such multiplicity that they became, if not her ordinary state of consciousness, as with Ramakrishna, then at least a spectacular visionary backdrop against which her everyday life unfolded. During this period she enjoyed a great stroke of luck or providence, meeting a priest who gave her visions the imprimatur of the Church, assuring her that they were indeed the work of God.

From now on, Christ would speak to Teresa repeatedly, directing her prayers and her actions. She enjoyed her first purely intellectual vision:

> One day when I was at prayer on the feast day of the glorious St. Peter, I saw Christ at my side — or, to put it better, I felt Him, for I saw nothing with the eyes of the body or of the soul, but it seemed that Christ was right beside me and that it was He who was speaking to me. Being completely ignorant that one could have such a vision, I felt extremely frightened at first, and could do nothing but weep; however, by speaking just a word to reassure me, He restored me to my usual state, quiet, greatly cheered and without any fear.[34]

In subsequent apparitions, she witnessed Christ hanging from the cross, Christ triumphant in the Resurrection, Christ displaying his bleeding hands, his crown of thorns, his cross. One day she handed Christ her rosary, and when it was returned, the wooden beads had been transformed into four large stones "far more precious than diamonds, beyond compare." (After Teresa's death, this rosary was pressed to the eyes of supplicants suffering from cataracts or blindness; miraculous cures ensued.) She saw devils clinging to a debased priest and worrying the corpse of a man who had died in mortal sin. Once she challenged the demons by thrusting a crucifix in their face, like some sixteenth-century Van Helsing, but ordinarily she took "no more notice of them than of flies." Often she saw Jesuits and members of other religious orders rejoicing in heaven or doing battle against infernal hosts. She visited hell. Heaven visited her, and she talked with the Blessed Virgin Mary and Saint Joseph.[35]

Almost always, these visions erupted while Teresa was at prayer. They were often accompanied or followed by sensations, mental, emotional, and physical, of nearly unbearable intensity, at once joyous and painful. These experiences, which Teresa might describe as the physical imprint of a spiritual agency, reached their peak in the most important and famous of her visions, known as the Transverberation (a term generally taken to mean "to strike through," but so obscure that it is not found in the *Oxford English Dictionary*). The event, commemorated each year in the Roman Catholic calendar, took place on August 27, 1559. Teresa describes what happened:

> I saw an angel beside me to my left, in bodily form. . . . He was not large but small, and most beautiful, with a face so fiery that he appeared to come from that highest order of angels who are all aflame. . . . I saw in his hands a long golden spear, and at the iron tip there seemed to be a little fire. It seemed to me that he thrust it several times into my heart, and it reached my entrails. When he drew out the spear he seemed to be drawing them with it, leaving me all on fire with the immense love of God. The pain was so great that it brought forth from me several moans; and yet so exceedingly sweet is this intense pain that there is no desire to be rid of it, nor is the soul content with anything less than God.[36]

The Transverberation is depicted by Bernini in his famous marble fantasia *The Ecstasy of Saint Teresa,* in the church of Santa Maria della Vittoria in Rome. What may strike the modern observer (and, judging by the statue's expression, Bernini as well) most forcefully is the sexual overtones of the sculpture, as the angel prepares to pierce the saint with his golden spear. Who doubts that this imagery can be linked to Teresa's prolonged celibacy and unconscious libidinal longings?

But analysis of this sort tells us next to nothing; one can hardly expect an imaginary vision (as Teresa herself would class the Transverberation), which of necessity draws on the symbolic language of the subconscious, to be antiseptically divorced from its subject's dreams and desires. To note sexual imagery in a vision is not to reduce it to erotic fantasy. In fact, *fantasy* may be entirely the wrong word, bearing in mind that when Teresa's body was examined after her death, doctors found a hole running through the center of her heart, precisely matching the path of the golden dart. In 1872, the heart was reexamined by physicians at the University of Salamanca, and the aperture was confirmed. That Teresa's heart could be examined three centuries after her death is in itself astonishing; it had resisted decomposition, a physical phenomenon often associated with the remains of holy men and women. Of course, the professors of Salamanca may have been mistaken, misled, or willfully duplicitous; and in any case the hole may be explained as a psychosomatic disturbance, a hysterical effect rather than a miracle. We cannot know for sure. But we may say with certainty that, for Teresa, the Transverberation was a paramount example of a vision brought on by prayer and culminating in rapture. And what a marvelous description of that rapture she provides: "leaving me all on fire with the immense love of God."

Indeed, Teresa stands alone among writers in providing a precise, polished account of her raptures and establishing their proper place within the world of prayer. In her *Life,* she likens the discovery and exploration of this world to the watering of a garden, which unfolds in four stages, each more filled with joy than the one that came before:

- *Stage I:* The water is drawn manually from the well, a tedious effort akin to the first, difficult steps of meditation.
- *Stage II:* The water is drawn mechanically from the well by means of a waterwheel. Teresa compares this method of aquaculture to the "prayer of quiet"; meditation has ceased, and only the naked will, yearning for God, remains.
- *Stage III:* The water flows naturally from a brook into the garden. Will, memory, and intellect fall silent; the one who prays is utterly passive. God is the gardener, "for it is He who does it all."
- *Stage IV:* The water comes as rain, freely bestowed by God, bathing the one who prays in "heavenly love," an experience of total union with God.[37]

Teresa places ecstasy in the fourth stage of prayer. While in ecstasy, she writes, "The soul feels with a magnificent and sweet delight that it is fainting almost wholly away in a kind of swoon, as breath fades and bodily forces wane."[38] Body and mind are paralyzed; one cannot move, read, or speak. Teresa could fall into rapture while standing, kneeling, or lying down, and her body would freeze in whatever position it happened to be at the time. Her hands and feet would grow ice cold, but her face would glow with preternatural light. According to eyewitnesses, sometimes she levitated, once so energetically that the entire community of nuns piled on her to keep her body from soaring away; another time, while receiving Communion, she began to ascend and clung desperately to an iron grille in order to remain earthbound. These transports shocked, embarrassed, and confused her; why would God's love for such a "vile worm" as her be so great that he would draw to him not only the soul but also the body? To her great relief ecstasy never lasted more than thirty minutes, although complete recovery could take hours, and the ordeal had its compensation in a superabundance of heavenly bliss.

In *The Interior Castle* (1588), her most extended treatise on prayer, Teresa replaces the metaphor of the garden with that of a castle. The seeker after God passes through seven chambers, or "mansions," within the castle of prayer on her way to the sacred nuptial chamber, where she enjoys a "spiritual marriage" with God. In the book's most famous simile, Teresa likens the soul to a silkworm, nourished on the mulberry leaves of the Church, dying in the cocoon of a "life hid with Christ in God," and reborn as a resplendent moth, ready to praise the Lord. With the precision of a lepidopterist, she describes what befalls this winged being in the realms of rapture. Two different forms of ecstasy await. In the first, God discerns our yearning for him, and he responds, in his infinite compassion, by inflaming the soul, cleansing it, uniting with it, and revealing to it eternal truths. This state may involve paralysis or the loss of sensory activity; nonetheless, the soul perceives "heavenly things," many of which will be remembered when rapture ends. In the second, the soul flies out of the body, and the ecstatic "feels as if he has been in another world, very different from that in which we live. . . . In an instant he is taught so many things at once that if he were to work for many years trying to grasp them with his imagination and thought, he could not succeed with a thousandth part of them." These two forms of rapture, she says, are "one in substance" but "interiorly experienced very differently." Both fade away in the last mansion of prayer, where raptures are few, replaced by a more quiet, steady, but equally blissful state. Ecstasy, then, is not for Teresa the highest form of prayer; it gives way in the end to serene equilibrium.[39]

Teresa never doubted the supernatural provenance of her visions and ecstasies. After all, they were a familiar part of the sixteenth-century grammar of the Faith; Jesus appeared to many cloistered nuns. Why wouldn't the savior come in person to bring solace or rebuke to those under his care? As for devils, they would seize any opportunity to do evil. What's more, as Teresa repeatedly pointed out, the visions came without volition on her part. When she was young and naive, she had indeed begged Jesus to appear to her, but nothing had happened. Only after she had spurned such desires did he deign to appear, often in circumstances that left her blushing. On occasion, sensing an impending ecstasy, she would scurry to her room or pretend that she was fainting from heart trouble; just as often, she would resist with all the power at her command. Many of her biographers cite this resistance as proof of the legitimacy of her ecstasies; certainly it demonstrates that there was no willful intent to deceive. The poet and novelist Vita Sackville-West, who wrote a perceptive study of the saint, advances a second reason to accept her visions at face value: Teresa was unable to manipulate them in any way. When once the saint tried to determine the color of Jesus' eyes, the vision evaporated on the spot. For Sackville-West, Teresa's scrupulousness "in never pretending to see or hear more than she actually believed she saw and heard, is extremely convincing, and rules out any suggestions that she could delude herself into imagining something which was not out 'there.'"[40]

Teresa was, in fact, terribly concerned with discriminating between authentic visions and raptures, sent by God, and the ersatz variety, implanted by demons or self-deception. Through her studies of this problem, she helped refine the art of discernment of spirits, a major preoccupation of the Church since patristic days. Teresa was acutely aware that many nuns were prone to self-delusion, as she made clear in a delicious pun: "They call it *arrobamiento* [rapture]; I call it *abobamiento* [foolishness]."[41] Real rapture, she says, may be frightening or painful, but the aftereffect makes one more detached from the world and more deeply in love with Christ. A devil-spawned vision would lead one away from Christ, toward the world. If the rapture brings us closer to God, how can it be anything but a gift from his hands?

Teresa set down rules for evaluating locutions as well. If the words come from God, they will shine with clarity and precision, and if they prophesy, the prophecies will come true. She reveals, speaking of her own locutions, that "I have proven many things that were told to me two or three years beforehand and all of them have come to pass; up until now not one of them has turned out to be a lie."[42] Above all, locutions from God will bestow great rewards upon the soul. Even if one forgets everything that happens during a rapture, the event resounds at the deepest levels of being. It makes its mark where it counts.

Without doubt, ecstasies made their mark on Teresa. Her ability to blend the nitty-gritty and the gossamer, to found monasteries and yet faint like a schoolgirl, to discipline her soul with an iron hand and yet feel it melt with love for God is perhaps unmatched in the history of religion. The most impressive offspring of this marriage of the mundane and celestial may be her writing, for reports circulated soon after the publication of *The Interior Castle* that Teresa had composed it while in a state of ecstasy, and we know with some certainty that she penned her most famous poem, "Vivo sin vivir en mí," just after a prolonged rapture in Salamanca. The first stanzas read as follows:

I live, yet not within myself,
and thus I live in hope.
I die because I do not die.

I live, yet far beyond myself,
in that I die of love.
For I live in the Lord,
who seized me for himself;
and when I offered my heart,
he placed on it this sign:
"I die because I do not die."[43]

We cannot attest to the objective veracity of this life "far beyond myself," the reliability of Teresa's visions, or the knowledge imparted to her during rapture. But we know that she reported her experiences as honestly and precisely as possible. Add to this her unflagging effort to separate true visions from false and the effect of rapture on her life, transforming timidity and doubt into strength and joy, and one might well conclude that her ecstatic prayer was a gift of supernatural proportions.

Saint Teresa of Ávila and Sri Ramakrishna stand alone. To be sure, a few of Ramakrishna's disciples enjoyed *samādhi,* and swooning joy, ersatz or real, was not unknown among other nuns of the Discalced Carmelites. But we celebrate Teresa and Ramakrishna for being out of the ordinary — not representative, but unique. They are the templates by which others cut their own devotional lives; they are the geniuses of ecstatic prayer.

Not all ecstasies are reserved for the select few, however. From the Greco-Roman rites of Dionysus to modern experiments with psychoactive drugs, ravishment in the spirit has been available to the masses as well. The greatest of all ecstatic prayer movements, born with the twentieth century and in its early years a watershed in the history of interracial prayer, is now a force around the globe, boasting hundreds of millions of adherents and expanding exponentially: Pentecostalism and its astounding core practice of glossolalia, speaking in tongues.

Speaking in Tongues

On the morning of April 18, 1906, the deadliest earthquake in U.S. history, measuring 8.25 on the Richter scale, ruptured the northern end of the San Andreas Fault, devastating San Francisco and much of the Bay Area. At least one thousand five hundred people died in the quake and subsequent fire. Tremors were felt as far south as Los Angeles, four hundred miles away. But breakfasters reaching for their newspapers that day did not read about the quake — that nightmare would be reserved for tomorrow's edition. Instead, they learned about another earth-shaking event that erupted at the same time, a spiritual convulsion of the highest magnitude that would lead to a revolution in American religious life. The front-page headlines of the *Los Angeles Times* screamed, "WEIRD BABEL OF TONGUES: New Sect of Fanatics Is Breaking Loose. Wild Scene Last Night on Azusa Street. Gurgle of Wordless Talk by a Sister." The report began as follows:

> Breathing strange utterances and mouthing a creed which it would seem no sane mortal could understand, the newest religious sect has started in Los Angeles. Meetings are held in a tumble-down shack on Azusa Street, near San Pedro Street, and devotees of the weird doctrine practice the most fanatical rites, preach the wildest theories and work themselves into a state of mad excitement in their peculiar zeal. Colored people and a sprinkling of whites compose the congregation, and night is made hideous in the neighborhood by the howlings of the worshippers who spend hours swaying forth and back in a nerve-racking attitude of prayer and supplication. They claim to have "the gift of tongues" and to be able to comprehend the babel.

This heated report, typical of news media confronting a religious event beyond their ken, scrambles facts and misrepresents intentions. The described event on Azusa Street did not entail wild theories, fanatical followers, or hideous howls. To understand what did transpire, let us travel six years back and one thousand five hundred miles to the east, to a Bible school in Topeka, Kansas, in the waning days of 1900.

Bethel Bible School, housed in a fantastic wedding cake of a building known to the locals as Stone's Folly, was founded by Charles Fox Parham (1873–1929), a charismatic preacher from Iowa who championed the classic evangelical doctrines of conversion and sanctification. First, Parham would say, you must experience your sinfulness, then turn your life over to Jesus and attain by grace a state of Christian holiness. After prolonged study of the Bible, Parham, along with other preachers of the age, added a further stage: baptism in the Holy Spirit, the overwhelming entrance of God's divine power into the soul, sealing both conversion and sanctification and readying the recipient for a life of Christian service. Here a problem arose: how could one recognize the arrival of this climactic third stage, of such burning importance to personal salvation? In December 1900, Parham set off on a three-day journey and asked his students at Bethel Bible School to ponder this question during his absence. Upon his return, he found to his astonishment that the students, poring over scripture, had unanimously agreed that the only reliable proof of baptism in the Spirit was glossolalia — speech delivered, under the influence of the Holy Spirit, in a language unknown to the speaker and, in most cases, to his or her listeners as well.

There is some evidence that Parham had already decided on glossolalia as the litmus test of Spirit baptism and that this tale of student inspiration is more fancy than fact. In any event, Parham and his students jointly proposed three New Testament precedents for speaking in tongues:

- At Pentecost, when the Holy Spirit descended with "a sound from heaven as of a rushing mighty wind," tongues of fire hovered over each of the apostles, and all "began to speak with other tongues, as the Spirit gave them utterance" (Acts 2:1–4).
- A few years later, in Caesarea, when Peter was preaching and the Holy Spirit descended upon Jews and Gentiles alike, "they heard them speak with tongues, and magnify God" (Acts 10:44–46).
- In Ephesus, when the Holy Spirit descended as Paul was baptizing disciples of John the Baptist, "they spake with tongues, and prophesied" (Acts 19:1–6).

Glossolalia did not end with the apostolic age. In the second century, the heretic Montanus and his followers would be seized by raptures and prophesy in unintelligible languages, and during the eighteenth and nineteenth centuries scattered evangelical groups also spoke in tongues. For the most part, however, it was an obscure phenomenon, little known and little appreciated, especially in the refined, restrictive Protestant culture in which Parham preached and wrote. Nonetheless, he embraced his new theory. To demonstrate its validity, he sponsored a New Year's Eve worship service to usher in the new century, during which, serendipitously, a student by the name of Agnes Nevada Ozman stepped forward to pray with Parham for baptism in the Holy Spirit. As he later recalled,

> I laid my hands upon her and prayed. I had scarcely repeated three dozen sentences when a glory fell upon her, a halo seemed to surround her head and face, and she began speaking the Chinese language and was unable to speak English for three days. When she tried to write in English to tell us of her experience she wrote the Chinese, copies of which we still have in newspapers printed at that time.[44]

At the time of her exaltation, Ozman was thirty years old. A photograph taken shortly before her death, some four decades later, reveals a small, sweetly smiling woman with a bun of white hair and a black Bible tucked under her arm: an unassuming appearance but a prodigious presence, for the modern Pentecostal movement dates its inception from the moment she spoke in tongues at Bethel Bible College.

Events soon accelerated. Parham departed on another brief journey and discovered, upon his return, that a festival of tongue speaking had broken out, concentrated in a room on the second floor of the college:

> The door was slightly ajar, the room was lit with only coal oil lamps. As I pushed open the door I found the room was filled with a sheen of white light above the brightness of the lamps.
>
> Twelve ministers, who were in the school of different denominations, were filled with the Holy Spirit and spoke with other tongues. Some were sitting, some still kneeling, others standing with hands upraised. There was no violent physical manifestation, though some trembled under the power of the glory that filled them.
>
> Sister Stanley, an elderly lady, came across the room as I entered, telling me that just before I entered tongues of fire were sitting above their heads.[45]

Parham dropped to his knees to praise God and to beg for himself the gift of tongues. God answered that if he would spread this ministry "with all the persecutions, hardships, trials, slander, scandal that it would entail," his wish would be granted. When Parham consented, "right then there came a slight twist in my throat, a glory fell over me and I began to worship God in the Sweedish [*sic*] tongue, which later changed to other languages and continued so until the morning."[46]

Soon others at Stone's Folly discovered that they possessed an additional gift, described by Saint Paul in 1 Corinthians 14 (RSV) as "the power to interpret," that is, a knack for translating these tongues into lucid English. Languages spoken while in the Spirit soon included Russian, Bulgarian, Norwegian, Italian, Polish, and fifteen others. Native speakers confirmed their identity. This was more than linguistic pyrotechnics, even more than the supernatural imprimatur of baptism in the Holy Spirit. It was, Parham soon realized, a ticket to missionary glory, for laborious years of language study were now a thing of the past: a missionary merely had to go into the field, receive the Holy Spirit, and dispense the gospel teachings in words that, even if opaque to him or her, would be transparent to the listeners.

Inspired by these breathtaking events, Parham spread abroad the news that a "latter rain" of the Holy Spirit had arrived in the American heartland. He achieved great success in Galena, Kansas, in 1903, and in Houston, Texas, in 1905–6, founding schools and ministries and winning thousands of adherents, many of whom spoke in tongues or engaged in faith healing. Parham's future seemed assured: millions would flock to his side; the entire nation might turn to the Lord. It was not to be. Parham's fall was as rapid as his ascent; in 1907 he was arrested for sodomy in San Antonio, and although charges were dropped, his reputation was ruined. No matter. He had made his mark first by proclaiming loudly and steadily the importance of speaking in tongues as rock-hard evidence of Spirit baptism, the highest fruits of Christian prayer; and second, unbeknownst to him, by inspiring his successor, for among the students at his Houston Bible school was one William Joseph Seymour (1870–1922), who would transform Pentecostal prayer from a local American experience into a worldwide movement, breaking down racial barriers in the process.

Seymour had the makings of a classic American folk hero. He was black, the son of ex-slaves; penniless; blind in one eye from smallpox; humble, generous, and kind. It is difficult to think of anyone more unlike Charles Fox Parham — white, well-to-do, ambitious, arrogant, and powerful. Parham was also a racial bigot who heaped praise on the Ku Klux Klan. When Seymour enrolled in the Houston school in 1905, Parham insisted that he attend classes by sitting in the hallway and catching whatever snatches of lecture filtered through the door. Jim Crow notwithstanding, Seymour heard enough to be convinced that Parham had unlocked a secret of tremendous proportions. He resolved to carry on the great work.

Shortly after, Seymour received an invitation to preach in Los Angeles. There he proclaimed the necessity of the new baptism and its accompanying glossolalia and was promptly locked out of the church for his pains. Undaunted, he moved his meetings to a four-room home at 214 North Bonnie Bray Street, an address now legendary in Pentecostal circles. On the evening of April 9, 1906, Seymour and seven others, in the midst of prayer, began to writhe in ecstasy and speak in tongues. A young woman spread the news through the neighborhood. Soon a crowd gathered and watched one of the seven, Jennie Moore (later to become Mrs. Seymour), play a piano and sing in Hebrew, although she had not touched the instrument or attempted the language until that evening. The raptures continued unabated for several nights. As one eyewitness reports, "They shouted three days and nights. It was Easter season. The people came from everywhere. By the next morning there was no way of getting near the house. As people came in they would fall under God's power; and the whole city was stirred. They shouted until the foundation of the house gave way, but not one was hurt."[47]

The collapse of the house on North Bonnie Bray Street led to a search for new quarters. An ugly, abandoned whitewashed wooden stable was located in one of the poorest sections of the city, planks were laid on nail kegs for pews, shoeboxes were piled high for a pulpit, and on April 14, 1906, the Azusa Street Mission was born, to the prurient disgust of the *Los Angeles Times* and the rampant joy of thousands who streamed through its doors in search of spiritual renewal.

Azusa Street meetings were integrated. Men and women of every race joined in the services, the ecstasies, and the glossolalia. On some nights blacks predominated, on others, whites; almost always Asian and Hispanic people attended. Newspaper, choir, business office — every corner of the mission witnessed different races working side by side. This cohesion, a rarity in evangelical circles at this time, was so remarkable that one observer declared, utilizing apocalyptic imagery, that "the color line has been washed away by the blood." A journal published by the mission proclaimed that "one token of the Lord's coming is that He is melting all races and nations together, and they are filled with the power and glory of God." Some of this racial harmony spread to other areas of the country. G. B. Cashwell, an evangelist from North Carolina, returned from a visit to Azusa Street to announce that "the people of God are one here." Few Edens survive for long, however; racial tensions soon cleaved the community, and in 1914 Seymour restricted the key positions at the mission to "people of Color," an act that he later explained was necessary "in order to keep down race war in the Churches."[48]

Parham played a role in this racial dissension, for he visited the Azusa Mission soon after its reputation began to spread and was not pleased with what he found, complaining that "Men and women, whites and blacks, knelt together or fell across one another; frequently, a white woman, perhaps of wealth and culture, could be seen thrown back in the arms of a big 'buck nigger,' and held tightly thus as she shivered and shook in freak imitation of Pentecost. Horrible, awful shame!"[49]

What actually transpired at Azusa Street Mission services was, if hardly the scandal that Parham imagined, extraordinary in its own right. Meetings lasted from early morning until late at night. Prayers of praise, prayers for the sick, testimonies, preaching, talking and singing in tongues, and miraculous healings unfolded in no set order, one event following another as the Spirit dictated. Seymour orchestrated the goings-on with a loose hand, usually keeping to the background, head bowed, deep in prayer. Here is one eyewitness account:

> The altar is on a plank on two chairs in the center of the room, and here the Holy Ghost falls on men and women and children in old Pentecostal

> fashion as soon as they have a clear experience of heart purity. Proud preachers and laymen with great heads, filled and inflated with all kinds of theories and beliefs, have come here from all parts, have humbled themselves and got down, not "in the straw," but "on" the straw matting, and have thrown away their notions, and have wept in conscious emptiness before God and begged to be "endued with power from on high," and every honest believer has received the wonderful incoming of the Holy Spirit to fill and thrill and melt and energize his physical frame and faculties, and the Spirit has witnessed to His presence by using the vocal organs in the speaking forth of a "new tongue."[50]

The old walls of Protestant church organization, in most denominations as rigid as steel, came crumbling down. Historian Vinson Synan points out that glossolalia lay at the center of this antinomian impulse: "Here was an experience that truly cast aside the constraints of human convention and gave free rein to the Spirit. In ecstatic speech the action of human agency was completely denied, and the basic structure of language itself was set aside."[51] One visitor remembered the sense of spiritual improvisation that governed, or at least guided, each meeting:

> No subjects or sermons were announced ahead of time, and no special speakers for such an hour. No one knew what might be coming, what God would do. All was spontaneous, ordered of the Spirit. . . . Suddenly the Spirit would fall upon the congregation. God himself would give the altar call. Men would fall all over the house like the slain in battle, or rush for the altar en masse, to seek God. The scene often resembled a forest of fallen trees.[52]

This casting off of the conventions of polite behavior in favor of spiritual renewal soon captured the attention of the outside world. Visitors flocked to Azusa Street from across the nation, spoke in tongues, and returned home to spread the word. Sister churches sprang up in Oakland, San Diego, Seattle, and the East. As the movement blossomed, Seymour sent missionaries to China, Japan, the Philippines, Egypt, India, South America, and Europe. He published a journal, *Apostolic Faith,* that reached fifty thousand subscribers. Mainstream Protestant churches, realizing that something special, perhaps miraculous, was unfolding, began to hold Spirit-filled prayer meetings alongside their conventional orders of service. A number of churches converted wholesale from mainstream to Pentecostal worship.

This success did not sit well with many established ministries nor with Pentecostals inclined toward racial segregation. Azusa Street was denounced for promoting false religion, for witchcraft, for devil worship.

Some mainstream Protestant groups tried to shut it down, enlisting the help of the Los Angeles government. The fire department came to investigate claims of a mysterious glow emanating from the building; the health department, to check out complaints of perilous overcrowding; the child welfare department, in response to reports of too many youngsters wandering the premises. Seymour and his followers weathered these storms, praying and exalting God. The Azusa Street Mission flourished for several years, and in its flowering, it changed forever the face of American religion. In time the initial impulse weakened. In 1936, fourteen years after Seymour's death, the mission closed down and the building was sold. It was razed three years later and the site, which should have been declared a historical monument, became a city parking lot.

Such is the tale of one of the more fiery religious movements in a nation known for spiritual conflagrations. But what was really going on at Stone's Folly and Azusa Street? What is it that happens when someone speaks in tongues? By all accounts, it is, both viscerally and spiritually, an overwhelming experience. A. J. Tomlinson, a Bible salesman and influential preacher in the early days of the movement, wrote extensively about what happened to him on January 12, 1908, the day he was baptized in the Spirit. He describes total loss of motor control; he slipped to the floor; his feet shook, his lips "moved and twisted about as if a physician was making a special examination." Then, he recalls, "my body was rolled and tossed about beyond my control, and finally while lying on my back, my feet were raised up several times, and my tongue would stick out of my mouth in spite of my efforts to keep it inside my mouth." He finally found himself levitating several inches off the floor. This was cause not for horror, but for bliss. "Oh, such floods and billows of glory ran through my whole being for several minutes! There were times that I suffered the most excruciating pain and agony, but my spirit always said 'yes' to God." This joy was followed by visions in which he traveled to Central America, Brazil, Chile, Russia, Japan, and elsewhere, witnessing the suffering of the native peoples and speaking in tongues. He wrestled with the devil, saw the future, witnessed "multitudes coming to Jesus."[53]

To balance this rather florid account, it is helpful to consider the more polished, if hardly more sedate, memoir of J. Rodman Williams, a respected scholar who at the time of his first ecstasy in 1965 was professor of theology at Austin Presbyterian Theological Seminary in Texas. Williams's initiation into glossolalia began as he was reading a testimonial from a pastor who had himself recently spoken in tongues:

> As I read and reread the letter . . . I found myself being overcome. I was soon on my knees practically in tears praying for the Holy Spirit, and pounding the chair — asking, seeking, knocking — in a way I never had done before. . . . Then I knew it was happening. *I was being filled with His Holy Spirit.* . . . Instead of articulating rational words I began to ejaculate sounds of any kind, praying that somehow the Lord would use them. . . . Wave after wave, torrent after torrent, poured out. It was utterly fantastic; I was doing it and yet I was not. . . . Tears began to stream down my face — joy unutterable, amazement incredible. . . . I knew I was on earth, but it was as if heaven had intersected it — and I was in both.[54]

Merging the accounts of Tomlinson and Williams, we arrive at the two indelible features of glossolalia: the sense of surrender to a greater power and the bliss that ensues. The body spasms and surreal mental effects seem epiphenomena, cast off as surrender and bliss unfold. Other accounts of glossolalia include descriptions of strange lights, flashes, electrical discharges; automatic writing; paralysis; the ability to sing or play musical instruments without previous instruction or practice; even hallucinatory experiences of death and resurrection. The trigger for these remarkable events varies widely: sometimes it is prayer, sometimes laying on of hands, sometimes there is no apparent catalyst. Nor can one predict who will be penetrated by the Spirit; some are granted the experience spontaneously, instantaneously; some seek for years and never receive the gift. But whenever and however it arrives, it always contains the two crucial ingredients of absolute submission and absolute exaltation.

Such is the event; what is the cause? Most Pentecostals harbor no doubts. Through intense and often prolonged prayer, they have been filled with the Holy Spirit, the third Person of the Trinity, and they have received a gift and a sign, the power to speak in tongues as the apostles did on Pentecost. They have experienced what Parham and others refer to as the "latter rain" (Joel 2:23), a second Pentecost. Earth reaches up to heaven, heaven descends to earth, and a momentary paradise results. As writer John Sherrill describes the experience, "It was healing, it was forgiveness. . . . My will was released, free to soar into union with Him."[55]

Non-Pentecostals may take a more skeptical view. Some consider it all an elaborate fraud, as in this 1907 assessment of events at a Memphis church:

> The pastor pretended to speak the language of the Spirit and the wise ones of the congregation got onto his curves and began using a strange, idiotic jargon, which was alike meaningless to them and the preacher. . . .

> The minister would proclaim "Hicks, hicks!" and the congregation would answer back, "Sycamore, sycamore, sycamore!" and such insignificant words, which lifted the congregation to the highest point of ecstasy, showing what has been contended for years, that the Negro's religion is sound instead of sense.[56]

Happily, not all who reject the conventional Pentecostal explanation are so scathing in their assessment. Carl Jung, in *On the Psychology and Pathology of So-Called Occult Phenomena* (1902), likened glossolalia to somnambulism; later he would see it as the collective unconscious erupting into consciousness. Some psychologists describe it as a pathology and find parallels in the ramblings of schizophrenics. Others explain it as cryptomnesia, the subconscious retention of a language encountered and then forgotten earlier in life. Others suggest that it is a regression to infantile language forms, an emotional escape mechanism, a complex symptom of cultural disaffection, or an altered state of consciousness. Some linguists argue that it employs the basic structural units of language but is not itself a language. Against these interpretations one must place the claim of eyewitnesses that along with unrecognizable languages, they have discerned a multitude of real ones, from Chinese to Hebrew, rolling off the tongues of those in ecstasy.

Evidence abounds that glossolalia exists outside Pentecostalism in a variety of settings, from classical Greek prophecy to Siberian shamanism. Many of these non-Christian examples include the uttering of strange, unclassified languages. It remains unclear, however, how closely such cases parallel Pentecostal glossolalia and whether examples stripped of the religious suppositions and accoutrements of Pentecostalism can be considered comparable. In any case, similarity of effect hardly proves identity of cause.

The findings of a study published in the *Journal of Religion and Health* in 1974 may be more instructive; research determined that Pentecostal prayer leads to tolerance, social openness, and efficient use of time. As William James might put it, glossolalia's "fruits for life" are many and satisfying. Not least, it has given us a new form of sacred language. In other traditions, prayer is often framed in a language, such as Sanskrit, Hebrew, Arabic, or Latin, especially suitable for sacred activities; in Pentecostalism, prayer gives birth to something never before witnessed, except by the apostles: a tongue co-created by God and human to offer praise on high, to drench the heart in joy, and, it may be, to confound the nonbelievers.

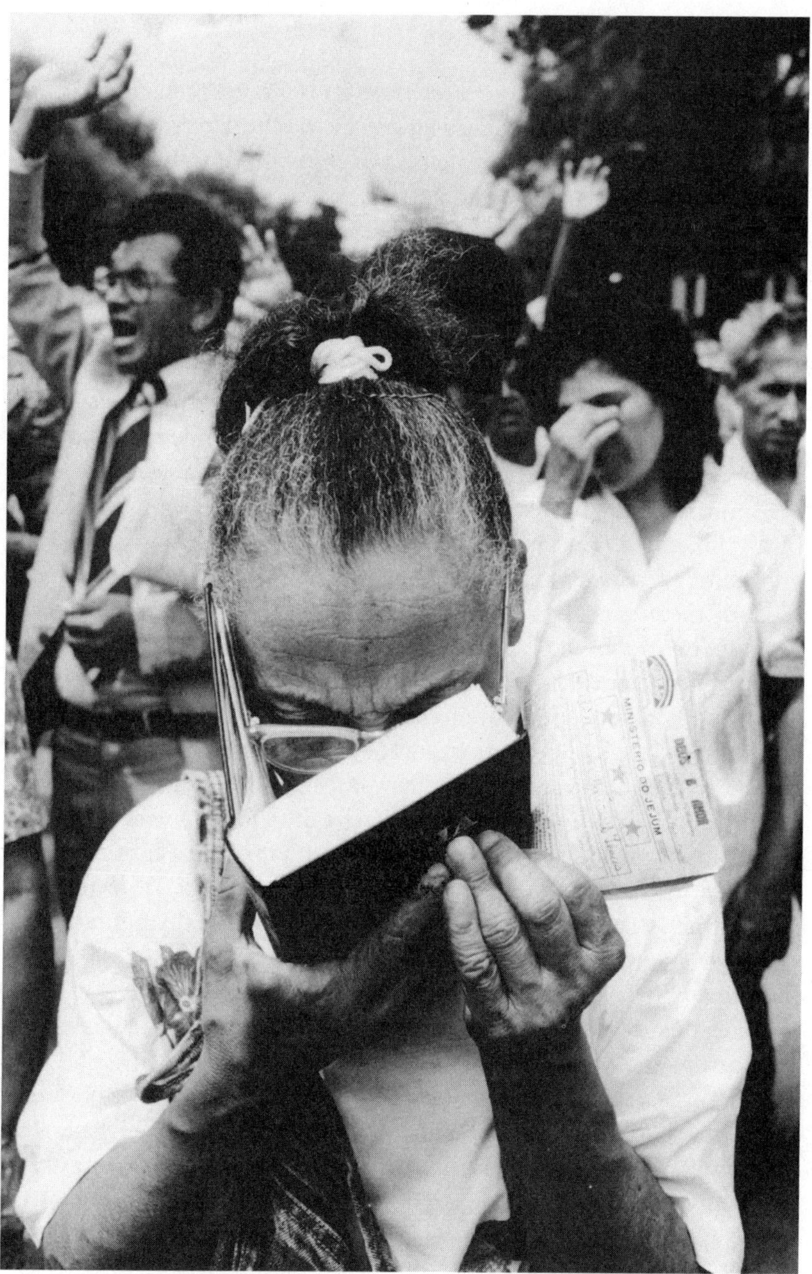

Brazilian Pentecostal believers praying on the street.

Vodun

If the democracy of ecstatic prayer finds its richest expression in Pentecostalism, the invasion of the worshiper by the third Person of the Holy Trinity, it achieves an equally intense and more catastrophic mode when divine invasion becomes divine possession. Witness the curious case of American avant-garde filmmaker Maya Deren (1917–1961). Born in the Ukraine, Deren came to the United States at the age of five. After college at New York University, she turned to the cinema, producing a series of experimental works characterized by innovative camera work and dreamlike narratives. These films rapidly established Deren as a major voice on the American art scene; a still from her first film, *Meshes of the Afternoon* (1943), which depicts her gazing out of a window, her face soft and lovely as a Renaissance Madonna, was widely reproduced and made her something of a poster child for the avant-garde. "She appeared like a Botticelli," noted Anaïs Nin in her diary.[57]

Deren first visited Haiti in 1947, planning to film native ritual dances. Most of these dances revolved around Vodun (also known as Voudon, Voudou, or voodoo), a blend of Catholicism and native African beliefs and practices centered on the worship of spirits, the most prominent of which are known as *lwa* (or, in Deren's orthography, *loa*). To some extent, this worship is a familiar matter of prayer and sacrifice — singing to the *lwa* or sacrificing animals to them. But the core ritual practice is decidedly unusual: spirit possession, whereby the subject enters an ecstatic trance and is inhabited by a *lwa,* who becomes for a time his or her animating principle. Vodun practitioners describe this process by means of a somewhat startling analogy, that of horse and rider: the human horse *(chwal)* is mounted by the spirit rider. What spectators see is a dancer — the ritual entails long stretches of drumming and movement — staggering about as if under tremendous physical pressure and then assuming the posture, look, and actions of the possessing divinity.

All this Deren knew by the time she had attended a number of Vodun ceremonies. What she did not anticipate was that she, a white American, a visiting artist, a complete outsider, with no roots in or deep connection to Haitian culture, would become the mount for the *lwa* known as Erzulie. In the Vodun pantheon, Erzulie is the goddess of love; Deren would also describe her as "Lady of Luxury" and, in a passage worthy of her most surrealist celluloid images, as "the dream impaled eternally upon the cosmic cross-roads where the world of men and the world of divinity meet."[58]

Deren's adventure began one warm evening — she never specified the date — as the sound of Vodun drums filled the air. At first the ceremony seemed like others she had witnessed. She chatted with the *houngan* (priest), took part in preliminary rituals, and heard prayers invoking Damballah, a benevolent spirit who appears in the form of a serpent. She sang and danced, swept up in the "glorious movement" of the night, when the *lwa* struck: "I take two steps and my left leg suddenly roots, numbly, to the ground, pitching me forward."[59] This forward stagger is a common sign that a *lwa* is attempting to mount. Deren continued to watch the ceremony, but now she was afraid. What was happening to her? She quit the ritual grounds, but then, mustering her courage, returned. To run away would be cowardice; it would mean that she was a dilettante, not a seeker.

Deren rejoined the dance; the assembly was now chanting prayer songs invoking Erzulie. These songs are not composed by the singers; they come directly from the *lwa,* who transmit them to human beings in dreams or during possession. Listening and swaying to the songs, Deren absorbed their power. The complicated, vigorous dance movements, which had felt exhausting and painful, now became easy and light; she found that she was standing outside herself, observing herself as if from afar. Looking around, she noticed that the other dancers had withdrawn, and then

> I realize, like a shaft of terror struck through me, that it is no longer myself whom I watch. Yet it *is* myself, for as that terror strikes, we two are made one again, joined by and upon the point of the left leg which is as if rooted to the earth. Now there is only terror. "This is it!" Resting upon that leg I feel a strange numbness enter it from the earth itself and mount. . . . I must call it a white darkness, its whiteness a glory and its darkness, terror. It is the terror which has the greater force.[60]

Then her awareness began to flicker; she watched herself first here, then there, "and whatever lay between these moments is lost, utterly lost. . . . in that dead space and that dead time." The drums beat, and she felt the white darkness flood up her legs. "'Mercy!' I scream within me. I hear it echoed by the voices, shrill and unearthly: '*Erzulie!*' The bright darkness floods up through my body, reaches my head, engulfs me. I am sucked down and exploded upward at once. That is all."[61]

Deren provides no account of the possession itself, only of its prelude. Possession is, for the possessed, beyond description, for when the *lwa* mounts, the soul of the horse wanders off, as it does in sleep or death.

She did, however, ask others what they had witnessed and, in particular, whether her ecstasy had qualified as an authentic possession. She was assured that it had, that Erzulie, inhabiting her body, had behaved as one might expect — acting the coquette, dancing gracefully, laughing and weeping, accepting and dispensing gifts, advice, and love.

What should we make of all this? Deren emphatically rejects the reductionist explanations forwarded by skeptics, theories bearing a close kinship to those advanced against the claims of Pentecostals. Possession by the *lwa,* she contends, has nothing to do with the popular notion that it provides a screen for orgiastic sexual activity. Nor does it relate to hysteria, for instead of releasing unconscious impulses, it institutes "a highly formalized, disciplined identity, that of the loa."[62] She concedes that parallels exist between possession and hypnotism — ability to climb impossible heights, imperviousness to pain, and so on — but she underscores the differences, above all, that hypnosis requires relaxed acquiescence, whereas possession takes place in spite of intense resistence.

As for her own personal beliefs, Deren circles around the issue, insisting that "as a metaphysical and ritualistic structure Voudon *is a fact,* and does exist, and . . . incorporates values with which I am in personal agreement, displays an organizational, psychic, and practical skill which I admire, and accomplishes results of which I approve." One senses that she has erected brackets around her affirmation: Vodun is real for her as long as she is in the Vodun cosmos, but whether these personifications, concretized in the *lwa,* have ontological autonomy — whether they exist on their own apart from human imagination — is a question around which she dances like a *lwa* handling its *chwal.* In any case, Vodun possession, despite the unremitting terror, so different from the explosive joy of Pentecostal baptism, contains its own reward, for it affirms the infinite abyss of the human soul, and this, writes Deren, "soothes all the diversity of singular fears, personal losses and private anxieties" associated with possession.[63]

Deren's experience with Vodun — the emotional intensity, the loss of control, the battles with skeptics, the ambiguities about its larger meaning — is familiar to any observer of ecstatic prayer. Reports of extraordinary events abound, yet upon close scrutiny, contradictions arise. In Robert Musil's novel *The Man Without Qualities,* the title hero, fascinated by descriptions of ecstatic experiences, describes this apparent conflict:

> They speak of an overflowing radiance. Of an infinite expanse, an infinite brilliance of light. . . . Of flashes of knowledge so swift that every-

> thing is simultaneous and like drops of fire falling into the world. And on the other hand they speak of a forgetting and no longer comprehending, of everything utterly sinking away. . . . They call it an undoing of the self, and at the same time they declare they live more fully than ever.[64]

And yet, the narrator insists, one cannot help but feel that something real is being conveyed: "If you could read straight through all these descriptions that men and women of past centuries have left of their states of divine ecstasy, you'd find that there's truth and reality somewhere there in all the printed words."[65]

This sense of "truth and reality" in ecstasy persists in spite of a continuing barrage from the skeptics. Both Ramakrishna and Teresa have been dismissed as mad or as victims of their own rampaging libidos; the experience of religious ecstasy has been ascribed, as we have already seen, to any number of causes, from infantile regression, to deliberate fraud, social dislocation, and biochemical agents.

To these objections to ecstasy four responses may be offered. First, it is the very incomprehensibility of the event that makes it so valuable, and that leads human beings, despite the sufferings involved, to engage in ecstatic prayer. Ecstasy carries us beyond this humdrum world into a foretaste of eternity. To ask why we engage in this form of prayer is, in a sense, to ask why a child spins until she grows dizzy and falls to the floor: it is to fly out of herself and into the secret heart of the spinning cosmos. Second, ecstasy has both a metaphysical and a moral function. For Ramakrishna, as his disciple Vivekananda puts it, visions and raptures were "milestones on the way to progress," steps toward *samādhi;* for Teresa, they were pathways to Christ; for Pentecostals, a way of receiving the Holy Spirit; for Deren, signs of the "imperturbable principles of cosmic good." Third, any number of things trigger religious ecstasy, and among them may well be the genuine presence of the numinous, as D. H. Lawrence indicates in this florid but informative passage from the novel *The Rainbow:*

> Then he pushed open the door, and the great, pillared gloom was before him, in which his soul shuddered and rose from her nest. His soul leapt, soared up into the great church. . . . Here in the church, "before" and "after" were folded together, all was contained in oneness. . . . Here the stone leapt up from the plain of earth, leapt up in a manifold, clustered desire each time, up, away from the horizontal earth, through twilight and dusk and the whole range of desire, through the swerving, the declination, ah, to the ecstasy, the touch, to the meeting and the consummation, the meeting, the clasp, the close embrace, the neutrality, the perfect, swoon-

> ing consummation, the timeless ecstasy. There his soul remained, at the apex of the arch, clinched in the timeless ecstasy, consummated.[66]

Finally, as Musil's narrator points out, raptures may be closer to our own experience than we realize or are willing to admit: "Aren't they, even though flickeringly veiled by the difficulty of expressing them at all, the same sensations one has even today when it chances that the heart — 'ravenous and satiated,' as they say! — suddenly finds itself in those utopian regions that lie somewhere and nowhere between an infinite tenderness and an infinite loneliness?"[67]

Perhaps we should be grateful for those, more intrepid than us, willing to enter these vast, uncharted regions and return with testimonies of grace given and received.

CHAPTER 7

The Contemplative

WORDS, LIKE ALL LIVING THINGS — and who can doubt that words have life? — contract or expand in response to their environment. Thus *car,* an ancient term (dating at least to the fourteenth century) that once meant any wheeled conveyance — chariot, wagon, carriage, truck — has shrunk in ordinary modern usage to designate the automobile, while *call,* formerly limited in meaning to a summons or a shout, has expanded to include a telephone chat, a poker challenge, and an umpire's ruling in baseball. Words reflect the world around them. When it comes to the lexicon of prayer, no word has undergone more dramatic alteration, in response to changes in its cultural environment, than *contemplation.*

The sacred character of contemplation is affirmed at the outset, for the term derives from Latin *templum* (temple or shrine). One senses this quality even when the word refers to the sense of pondering, as in Rembrandt's painting *Aristotle Contemplating a Bust of Homer* (1653). Although there is nothing specifically religious about the scene, the canvas evokes, through the wonder in the philosopher's eyes and the absolute stillness of his pose, metaphysical mysteries of time, death, and eternity. In classical Athens and Rome, and during the patristic centuries of the church, contemplation designated the highest activity of the mind, the function of the intellect when released from the burden of passions, desires, and discursive reason: in effect, the flight to God. As such, contemplation can be said to contain and complete all forms of prayer. This understanding flourished in the High Middle Ages, as evidenced in the following lovely passage from Richard of St. Victor (d. 1173):

> Thinking roams about, meditation investigates, contemplation wonders. Thinking arises from the imagination, meditation from the reason, con-

> templation from the intelligence. Behold these three, imagination, reason, intelligence. Intelligence takes the highest place, imagination the lowest, reason lies between them. Everything which comes under the view of the lower sense, comes necessarily also under the view of the higher sense. . . . Behold then how wide is the extent of the ray of contemplation; for it embraces all things.[1]

Beginning in the seventeenth century, contemplation fell under the microscope of modern scholasticism, and more technical definitions arose. Terms such as *acquired contemplation, infused contemplation, the prayer of quiet, the prayer of union, the prayer of spiritual marriage,* and the like began to proliferate. These are not meaningless distinctions; the modern scholastics were canny men, and their taxonomy corresponds to genuine if sometimes overlapping interior experiences. But all this parsing of prayer had an unforeseen result: the net effect was to turn the analysis of prayer, obviously a useful study, into a dry academic exercise, divorced from the considerably more messy adventures of real contemplatives in their monastic cells.

In recent years, a strong reaction to this taxonomy has set in, and scholastic classifications, for the most part, now hold little claim on contemplatives or those who study them. This change has breathed new life into writings on the subject, as the work of Thomas Merton amply demonstrates, but this intellectual housecleaning has not been entirely beneficial. Suddenly the meaning of contemplation has stretched, like Turkish taffy, until it has become all things to all people. Watching birds in flight, soaking up the sun, listening to a Joni Mitchell ballad — all this has become part of the current contemplative stock-in-trade. None of this is particularly objectionable and such examples may not have raised too many medieval eyebrows, but the same cannot be said of the commercialization of contemplation. Nowadays beauty spas offer, alongside body wraps and pedicures, a session in a "contemplation chamber," complete with incense and calming music, and a number of mega-corporations teach contemplative techniques as one tool in the arsenal for minding the bottom line. Contemplation, like the closely allied practice of meditation, has become a magical elixir that promises, if not eternal life, at least a beautiful body and a padded wallet.

What explains contemplation's shifting colors, its chameleon-like character? The answer lies at least partially in its peculiar nature as a wordless form of prayer. Teresa of Ávila described contemplation as a "close sharing between friends" (that is, oneself and God), a kind of communion of heart to heart. Unfolding beyond discursive thought, contemplation resembles music more than any other form of prayer.

Like music, it defies pigeonholing or clear-cut definition. We may approach it as pure technique, as a finely tooled method for encountering God, but many great contemplatives have had no interest in technique. We may approach it as a mental art, usually associated with silence and stillness, but classical Indian dance, *bhāratanātyam,* employs music and movement to achieve divine union in a contemplative art par excellence. We may approach it as a quasi-mathematical abstraction, as Plotinus does in calling it the "flight of the alone to the Alone," but this lofty expression does little to abate our ignorance.

The mysterious reality is that contemplation, unlike other forms of prayer, is not an event in life. It is a way of life. A photo of someone in contemplation, comparable to the image of Ramakrishna in ecstasy described in the previous chapter, reveals nothing of value. One seeks in vain for distinguishing marks akin to the ecstatic's rolled-back eyes or sagging limbs. The contemplative is the most invisible of beings; thus the ancient monastic formulation that the contemplative enjoys a life "hidden in God." His contemplation is his life. No one appreciated this better than Emily Dickinson, most invisible of poets, who passed her years in the Yankee cloisters of an Amherst manse:

I dwell in Possibility —
A fairer House than Prose —
More numerous of Windows —
Superior — for Doors —

Of Chambers as the Cedars —
As Impregnable of Eye —
And for an Everlasting Roof
The Gambrels of the Sky —

Of Visitors — the fairest —
For Occupation — This —
The spreading wide my narrow Hands —
To gather Paradise — [2]

Contemplation is a matter of windows, doors, the open sky — symbols of possibility — a matter of spreading wide the hands to "gather Paradise." Is it any wonder that those with the most contemplative experience rarely speak of contemplative prayer? They prefer to talk of the contemplative life, of a pattern of behavior that embraces all modes of prayer but is characterized, above all, by *openness:* to God and to the world.

Contemplation, they say, is like being in love. The borders of one's being melt; lover and beloved unite. The contemplative life may entail an austere effort of bare attention or a rapturous surrender to God. It may include silence or song, stillness or dance, solitude or companionship, self-collection or wild abandon. Every element finds its place in the grand festival; contemplation is the prayer that wears a thousand carnival masks; it is the Mardi Gras of prayer. Let us meet some of the revelers.

The Warrior

Nowhere is contemplation's extravagant, even seriocomic nature more apparent than in the life of Abba Antony of the Desert (251–356). Of the contemplatives of Christian antiquity, that legion of men and women who sought the intimate company of God at almost any price, he is at once the most remote, the most mysterious, and the most influential. To modern eyes, he may appear a monstrosity or a fool: how else to describe a man who locked himself in a ruined fortress for twenty years while wrestling with demons and undertaking ascetic rigors that make one blanch? Antony wore ragged clothing, he wallowed in dirt and filth, no doubt he stank. Contrary to legend, he did know how to read and write, but clearly he was rough, not just around the edges but straight through to the core. He was, to put it simply, a man of the desert. Yet his harsh figure and extravagant acts were entirely consistent with contemplation. For the monks of Egypt and the Sinai, the contemplative life was a struggle, a bout, an athletic competition, or even a war. "You have entered on a fine contest" read the first words of Athanasius's *Life of Antony* (c. 360), our primary source of information about the saint's life. The monk competed against his fellows, to see who would prove first in discipline and foremost in virtue; against the devil, who sought at every turn to thwart the holy life; and against his own corrupt nature, his tendency toward lust, gluttony, and acedia. To be a contemplative was to don armor and shield, to be a warrior for Christ.

For Antony, the call to arms came much as it did for the Russian pilgrim one thousand five hundred years later: through overhearing a scriptural passage read aloud in church. In the pilgrim's case, as you may recall, the text in question was Saint Paul's exhortation to the Thessalonians to pray without ceasing. What befell Antony was even more dramatic, for he heard Christ himself demand that "if thou wilt be perfect, go and sell that that thou hast and give to the poor, and thou shalt have treasure in heaven" (Matthew 19:21). According to Athanasius, Antony felt "as if the passage had been read on his account." Although only twenty years old, orphaned, and thus responsible for the welfare of his younger sister, he responded with alacrity. He sold his land—"three hundred acres, productive and very fair"[3] — and the bulk of his other possessions and distributed the proceeds to the poor, retaining just enough to support his sister. But was this a sufficient response to Christ's call? Returning to church, he heard a second gospel saying delivered from the pulpit, as if in direct answer to his concerns: "Take therefore no thought for the morrow" (Matthew 6:34). Antony was thunderstruck; half measures would no longer suffice. Immediately he disposed of the remainder of his estate, put his sister in the care of trusted friends, and resolved to undertake what was commonly known as "the discipline": rigorous, painful training in self-mastery and prayer.

Antony adopted a moderate course — moderate, that is, by monastic standards of the day, although it will strike many today as extreme. He turned his back on his past life, resolving never again to think of his sister or other relatives. Remaining at first in his native village, he sought out experts in prayer and absorbed their knowledge. Like the Russian pilgrim more than a millennium later, he was "constant in prayer, knowing that a man ought to pray in secret unceasingly."[4] Unfortunately, Athanasius does not tell us the content of these prayers, but it is likely that they consisted largely of meditating on scripture and reciting the Lord's Prayer and the Psalms.

All this sat well with fellow ascetics, who bestowed upon him the happy name of "God-loved." It seems, however, that Antony's labors did not please the devil. As Athanasius puts it, "The devil, who hates and envies what is good, could not endure to see such a resolution in a youth, but endeavoured to carry out against him what he had been wont to effect against others."[5] Antony's battles against the Evil One constitute one of the great mythological tales in the Christian canon. A sense of their frightening intensity and lurid brightness can be gleaned from the many artistic depictions of the conflict. Hieronymus Bosch's triptych *The Temptation of Saint Antony* (1500) presents a truly nightmarish picture, depicting the saint under assault by a galaxy of cavorting demons and other hideous creatures, including a fish sprouting human hands and a harp-playing harpy. Other portraits by Solvado, Callot, Huys, Tintoretto, and Grünewald address the same theme, each with its own hallucinatory horrors. Our old friend Dali joined the fray, painting in 1946 a naked, kneeling Antony brandishing a cross before a caravan of approaching monstrosities, mostly elephants with impossibly spindly legs bearing on their backs an array of phallic symbols (obelisk, tower, trumpet). Dali executed this fever dream for an international competition, sponsored by an American film company, to produce the best modern *Temptation*. The winner was Max Ernst, who submitted a rich, barbaric landscape in which hairy, fanged demons assail the saint in a primordial swamp ringed by cliffs of rock, vegetation, and rotting human flesh. Like almost all images of Antony's temptation, Ernst's painting is unspeakably grotesque.

What these pictures cannot convey is the increasing intensity of the demonic attacks. At first the devil attacked Antony with tantalizing memories of his parents, his sister, his favorite foods. When these failed to sway the saint, the devil appeared as a lustful woman. Antony spurned her advances and increased his mortifications. Henceforth he ate but once a day, slept on bare earth, and spent the night immersed in prayer. More important, he accepted fully the goal that would become that of all Christian contemplatives. Athanasius puts it thus: "He eagerly endeavored to make himself fit to appear before God, being pure in heart and ever ready to submit to His counsel, and to Him alone."[6] This intense preparation for the presence of God lies at the core of the contemplative mission.

Longing for an isolated environment more conducive to prayer and sacrifice, Antony moved out of his home and into a nearby tomb. There the devil began a third stage of torments, assaulting the saint with whips, earthquakes, and a plague of demons who took the form of wild beasts — asps, leopards, lions, wolves, scorpions, bulls. They raked Antony with teeth and claws but failed to disturb his mind, which remained "unmoved and even more watchful." Indeed, he retained enough wit to note that the devil was overplaying his hand; if the powers of darkness truly ruled, a single wild beast would have sufficed. Nonetheless, there seems little doubt that Antony — bloodied, torn, and exhausted — was in a perilous state. The future looked bleak, for were not the devil's resources inexhaustible? Suddenly, in a glorious deus ex machina, the roof of the tomb opened and God descended as a beam of light. In a flash Antony's pains vanished, the demons fled, and the tomb walls, wrecked by the assault, rejoined into a solid edifice. In a moment of high comedy the exhausted saint, instead of falling to his knees in worship, demanded to know just where God had been all this time. The Lord replied, "Antony, I was here, but I waited to see thy fight; wherefore since thou hast endured, and has not been worsted, I will ever be a succor to thee, and will make thy name known everywhere."[7]

The next day Antony quit the tombs for yet more remote quarters. Here began the most fantastic portion of his tale. Walking toward distant mountains, he stumbled across an empty fortress filled with reptiles and decided to call it home. The beasts fled, and Antony sealed himself inside the ruins. He remained there, utterly alone, for twenty years. Every six months devotees left him a new supply of bread and water. Apart from these furtive visits he heard no one, saw no one, touched no one, addressed no one. During these two decades of isolation, Antony perfected the prototype of the Christian contemplative: a man or woman who withdraws from the world (but, as we shall see, usually not as completely as Antony) in order to do combat with darkness, within or without, and come face to face with God. These years witnessed, too, the perfection of prototypical contemplative tools. Fasting, wakefulness, silence, and other austerities weakened the grip of worldly passions; recitation of the Psalms and the Lord's Prayer defended against demons; frequent recourse to other forms of prayer — petition, thanksgiving, even mantra-like repetition of simple phrases — although rarely or never mentioned by Athanasius, no doubt played their part in strengthening heart and mind; and the naked love of God, directing the will toward holiness, sustained the saint through years of aridity and suffering.

Antony entered his fort at the age of thirty-five, in about 286 C.E. During his entombment, his circle of devotees increased dramatically. Over the years they grew restless, eager both for instruction from the master and for his very presence, which conveyed *baraka* (spiritual power). By 306 they had waited long enough. Arriving en masse, they tore down the fortress door. What followed has the quality of a miracle or a fairy tale:

> Antony, as if from a shrine, came forth initiated in the mysteries and filled with the spirit of God. Then for the first time he was seen outside the fort by those who came to see him. And they, when they saw him, wondered at the sight, for he had the same habit of body as before, and was neither fat, like a man without exercise, nor lean from fasting and striving with the demons, but he was just the same as they had known him before his retirement. And again his soul was free of blemish, for it was neither contracted as if by grief, nor relaxed by pleasure, nor possessed by laughter or dejection, for he was not troubled when he beheld the crowd, nor overjoyed at being saluted by so many. But he was altogether even as being guided by reason, and abiding in a natural state.[8]

Nor was the change limited to Antony alone, for his power soon transformed his world: "Through him the Lord healed the bodily ailments of many present, and cleansed others from evil spirits. And He gave grace to Antony in speaking, so that he consoled many that were sorrowful, and set those at variance at one, exhorting all to prefer the love of Christ before all that is in the world." From this time on Antony, or at least the ascetic movement of which he became the legendary symbol, dominated the religious landscape of his age. He urged on the faithful, thundered against heretics, and planted monasticism firmly in the deserts of the Egyptian Thebaid. "And thus it happened in the end," writes Athanasius, "that cells arose even in the mountains, and the desert was colonized by monks, who came forth from their own people, and enrolled themselves for the citizenship in the heavens."[9] Demonic attacks continued to plague Antony — the Archfiend, it seems, never gives up the battle — but all were successfully repelled. Sustained, too, were the miraculous healings, along with other paranormal powers, most notably clairvoyance. By the time of his death Antony was famous throughout the Middle East, and even Emperor Constantine sought his advice. He was buried, in keeping with his character, in an anonymous grave; Athanasius, although an influential bishop, did not know the location.

Thus the career of Abba Antony of the Desert. What do we make of it? Many will feel uneasy about the details — demonic assaults, heavenly intercessions — although such events still are matters of course, or at least of belief, in most religions. In any case, these fantastic elements are essential to the mythic qualities of the tale, and it is the myth of Antony that matters: Antony as slayer of demons and slayer of the ego, as soldier of God and servant to all who seek God. In this myth, prayer and spiritual combat go hand in hand; this twin movement of surrender of self and surrender to God reveals, even allowing for hyperbole on the part of the adoring Athanasius, a man of extraordinary spiritual attainment. The qualities that Antony exemplifies — equilibrium, moderation, fortitude, self-mastery, faith — will ever be counted among the high contemplative virtues. Antony, however, would have said that he did not possess them. He possessed nothing; he was but a destitute monk; what others perceived as his goodness was merely the goodness of God, reflected in an inadequate mirror. One is reminded of Mother Teresa of Calcutta, spiritual descendant of Antony, who said that "I am but a pencil with which God writes as He wills."

Antony not only helped establish the rationale and rules of the contemplative life; he also had a hand in determining its daily rhythms. His template for this life combines prayer and scriptural study, prayer and physical labor, prayer and ascetic disciplines, prayer and battle with demons. The goal of these disciplines is summed up in one word: *purity*. This term is often associated with Antony, for whom it meant the radical restructuring of the human being, removal of the stains inflicted by sin, and restoration by grace of original innocence. The importance of purity permeates that small but precious treasure trove, the seven extant letters written by Antony. Here he writes of the rewards of spiritual battle: "The mind is taught by the Spirit and guides us in the actions of the body and soul, purifying both of them, separating the fruits of the flesh from what is natural to the body, in which they were mingled, and through which the transgression came to be, and leads each member of the body back to its original condition, free from everything alien that belongs to the spirit of the enemy."[10]

This is closely akin to Platonic teachings about the goal of contemplation. In the *Phaedo,* Socrates explains that the aim of life is *sophia* (wisdom), "for it is wisdom that makes possible courage and self-control and integrity or, in a word, true goodness." The path to this lofty end entails purgation, the eradication of fear, lust, and the other passions, and the acquisition of perfect balance of mind and body — the exact state that Antony attained after twenty years of battling demons. These demons lurked within as well as outside the saint; as historian Peter Brown puts it, "The demonic stood not only for all that was hostile *to* man; the demons summed up all that was anomalous and incomplete *in* man." Slaying demons is violent work, but it is also an act of love. Wielding the sword of contemplation, one simultaneously repels the demonic and gravitates toward the holy. It is all one action: the expulsion of evil, the embrace of the true, the beautiful, and the good — of God, Antony would say — the recollection of lost wisdom, of "the realm of the pure and everlasting and immortal and changeless." Antony stands, then, as the son of ancient Greek contemplation and the father of Christian contemplation, an exemplar for pagans and baptized alike, proof that battles of flesh, mind, and spirit all have a role to play in the life of the contemplative.[11]

The Lover

Antony both inspires and repels. One wants to watch and admire him rather than follow him. He paints the contemplative life in broad, violent strokes — seek solitude, pray the Psalms, combat demons — a prescription that suited the harsh climate of the Egyptian desert and its rough inhabitants but might have proved too fierce to nurture the contemplative life under less extreme conditions. Fortunately, others of a gentler disposition — less martial, more domestic — appeared later, among them Augustine (354–430), John Cassian (c. 360–c. 430), Benedict of Nursia (c. 480–c. 550), Gregory the Great (c. 540–604), Bernard of Clairvaux (1090–1153), Richard of St. Victor (d. 1173), Hildegard of Bingen (1098–1179), and Bonaventure (c. 1217–1274). Each added to our storehouse of knowledge about contemplative prayer and its application in everyday life, often in writings of exceptional profundity and beauty. But none of these men and women produced what we might call in the modern sense a guidebook — compact, comprehensive, eminently practical — to the contemplative life, or at least not one that enjoys widespread popular appeal today. Benedict comes closest in his celebrated Rule, but that volume was composed for, and is still largely applicable to, cloistered monks and nuns. When the breakthrough came, it arrived in the most unlikely of places: not in the great monasteries of Cluny or Cîteaux or in the great centers of learning such as Paris or Bologna, but in the bucolic East Midlands of England, among shepherds and cheese makers, in the second half of the thirteenth century, at the same time that Chaucer was writing his *Canterbury Tales.*

The identity of the author of *The Cloud of Unknowing* — for that is the name of our guidebook — remains a mystery. Some scholars argue, on the basis of the book's concluding blessing, redolent with liturgical language, that the author was a priest, a Dominican friar, or a Carthusian. In any event, we know that his language echoes the dialect of central England, a soil that would later produce Newton, Tennyson, and Dryden, and that he was intimately familiar with the prayer practices of the medieval English church, including the Divine Office, *lectio divina,* meditation, and silent prayer. His manner is blunt and powerful, like a ploughman or a hunter who had donned the habit, and he dislikes verbosity, in himself and others. The *Cloud* is only thirty thousand words long, divided into seventy-five succinct chapters, and, in one of its most famous passages, the author advises readers to pray in words of one syllable, for "short prayer penetrates heaven."[12] He is, in sum, a solid Englishman who has a vital message to deliver and goes about his business briskly, even brusquely.

His message, the importance of contemplative prayer and how to practice it, has roots in a sixth-century Neoplatonic text, *The Mystical Theology* of Pseudo-Dionysius the Areopagite (fl. c. 500). *The Mystical Theology,* dense and often obscure, provides in a few thousand words (far surpassing the *Cloud* in brevity) a map of the mystical ascent to God, with a pronounced emphasis on God's utter mystery and otherness. We cannot know God, says Pseudo-Dionysius, for he lies beyond all description, all intellection, all imagining. "The Cause of all is above all. . . . It is nothing known to us or to any other being. It falls neither within the predicate of nonbeing nor of being. . . . There is no speaking of it, nor name nor knowledge of it."[13]

How, then, shall we encounter this Being beyond all beings? By surrendering everything we know or imagine, by "renouncing all that the mind may conceive" in an act of self-abnegation — akin to Saint Antony's self-surrender but in a higher key. Now even the intellect must be abandoned in order to "be uplifted to the ray of the divine shadow which is above everything that is." This liberation from all created things and this accession to divinity takes place, Pseudo-Dionysius says, in a special realm of existence that he calls "the truly mysterious darkness of unknowing,"[14] the state of being that the author of the *Cloud* would describe seven centuries later in the more memorable metaphor of the cloud of unknowing.

The author of the *Cloud* improves on Pseudo-Dionysius in another way as well; in place of his predecessor's rather unappealing generic prescription of "absolute abandonment" as the key to contemplation, he offers an attractive and specifically Christian counsel: the way to God is the way of love. He agrees with Pseudo-Dionysius that God can never be reached through the intellect, for God is beyond all conceptions. Only love can bridge the gap. Through "the everlasting miracle of love," the author writes, "one loving soul by itself, through its love, may know for itself him who is incomparably more than sufficient to fill all souls that exist."[15] *Amor ipse intellectus est* (Love itself is understanding), as the twelfth-century Cistercians used to say.

Unfortunately, not everyone qualifies to tread this path. The *Cloud* opens with one of the most thunderous warnings in the annals of literature:

> I charge and beg you, with all the strength and power that love can bring to bear, that whoever you may be who possess this book (perhaps you own it, or are keeping it, carrying it, or borrowing it) you should, quite freely and of set purpose, neither read, write, or mention it to anyone, nor allow it to be read, written, or mentioned by anyone unless that person is in your judgment really and wholly determined to follow Christ perfectly.[16]

As for the "loud-mouthed, or flatterers, the mock modest, or fault-finders, gossips, tittle-tattlers, talebearers, or any sort of grumbler,"[17] it would be better if they never saw the book, for it would mean nothing to them. One might presume from this sweeping dismissal that the author limits his counsels on the contemplative life to an elect few, perhaps to professed monks. But this is not so: he takes pains to emphasize that anyone, whether cloistered in a monastery or active in the world, may undertake what he calls "the work." The prerequisites are a clean conscience, adherence to the ordinary religious duties prescribed by the

Church, and a burning zeal for contemplative encounter with God. With these in place, one may undertake contemplative prayer, a project that proceeds on three levels simultaneously.

1. *Training in the virtues.* A contemplative must be a saint or at least on the path to sanctity. The author of the *Cloud* pulls no punches; Antony's martial spirit colors his voice as he declares, "Pause for a moment, you wretched weakling, and take stock of yourself. Who are you, and what have you deserved, to be called like this by our Lord?"[18] The contemplative must long for God with all his might; he must beware of the devil's wiles; he must cleanse mind and heart, especially by cultivating humility. He must treasure every moment of prayer, including *lectio divina*, meditation, and private devotions, uniting himself with Christ and all the saints. This rigorous program may be easier than it seems, for when we order our being by making God the sun around which our desires orbit, virtue necessarily ensues. Virtue gives rise to contemplation; contemplation nurtures virtue.

2. *Perfection of the contemplative method.* Once a foundation of virtuous living has been established, a person is ready to engage in contemplative prayer. The *Cloud* author describes contemplation as "a simple steadfast intention reaching out towards God," or, more vividly, as "a sharp dart of living love." We will find, to our likely dismay, that instead of arriving at God, our longings achieve only darkness, the "cloud of unknowing." Our job is to stay within this cloud, to yearn, to pray, and to await, while enveloped in darkness, the presence of God. This work, the author assures us, is easy and quick: easy, because once we arrive in the cloud, we need only remain open to God, who may graciously descend to our level and surround our love with his own; quick, because propelling a dart of love toward the cloud is "neither shorter nor longer than a single impulse of your will."

Contemplation is a return to Eden, for it is the labor that Adam and Eve performed before the Fall. It is what we would all do, all the time, if not for original sin. As things stand, however, we will never in this lifetime experience an unclouded vision of God; the beatific vision is reserved for heaven alone, and the way back to Eden is blocked by an angel with a flaming sword. But we may through contemplation enjoy an awareness of God so glorious, even in its limited scope, that it will prove more beneficial than catching a glimpse of the angels and saints or hearing some bars of the "happy music of the blessed."[19]

3. *Abandonment of earthly things.* One major impediment must be overcome before our "blind outreaching love" can attain the strength and intensity needed to penetrate the cloud of unknowing. We must en-

ter a second cloud, "a cloud of forgetting," placing it between ourselves and all created things — not only vices and distractions that one might expect to be obstacles to prayer, but even thoughts of the saints, the Blessed Virgin Mary, and heaven. Here again the author of the *Cloud* speaks bluntly, almost brutally: all these reminders of created things must be "trampled down." If any thoughts arise during prayer, they are to be summarily crushed. If thoughts continue to plague us, we must simply ignore them and continue in our naked intention toward God. If these mental phantoms prove overwhelming, a third strategy is advised: we should admit our weakness, "cower down . . . like some cringing captive overcome in battle," and God, who is ever merciful, will come to our aid.[20]

Contemplation makes extraordinary demands on its practitioners. To reject all worldly thoughts while praying is a grueling enterprise; the mind is capricious (often likened to a monkey) and eagerly seizes any opportunity for woolgathering. The *Cloud* author addresses this problem by turning to the time-honored method of repetitive prayer, urging contemplatives to coalesce all their desire for God, all their ardor to pierce the cloud of unknowing, in the repeated utterance of a short word, preferably of a single syllable. He proposes *God* or *love*. This word plays a dual role: it suppresses thought under the cloud of forgetting, stopping the mind's restless habits of association, fantasy, and analysis, and it frees the naked will to penetrate the cloud of unknowing in an act of perfect love. With the help of this tool and aided by grace, the possibility exists of attaining "perfect contemplation."

Despite its brevity, down-to-earth prose, and nuts-and-bolts practical advice, *The Cloud of Unknowing* fell into obscurity soon after its appearance; as recently as 1961 a new edition of the book declared that "for most English-speaking Christians, *The Cloud of Unknowing* is not even a name." Yet recently the work has become one of the most influential Christian contemplative texts and a staple in the religion section of many bookstores. Two reasons explain this resurgence: an ample supply of good new translations, rendering the author's East Midlands dialect ("In the name of the Fader and of the Sone and of the Holy Goost") into forceful modern idiom, and the startling explosion of interest in practical spirituality that marked the second half of the twentieth century. The *Cloud*'s newfound success has not come without a price, however. As it has entered the mainstream, it has been adopted — and sometimes adapted beyond recognition — by many popular movements of the day. A 1957 edition by Ira Progoff, a depth psychologist, weds a mellifluous translation of the text with a wildly speculative introduction that attempts to wrench the core message of the *Cloud* out of its religious context, informing the bewildered reader that the *Cloud*'s "references to the Bible, to Jesus, and to the nature of God, have only a transitory significance"![21]

A more subtle appropriation emerged a few decades later, via the combined efforts of three Catholic monks, Fathers William Meninger, M. Basil Pennington, and Thomas Keating. Their adaptation, developed through years of study, writing, and prayer, came to be known as "centering prayer." As summarized in Pennington's 1980 bestseller, *Centering Prayer: Renewing an Ancient Christian Prayer Form,* this method entails distilling the *Cloud*'s seventy-five chapters into three basic steps or rules:

> *Rule 1:* At the beginning of the Prayer we take a minute or two to quiet down and then move in faith to God dwelling in our depths; and at the end of the Prayer we take several minutes to come out, mentally praying the "Our Father" or some other prayer.
>
> *Rule 2:* After resting for a bit in the center of faith-full love, we take up a single, simple word that expressed this response and begin to let it repeat itself within.
>
> *Rule 3:* Whenever in the course of the Prayer we become *aware* of anything else, gently return to the Presence by the use of the prayer word.[22]

It's easy to discern in this program the bare bones of the teaching of the *Cloud,* especially the effort to suppress awareness of created things and the use of a single prayer word. But one misses the boldness of the original, here replaced by painfully polite expressions ("the center of faith-full love"). No hint of the cloud appears, no reference to blind praying into a never-ending darkness. For the author of the *Cloud,* contemplative prayer is an arduous trial with an uncertain end; the centering prayer movement, for better or for worse, has turned it into a comfortable exercise with a foregone conclusion. Through centering prayer, Pennington writes, we attain "a constant, abiding joy and Presence."[23] These buoyant certainties have little in common with the *Cloud*'s hard-eyed realism and seem rather to partake of the Zeitgeist of the late twentieth century, with its spiritual eclecticism and optimism, much as the *Cloud*'s tone reflects the hard daily life and exquisite intellectual order of medieval Europe.

"My Vocation Is Love"

The Cloud of Unknowing and its descendants by no means exhaust the variations of contemplation in the key of love. In a sense, all Christian prayer depends on love. If, as the New Testament proclaims, "God is love" (1 John 4:8) and if only like can know like, then through love alone can we reach and know God. This perception has evolved over the centuries of Christianity into a form of contemplation characterized by what we may fairly call "the intoxication of desire." Three medieval women — Hadewijch (c. thirteenth century), Mechtild of Magdeburg (c. 1207–1282), and Gertrude of Helfta (1256–1301) — are representative; but this mode of contemplation would reach its apex in the life of the young woman whom Pope Pius X declared "the greatest saint of modern times": Thérèse of Lisieux (1873–1897). That designation may be in dispute — some would accord it to Mother Teresa of Calcutta — but certainly Thérèse is the most popular saint of modern times, her image de rigueur in devout Catholic households, her autobiography, *Story of a Soul,* a perpetual bestseller; and her life and works the subject of more books than any other contemporary Catholic figure, written by authors as diverse as Dorothy Day *(Thérèse)* and Vita Sackville-West *(The Eagle and the Dove).* Much of Thérèse's fame is due to her intense piety, her physical beauty, and her death from tuberculosis at the age of twenty-four. Her life is something of a fairy tale told backward, a reverse Cinderella story in which our heroine exchanges golden slippers for rough monastic sandals and embraces a life of self-denial and suffering. Yet like the original, this tale has a happy ending, suffused with prayer and sealed by love, in which death itself plays the fool.

As a young child Thérèse Martin knew nothing but affection. "My first memories," she writes, "are of smiles and the most tender caresses."[24] She dwelt in the plush bosom of late-nineteenth-century French mercantile society, a pampered princess holding court over her four older siblings (four others had died before she was born) and adoring parents in a sheltered realm of overstuffed mahogany and damascene furniture, silk and brocade dresses, well-bred manners, and well-cooked meals. Was she stifled by this warm but banal environment? Some of Thérèse's biographers have marveled that anything extraordinary could grow under such conditions. But the close-knit family life instilled in her an unshakable belief in the power of love, and the family's unflagging religious devotions — daily Mass, praying the rosary, fasting, keeping the Sabbath — taught her the closeness of God and the fragile beauty of earthly things. The dream soon fractured — she suffered from severe childhood illnesses, and her mother died when she was only age four — but overall it was a happy childhood, surrounded by doting relatives and filled with deeply felt if unexceptional pleasures.

On Christmas night, 1886, at the age of thirteen, Thérèse experienced what she called a conversion, a sudden deepening in her love of God and her desire for prayer. "I was a witness to that sudden change," remembered her sister Celine, "and I thought I was in a dream . . . her soul could be seen to develop and grow in the practice of zeal and charity." Thérèse didn't write at length about her conversion, but the little she reveals points to a life-changing event: "Satisfied with my good will, Our Lord accomplished in an instant the work I had not been able to do during years. Love and a spirit of self-forgetfulness took complete possession of my heart, and thenceforward I was perfectly happy." The immediate fruit of "this radiant night" was a conviction that God had called her to be a cloistered nun, following in the footsteps of her two older sisters, both of whom had received the veil at the Carmelite monastery in Lisieux. Thérèse brooked no opposition to this summons; when local ecclesiastical officials reasonably advised her to wait until she turned twenty-one, she rushed off to Rome, father in tow, to beg Pope Leo XIII to intervene. Never shy, she sought out the pontiff during his general audience, clutched his legs, and whispered in his ear, in violation of the rule of absolute silence, her passionate plea. The pope, no doubt bewildered by so much teenage ardor, muttered a genial "If God wills." God did will, the objections of the local officials evaporated, and Thérèse entered Carmel (the designation for all Carmelite monasteries) four months later.[25]

Even before entering the monastery, Thérèse had entered upon the hard road of self-giving and self-denial. She would live for others, she would love them through the intensity and splendor of her prayers. She vowed to take up impossible cases — reprobates, murderers, the greatest of sinners — and reclaim their souls. In the summer of 1887, when she was only fourteen, she read in the newspaper *La Croix* about Henri Pranzini, sentenced to the guillotine for the triple murder of two women and an eleven-year-old girl. Thérèse resolved to bring this vagabond-thug to God, declaring him her "first child" and entering an intense cycle of prayer, personal sacrifice, and attendance at Mass. She was certain she would succeed; God could not reject prayers so passionate and pure: "I was convinced to the depths of my heart that our desires would be granted, but to give me courage to go on praying for sinners I told God I was sure he would pardon poor unfortunate Pranzini and that I would believe it even if he did not go to confession or show any signs of repentance. I had such confidence in Jesus' infinite mercy . . ."[26] On the morning of his death, Pranzini, who showed no hint of repentance, refused to see a priest. Then, just when all seemed lost, the miracle occurred: at the public execution — attended by thirty thousand onlookers — the murderer ascended the scaffold and, a moment before offering his neck to the blade, seized a crucifix proffered by the attending priest and kissed it three times. When Thérèse read this in the next day's newspaper, "tears betrayed my emotion and I was forced to run from the room." God had spoken, and henceforth Thérèse would be a missionary of love.[27]

Once in the monastery, Thérèse wrote poems, plays (in which she also acted), and her famous memoirs. Her most precious undertaking, however, remained the salvation of souls through prayer. In order to succeed in this tremendous enterprise, she needed to purify her heart, give herself unflinchingly to God. In June 1895, she did so in her astounding "Act of Oblation to Merciful Love":

> In order to live in one single act of perfect Love, I OFFER MYSELF AS A VICTIM OF HOLOCAUST TO YOUR MERCIFUL LOVE, asking you to consume me incessantly, allowing the waves of *infinite tenderness* shut up within You to overflow into my soul, and that thus I may become a *martyr* of Your *Love,* O my God! . . . I want, O my *Beloved,* at each beat of my heart to renew this offering to You an infinite number of times, until the shadows have disappeared and I may be able to tell You of my *Love* in an *Eternal Face to Face!*[28]

The peculiar orthography, with its exclamation marks, capitals, and italics so reminiscent of a teenage diary, reveals the high pitch of Thérèse's emotions but may obscure the gravity of her intentions. Yes, she was young, and in her youthful fervor she yearned to become love itself, nothing but love, immaculate love. How would she use this love to save souls? Was prayer enough? Her ambition soared; she dreamed of becoming a priest, a soldier, a nurse, a martyr, an apostle, a missionary lifting people to heaven by lowering them to their knees in prayer. But how could she, a young woman, an enclosed nun, accomplish these mighty deeds? She pored over the New Testament, especially Saint Paul's letters to the Corinthians on the nature of love, and discovered the answer:

> *Charity* gave me the key to my *vocation.* I understood that if the Church had a body made up of different members, the most necessary and most noble of all could not be lacking to it, and so I understood that the Church *had a Heart and that this Heart was* BURNING WITH LOVE. *I understood it was Love Alone* that made the Church's members act, that if *Love* ever became extinct, apostles would not preach the Gospel and martyrs would not shed their blood. I understood that LOVE COMPRISED ALL VOCATIONS, THAT LOVE WAS EVERYTHING, THAT IT EMBRACED ALL TIMES AND PLACES . . . IN A WORD, THAT IT WAS ETERNAL!

> Then, in the excess of my delirious joy, I cried out: O Jesus, my Love . . . my *vocation*, at last I have found it . . . MY VOCATION IS LOVE![29]

Love encompassed every work and every way of life; in love she would travel all roads at once, be soldier and peacemaker, apostle and hermit, priest and nun. Through the austere life of a cloistered Carmelite, devoted to contemplative prayer, the *opus Dei*, and menial chores — that is, to the love of God in mind, heart, and body — she would help Jesus save the world.

Thérèse spent the rest of her short life in prayer for others. She prayed especially for priests and for missionaries, who undertook work in foreign lands forever barred to her; she prayed for family and friends, her religious sisters, the Church; and always, she prayed for lost souls. At times her devotions approach the erotic. While still living at home she would write of a moment of nearness to God, "Ah, how sweet was that first kiss of Jesus! I FELT that I was LOVED"; in Carmel, her insight would deepen and her language grow more assured, more adult: "I know, O my God! that *the more You want to give, the more You make us desire.* I feel in my heart immense desires and it is with confidence I ask You to come and take possession of my soul."[30] Thus the virginal kiss matures into complete self-abandonment to the divine presence; the intimations may be passionate, but the intentions are entirely chaste. The contemplative, stripped of all senses, returns continually to the innermost chambers of the heart and there awaits the approach of her Lord, divine love incarnate. One can read this universal contemplative act as analogous to a woman awaiting her lover, and interpretations of this sort abound in examining the lives of other contemplatives, but Thérèse reads it in another way: as the innocent delight of a child awaiting her father in perfect trust. For Thérèse, this capacity to love God with the limitless heart of a child was so important that she took her case to the realm of the spirits: "I presented myself before the angels and saints and I said to them: 'I am the smallest of creatures; I know my misery and my feebleness, but I know also how much noble and generous hearts love to do good. I beg you then, O Blessed inhabitants of heaven, I beg you to ADOPT ME AS YOUR CHILD. *To you alone will be the glory* which you will make me merit, but deign to answer my prayer.'"[31]

Thérèse called this method of spiritual childhood the "little way." It was not a feeling but a work, a labor of love.

> What this child asks for is Love. She knows only one thing: to love you, O Jesus. Astounding works are forbidden to her; she cannot preach the

Image of Saint Thérèse at an outdoor Mass, World Youth Day, Paris, August 1997.

> Gospel, shed her blood. . . . how will she prove her *love* since *love* is proved by works? Well, the little child *will strew flowers*. . . . Yes, my Beloved, this is how my life will be consumed. I have no other means of proving my love for you other than that of strewing flowers, that is, not allowing one little sacrifice to escape, not one look, one word, profiting by all the smallest things and doing them through love.[32]

Strewing flowers, Thérèse recapitulates the soldiering of Saint Antony of the Desert in a gentler, more feminine mode. The discipline remains fierce, "not allowing one little sacrifice to escape, not one look, one word." She embraces the sufferings of Carmelite life — lack of sleep, lack of freedom to talk or travel, lack of intimate human love — and the sufferings of her own deteriorating health.

As tuberculosis ravages Thérèse's body, new miseries strike: doubts about her profession, about the goodness of creation, even about the intentions of God. In the woods outside her window she sees a "black hole" and declares, "I am in a hole just like that, body and soul. Ah! what darkness." Yet this storm too she weathers, through prayer and confidence in the primacy of love. After all, she points out on her deathbed, Jesus died in anguish as a "Victim of Love," and so might she. "To die of love does not mean to die in transports." It does mean, however, that love will be one's condition in the next world as well as in this vale of tears; a realization that led to Thérèse's most famous saying: "I want to spend my heaven doing good on earth." Contemplative love, it seems, is an eternal project.[33]

Counterparts to the Christian understanding of contemplation as a path of desire and love can be found in many other faiths; the approach is so ubiquitous that we may even say that love is the principal note of that prayer, characterized by abandonment, openness, and surrender to the divine, that we have designated as contemplation. But a radically different approach has also wielded tremendous influence. Let us now turn to contemplation as a way of knowledge.

The Knower

The belief that self-knowledge can be a contemplative path has been around for many thousands of years. *Gnōthi se auton* (Know thyself) reads the inscription on the Temple of Apollo at Delphi, home of the oracle and *omphalos* (navel) of the world. That this injunction appears on a sacred building confirms that the desired knowledge was no mere gathering of facts but rather salvific: the key to a right relationship between human beings and the gods, the means to self-transformation in the light of eternal truth, a revelation of the true order of the cosmos. Self-knowledge involved more than self-analysis; it demanded withdrawal from the world into the deepest regions of the soul in search of divine truth — in short, it was a contemplative practice. The project of self-knowledge was taken up by Socrates (c. 470–399 B.C.E.) and his followers, for whom it epitomized the quest for wisdom (although the command "Know thyself," ascribed to Socrates, appears nowhere in the dialogues of Plato; the closest approximation comes in *Apology* 38a, where Socrates declares that the unexamined life is not worth living). In the *Meno,* Socrates establishes that self-knowledge brings contact with divine reality. He summons a slave boy, bright but uneducated, and by drawing figures in the sand and interrogating the boy about them, demonstrates that every human being possesses an innate understanding of geometry. "The truth about reality," Socrates explains, "is always in our soul." The process by which this truth becomes known he calls recollection. The task of the philosopher and all right-minded human beings is to recollect the perfect truths embedded in the soul. In the *Phaedo,* Socrates expands upon this precept, describing a process clearly akin to Christian contemplation by declaring that when the soul investigates "by itself," through pure intellect or vision, "it passes into the realm of the pure and everlasting and immortal and changeless. . . . and this condition of the soul we call wisdom." A soul accustomed to these investigations will, at the moment of death, enter "into the presence of the good and wise God." The aim of life, then, is the discovery, study, and contemplation of divine reality; the search for self-knowledge is the search for wisdom, and wisdom is, at its highest reaches, divine.[34]

Approximately one hundred years after Socrates' death, the Stoic philosophers of Greece presented their own variation on the theme. Wisdom, they believed, was to live in harmony with universal law, to control that which can be controlled (such as emotions), and to accept that which is beyond control (weather, death, the machinations of fate). To this end, they engaged in exercises that historian Pierre Hadot has termed "philosophical therapeutics." Some have a familiar contemplative ring, such as reading, study, the suppression of lusts; most significant is a discipline known as *prosoche* (attention), which Hadot describes as "a continuous vigilance and presence of mind, self consciousness which never sleeps, and a constant tension of the spirit." We may learn from the past and plan for the future, but the great focus of our attention must be the present moment. Thus Marcus Aurelius: "Everywhere and at all times, it is up to you to rejoice piously at what is occurring *at the present moment,* to conduct yourself with justice towards the people who are *present here and now,* and to apply rules of discernment to your *present* representations, so that nothing slips in that is not objective."[35]

Openness to the present saves us from deceit and unreality; it reveals things as they are, not as we wish them to be. To respond appropriately, however, our attention must encompass not only the present moment but also the universal laws (the "rules of discernment" mentioned by Marcus) that should govern our response. We must see every passing moment in the light of eternity. The Stoic — or anyone who attains this level of *prosoche* — "lives constantly in the presence of God and is constantly remembering God, joyfully consenting to the will of universal reasons, and he sees all things with the eyes of God himself."[36] The Stoic is the contemplative par excellence.

Stoicism wielded tremendous influence on the early Christians. Stoic emphasis on attention — to oneself, one's neighbors, and God — became a staple of contemplative practice, as we see both in the story of Saint Antony (recall his serene equilibrium after twenty years of immurement, unmistakable evidence of the remembering of God and self) and in numerous accounts of other Desert Fathers. A typical admonition comes from Saint Dorotheus of Gaza (c. 505–565): "Let us pay heed to ourselves and be vigilant, brothers. Who will give us back the present time if we waste it?" This vigilance bears fruit when directed toward God as well as oneself, as Diadochus of Photice (died c. 468) exhorts: "What distinguishes a man who is virtue's friend is that he constantly consumes everything that is earthly in his heart by means of the remembrance of God, so that, bit by bit, the evil in it is dispersed by the fire of the remembrance of the Good, and his soul returns in perfection to its natural brilliance; nay, even with increased splendor."[37]

A thousand years after Diadochus, the Russian pilgrim, thumbing through the *Philokalia,* would encounter a torrent of advice on the relationship of attention to prayer. One notable passage comes from Saint Nicephorus the Solitary (d. 1340), monk of Mount Athos, who spoke of its role in contemplation:

> Attention is the beginning of contemplation, or rather its necessary condition: for, through attention, God comes close and reveals himself to the mind. Attention is serenity of the mind, or rather its standing firmly planted and not wandering, through the gift of God's mercy. Attention means cutting off thought, it is the abode of remembrance of God and the treasure-house of the power to endure all that may come. Therefore attention is the origin of faith, hope and love.[38]

Four centuries later, the French Jesuit Jean-Pierre de Caussade (1675–1751), in a series of letters to Visitation nuns at Nancy in eastern France, would elaborate his own system of holy attention based on "abandonment" to the will of God. How does one attain this abandonment? By remaining attentive to the present moment and accepting everything that comes one's way as directed by God for one's edification. "Every moment we live through is like an ambassador that declares the will of God," writes de Caussade. "We can find all that is necessary in the present moment." Come what may — pain or pleasure, failure or success, sorrow or joy — the present moment will contribute to spiritual growth if embraced with love and obedience. This practice is remarkably similar to the spiritual exercises of the Stoics; to de Caussade, however, self-abandonment not only opens the mind and heart to the will of God but is a prerequisite to any form of prayer: "What makes us holy is the presence of God through the dwelling of the Holy Trinity in the depths of our hearts when we give them up to God's will. Now, contemplation produces this close union of us with God, as indeed do other acts. . . . But contemplation stands supreme, for it is the most effective means of achieving this union, if God wills it."[39]

But exactly how does one discern the will of God in each passing moment? Unfortunately, de Caussade remains vague on this crucial matter, although he does suggest using the self as a kind of barometer of God's will. For instance, if it is God's wish that we read a book, then reading will "exert a mystical power in the depths of the soul," but if God wishes us to do something else, then reading will prove "useless and detrimental."[40] Our job is to remain attentive to our inner state and thus discern our spiritual duties. If these are carried out with pure intention and humble detachment, divine grace will descend and we will attain perfect sanctity.

It is difficult to imagine a more radical proposition than this: everything that happens to us reveals, brightly or obscurely, the will of God. There seems a touch of Voltaire's *Candide* here, for if God's will is always available to us, if "every current . . . thrusts us onward in our voyage to the infinite" and if "everything . . . without exception, helps us towards holiness," then this is indeed the best of all possible worlds. The difference between de Caussade and Pangloss, of course, is that de Caussade's point of view is not the product of ignorance and gullibility but of suffering and hard labor. To see God's hand in every event and to discern which way that hand is pointing requires tremendous resources of will, intelligence, and faith. It demands the "constant vigilance" of which Marcus Aurelius spoke, and it almost certainly demands a sea change in one's way of life. De Caussade remarks that "God takes away everything from us if we give ourselves entirely to him."[41] The enormousness of the task is staggering, and the history of contemplation, if not of Western religion, may be defined as the effort to meet it. One way to effect this sea change, or *metanoia*, is to lead a strictly cloistered life; de Caussade's letters are addressed to traditional nuns, immersed in a world of ritual and prayer, of obedience and humility, of daily examination of conscience. In this spiritual climate, as we saw with Thérèse of Lisieux, the call to abandon all for the will of God seems a natural extension of sacrifices and practices already assumed.

"Where Is This I?"

Nonetheless, very few of us can be — or even desire to be — monks or nuns. Is there no other way of life that may lead to self-knowledge? One intriguing answer to this question emerged during the first half of the twentieth century among the hills of southern India, in a teaching propounded by the celebrated Indian saint, the sage of Arunachala, Sri Ramana Maharshi (1879–1950). According to Sri Ramana, anyone, anywhere, can follow the path of self-knowledge. The only tool required is relentless self-inquiry, which by itself is enough to discover one's true self and to find that this self is steeped in divinity.

How Sri Ramana stumbled on this radically simple formula constitutes one of the remarkable stories in modern religious history. The revelation came upon him without warning, in the space of about half an hour, on a July day in 1896 in the city of Madurai in southwest India. Venkataramana Iyer, as he was known at the time, was sixteen years old and a student at Mission High School. He was, by all accounts, a normal teenager. On the day in question, he returned home from school and lay down to rest in an upstairs room, when suddenly he was overcome by vertigo and became convinced that he was about to die. Here the tale takes an extraordinary turn, for rather than call for help, Venkataramana opted, in a decision worthy of Socrates, to stay put and investigate his own death in order to discover its nature and meaning. He lay on the floor, assuming the aspect of a corpse — motionless and silent, face and limbs stiff as if rigor mortis had set in. Contemplating his condition, he concluded that he was not his body but an immortal spirit. He remembered, years later, his thoughts at that time:

> Well, this body is now dead. It will be carried to the funeral pyre and there reduced to ashes. But do I die with the death of this body? Is the body I? It is silent and inert; but I feel the full force of my personality and even the voice of the "I" within me, apart from it. So I am the Spirit transcending the body. The body dies but the Spirit that transcends it cannot be touched by death. That means that I am the deathless Spirit.[42]

At another time he expanded upon this realization, describing his new awareness as "a powerful, living Truth that I experienced directly, almost without thinking. . . . From that moment, all attention was drawn as if by powerful magic to the 'I' or the 'Self.' The fear of death was permanently extinguished. From this time on I remained fully absorbed in the 'Self.'"[43]

As one might expect, absorption in the absolute did not lend itself to school studies, and within a few months Venkataramana had fled to the sacred mountain of Arunachala, long revered as a manifestation of Śiva. There he shaved his head, stripped to a loincloth, and began to meditate. For four years he maintained utter silence, passing each day in contemplation. A circle of devotees began to gather, feeding him, sheltering him from the rain, removing the insects that infested his skin, and bestowing on him the honorific of Ramana Maharshi (Ramana Great Seer). His disciples plied him with questions about the spiritual life, and at last he began to respond, at first in writing, then with spoken instructions. In time an ashram coalesced about him, and tens of thousands of people flocked to hear him teach or simply to bask in his presence. By all accounts, his mien was unforgettable: he spoke in a gentle, quiet voice, radiating a kindness and peace that affected all around him. W. Somerset Maugham visited the ashram in early 1938 and in his novel *The Razor's Edge* made Sri Ramana the model for the holy man, Shri Ganesha, here visited by the protagonist, Larry Darrell:

> Shri Ganesha sat in the attitude of meditation on a raised dais covered with a tiger skin. "I've been expecting you," he said . . . he looked at me without speaking. I don't know how long the silence lasted. It might have been for half an hour. I've told you what he looked like; what I haven't told you is the serenity that he irradiated, the goodness, the peace, the selflessness. I was hot and tired after my journey, but I began to feel wonderfully rested. . . . What he taught was very simple. He taught that we are all greater than we know and that wisdom is the means to freedom. He taught that it is not essential to salvation to retire from the world, but only to renounce the self. He taught that work done with no selfish interest purifies the mind and that duties are opportunities afforded to man to sink his separate self and become one with the universal self. But it wasn't his teaching that was so remarkable; it was the man himself, his benignity, his greatness of soul, his saintliness. His presence was a benediction.[44]

That a holy man's or woman's very presence confers blessings is widely attested in a multitude of faiths. The explanation usually runs like this: the devotee contemplates the saint while the saint contemplates God, and some of God's presence rebounds upon the devotee. Sri Ramana believed that his most important teachings were transmitted in this way, through a silent radiance that filled his disciples with the light of wisdom. "A realized one sends out waves of spiritual influence," he says, "which draw many people towards him. Yet he may sit in a cave and maintain complete silence. We may listen to lectures upon truth and come away with hardly any grasp of the subject, but to come into contact with a realized one, though he speaks nothing, will give much more grasp of the subject."[45] Fortunately for us, Sri Ramana did not resort exclusively to silent transmission, and over the decades he spoke at considerable length about the means to discover the true self. He recommended all forms of prayer, including meditation, devotional acts, and repetition of the name of God. He offered petitionary prayers throughout his life and spoke favorably of surrender to God's will in words that echo those of de Caussade and Bill Wilson of Alcoholics Anonymous.

Above all other practices, though, Sri Ramana favored the form of meditation that he called *vichara* (self-inquiry), which he considered the only infallible means of arriving at knowledge of the self. *Vichara* can be described as contemplation of the mind by the mind. It consists in asking, "Who am I?" at every turn, tracing the "I-thought," as Sri Ramana termed it, to its source. At first this work is difficult and exhausting, "an intense activity of the entire mind to keep it steadily poised in pure Self-awareness." As the process becomes more familiar, however, discursive thought ends and the mind spontaneously realizes its independence from the body and its immortal nature: "The thought 'I am this body of flesh and blood' is the one thread on which are strung the various other thoughts. Therefore, if we turn inwards enquiring 'Where is this I?' all thoughts (including the I-thought) will come to an end and Self-knowledge will then spontaneously shine forth."[46]

Sri Ramana offered a somewhat more detailed description of this method to British journalist Paul Brunton, who crisscrossed India between the two world wars, interviewing spiritual masters. Brunton's impression of Sri Ramana, recounted in *A Search in Secret India,* is reminiscent of Maugham's fictional Shri Ganesha:

> The Maharishee's body is almost nude, except for a thin, narrow loincloth . . . If he is aware of my presence, he betrays no hint, gives no sign. His body is supernaturally quiet, as steady as a statue. . . . One by one, the questions which I have prepared in the train with such meticulous accuracy drop away. . . . I know only that a steady river of quietness seems to be flowing near me, that a great peace is penetrating the inner reaches of my being, and that my thought-tortured brain is beginning to arrive at some rest.[47]

Eventually Brunton does ask his questions, which concern the usefulness of science, the odds of the eruption of another world war, and the way to enlightenment. Sri Ramana listens patiently, then steers his interlocutor toward the true nature of the self and how to attain it. He urges Brunton to follow "the 'I' thread," which he calls the "primeval thought," as far into his mind as he can, until finally it vanishes, and all that remains will be "consciousness which is immortal." This method, he assures Brunton, cannot fail, for "the very attitude of enquiry will eventually draw the answer to you out of the depths of your own being." The result will be a state of detachment, purity, and serenity, of wisdom attained and innocence regained: "When a man knows his true self for the first time, something else arises from the depths of his being and takes possession of him. That something is behind the mind; it is infinite, divine, eternal. Some people call it the kingdom of heaven, others call it the soul, still others call it Nirvana, and we Hindus call it Liberation; you may give it what name you wish."[48]

One can quarrel with the theological exactness of Sri Ramana's equating of nirvana, liberation, and Jesus' teaching on the kingdom of heaven. Dwelling in isolated Arunachala, he had little exposure to religions other than his own. But these broad comparisons underscore the universal applicability of his central idea: that behind the experience of "I" lies "something else" — something that he calls "the true self." Contemplation of the mind by the mind, a method available to all, will reveal this truth and transform our being. "Know the real self," he said, "and then the truth will shine forth within your heart like sunshine. The mind will become untroubled and real happiness will flood it, for happiness and the true self are identical."[49]

According to Maugham, Brunton, and many others, the proof of this assertion could be discerned in Sri Ramana's serene, gentle, fatherly presence, in the balance of his mind and the power of his voiced and voiceless teaching. Here he stands as brother to Saint Antony of the Desert, "neither contracted as if by grief, nor relaxed by pleasure, [but] was altogether even as being guided by reason, and abiding in a natural state." Sri Ramana sustained this equanimity for nearly six decades, from his initial revelation in 1896 to his death from cancer on April 14, 1950. Late in his life he suffered from numerous physical ailments, and his last days were terribly painful, but according to eyewitnesses he maintained his serene disposition until the end, declaring, "They take this body for Bhagavan and attribute suffering to him. What a pity! They are despondent that Bhagavan is going to leave them and go away, but where can he go and how?" He could go nowhere, for only the Self exists, and it abides everywhere.[50]

The Artist

"The canons of art," said Alfred North Whitehead, "are merely the expression in specialized forms of the requisites for depth of experience." The more profound the art, the deeper the experience it reflects or intuits. The greatest art seems to touch on the eternal, the necessary, the irreducibly real; it has something of God in it; it is first cousin to contemplation. Thus Wittgenstein, a man for whom philosophy was nothing if not an art, could write that "the work of art is the object seen *sub specie aeternitatis*."[51] The attempt to portray the world in the light of eternity is especially evident in certain cultures — Egyptian, Byzantine, Navajo — where religious principles guide aesthetic considerations and every stroke of the brush or movement of a dancer's limbs is determined by a concern for beauty that expresses eternal spiritual values.

Nowhere is this fusion of aesthetics and spirituality more apparent than in the Zen arts of Japan, contemplative practices of the first order and vehicles that manifest ultimate realities. Tea ceremony, archery, architecture, gardening, Nōh drama, calligraphy, ink drawings, all become means to attain and demonstrate "suchness," the spiritual reality inherent in every thing or act. When spiritual realization (satori in Zen) merges with artistic genius, we may, as D. T. Suzuki summarizes it, "attain a glimpse of things eternal in the world of constant changes; that is, we look into the secrets of Reality."[52] That this vision can be discerned in, say, a Zen monastic garden is almost a commonplace; the balanced modulation of rock and raked sand, moss and bush inspires meditation; each element in the composition seems inevitable, perfectly disclosing its own essential nature. To the practicing Buddhist, each embodies dharma, ultimate truth.

What astonishes is that the same spiritual-aesthetic principles might lend themselves to poetry. Who would think that words could express the wordless? That language could point beyond itself to the silent, eternal matrix from which it and all else springs? Yet this is precisely what Zen poetry, or haiku, attempts to do. Haiku has become very popular in the United States and other Western nations, where it is often taught to schoolchildren as an easy way of introducing them to verse, based on the assumption that its brevity makes it childlike. But haiku is no more childlike than a Shakespeare sonnet, a Blake miniature, or any other condensed work of art. Like these, its beauty and sublimity depend on strict adherence to form; each poem must be three lines long, with each line containing, successively, five, seven, and five syllables. According to R. H. Blyth, a leading Western analyst of the form, haiku represents "artistic asceticism." Like most asceticism, it contains a religious motive, which Blyth finds clearly enunciated in a line from Henry Vaughan's (1621–1695) poem "The Retreat": "Felt through all this fleshly dress / Bright shoots of everlastingness." It is haiku's job to contemplate the everlastingness inherent in the fleshly dress of this world.

Haiku first emerged in twelfth- or thirteenth-century Japan, but for many years it was little more than decorative verse, sparkling with bon mots and lovely imagery. The revolution came with Matsuo Bashō (1643–1694). Son of a samurai, Bashō was trained as a member of the warrior caste, but a number of events — the death of his master, an unhappy love affair, the onset of wanderlust — turned him toward literature. He began to publish poetry, took up Zen meditation, and finally, in 1684, set off on the foot journeys across Japan that made him famous. He described his travels in a series of books — *The Records of a Weather-Exposed Skeleton, The Records of a Travel-Worn Satchel, The Narrow Road to the Deep North* — filled with limpid prose descriptions of the countryside and its inhabitants as well as hundreds of haiku of exceptional beauty.

Bashō's contemplative approach is revealed in an anecdote about his early days as a poet. One day, while he and a student watched dragonflies flitter across a field, the student composed a haiku that ran as follows:

Red dragonflies —
Remove their wings,
and they are pepper-pods.

To this Bashō replied, "There is nothing of haiku there. To be haiku, your poem should read:

Red pepper-pods —
Add wings
And they are dragonflies."

The student strips the dragonfly of wonder, turning it prosaic; the poet contemplates the numinous in this lowly insect.[53]

To achieve contemplative depth, Bashō relied on special techniques. First, haiku dispenses with punctuation and often with words typically required by grammar. This dissolving of rules thrusts the reader into an unmapped world where allusion and intimation reign. Second, *renso* (association of ideas) creates a web of unexpected relationships (between a pepper pod and a dragonfly, for example) that disrupts logic and points to the numinous gaps and links between all things. Third, almost all haiku suggest a *ki* (season of the year; summer in the dragonfly haiku). Everyone, it is believed, carries a cargo of emotional and intellectual responses to different times of year; triggered by seasonal imagery, these responses add depth and unpredictability to the experience of the poem. The end result of this complex aesthetic is a quality known as *sabi,* the "suchness" of embodied existence, the way in which every finite thing — a cherry blossom, a rushing river, a urinating horse, to cite three well-known images used by Bashō — suggests the sublime enigma of exis-

tence. There is in *sabi* (derived from *sabishi,* "solitary") a hint of solitude and a touch of melancholy, an intimation of the evanescence of earthly things in a vast, unfathomable cosmos. The most famous of Bashō's haiku, the one that initiated his poetic revolution, epitomizes this poignancy:

Old pond
A frog leaps in.
Plash!

According to D. T. Suzuki, "This sound coming out of the old pond was heard by Bashō as filling the entire universe. Not only was the totality of the environment absorbed in the sound and vanished into it, but Bashō himself was altogether effaced from his consciousness. Both the subject and the object, *en-soi* and *pour-soi,* ceased to be something confronting and conditioning each other."[54]

This poem marked a turning point in Bashō's life. From now on, his haiku would express absorption in the infinite. He wrote another poem to enunciate his artistic vision:

The origin of all art:
A rice-planting song
In the inmost field of all.

Amidst the humblest of crops, in the tiniest patch of cultivated ground, a song emerges; here, in a place of purity and simplicity, where infinite and finite meet, haiku comes to life. The task of the poet is to seek out these landscapes, catch these moments in his net of words, and reveal to others the wordless mystery of life.

In addition to the poets of Japan, many English-language poets, such as Donne, Keats, Wordsworth, Dickinson, Eliot, Pound (who was considerably influenced by haiku), and William Carlos Williams can be called poetic contemplatives. One who plunged especially deeply into contemplative realms was Gerard Manley Hopkins (1844–1889). His work may be described as the most perfect attempt to transcend language by means of language, to fuse the glittering surface and divine depth of words, to incarnate, in each poetic image, the heavenly force that inspires and sustains it.

Born in Stratford, England, the oldest of nine children, Hopkins was a studious youth who blossomed, at Oxford, into a brilliant scholar of Greek and Latin. At the same time he began to study theology and reli-

Opposite: *Zen rock garden.*

gious history, and in 1866, at the age of twenty-two, he became a Roman Catholic and, two years later, a Jesuit. The rest of his brief life he divided between two occupations, poet and priest. This twin vocation proved immensely fruitful, producing some of the finest religious poetry in the English tongue. Immersed in sacerdotal duties in London, Glasgow, Dublin, and elsewhere, Hopkins never bothered to publish his major poems, and his reputation remained obscure until the early twentieth century, some thirty years after his death, when his friend, the British poet laureate Robert Bridges, brought his work to public attention.

The core of Hopkins's approach to poetry lies in what he termed *inscape.* A precise definition of *inscape* is notoriously difficult, as Hopkins never offered a clear explanation and seemed to vary its meaning to suit the circumstances. We may say, however, that the term represents the individuality, the "thusness" or (following Bashō) "suchness" of any being or thing that sets it apart from others. Inscape is also a form of prayer — the way in which each thing praises God, whether or not it knows it:

> The sun and the stars shining glorify God. They stand where he placed them, they move where he bid them. "The heavens declare the glory of God." They glorify God, *but they do not know it.* The birds sing to him, the thunder speaks of his terror, the lion is like his strength, the sea is like his greatness, the honey like his sweetness; they are something like him, they make him known, they tell of him, they give him glory, but they do not know they do, they do not know him, they never can, they are brute things that only think of food or think of nothing. This then is poor praise, faint reverence, slight service, dull glory. Nevertheless what they can *they always do.*[55]

Only human beings can perfect this praise: "Man can know God, *can mean to give him glory.* This then was why he was made, to give God glory and to mean to give it: to praise God freely, willingly to reverence him, gladly to serve him. Man was made to give, and meant to give, God glory."[56]

The sole purpose of poetry is to disclose inscape: "Poetry is in fact speech only employed to carry the inscape of speech for the inscape's sake — and therefore the inscape must be dwelt on,"[57] runs this typically muddy explanation from his journals. If we discern the inscape of a thing, we see it perfectly, praising God; and if we can capture this inscape in poetry, we transmit, elevate, and perfect this praise.

To perceive inscape is a contemplative act; it requires spiritual acquiescence to God's truth as revealed through the natural world; this act in turn demands a special openness on the part of the observer, a quivering yet quiet readiness that seems to characterize most contemplative states. One is reminded of Bashō's approach to haiku; both he and Hopkins, although each inhabited a different religious cosmos, tried to see and describe the sublime mystery present in everything. But the artistic results of each poet's exploration differ strikingly. Bashō's poems are spare, laconic, almost bony; Hopkins's are lush, passionate, dazzling, as shown in one of his most famous sonnets, "God's Grandeur":

> The world is charged with the grandeur of God,
> It will flame out, like shining from shook foil,
> It gathers to a greatness, like the ooze of oil
> Crushed. Why do men then now not reck his rod?
> Generations have trod, have trod, have trod,
> And all is seared with trade, bleared, smeared with toil;
> And wears man's smudge and shares man's smell: the soil
> Is bare now, nor can foot fell, being shod.
> And for all that, nature is never spent;
> There lives the dearest freshness deep down things;
> And though the last lights off the black West went
> Oh, morning, at the brown brink eastward, springs –
> Because the Holy Ghost over the bent
> World broods with warm breast and with ah! bright wings.

This sonnet, like Bashō's haiku, follows strict compositional laws, yet the result is riotous, flashing with energy, electric with God. The pyrotechnics include the repetitive march of "have trod, have trod, have trod"; the alliteration, reversed at the conclusion, of "World broods . . . warm breast . . . bright wings"; and the rhyming crescendo of "seared . . . bleared, smeared." The richness of Hopkins's language reflects his incarnational theology, his belief that the world is the "word, expression, news of God."[58] We may fail to see the glory before us ("why do men then now not reck his rod?"), blinded by the "trade and toil" of the world; but nonetheless, in nature abides "the dearest freshness deep down things" (an echo of Bashō's "inmost field of all") and the presence of God, in the Person of the Holy Ghost.

Hopkins's exploration of inscape may seem a far cry from the spiritual combat of Saint Antony of the Desert, the cloistered ardors of Saint Thérèse, or the intellectual serenity of Sri Ramana Maharshi. As we said at the outset of this chapter, the prayer of the contemplative assumes a multitude of forms; warfare, love, intellect, and art do not exhaust its fields of play. Nonetheless, it holds to a single goal, embracing all things in order to discover the one essential thing, "the realm of the pure and everlasting and immortal and changeless." Here the seeker may find God seated on a golden throne or at play in the dust motes stirred up by a kitchen broom. He tastes ultimate reality, whether set apart from or caught up in the world in which he dwells; and in this tasting lies the source of contemplation's eternal appeal and harlequin career.

PART III

The Land of Spices

In Part III we explore the relationship of prayer to culture. Chapter 8 describes the exceptional role that prayer plays in traditional societies, where religion suffuses every aspect of life, and Chapters 9 and 10 the subtle or dramatic shifts that occur when prayer must negotiate its role in a modern, secular environment.

The transition from tradition to modernity has been the subject of much controversy. As we saw in Chapter 1, a number of influential nineteenth- and early-twentieth-century thinkers such as Tylor, Frazer, and Freud posited that religion (and thus prayer) evolved from primitive to civilized forms, from crude to refined expression, from ignorance to illumination. Another view, put forward by the French metaphysician René Guénon and a handful of other philosophers, reverses this idea: history is not progress but decay, a fall from a golden age ruled by religious truth and crowned by prayer into our present woeful condition of godless confusion. The modern world's principal task and its most fervent prayer, these philosophers say, must be to recover the past in its pristine wholeness.

The third perspective on tradition and modernity occupies the middle — and in our view, the higher — ground. Its advocates include John Henry Newman and T. S. Eliot. Here the movement from traditional to modern culture is seen neither as an ascent into light nor a descent into darkness, but rather as an unfolding, in a multiplicity of ways, with detours and dead ends as well as new avenues and vistas of eternal truth. Newman, writing as a theologian, describes this process as "the development of doctrine" whereby religious verities, eternally present, gradually become articulated and understood. Eliot, writing as a poet, offers a parallel vision in which all literature, past and present, "has a simultaneous existence and composes a simultaneous order." The modern poet neither denies nor worships the past; his or her work adds to and modifies the canon and thus contributes to "the main current." Tradition is not static, modernity is not irreversible, secularism is not final. Applying this view to the story of prayer, we may say that the truths of tradition — vividly realized, as we will see, in the cultures of ancient Scotland, native America, medieval Europe, and elsewhere — can take on new and unexpected life, sometimes vibrant, sometimes vitiated, in our own postmodern world.

CHAPTER 8

Prayer and Tradition

AMONG HISTORY'S GREAT WALKERS — Johnny Appleseed, John Muir, Robert Falcon Scott — few tramped for as many years or to such worthy effect as Alexander Carmichael (1832–1912). For nearly half a century this gentle Scottish scholar crisscrossed the meadows and moors, mountains and islands of northern Scotland, clad in full Highlands regalia, with kilt, sporran, and *sgian dubh* (dagger), a walking stick in his right hand and a notebook in his left, sleeping under the stars or in rude shepherds' huts, knocking at a cottage here and a manor house there, and courteously begging, when the door cracked open, for a chance to explain his quest. His mission was to seek out, collect, and preserve the vanishing Gaelic folklore — hymns and tales, incantations and curses, and above all, prayers — of this remote Highlands region, where the corrosive culture of modernity had not yet won the day.

Hearth and Heath: The Carmina Gadelica

By all accounts, Carmichael was a congenial, even a lovable man, and many a crofter, notoriously close-mouthed to strangers, poured out precious lore to this polite visitor from the world of learning. The Reverend Doctor Kenneth MacLeod, a scholar who knew Carmichael well, remarked that other researchers "could get the heroic tales and ballads, the things which were recited in public at the *ceilidh;* only Alexander Carmichael could have got the hymns and the incantations, the things that were said when the door was closed, and the lights were out." The reason for his success, MacLeod explains, is that Carmichael was "one of ourselves . . . one who saw with our eyes, who felt with our heart, and who reproduced our past because he loved it himself and was proud of it."[1] A Gael through and through, Carmichael was not so much studying a foreign culture as visiting friends. His "beautiful mania" for elusive lore and his love for things Gaelic spilled over into generosity to all who spoke the tongue and lived the ancient ways; stories abound of how he offered lodgings to homeless students and cash to bankrupt friends, while he himself, with his wife and children, teetered on the brink of poverty. He struggled mightily for Gaelic rights and helped abolish the tax on herding dogs and horse-drawn carts, a campaign that may strike modern ears as quaint but that, 150 years ago, rescued countless peasants from financial ruin.

The result of Carmichael's gallant half century of foot travel is the *Carmina Gadelica*, a six-volume compendium of Gaelic lore, a triumph of the ethnographer's art with its literary elegance and physical sumptuousness (the first edition is richly illustrated with swirling, intertwining letters from a Celtic bestiary alphabet, printed on thick, creamy, gilt-edged paper, and bound in crimson cloth). This landmark work took even longer to publish than to compile: the first volume appeared in a limited edition in 1901 and the last in 1971. Three generations of Carmichaels participated, including Alexander's wife, who managed the family finances, raised four children, and urged her husband onward when he felt inadequate to his task; his daughter Elizabeth, who transcribed the manuscripts, corrected the proofs, and later edited the *Celtic Review*, a spearhead of the Gaelic revival in Scotland; and his grandson James, who edited the third and fourth volumes and whose plans to complete the series were thwarted by his death in action during World War II. The *Carmina Gadelica* is thus a family project and shares some of the characteristics of the best works of that type: warmth, vitality, generosity of heart, and an appreciation for the moral and spiritual traditions that help sustain any living culture, whether that of family, clan, country, or civilization.

The *Carmina Gadelica* makes clear that in the case of Gaelic culture, these traditions were primarily religious, and the heart of this folk religion was prayer. "Religion, pagan or Christian, or both combined, permeated everything," Carmichael writes, "blending and shading into one another like the iridescent colours of the rainbow. The people were sympathetic and synthetic, unable to see and careless to know where the secular began and the religious ended."[2] It may have been carelessness, or it may have been their ever-present goodness. One turns from the *Carmina Gadelica* with the sense of having visited an enchanted land, populated by saints and seers, oracles and holy fools, in love with God and God's creation, a people who would give their last scrap of bread to a passing stranger. Carmichael remembers:

> During all the years that I lived and travelled among [the Highlanders and western Islanders], night and day, I never met with incivility, never with rudeness, never with vulgarity, never with aught but courtesy. I never entered a house without the inmates offering me food or apologising for their want of it. I never was asked for charity in the West, a striking contrast to my experience in England, where I was frequently asked for food, for drink, for money, and that by persons whose incomes would have been wealth to the poor men and women of the West.[3]

In the life of the Highlanders, every moment, every action, every atom of creation was blessed, cursed, praised, thanked, abjured, invoked, beseeched, or otherwise drawn into the realm of prayer. The *Carmina Gadelica* includes prayers tailored to dawn, midday, dusk; prayers for milking the cow or healing the eyes; prayers for the new year and prayers for harvest; prayers for the sun and prayers for the moon; prayers for protection at home and abroad; prayers for the animals and vegetables of farm, field, forest, and sea; prayers to the angels and to the saints, to husband or wife, to parents, children, ancestors, and descendants — to everyone and everything in the great festival of creation. What strikes the reader, apart from the prayers' variety of subject, is their great beauty, their entrancing cadences and gnomic intelligence. There is some evidence that Carmichael added a coat or two of literary gloss to some of the material, restructuring here, merging variant retellings there. This artful embellishment is a mixed blessing; it damages the value of the work as raw ethnographic record but adds fluency and clarity, making the whole more accessible to the general public. Three examples will serve to indicate the work's characteristic notes and range and reveal how, in a traditional culture, prayer can illumine every aspect of the household and its surroundings.

Blessing of the Kindling (Beannachadh Beothachaidh)

I will kindle my fire this morning
In presence of the holy angels of heaven,
In presence of Ariel of the loveliest form,
In presence of Uriel of the myriad charms,
Without malice, without jealousy, without envy,
Without fear, without terror of any one under the sun,
But the Holy Son of God to shield me.
    Without malice, without jealousy, without envy,

Without fear, without terror of any one under the sun,
But the Holy Son of God to shield me.

God, kindle Thou in my heart within
A flame of love to my neighbour,
To my foe, to my friend, to my kindred all,
To the brave, to the knight, to the thrall,
O Son of the loveliest Mary,
From the lowliest thing that liveth,
To the Name that is highest of all
O Son of the loveliest Mary,
From the lowliest thing that liveth,
To the Name that is highest of all.[4]

The Gaels believe that prayer begins at the hearth, the pith of the home, and radiates out into every avenue of life. The first work of the day, after a prayer of awakening, is to kindle the fire, filling the living quarters with warmth, light, and the promise of food. This ritual, a simple act requiring no more than matches and tinder, draws into its orbit even the "holy angels in heaven." As the woman who recites this prayer lights the fire (kindling being always a woman's task), a corresponding flame warms her heart. Sanctification of the morning fire is an ancient practice and this woman's prayer is also very old, its antiquity vouchsafed by the feudal imagery (brave, knight, thrall), the naming of the angels — a lore largely forgotten in the modern world — and the incantatory repetition, a sure sign of oral origins.

Charm for a Bursting Vein (Eolas Sgiucha Feithe)

The rune made by the holy maiden Bride
To the lame mariner,
For knee, for crookedness, for crippleness,
For the nine painful diseases, for the three venomous diseases,
Refuse it not to beast, deny it not to dame.

Christ went on a horse,
A horse broke his leg.
Christ went down,
He made whole the leg.

As Christ made whole that,
May Christ make whole this,
And more than this,
If it be His will so to do.
The charm made by Columba,
On the bottom of the glen,

For bursting of vein, for discoloration of bone —
Thou art ill to-day, thou shalt be well to-morrow.[5]

This charm contains many elements found in "Blessing of the Kindling" — petition, archaism, the conviction that divine power is active in the world — but adds something older and startling, the flavor of paganism. Carmichael classifies "Charm for a Bursting Vein" as an incantation, that is, a magical spell. It begins with a rune, a potent gesture, phrase, or song, here made, against all expectation, by a Christian saint. As the legend goes, Saint Brigid of the Isles ("the holy maiden Bride") was born the daughter of a druid and a Gaelic deity, but on the eve of the first Christmas she miraculously flew from the Scottish isle of Iona to Bethlehem, where she assisted at the holy birth and served as Jesus' foster-mother during infancy. Her odyssey thus recapitulates that of the Gaelic people from paganism to Christianity. "Charm for a Bursting Vein" exemplifies the "baptized" paganism that runs through the *Carmina Gadelica*, erupting in Christian love charms, fairy incantations, prayers for second sight, and spells against the evil eye.

New Moon (Gealach Ur)

I am lifting to thee my hands,
    I am bowing to thee my head,
I am giving thee my love,
    Thou glorious jewel of all the ages.
I am raising to thee mine eye,
    I am bending to thee my head,
I am offering thee my love,
    Thou new moon of all the ages![6]

This prayer of praise and submission typifies the reverence for nature, sometimes rising into adoration, that courses through the *Carmina Gadelica.* Sun, moon, and stars, fire and thunder, rose and milkweed, wren and rat, every corner of the natural order is drawn into the prayer life of the Gaels. One of Carmichael's island contacts, Mor MacNeill, a woman "poor and old and alone, but . . . bright of mind and clean of person," attests:

> in the time of my father and of my mother there was no man in Barra who would not take off his bonnet to the white sun of power, nor a woman in Barra who would not bend her body to the white moon of the seasons. No, my dear, not a man nor woman in Barra. And old persons will be doing this still, and I will be doing it myself sometimes. Children mock at me, but if they do, what of that? Is it not much meeter for me to

> bend my body to the sun and to the moon and to the stars, that the great God of life made for my good, than to the son or daughter of earth like myself?[7]

The image of Mor MacNeill on the rocky shores of Barra, bowing to the Highland moon, is romantic, almost dreamy, an illustration by Maxfield Parrish. But the impulse behind it is classical, lucid, and universal. The *Carmina Gadelica* reveals a coherent religious culture, knit together by prayer. That hackneyed saying "The family that prays together, stays together" contains much truth, and in traditional cultures, prayer serves as just such a binding agent. Shared table graces, morning and evening prayers, and the sacramental prayers of marriage and baptism join husband to wife, parent to child, and sister to brother in a common language of sign and symbol. Prayer binds neighbor to neighbor, too, through the collectively recited words of church services, yearly and seasonal festivals, and blessings conveyed for health and well-being. When the fishermen of the Scottish isles walk down to the sea to beg God for a successful harvest of fish or seaweed, they do so en masse, in a group ritual shaped and sealed by prayer. And prayer binds humankind to nature. "When a man has taken his herd to the pasture in the morning, and has gotten a knoll between himself and them," writes Carmichael, "he bids them a tender adieu, waving his hands, perhaps both hands, towards them, saying:

> 'The herding of Bride to the kine,
> Whole and well may you return.
>
> The prosperity of Mary Mother be yours,
> Active and full may you return.'"[8]

This is more than a plea for protection for one's sheep; it is a declaration of relationship, of the shepherd's tender regard for his flock, a central image in the Gael's Christian faith. It defines the shepherd's role: as viceroy of Christ in meadow and valley, he tends his flock in imitation of his Lord. His simple prayer, in conjunction with a dozen others uttered in the course of a day, enunciates his convictions, determines his actions (whether they run with or against his convictions), and defines his sense of self.

The prayer-drenched life of the Gaels finds a counterpart in many other long-standing cultures. To this day, the Brahmans of India, millions strong, say prayers akin to those of the *Carmina Gadelica*. From the instant of birth, Brahman men (and to a lesser degree, women) are enmeshed in an intricate web of propitiation, thanksgiving, petition, oblation, and adoration, enveloping every imaginable aspect of life and continuing until the grave and beyond — for the fate of the souls of the deceased can be altered through prayer. Mor MacNeill, watching her Gaelic brethren doff their bonnets to the sun, might well appreciate the following Brahmanic prayer, directed every morning, while standing outside with arms extended, toward the same heavenly body: "May all in this world be happy, may they be healthy, may they be comfortable and never miserable. May the rain come down in the proper time, may the earth yield plenty of corn, may the country be free from war, may the Brahmans be secure, may the sonless gain a son, may those who have sons gain grandsons, may those without wealth gain wealth, and all live for hundreds of years."[9]

Judaism, too, has its prayers of the hearth — indeed, the home is the locus of many important Jewish rituals — morning and evening recitations and blessings for washing hands, for meals, for holy days, even for the new moon. This last blessing differs from the Gaelic lunar prayer by directing adoration away from the moon and toward God, who ensures its monthly renewal:

> Blessed art thou, O Lord, our God! King of the universe, who with his word created the heavens, and all their host with the breath from his mouth; a decree and appointed time he gave them, that they should not deviate from their charge; they rejoice and are glad when performing the will of their Creator. Their Maker is true, and his work is true; he also ordained that the moon should monthly be renewed; a crown of glory for those who have been upheld by God from the womb, for they are also hereafter to be renewed like her to glorify their Creator, for the glorious name of his kingdom. Blessed art thou, O Lord! who renewest the months![10]

The Talmud declares that "It is forbidden to a man to enjoy anything of this world without a benediction, and if anyone enjoys anything of this world without a benediction, he commits sacrilege."[11] As a result, in traditional Judaism almost every conceivable event claims a *berakhah* (blessing):

> *Before eating meat, eggs, fish, or cheese:*
> Blessed art thou, O Lord, our God! King of the universe,
> through whose word everything was called into being.
>
> *When putting on new clothes:*
> Blessed art thou, O Lord, our God! King of the universe,
> who clothest the naked.

During a thunderstorm:
Blessed art thou, O Lord, our God! King of the universe,
whose power and might fill the universe.

Upon hearing good news:
Blessed art thou, O Lord, our God! King of the universe,
who art good and beneficent.

Upon hearing bad news:
Blessed art thou, O Lord, our God! King of the universe,
who art a righteous judge.[12]

Above all, these *berakhot* express gratitude to God, fount of all blessings. They affirm our relationship to God as worshipful dependents, our very existence contingent on divine mercy. Strict rules govern the uttering of *berakhot.* Every devout Jew is expected to say at least one hundred per day. One cannot bless needlessly or in vain — a restriction that produces some curious dilemmas, for example, saying a *berakhah* over food that subsequently tumbles to the floor and is no longer edible. These complications arise with some frequency: what to do when faced with a strawberry rhubarb crumble, a mixture of foods that invite different *berakhot*? Jewish scholars relish these conundrums and have evolved solutions for just about every problem. A recent guide to *berakhot* bristles with flow charts offering helpful advice; a diagram of a blessing over cooked grains, for example, forks and forks again depending upon the answer to various questions: Are the grains milled, chopped, or whole? If milled, do they adhere to one another or not? If not, is part of the kernel removed or not?[13] The intricacies of *berakhot* may amuse or madden us, but how satisfying it must be to have a blessing at hand for every occasion, how wonderful to stroll down the street in an orthodox Jewish neighborhood where such blessings ring out day and night. To greet whatever may come with the appropriate prayer has been the rule for nearly every culture in every land. We are the outsiders looking in, and we wonder with good reason what we might be missing.

The Temple

From what source pours the river of prayer that rushes through every nook and cranny of traditional life? In one sense, there is no single wellspring; prayers originate in particular locales under particular circumstances — as we have seen, a Gaelic kelp farmer may coin a devotional verse as he strolls along the shore; prayer, like God in the famous formula, can be fairly described as a sphere whose circumference is everywhere and whose center is nowhere. Wherever you find yourself, there you pray.

But our Gaelic peasant might give a different account of the matter. The shore gives birth to many a prayer, and so do sea and field, stable and smithy. All locales harbor the seed of prayer. But these places remain outposts, subsidiary oratories anchored by belief and practice to a firmer, more permanent structure. We may pray in the bedroom at dawn, in the fields at midday, in the kitchen at dusk. But we are able to pray there because we pray also in a more powerful place, where prayer goes on endlessly, day and night. Prayer does have a wellspring, and its name is the temple.

By temple we mean church, synagogue, mosque, fire altar, or any holy sanctuary where heaven meets earth. Often the temple marks the epicenter of prayer in a literal sense: thus Muslims, no matter where they are or what their occupation, prepare for *ṣalāt* by turning toward Mecca, pole star of Islam, home of the Ka'ba, where Adam uttered the first human prayers. But the temple is more than a place on the map and the lodestone of devotion: it is the womb of culture, history, learning, commerce, science, and the arts. As the place where heaven and earth commingle, it exists both inside and outside of time: the rites that unfold within its walls are eternal and everlasting, and they stir God to action; and yet these same rites have an immediate effect upon the everyday worlds of politics and commerce. This is true of the town churches and wayside chapels of the Scottish Highlanders, of the synagogues of the Jews, and of every other house of prayer (what an apt designation!). Thus Thomas Merton describes the medieval town of St. Antonin in southwest France, where he lived as a child:

> Here, in this amazing, ancient town, the very pattern of the place, of the houses and streets and of nature itself, the circling hills, the cliffs and trees, all focused my attention upon the one, important central fact of the church and what it contained. . . . The church had been fitted into the landscape in such a way as to become the keystone of its intelligibility. . . . The whole landscape, unified by the church and its heavenward spire, seemed to say: this is the meaning of all created things: we have been made for no other purpose than that men may use us in raising themselves to God, and in proclaiming the glory of God. . . . Oh, what a thing it is, to live in a place that is so constructed that you are forced, in spite of yourself, to be at least a virtual contemplative![14]

In St. Antonin, the church makes every citizen a contemplative. It is the geographic hub from which streets radiate, like rays from the sun; it is the spiritual hub, from which souls draw meaning, instruction, and direction. Great civilizations have sprung from such centers of prayer. Etymology states the case: both *cult* and *culture* derive from the Latin *cultus* (cultivation). What is being cultivated? Nothing less than humankind's relationship to creation and Creator. Every human culture (except possibly our own, as we will see in the next chapter) has breathed the air of the temple and its religious understanding of the cosmos. That does not mean, of course, that this understanding remains static; a religion may mature or degenerate, sometimes in tandem with the very culture that it inspires. Nonetheless it remains true, as T. S. Eliot has observed, that culture is "the incarnation . . . of the religion of a people."[15] Religion orders culture; prayer is both the fruit of this culture and its guiding soul. The evidence from the *Carmina Gadelica* speaks forcefully: a peasant plants his crops or tends his sheep in the sight of God and through the blessings of God, and he answers God's munificence by offering prayers and hymns of thanksgiving and praise, word craft that becomes the flower of Gaelic culture, embodying its deepest values.

Nowhere is the interdependence of prayer and culture more apparent than in the Cathedral of Notre Dame de Chartres, archetype of the temple as culture-bearer, located some three hundred miles northwest of St. Antonin. Chartres Cathedral is above all a house of prayer: domicile of the Eucharist, abode for the sacrifice of the Mass (the Christian ritual prayer par excellence), home base for a multitude of worshipers offering both corporate and private prayers. Its very edifice is a monumental prayer in stone and stained glass, with its flying buttresses and arches straining toward God and its windows depicting scenes from sacred history, flooding the interior with transfigured light that prefigures the glories of paradise. The entire structure, constructed according to musical proportions, conveys the belief, as art historian Otto von Simson puts it, that "beauty was . . . the radiance of truth, the splendor of ontological perfection and that quality of things which reflects their origin in God."[16]

In its heyday Chartres Cathedral was a nexus of Gothic culture, home of the legendary School of Chartres, an international network of eminent scholars who pursued advanced studies in rhetoric, logic, grammar, cosmology, and other disciplines. Nor was education limited to the intellectual elite; every aspect of the cathedral and its enclosed life — homilies, liturgical readings, plainchant, stained glass, sculpture, flagstone labyrinth, and so on — imparted both information and meaning to believers of every social stratum, revealing to all their place and role in a vast hierarchical cosmos made safe, almost cozy, by the overshadowing love of God. Even today, with the local Gothic culture reduced to plastic gargoyles hawked in souvenir shops along the structure's perimeter, a few minutes spent inside the cathedral are sufficient to reorient one's perspective, if not one's being. The windows and arches, the gemlike chapels, the penetrating atmosphere of sanctity still work magic; one never feels like a stranger in Chartres Cathedral; it is the outer world that seems alien; inside one feels that one arrived, if not home, at least where one can find one's way.

Chartres has cousins all over the world: Thebes in Upper Egypt, Borobuḍur in the forests of Java, Puri Jagannātha in eastern India. Each is a great temple city, a beehive of ritual prayer and cultural industry. Usually, an imposing edifice lies at the center of these cities, perhaps an architectural prodigy of size, such as Saint Peter's in Rome, or of intricacy, such as Naṭarāja Temple in South India, or of location, such as Macchu Picchu. Some of these establishments swell, in time, into the equivalent of small nations devoted principally to prayer, the most famous being Mount Athos, a quasi-autonomous state of twenty monasteries and some one thousand five hundred monks, situated on a thickly wooded mountainous peninsula in the Aegean Sea. But houses of prayer need not be vast, ornate, or even permanent; they may be spare, transitory, and small, like the structures assembled, employed, and dismantled during that most impressive of all Plains Indian religious ceremonies, the Wiwanyag Wachipi or Sun Dance.

The Sun Dance

The Sun Dance, a ceremony that originated among the Plains Indians some three or four hundred years ago, is in essence an extended prayer to Wakan Tanka (God or the "Great Mysterious"), entailing the erection of a sacred tree, around which dancers offer sacrifice, petition, and thanksgiving over the course of several days. The tree is always a cottonwood, as the Lakota Sioux holy man Black Elk explains: "Perhaps you have noticed that even in the very lightest breeze you can hear the voice of the cottonwood tree; this we understand is its prayer to the Great Spirit, for not only men, but all things and all beings pray to Him continually in differing ways."[17]

The tree stands in the middle of the dancing arena, a large space encircled by a shade arbor or, in more recent years when the ceremony has been performed at tribal fairgrounds, by bleacher seats. Within the dance arena stand colored flags marking off the cardinal directions, along with singing platforms, a buffalo robe bed, and an altar containing a pipe rack and a buffalo skull. Outside the arena a number of other structures are

Sun Dance (Cree).

scattered, among them a tepee where dancers dress or rest, tents for visitors and officials, and a sweat lodge — a small, low building of curved willows covered by blankets and furs and containing a pit filled with superheated rocks — used for the *inipi* (purification rite). These buildings and the dancing arena together constitute a house of prayer, analogous to a Christian church or Islamic mosque.

Here an elaborate ritual sequence unfolds, traditionally running four days, although dances of twelve days or even longer have taken place. The centerpiece of the Sun Dance is the flesh sacrifice. Usually, wooden skewers or eagle claws are inserted into the chest of the dancers — almost always male — and a rope is then tied to the stick or claw, connecting it to the sacred tree. The dancer pulls backward, while praying and blowing on eagle-bone whistles, until the flesh rips and the skewer snaps free. The process can take minutes or hours, depending on the depth of the piercing. Some dancers drag buffalo skulls tied to ropes attached to the flesh of their backs. Others cut out small pieces of flesh from their arms as gift offerings.

Almost all religions make use of ascetic practices — fasting, sleeplessness, and the like — but few involve actual sacrifice of one's own blood or flesh. Predictably, early witnesses of the Sun Dance described its core ritual activity as "torture," a term still commonly used to this day, even by some Native American writers. Even more predictably, the federal government was alarmed by the practice and condemned it on moral and political grounds (it was considered not only cruel but conducive to native unrest). The first official ban occurred in 1881, and in 1904 the Department of the Interior outlawed the Sun Dance throughout America. Nonetheless, it continued sub rosa, conducted by small groups in outlying areas free from official interference. It reemerged in 1928 under government supervision and often took the form of a tourist attraction, usually without flesh piercings. Only in the last decades of the twentieth century did the dance once again flourish, as it does to this day, leading one scholar of Sioux religion to prophesy that "it will not be sit-ins at the Bureau of Indian Affairs in Washington or sieges at Wounded Knee which will gather and direct the power for most reservation Sioux. It will be Sun Dances; it will be sacrifices, healings, visions, and purification."[18]

Whence derives the power of the Sun Dance? According to Black Elk, the rite first appeared in a vision granted to a Sioux named Kablaya (Spread), who declared that "this new way of sending our voices to *Wakan-Tanka* will be very powerful; its use will spread, and, at this time of year, every year, many people will pray to the Great Spirit."[19] As this statement makes clear, the entire Sun Dance, from initial selection of the sacred cottonwood tree to concluding processions and postdance celebrating, is conceived as a single offering to the Great Mysterious. Kablaya continues:

> O Grandfather, Father, *Wakan-Tanka,* we are about to fulfill Thy will as You have taught us to do in my vision. This we know will be a very sacred way of sending our voices to You; through this, may our people receive wisdom; may it help us to walk the sacred path with all the Powers of the universe! Our prayer will really be the prayer of all things, for all are really one; all this I have seen in my vision.[20]

The great prayer of the Sun Dance gathers all the powers of the cosmos and channels their blessings to the Sioux. According to Black Elk, who has a flair for symbolic interpretation, almost every element in the dance has cosmic significance; thus, the sacred pipe smoked during the proceedings represents the universe, while the tobacco and other herbs heaped into the bowl represent its constituent parts, ignited by fire and offered to Wakan Tanka as a sacrifice of smoke rising to heaven. So too the flesh offerings are gifts to God and, at the same time, a metaphor for spiritual liberation: "the flesh represents ignorance, and, thus, as we dance and break the thong loose, it is as if we were being freed from the bonds of the flesh. . . . we become broken and submit to the Great Spirit." As Black Elk describes it, the Sun Dance is the vehicle for the transformation of a people, a society, and a culture, as petitions ascend and blessings descend. The people sing, "Wakan-Tanka be merciful to me. We want to live!" and in return, God sends wisdom and goodness: "The light of *Wakan-Tanka* is upon my people . . . making the whole earth bright."[21]

The prayers of the Sun Dance, through the courage and self-sacrifice of the dancers, reestablish the proper relationship between all beings so that each fulfills its ordained role. The same prayers remind human beings of their role as intermediaries between heaven and earth; they strengthen the "hoop of the nation," the harmony and fruitfulness of the social structure; they affirm Sioux values such as humility, generosity, and courage; and they shower well-being, fertility, healings, and visions upon the people. The prayers demonstrate, in sum, that sacrifice, praise, petition, and thanksgiving form a sure path to human rectitude and a channel for divine mercy.

Icons

The influence of the temple — whether a Gothic cathedral or a Sun Dance lodge — radiates, as we have said, in all directions to permeate and condition every sphere of human activity. Now the first thing that strikes most visitors to Chartres Cathedral is the magnificence of the stained glass, sculptured porticoes, and flying buttresses; and students of the Sun Dance are quick to notice the rich array of crafted items in the ceremony, including eagle-bone whistles, animal-skin drums, cherrywood pipe racks, prayer flags, tents and arbors, sage or rabbit-skin anklets, wristbands and headbands, rawhide effigies, feathered headdresses, and more, saturated with meaning and painted, carved, dyed, or woven to a high degree of beauty. Chartres and the Sun Dance together reveal that of all endeavors shaped by the temple and its prayers, the most persistent and pervasive may be that of art.

Theology may explicate the ways of God, but art clothes sacred truth in concrete form, escorting us through color, texture, shape, sound, movement, narrative, and verse into the felt presence of the divine. Art, one might say, is the handmaiden of prayer, as prayer is the handmaiden of faith. "The work of art," says Wittgenstein, as we saw in Chapter 7, "is the object seen *sub specie aeternitatis*," that is, "under the appearance of eternity" (Michelangelo calls it "a shadow of the divine perfection"). Wittgenstein's definition may apply only loosely to modern and post-modern art (see Chapter 10), but it certainly fits those traditional arts associated with prayer, such as Gregorian chant, *bhāratanātyam* (the oldest form of classical Indian dance), and *shōdō* (Zen calligraphy). It seems particularly apt as a description of Byzantine icon painting, a discipline preceded by prayer, practiced with prayer, and designed to transport both artist and beholder to the threshold of eternity. Icon painting is the opposite of art for art's sake, for in intention, execution, and disposition, it is art for prayer's sake — or better yet, art for God's sake, through the medium of prayer.

According to legend, the first icon (Greek *eikon*, "image or likeness") came from the hand of the evangelist Saint Luke. Another story traces the form back to an image called the *Acheiropoietos (Not Made by Human Hands)*. As the tale goes, Abgar, king of Edessa in Mesopotamia, commissioned a portrait of Christ but could not find an artist equal to the task. Jesus, hearing of the difficulty, pressed a linen to his face and miraculously transferred his features to the cloth, which he then dispatched to the faithful king. The *Acheiropoietos* thus demonstrates, as theologian Vladimir Lossky writes, the "dogmatic principle of iconography": the painted image, executed with a holy intent, in an atmosphere of devotion and prayer, conveys the essence of the divine.[22] Certainly, the *Icon Not Made by Human Hands*, which remains to this day a favorite subject of iconographers, could never be mistaken for a sentimental approximation of God, for it depicts a stern, even frightening Christ, mouth grimly set and thick eyebrows arched in righteous anger, the only hint of softness being four long braids of hair tumbling over the holy shoulders. The *Acheiropoietos* grates on us, confounding expectations of a gentle, accommodating Jesus. It captures the profound seriousness and strangeness of divinity and challenges the beholder — as do all icons — to move beyond habitual expectations toward a new apprehension of God made man.

The authoritative theory of icons and their relationship to prayer was put forth during the Seventh Ecumenical Council in 787:

> We decree with all exactitude and deliberation that one should make room, next to the reproduction of the precious life-giving Cross, for holy and venerable icons made in colors, in mosaic, or in some other material . . . [of] Our Lord, God, and Savior Jesus Christ or of the Immaculate

> Lady, the Holy Mother God, of the venerable angels, and of all holy people. For in the measure that these are continually represented and contemplated in image, those who contemplate them raise themselves toward the memory and the desire for their prototype.[23]

An icon, then, is an image that points beyond the painted surface, guiding the attention of "those who contemplate" toward the "prototype" depicted. Contemplation, in this context, may include not only veneration of the image but also a bouquet of prayers — adoration, thanksgiving, petition, and meditation — offered to the holy figure represented. If the beholders pray with sufficient sincerity and purity, a miracle of sorts may result: they may find themselves standing in the presence of the prototype. Pavel Florensky, an Orthodox scholar of iconography who was martyred by the KGB in 1937, tells us that "at the highest flourishing of their prayer, the ancient ascetics found that their icons were not simply windows through which they could behold the holy countenances depicted upon them but were also doorways through which these countenances actually entered the empirical world. The saints came down from the icons to appear before those praying to them."[24]

This astonishing assertion depends on an understanding ubiquitous in traditional sacred art (one finds it in Navajo sand painting as well as Byzantine iconography): an image portrays not only the appearance but also in some mysterious way the living presence of what is depicted. Every icon, as Florensky puts it, is also an annunciation. Hence in every icon of Christ, Christ dwells; when we venerate an icon of the archangel Gabriel, this immortal being, wings spread and scepter in hand, stands revealed before us in all his glory.

It follows that an icon occupies space in a very strange way. To all appearances it is an ordinary object, hung on a wall or propped in a corner like any other devotional aid, and yet its borders enclose space that is not of this world. The icon contains divine space in which divine beings dwell. This explains why icons rest on lecterns in Orthodox churches; they are analogous to holy scripture, in which the word of God dwells. It also explains the icon's singular appearance. Look at one, and you instantly notice that something is awry. Nothing casts a shadow, buildings tilt in gravity-defying ways, human figures display impossibly elongated torsos and limbs. These distortions serve a spiritual goal. The peculiar perspective, with buildings and mountains curved toward the figure of Christ, and the directionless flood of light (the same divine illumination that surrounded the great Russian mystic Saint Seraphim of Sarov) suggest that we are no longer on the profane earth but in a precinct of paradise. Natural laws — of gravity, the density of matter, and the decay of flesh — have been repealed. The grace of God rules all. Colors assume symbolic value: white for purity, blue for transcendence, purple for wealth or power, and black for the mysterious otherness of God. Within the frame of the icon, heaven stands revealed.

For this divine action to unfold, the icon must be the fruit of intense devotion, hard labor, and continuous prayer. The iconographer strives for holiness, not artistic recognition. Principles of Beaux Arts have no authority in this sanctified calling: originality counts for nothing, and the best iconographers build upon, rather than rebel against, the creations of their predecessors. Inspiration means submission to the Holy Spirit rather than the dictates of individual genius. A dedicated iconographer adheres to a strict moral and religious code, which may include the following provisions:

> Let it be known, then, that the icon painter shall be meek, humble, and reverent, neither filled with vain talk, nor empty laughter, not quarrelsome, not envious, not a drinker of spirits, not a thief nor a murderer; and above all things, that he shall sustain in great mindfulness a pure chastity of soul and body . . . and that always and everywhere the icon painters shall attend constantly to their spiritual fathers, telling them everything always and living always according to their teachings about fasting and prayer and all the ascetic disciplines.[25]

The *Hermeneia (Painter's Manual)* by the Greek Orthodox monk Dionysios of Fourna (c. 1670–?) offers a practical guide to the painting of icons, perusing matters as diverse as how to bake and mix gypsum, how to color a narthex, and how to depict the vanities of the world. It begins with an invocation to Mary, Mother of God, whose intercessions open the way to the "pleasures of eternity"; this is followed by a plea to "all painters, and to others who love instruction" to "pray for us to the Lord, so that we may be delivered from the fearful condemnation of the slothful servant."[26] These preliminaries hint at the main argument of the book — that an iconographer can master his or her craft only by means of prayer. Dionysios instructs the novice to draw until he or she acquires rudimentary skills and then to approach a priest to request prayers for guidance and protection before a Marian icon known as the *Hodigitria* (traditionally ascribed to Saint Luke the Evangelist). After offering petitions, the priest must make the sign of the cross on the painter's forehead and then recite the following words of praise and supplication:

> O Lord Jesus Christ Our God . . . who imprinted the sacred shape of Thine immaculate face on the holy veil and, by means of this, healed the illness of Abgar and enlightened his soul with the full knowledge of God . . . enlighten and bring wisdom to the soul and heart and mind of this Thy servant [name] and so direct these hands that they may depict — most perfectly beyond all reproach — the forms of Thy person, of Thine All-Holy Mother, and of all the saints; to do so to the glory, splendor and beauty of Thy holy church, and for the remission of the sins of all who truly revere and devoutly kiss and so bring honor to Her.[27]

Here we have a golden chain of prayer: the painter, in company with the priest, bows before the *Hodigitria*, an image linked to the apostolic era and thus to the immediate presence of Christ; the priestly prayer tells the story of the *Acheiropoietas*, asking that Christ bestow wisdom and insight on the iconographer, so that he or she may produce works that will, in turn, inspire veneration and prayer on the part of the faithful, leading to their salvation and, God willing, their sanctity. This is the imperative claim of the icon: born in prayer, it gives birth to prayer for the good of all humankind.

The Word

In the realm of tradition, what holds for the image holds for the word. Spoken and written prayer is literature bending its knee:

> O father! Great man!
> King of this earth,
> Favor me each day with nourishment.
> Give me good water and sweet sleep.
> I am poor. Art thou hungry?
> Here is a morsel from my poor table.
> Eat it if you wish.[28]

Praise, petition, self-humbling, and sacrifice: how much is packed into this brief Patagonian prayer! And yet whatever beauty it possesses serves only a spiritual mission. What John Henry Newman says of good preaching can be said with equal force about spoken or written prayer: that the aim should determine the manner, that a fine style is beside the point, that one should address God like a marksman taking aim at a target:

> We ask questions perhaps about diction, elocution, rhetorical power; but does the commander of a besieging force dream of holiday displays, reviews, mock engagements, feats of strength, or trials of skill, such as would be graceful and suitable on a parade ground when a foreigner of rank was to be received and *fêted;* or does he aim at one and one thing only, viz., to take the strong place? Display dissipates the energy, which for the object in view needs to be concentrated and condensed. We have no reason to suppose that the Divine blessing follows the lead of human accomplishments. Indeed, St. Paul, writing to the Corinthians, who made much of such advantages of nature, contrasts the persuasive words of human wisdom "with the showing of the Spirit," and tells us that "the kingdom of God is not in speech, but in power."[29]

Concentrating and subjugating the faculty of verbal imagination appears to free the creative impulse. Traditional spoken and written prayers display a breathtaking variety of forms, including invocation, proclamation, exorcism, novena, meditation, hymn, didactic wisdom, and lament. They may be intricate and lengthy like Psalm 119 ("Blessed are the undefiled in the way . . ."), whose 176 lines are structured according to an alphabetical acrostic. Or they may be as short and sharp as a dagger, like this Sumerian prayer dating from about 2000 B.C.E.: "O God, our sins are many; strip us of them like a garment." They may conjure or abjure, curse or jest, praise or blame, plea or give thanks; they may be joyous, bitter, calm, choleric, charitable, or vindictive; they may burst forth at any hour, under any circumstance, in any place.

Every prayer tradition exhibits this peacocklike variety and splendor, and every prayer tradition is in this sense all-encompassing, and in addressing universal human needs (to praise, to plea, to be forgiven), may conceal its geographic and historical particulars. Yet every prayer tradition exhibits this variety and this comprehensiveness in its own peculiar fashion. An unidentified psalm-in-a-bottle quickly discloses its provenance to anyone familiar with the rhetorical strategies and tropes of Hebrew prayer, its couplets and strophes, parallelisms, antiphonal dialogues, alphabetic acrostics, paradoxes, metaphors, meters, and puns. We might recognize a Hebrew prayer by the way it raises its edifice upon what seems at first no more than a simple redundancy:

> Bless the LORD, O my soul:
> and all that is within me, bless his holy name. (Psalm 103:1)
>
> Lift up your head, O ye gates;
> and be ye lift up, ye everlasting doors;
> and the King of glory shall come in. (Psalm 24:7)

and develops its theme by small variations:

> O give thanks unto the LORD, for he is good: because his mercy endureth forever.
> Let Israel now say, that his mercy endureth forever.
> Let the house of Aaron now say, that his mercy endureth forever.
> Let them now that fear the LORD say, that his mercy endureth forever. (Psalm 118:1–4)

Repetition in this case is not merely incantation, for it permits development. A repetition with variation can intensify or provide an impelling direction to a narrative:

> Thou hast breached all his walls;
> thou hast laid his strongholds in ruins. (Psalm 89:40 RSV)

As biblical interpreter Robert Alter observes, "If something is broken in the first verset, it is smashed or shattered in the second verset; if a city is destroyed in the first verset, it is turned into a heap of rubble in the second."[30]

No one has yet succeeded in counting all the varieties of parallelism or all the other poetic structures in biblical prayer, but they have a palpable effect. We know the sound of a biblical prayer when we hear it, even if we are not well versed in the theory of biblical poetry. We instantly recognize the familiar address with which it begins ("My God, my God," Psalm 22:1) and the characteristic ways in which it ends, whether circling back to the beginning (Psalm 8:1 and 8:9: "O LORD our Lord, how excellent is thy name in all the earth!") or offering the entire prayer as sacrifice ("Let the words of my mouth, and the meditation of my heart, be acceptable in thy sight, O LORD, my strength, and my redeemer," Psalm 19:14). To the extent that the Bible still informs our culture, we have an instinct for this kind of prayer, an ear for the particular cadence of dialogue between the God of Israel and his people.

It is characteristic of traditional prayer to make the most of available resources for literary invention, while concealing the name of the inventor. As we have noted earlier, most scholars now agree that the psalms ascribed to King David were composed by numerous hands. Authorial anonymity, or in this case, pseudo-epigraphy (attributing an unsigned work to a cultural hero who may not have an actual role in its composition), is common in cultures that make no fetish of individuality, in which established artistic canons are faithfully preserved and the touchstone of art is truth rather than individual self-expression; it is rare to find a signed creation, rarer still to find anything like the idea of copyright or intellectual property where prayer is concerned. Yet traditional prayer is far from impersonal; far from the abstract, abstruse prayers to the All, the Absolute, or the World Soul of which modern theosophical and transcendentalist philosophers are fond. We would venture to say that traditional prayer is the product of individual genius wedded to collective wisdom, and counting itself little in the match. In oral cultures, the author of a prayer fades to a vanishing point; in literate cultures, the author's role is nearly as subdued. King David was a real personality, and his personal history is stamped on the Psalms, whoever may have actually composed them; but his personality is not the main concern. Rather, it is David the archetypal king and personification of his people whose profile shines forth from the Psalms.

The boundaries of traditional prayer can be elastic enough to permit new prayer forms to arise, faithful to original insights but responsive to a changing culture. At a sophisticated stage of literary composition, there is considerable scope for invention. Creations that are deeply conservative in structure or content can venture into fresh, startling territory. One thinks of the poems of Rūmi, full of personal detail, which endured as prayers only by being enfolded into the living tradition of the Mevlevi dervishes; or of the Eucharistic prayers of Saint Thomas Aquinas, which forged a new language of adoration, yet quickly grafted themselves onto the living tree of Catholic tradition. The faithful who sing Thomas's "Tantum Ergo Sacramentum" or "Pange Lingua" are made conscious not of the scholastic giant who composed them but of the sacrament to which the words direct their vision.

There are, however, cases in which the elasticity of traditional prayer is put to the test: the *Confessions* of Saint Augustine, an extended literary prayer of vast subtlety and complexity, stretched the boundaries of traditional prayer far enough to inspire a new genre, that of personal memoir. The *Confessions* was unusable as a precedent for Christian prayer, yet in its fidelity to the tradition of the faith it contributed to the organic development of the overall culture of Christian prayer and fostered the composition of intimate prayers for private devotion (Saint Anselm, Lancelot Andrewes, and many others).

Tradition dies if it remains static, but it also dies if growth is forced upon it on the basis of principles external to its essence. The matter of translating traditional prayers — a topic of lively debate these days — is fraught with such dangers. Some make the case that it is better not to translate prayer at all. Many feel that there is no better way to preserve the sense of the sacred than to pray in the language of one's ancestors, a language set apart for that purpose, undefiled by the marketplace and undeformed by passing fads. A common hallowed tongue permits believers of diverse ethnic and national backgrounds to pray in unison and therefore to belong to a common culture. The Muslim who rolls out a prayer carpet by a Cairo curbside for morning prayer is aware that his or her brothers and sisters in America and Asia praise God in the same Arabic words.

Nonetheless, the stream of traditional prayer flows through many channels, and a good case can be made for the simplicity, directness, and transparency of praying in one's vernacular language, provided translators are sufficiently immersed in the given tradition to serve its underlying vision. Much depends upon whether translations or new compositions are made during a period when the vernacular is robust enough to become virtually a sacred language in its own right. Old Church Slavonic provided a language of prayer fully the match of its Byzantine models. Similarly, the 1549 prototype of the Book of Common Prayer, crafted by Thomas Cranmer, archbishop of Canterbury, not only forged the identity of the Church of England and uprooted its Roman Catholic antecedents, but it also gave the English-speaking world a language of prayer, a standard of poetic composition, and a storehouse of maxims and figures of speech such as "ashes to ashes, dust to dust." From its formal authorization in 1662 until the present, proposals for revision (and in recent times, alternative forms of worship) have unfailingly provoked intense argument among the churches of the Anglican Communion. Understandably so, for each step away from the ancient model risks rupture with the past; yet not to take such a step risks stagnation. Traditional prayer has always lived with such tensions and cannot live without them. For the life of tradition is not just conservation of past forms, but also organic development and faithful change.

Theocracy

If we conceive of traditional culture as occupying a series of concentric rings, with the hearth at its center and encompassing, in its annular expansion, the major realms of human endeavor — family life, labor (farming, fishing, hunting), commerce, ritual activity, the arts, and so on — we must sooner or later arrive at the outermost ring, the retaining wall that safeguards and binds all that lies within. In one sense, this wall is prayer itself, which regulates the daily round, fosters the arts, crowns ritual, and, in general, grounds traditional society in the *Urgrund* of God. In another sense, however, the retaining wall is what we commonly call government, the regulator of public (and often private) activity throughout society. The first thing to note about government in traditional cultures is that it takes many forms. In smaller communities political power might reside with a chief, holy man, clan or family leader, council of elders, or some combination of the foregoing. The culture of the *Carmina Gadelica* blossomed under local rule; larger governmental structures may have lurked in the background, but effective authority resided within the family, clan, and parish. A very different arrangement held sway in the quasi-traditional society of ancient Athens, with its oligarchy of nine *archons* giving way to a modified democracy. Despite this variety, however, one form of government capable of coexisting with a number of social structures predominated in traditional culture and profoundly affected the role of prayer: theocracy, a term coined by the first-century historian Josephus to designate rule by God or the gods (or, in effect, God's earthly manifestations or representatives).

Many scholars recognize three basic types of theocracy: rule by priests or prophets, by a divine monarch, or by divine law.[31] The first type, relatively rare, occurred now and then in the history of ancient Israel (for instance, during the rule of the prophet Moses, who, according to Josephus, ascribed "dominion to God") and more recently in Tibet, which until the Chinese invasion of the 1950s was governed by an oligarchy of monks led by the Dalai Lama. The second type, rule by a divine or divinely appointed monarch, is exemplified by the world's first nation-state, ancient Egypt, whose pharaoh governed as the incarnation of Horus, "the Great God," and son of Re, the sun god; during the Reformation, Henry VIII transformed England into a theocracy of sorts by adding to his monarchical office the role of head of the Church of England. Most theocracies, however, locate their source of power in divine law or the divine will. In a sense, as scholars have noted, every theocracy derives power from these sources, because every ruler — prophet, pharaoh, monk, or king — is answerable to God or divine truth (thus a Jewish prophet is subject to Mosaic law, and the Dalai Lama to the Buddha's dharma). Societies that have made divine law the explicit basis of theocratic rule include Puritan New England, the papacy of the High Middle Ages, the early Mormon Church, and Islam throughout much of its history.

Theocracy is, then, a political system with a long and venerable history; nor is that history dead. The most important political development on the world stage during the past half century may be the rise of Islamic fundamentalism, which includes as a core tenet the establishment of a Muslim state governed by Shariah (Muslim law). The present theocratic governments of Saudi Arabia, Sudan, and Iran constitute three of the movement's more notable successes. All three, as is well known, suppress various political and religious rights — freedom of assembly, freedom of the press, freedom of worship (at least for non-Muslims), to name a few — taken for granted by those weaned on the liberties of modern liberal democracies. Theocracies of the past, with one or two exceptions, have an equally poor record in this regard.

What is the relationship of theocracy to prayer? A nuanced response is required, for prayer thrives in theocracies — or so it would appear at first glance. One reason for the rise of Wahhabism, the nineteenth-century fundamentalist movement that led to the modern theocratic Saudi state, was a desire to reinvigorate Muslim religious life, which in large measure means Muslim prayer life, and the vigorous devotion that characterizes Saudi society speaks to their success. The same is true of other Islamic theocracies, most notably Iran. Theocracy protects the autonomy of prayer against a number of outside forces — not least, many modern Muslims (and others) would argue, the depravities of Western consumerism, which (they might go on to say) would substitute boutiques for houses of prayer and Hollywood films for holy scripture. Be this as it may, little doubt exists that in the past theocracies have provided strong patronage for religious arts, including those associated with prayer — witness the temple and funerary painting and sculpture of ancient Egypt or the church mosaics of Byzantium. Theocracies have also blocked secular powers from usurping ecclesiastical prerogatives. For example, in the investiture controversy of the eleventh century, Pope Gregory VII, who perceived the papacy as the absolute authority in all spheres, religious and secular, clashed with the German monarch Henry IV over the appointment of bishops, a tug-of-war that culminated in the celebrated "Walk to Canossa," where the penitent king stood for three days, barefoot in the snow, to beg forgiveness from the pontiff.

At the same time, theocracy harbors forces that can be inimical to prayer. While the official state religion flourishes, other traditions may be suppressed; in Saudi Arabia, it is illegal to display a Bible or a crucifix in public (a ban curiously mirrored by recent efforts of the French government, historically wedded to secular humanism, to prohibit Muslim head coverings and large Christian crosses in public schools). Equally troubling is the danger of the concentration of power in a single person or in a small group of aristocrats, which typifies a theocracy. The reign of Akhenaton, pharaoh of Egypt (r. 1353–1336 B.C.E.), exemplifies this problem. A religious genius, Akhenaton stunned Egypt by introducing both a radical monotheism, directed toward the Aton (Sun Disk), which overturned a thousand years of Egyptian polytheism (and, according to Freud's doubtful theory, inspired Moses to bring the concept of the One God to the Hebrews), and a new aesthetic, colorful and naturalistic, that helped infuse his new teaching into every aspect of Egyptian royal life. His "Hymn to the Sun" epitomizes his art:

> Thy dawning is beautiful in the horizon of heaven,
> O living Aton, Beginning of life!
> When thou risest in the eastern horizon of heaven,
> Thou fillest every land with thy beauty;
> For thou art beautiful, great, glittering, high over the earth;
> Thy rays, they encompass the lands, even all thou hast made.
> Thou art Re, and thou hast carried them all away captive;
> Thou bindest them by thy love.
> Though thou art afar, thy rays are on earth;
> Though thou art on high, thy footprints are the day.

Yet the same poem reveals a degree of self-approbation that, at least in hindsight, foreshadows the coming disaster:

> There is no other that knoweth thee,
> Save thy son Ikhnaton [Akhenaton].
> Thou has made him wise in thy designs
> And in thy might. . . .
> The son of Re, living in truth, lord of diadems,
> Ikhnaton. . . .[32]

Akhenaton's reign promoted, in the view of many Egyptologists, the most traumatic event in the history of ancient Egypt — the identification of divine will with the person of the pharaoh. Even high court officials, often men of robust individuality, would describe themselves (as we know from temple inscriptions) as "created" by Akhenaton, to whom they owed their very being, and all cultic activity became the exclusive province of the royal family. Akhenaton proclaimed himself and his wife, Nefertiti, high priests of Aton, usurping the role of the traditional priesthood. The other gods of the Egyptian pantheon were downgraded, if not banished. Prayer became, at least within the sphere of Akhenaton's influence (which perhaps did not extend far beyond his new capital city, Akhetaton), exclusively a matter of worshiping the Aton and its divine manifestations, pharaoh and wife. Akhenaton's revolution was bold, brilliant, and short-lived; soon after his death, his son Tutankhamun restored the traditional gods and began to obliterate his father's palaces and temples; and prayer, which for a time had flowed into such constricted but lovely channels — and adumbrated the monotheism that

Akhenaton offering a sacrifice to Aton, the sun god. Egypt, 1350 B.C.E.

would later become the world's dominant theology — returned to its older, wider, customary course.

Power and prayer, as the story of Akhenaton reveals, make uneasy bedfellows. Prayer confers power — witness the miracle stories associated with saints throughout the world — but power, in turn, can set its teeth on prayer. This does not mean that we should abolish all law, all hierarchy, all distinction between orthodoxy and heterodoxy in the world of prayer. Like every creative act, prayer needs to be cultivated, shaped, deepened, strengthened, even perfected, and this requires will, discipline, and the rule of law. But it is, perhaps, not the law of the state — coercive, imperious, and inflexible — but the law of God — loving, subtle, and forgiving — that alone produces prayer worthy of the name. "Render therefore unto Caesar the things that are Caesar's; and unto God the things that are God's." Who among us, surveying the blighted history of theocracy, would conclude that prayer should be rendered to Caesar?

CHAPTER 9

Prayer and the Modern Arts

THE CROFTERS AND FISHERS of the *Carmina Gadelica* lived in a world steeped in prayer, but they also lived on the brink of cultural devastation. By the beginning of the twentieth century, reverence for sun and moon had become, as Alexander Carmichael notes, "a matter of form rather than of belief." The fairies and selkies had withdrawn to the shadows, and those who remembered the ancient ways took pains to hide their knowledge. One old man disclosed to Carmichael a "going to sleep" prayer; a day later, he hiked twenty-six miles to catch up to the folklorist and begged him not to publish it, declaring, "I should not like cold eyes to read it in a book."[1] Carmichael himself thundered against the decay of Gaelic life, spreading blame over the Reformation, a repressive school system, draconian British policies, and the arch-villainous "spirit of the age." The collapse of the indigenous Highlands culture reminded him of the destruction wrought upon Native Americans across the ocean.

Carmichael would be yet more dismayed if he could revisit his beloved Gaels a century later. English poet Kathleen Raine, who walked many of the same paths as Carmichael, recalled in the late twentieth century that she "first visited the Western Isles before television had reached them; now the same people as then used to sit round the walls of the kitchen to sing and hear stories from the Bard of the Isle, sit on the same chairs and settles watching whatever flickers on that hypnotic screen." The glories of Gaelic culture had fallen prey to "the hypnotic twaddle of the mass-media," to "a trashy materialist ideology bringing in its train discontent, vulgarity and loss of identity."[2]

That the *Tonight Show* (or its British equivalent) has usurped the nighttime *ceilidh* is not news; it marks but the latest stage in a complex process of cultural change that began, in most Western nations, somewhere around the Renaissance, when the hierarchies and dogmas of the Christian Middle Ages began to lose their footing. Over the past five hundred years, attrition of traditional customs around the globe has affected not only Christian but also Buddhist, Hindu, Islamic, and animist cultures, shrinking, if not utterly exterminating, innumerable prayer practices of surpassing beauty and spiritual depth. But it may not be the unmitigated catastrophe that Alexander Carmichael and Kathleen Raine imagine. One can argue that half a millennium of evolution has rained both curse and blessing upon the world of prayer; that the death of one form of devotion or petition often gives birth to another; that the ecology of human prayer as a whole, and each of its small coherent ecosystems, is so complex that it is foolhardy to pass summary judgment; and that the future may bring a more abundant harvest than we can imagine. To justify this assertion, we will look at what has happened to prayer in art and literature during the fall of tradition and the rise of modernism.

Painting

To trace prayer through the history of art is to track a bird of paradise through a sunset sky: one glory tends to obscure the other, and we must be content with occasional glimpses of our quarry. During the age of the icon, lasting roughly from 787, when the Seventh Ecumenical Council reaffirmed the veneration of holy images, to the fourteenth-century birth of the Renaissance, Western art was the handmaiden of faith, and painting the sacramental art par excellence: an outward and visible sign of an inward and invisible grace. Commissioned as prayer offerings and created by artists who themselves prayed, sometimes day and night, icons proliferated in churches, monasteries, and private homes, fostering prayer in all who venerated them. These holy images were themselves material prayers, in which the three kingdoms of creation — animal (egg tempera), vegetable (birch panel), and mineral (gold highlights) — were uplifted, transfigured, and deified in the light of Christian faith. To millions of the faithful, icons were as essential to daily life as food or drink.

All this changed with the Renaissance. Art discovered the third dimension, the pull of gravity, the ravages of time. Suddenly parallel lines met in the distance, trees cast shadows, and faces erupted in pimples and warts. The corporeal world of corruption, sin, and death usurped the spiritualized world of resurrection, purity, and eternal life. The rationale behind these changes, as art historian Mahmoud Zibawi has pointed out, is neatly summarized in the eleventh canto of Dante's *Inferno:*

> . . . Nature takes her course
>
> from the Divine Intellect and from its art;
> and if you check your *Physics,*
> you will find, not many pages along,
>
> that your art as far as it is able,
> follows Nature as the student does the master;
> so that your art is to God like a grandchild.[3]

Dante is building on Aristotle's contention (in *Physics,* book II, part 2) that art imitates nature. As nature imitates (that is, takes direction from) God, it follows that art also, albeit one step removed, imitates God. For Dante, art continues to serve a Christian purpose, but its method will be that described by the celebrated pagan philosopher, taking as its model the natural world rather than a supernatural "new heaven, new earth," and verisimilitude, rather than abstraction, as its method. The rule of iconography has been decisively overturned. From now on, painting about prayer will unfold in the light of the sun rather than in the uncreated light of Mount Tabor.

Dante guards the gates of the Renaissance in tandem with his almost exact contemporary, the painter and architect Giotto di Bondone (1266–1337). In Giotto we perceive the first mature signs of this new, earthy aesthetic. His most famous biographer, Giorgio Vasari, describes the break with tradition: "[Giotto] began to draw so ably from life that he made a decisive break with the crude traditional Byzantine style and brought to life the great art of painting as we know it today, introducing the techniques of drawing accurately from life, which had been neglected for more than two hundred years."[4]

Giotto's portrait of Dante (c. 1337) epitomizes the new style by emphasizing the poet's long face, curved nose, jutting chin, and haughty, melancholy mien. It is a purely individual portrait, without a hint of the formal canons of iconography. The same realism emerges in Giotto's famed portrait of Saint Francis of Assisi: here again, the haggard, birdlike face, exhausted eyes, and protruding ears suggest an authentic likeness rather than an idealized or spiritualized image. Both pictures churn with emotion — the sorrow of the exiled poet, the suffering of the stigmatic — gone forever is the cool, dispassionate glance of the Byzantine icon saints.

This is not to suggest that Giotto's paintings are unflaggingly realistic. Many, such as *The Ecstasy of Saint Francis,* which shows the great saint levitating in a puffy pink cloud, arms raised in the *orans* prayer position, depict events as uncanny as those found in any icon. But even in Giotto's depictions of supernatural episodes, one perceives a deep respect for the natural order. In *Saint Damian's Crucifix Speaks to Saint Francis*, the saint kneels, leaning forward, and we feel the awkwardness of his posture, conveyed by the long bow of his back and his inclined body, painted as a vast slab of reddish white robes. This saint is a flesh-and-blood being, not a wraith. Giotto uses naturalistic details — Francis's intense gaze, upturned toward heaven; his curved hands, fingers elongated as if straining for God — to present an atmosphere of intense, electric prayer. This mudra of the beseeching saint, heartbreaking in purity and beauty, exemplifies the Renaissance vision: art, as Dante suggests, will serve God best by depicting the world as it is. Henceforth paintings about prayer will unfold in everyday time and space, the world in which we live and move and have our being. From now on, even a praying saint is one of us.

Sometimes the praying saint turns out to be a painter as well. Fra Giovanni of Fiesole (1400–1455), better known as Fra Angelico of the Order of Preachers (the Dominicans), enjoyed, at the monastery of San Marco in Florence, a life remarkable both for spiritual purity and artistic fecundity. His reputation for sanctity rests largely on the writings of Vasari, who reports that the holy friar "shunned all worldly intrigues, lived in purity and holiness, and befriended the poor as much as his soul is now, I believe, befriended by heaven." Vasari recounts that Fra Angelico commenced each painting with a prayer, wept copiously when depicting scenes of Christ's Passion, and never retouched his work, believing that his initial efforts best conformed to the will of God. Though this has the flavor of pious legend, there may be something in it, for Vasari received much of his intelligence from a friar at San Marco who, in his youth, had been acquainted with close friends of the painter. According to Vasari, Fra Angelico not only practiced a prayerful life but considered it indispensable for anyone who would wield the brush, along with a quiet, untroubled life; he liked to say that the man who occupies himself with the things of Christ should live with Christ.[5]

Vasari himself draws from this sensible advice the more doubtful conclusion that godliness is a prerequisite for artistic success, arguing in his *Lives of the Artists* that "the rare and perfect talent that Fra Angelico enjoyed neither can nor should be granted to anyone who does not lead a thoroughly holy life."[6] Perhaps this explains the brevity of Vasari's biography of Fra Filippo Lippi (1406–1469), a contemporary of Fra Angelico who was as famous for his salacious sexual exploits as for his splendid altarpieces and panel paintings. In any event, Fra Angelico's paintings exude the calm intelligence and deep sympathies of a lifetime spent with Gospels, Mass, and daily prayer. Many depict people in postures of prayer: Saint John kneeling at the foot of the Cross; one of the Magi prostrate before the baby Jesus; Saint Dominic, chin in hand, sitting in meditation beneath an image of the Passion.

One important source for Fra Angelico's knowledge of these prayer positions, in addition to his own prolonged monastic experience, was almost certainly *The Nine Ways of Prayer of Saint Dominic,* a book published about half a century after the saint's death in 1221 and widely read and studied in Dominican circles. This curious volume, assembled from the testimony of eyewitnesses who spied on Dominic while he was rapt in adoration, is an invaluable guide to prayer as it was practiced in medieval and Renaissance Italy. The saint is seen bowing or kneeling before the altar; prostrating himself in the dust; flagellating himself with an iron chain; standing with arms stretched sideways in cruciform position or extended high over his head like an arrow aimed at heaven; reading, laughing, crying, and talking to invisible companions; and shooing away devils as he meditates in the countryside. Much leaps out from this entertaining presentation: the blend of sober and manic actions; the sense that the miraculous is just around the corner; the use of pain to awaken attention and do penance; and, of course, the remarkable variety of postures, in which every part of the human anatomy — hands, feet, arms, legs, face, head, torso, all but the profane regions of reproduction and excrement — participates in prayer. Was, then, Renaissance Italy a land of praying virtuosos, a paradise of prayer? Alas, no, if only because the techniques of Saint Dominic and his spiritual kin, although not denied to the populace at large, were practiced almost exclusively by members of religious communities.

We can say with some certainty, however, that at least in the Dominican monastery of San Marco, prayer blossomed. How could it not, with such powerful inducements? The friars who wandered its halls encountered these hieratic postures countless times each day, whenever they turned a corner or ascended a staircase and found themselves facing one of Fra Angelico's majestic frescoes. A case in point is the painter's most famous image, *The Annunciation,* situated on the wall of the south floor of the upper corridor of the monastery. Here the Virgin sits on a stool, arms folded on her breast, while the archangel Gabriel genuflects before her: though taking distinctly different prayer stances, both figures convey humility, obedience, and serenity, quintessential Christian and monastic virtues. In keeping with the Renaissance aesthetic, there is nothing otherworldly about this encounter. Virgin and angel meet in a colonnaded palazzo or cloister, reflecting the architecture in which the monks worked and prayed. The portraiture is delicate but realistic: we can see the flush on Mary's cheek, the sheen in the angel's wings. Fra Angelico's many other frescoes repeat and add to this lesson. The holy painter's oeuvre, a visual counterpart to the written text of *The Nine Ways of Prayer of Saint Dominic,* thus constitutes a prayer manual in its own right, and a vital element in the spiritual formation of generations of Dominicans.

Fra Angelico, writes Vasari, "would choose only holy subjects" for his art. The same was true of other medieval and early Renaissance painters and, of course, of Byzantine iconographers. As Europe passed through the three-pronged revolution of the Renaissance, the Reformation, and the Enlightenment, however, many humanistic disciplines, including the arts, stepped away from traditional models. Painting followed suit, with biblical or hagiographic motifs giving way to landscapes, still lifes, scenes from pagan mythology, and images of everyday life. Where did prayer fit into these new emphases? Artists working in other disciplines quickly found new modes of prayerful expression, such as the polyphony of Byrd, the baroque counterpoint of Bach, and the *pensées* of Pascal. But could one depict prayer in painting without recourse to Vasari's "holy subjects"? The attempt to meet this challenge has, in one way or another, set the agenda for the visual arts in relation to prayer for the past four hundred years.

The first important effort to depict prayer in a new way emerged in the short career of the Dutch master Johannes Vermeer (1632–1675). Vermeer stands, to borrow Wilde's phrase, in symbolic relationship to his age, for he was deeply religious — a convert to Catholicism who filled his canvases with Christian allegory and symbol — yet also at home with the revolutionary tools and techniques of Enlightenment science, almost certainly employing a camera obscura for some of his works and counting among his companions the great optician, microscopist, and discoverer of the world of protozoa, Antonie van Leeuwenhoek. Vermeer specialized in domestic scenes, most portraying women as they performed mundane tasks — pouring milk, stitching lace, playing the virginal (an early harpsichord) — in the drawing rooms and kitchens of seventeenth-century Delft, and it was by depicting these humble occupations that he worked his aesthetic revolution.

Let us consider, by way of example, *Woman Holding a Balance* (c. 1662–1665), a painting executed at the height of Vermeer's powers. This canvas depicts a pregnant woman standing at a table, a jeweler's balance in her right hand. Behind her hangs a painting of the Last Judgment, the only obvious religious note in the composition. At first glance, the picture seems no more than a beautifully realized depiction of an everyday event, a merchant's wife weighing her valuables. But in fact the painting swims with spiritual allegory. The woman stands before the painting in such a way that the elements of the apocalyptic vision surround her: the figure of Christ floats above her head, the souls of the elect rejoice before her, and the souls of the damned cower behind her. She is, then, intimately involved with this cosmic judgment. Given this clue, what do we make of the balance clutched in her hand? On the table before her lie gold coins and a box of jewels, but the scales are empty. She is weighing something other than material wealth. The analogy to the Last Judgment becomes clear: she is weighing her soul, as Christ weighs the souls of the dead, and the scales tell us that her soul is weightless, free of material dross, a thing of pure grace. The woman is in fact an icon of Mary; thus the blue cloak and white veil, traditional garb of the Virgin, an identification underscored by her rotund belly. *Woman Holding a Balance* is nothing less than a secular Annunciation, sharing with Fra Angelico's masterpiece in the corridor at San Marco a nearly palpable sense of God's quickening presence.

Thus does Vermeer transform a domestic scene into a Christian vision of the Virgin of Delft. In so doing, he tells us something about the place of prayer in the seventeenth-century Netherlands. The window in the painting floods the room with light, an allusion not only to the fecundating power of the Holy Spirit two thousand years ago in the town of Nazareth, but to the ever-present power of God to illuminate the soul. The woman's relaxed face and lowered eyelids express the peace of accepting God's word. She is alone, at rest, enfolded in silence. *Woman Holding a Balance* proclaims that the harmony, grace, and purity of Mary — the high fruits of the contemplative life — can be found even among the familiar accoutrements of a bourgeois urban Dutch household.

Vermeer's discovery of what we might call contemplative painting was a watershed in the history of art, but several centuries would pass before its full effect became evident. From the seventeenth through the nineteenth centuries, prayer remained a popular theme of artists, but the results, for the most part, were garish or maudlin, veering toward the kitsch that proliferates at church bazaars and religious shrines. Every so often, though, a painter would arise who captured something authentic about prayer, often in portrayals of ordinary folk in moments of petition or pious reflection. An outstanding example is *Old Woman Praying* by Nicolaes Maes (1634–1693). Here an elderly peasant, most likely a widow, prays alone over a scanty meal of bread, fish, and wine (or water; the jug is covered). A Bible rests in the window alcove at her side. In the woman's furrowed brow and ardent introspection we read the suffering that she faces each day, as well as the courage, patience, and resolve that she receives, through prayer, to help her in her struggles. In a sense, the painting is a Vermeer canvas turned inside out: we have a woman by herself in a domestic setting, attending to the daily round, but the painting is set at night, with flocking shadows in place of the flooding light that signals for Vermeer the immediate presence of the divine. Only the Bible and the symbols of the Eucharist — bread, wine, fish — suggest that God is near. The painter focuses on the human side of the equation, the woman's sacrificial offering of her own flesh, wrinkled with age, bent without fail day after day over her labors and devotions. This is a prayer study stripped of the numinous, an image harshly realistic but nonetheless filled with a strong, steadfast faith.

Maes's teacher, Rembrandt van Rijn (1606–1669), gives us a third alternative: a painting that explores prayer not as divine manifestation or as human habit but as an attribute of nature. His *Saint Francis Beneath a Tree Praying*, an etching and drypoint of the saint in rapture, is based on a passage in Saint Bonaventure's *Life of Francis:*

> After that [Francis] began to seek out solitary places, well suited for sorrow; and there he prayed incessantly with *unutterable groanings* (Rom. 8:26). After long and urgent prayer, he merited to be heard by the Lord. One day while he was praying in such a secluded spot and became totally absorbed in God through his extreme fervor, Jesus Christ appeared to him fastened to the cross. Francis's *soul melted* (Cant. 5:6) at the sight. . . . From that time on he clothed himself with a spirit of poverty, a sense of humility and a feeling of intimate devotion.[7]

The painting emphasizes the primeval density of the forest. The saint, bearing the sharp, fierce features of a woodland gnome, blends into the foliage, a small gnarled creature beside a large gnarled tree. Behind the trunk looms the focus of his ecstasy, the miraculous crucifix described by Bonaventure. This object has a supernatural provenance, but Rembrandt draws it as a part of nature, a column of wood that rises from the tree's base like a second trunk. Saint, tree, and crucifix stand in a swirling black mass of lines intertwined into a tumultuous, organic whole. One gets the impression that "Francis's *soul melted*" (Bonaventure's expression) not so much into God as into the earthy muck that surrounds the saint. Francis's prayer becomes a natural event rather than a supernatural revelation; prayer has rarely seemed more earthbound.

If prayer can flourish in a forest bower, why not in a flowered boudoir? *Madeline After Prayer* by the Pre-Raphaelite Daniel Maclise (1806–1870), a work based on John Keats's "The Eve of St. Agnes," depicts a lovely young woman undressing beside her bed in a richly appointed medieval room, crammed with tapestries, holy statues, musical instruments, stained glass, and ornately carved furniture. A Bible lies open on a stand nearby; the woman has just been reading scripture and her face bears a pensive look, eyes downcast, lost in thought. We take her to be a contemplative of sorts, a conjecture supported by her name, for Madeline derives from Mary Magdalene, who is said to have traveled after Christ's Resurrection to southern France, where she donned the clothing of a cloistered hermit and passed her remaining years in solitary prayer. But this portrait must predate the Magdalen's conversion, for the bared shoulders, exposed upper bosom, and luxuriant sweep of red hair, spangled with pearls, suggest the prostitute Magdalene, unredeemed, enslaved to the flesh, an identification reflected in the ardent reds and creams of the sumptuous furniture and hangings. Here, then, stands a sensualist who has just this moment tasted a holier way of life. The transcendent world is intimated but not shown; we see not prayer itself, but the aftermath of prayer. A new woman is being born before our eyes; we are witnessing that most hidden of events, the subtle workings of grace in a fallen soul. Maclise's painting, for all its romantic voluptuousness, is a masterpiece of refined religious psychology.

The canvases of Maes, Rembrandt, and Maclise offer three distinct post-Vermeer approaches to the painting of prayer. Each in its own way extends the quest to praise God and to distill onto canvas something of the divine presence by means of representational realism and an emphasis upon natural or domestic realms. This quest was by no means completed — new avenues opened, for example, in the work of Van Gogh and Gauguin — when the radical turn toward abstraction swept the plastic arts in the late nineteenth and early twentieth centuries. A new way of looking at contemplative painting arose, bringing with it a new challenge: would it be possible to paint naked prayer, pure prayer, prayer unadorned by representational imagery?

Cubism laid the groundwork for this high ambition. This art movement, which thrived during the first decades of the twentieth century, attempted to fragment reality in order to discover its underlying structures and rhythms — what the French poet Guillaume Apollinaire (1880–1918) termed its "metaphysical forms." This links cubism to the antirealist canons of Byzantine iconography, leading Apollinaire to observe that "contemporary art, even if it does not directly stem from specific religious beliefs, nonetheless possesses some of the characteristics of great, that is to say, religious art. . . . [This] is the art of painting new structures out of elements borrowed not from the reality of sight, but from the reality of insight. All men have a sense of this interior reality."[8] Cubism's structural analysis does parallel in some ways the Byzantine aesthetic, notably in rejecting perspective in order to transmit "the reality of insight" rather than the "reality of sight." The cubists discovered much about the nature and interplay of space, light, color, and form, and their canvases express vividly the fracturing of the self in modern times. It can be argued that this method of interior investigation, this communion with the inner form, is itself a kind of prayer, an expression of the search for deeper truth, and in the history of painting it opened the door to further experiments in abstract articulation of the spirit. At the same time, it is prayer in an attenuated mode, lacking a transcendental dimension. More akin to anatomy than iconography, it reveals the hidden structures of reality without reaching their ontological ground.

In the work of Wassily Kandinsky (1866–1944), abstract art realizes its spiritual potential. Born in Russia, Kandinsky spent his childhood surrounded by icons, in museums and at home, and he acknowledged Byzantine art as a primary influence on his own; a photograph of his Paris studio discloses a primitive icon of Mother and Child resting on a table alongside a can of brushes. An intense religiosity runs through all of his writings — he was the most prolific author among major modern artists — and his wife, interviewed ten years after his death, remembered him saying, "Strange that there are people who do not believe!"[9] But how did this faith, inchoate though it may have been — he rarely attended church services or other formal religious events — express itself in painting, and to what extent can his paintings be considered prayers?

At least once, in his *Reminiscences* (1913), Kandinsky links art to prayer. He describes an early period in his life, when he was still painting representational scenes, mostly landscapes, and feeling acute distaste at the result. More satisfying, he found, was his quest for what he terms "the compositional element": "The word *composition* moved me spiritually, and I later made it my aim in life to paint a '*composition.*' This word affected me like a prayer."[10] He developed an inclination toward "the 'hidden,' the concealed," all the spiritual forms within images that he meant by the word *composition* that lead, he believed, to the discovery of new worlds of spiritual truth. The breakthrough came some years later in his studio in Munich:

> It was the hour of approaching dusk. I came home with my paintbox after making a study, still dreaming and wrapped up in the work I had completed, when suddenly I saw an indescribably beautiful picture drenched with an inner glowing. At first I hesitated, then I rushed toward this mysterious picture, of which I saw nothing but forms and col-

> ors, and whose content was incomprehensible. Immediately I found the key to the puzzle: it was a picture I had painted, leaning against the wall, standing on its side. The next day I attempted to get the same effect by daylight. I was only half-successful: even on its side I always recognized the objects, and the fine finish of dusk was missing. Now I knew for certain that the object harmed my paintings.[11]

What should replace the object? The answer came to him instantly: pure form, pure color, pure abstraction. But how to shape these elements? For Kandinsky, the solution was to open himself to spiritual guidance, a process with at least some kinship to contemplative and ecstatic prayer: "All the forms which I ever used came 'from themselves,' they presented themselves complete before my eyes, and it only remained to me to copy them, or they created themselves while I was working, often surprising me." In time he learned to guide or "bridle" this creative flow, arising — or descending — from some unknown dimension. As he concentrated, he found that "my capacity for absorbing myself in the spiritual life of art (and thus, too, of my soul) increased so greatly that I often passed external phenomena without noticing them." Out of these experiences grew his famous abstractions, geometrical and organic forms rotating, pulsating, vibrating — Kandinsky's canvases always display a sense of movement — on a multicolored background. These works, Kandinsky says, represent the "inner life" of painting; as such, he saw them as Christian art that opened (shades of Pentecostalism) to "the revelation of the Holy Spirit." Painting was a means for channeling divine truths, and "as regards me personally," Kandinsky writes, "I love every form which necessarily derives from the spirit, which is created from the spirit. Just as I hate every form which is not."[12]

This surrender of self-will, this eagerness to enter the inner life of the picture (Kandinsky spoke of his wish to "revolve" in the painting, as if inhabiting it and seeing it from within), this porosity toward spiritual influences, this embrace of the Holy Spirit betoken a method of painting that is remarkably similar to prayer. The culmination of this openness appears to be a painterly deification of sorts, an artistic counterpart to the divinization sought by Orthodox mystics: the painter becomes a god or demiurge, molding his or her own cosmos from the raw elements of color and form. "The creation of works of art," Kandinsky grandly declares, "is the creation of the world."[13]

Constantin Brancusi (1876–1957) made no such extravagant claims, although many of his gnomic comments about art resemble those of his Russian predecessor. Born into a peasant family in Romania, Brancusi

Wassily Kandinsky at the canvas.

spent his early years as a shepherd and dyer and remained illiterate until late adolescence. He began working in an academic style, first in Romania and then in Paris. His breakthrough into the simple, geometrical forms that would characterize his later work came in 1907, when he received a commission to erect a funeral monument for a well-known Romanian citizen. The contract stipulated a bust of the deceased atop a seven-foot pedestal, with an "allegorical figure" of a woman mourning at the base. The bust, a sensitive and faithful likeness, exhibited no extraordinary characteristics. But in the mourning woman, Brancusi discovered his artistic path. He shaped an elongated nude, kneeling in prayer, leaning forward, head down, as if carrying the weight of the world's sorrow on her back. At first, Brancusi says, she had outstretched arms. But "it looked to me as if instead of praying, she was cold." So he lopped off one arm and pressed the other against her chest. "I understood then that realism was not essential to expression."[14] The facial features are small, insignificant. This is no particular woman, but Woman bowed in sorrow and awe before the mystery of death. Brancusi called the figure *The Prayer.*

Cutting off the woman's arm proved to be an act not of brutality, but of spiritual insight. From now on Brancusi would remove extraneous elements and bore into the essence of things. He revered the methods of the iconographers and in some ways modeled himself after them:

> I met icon-makers during my youth in the country. I remember that an icon-maker before starting to paint, or a maker of wooden crosses before starting to carve, would fast for a few weeks in a row. They prayed continually that their icons and crosses would be beautiful. Before it is begun, the creation of any artist needs a pre-established orphic atmosphere. Today painters work with a beefsteak and a bottle of wine by their side. The sculptor holds a chisel in one hand and a glass in the other. . . . This kind of thing is no longer pure art; it is art governed by the earthly forces of alcohol and over-eating. I am vegetarian, maybe even because of the memory and example of the icon-painters and cross-makers of long ago.[15]

Flight, Brancusi's favorite motif, bears a close affinity to prayer. The sinuous form of *Bird in Space,* an elongated ovoid — egg, bird, and bird in flight all at once — occupied him for two decades, at various times appearing in marble, bronze, and plaster. Art historian Roger Lipsey has observed that the form of this sculpture "traces an itinerary between unformed matter and immaterial light, and occupies the midpoint between matter and spirit."[16] That is precisely the place of prayer, seated in the flesh and yet yearning toward God. As Brancusi's work deepened, it seemed more and more a search for the eternal. His whole life was, he believed, a movement toward fulfilling this call:

> During my childhood — I slept in bed.
> During my adolescence — I waited at the door.
> In my maturity — I have flown toward the heavens![17]

Photography and the Movies

During the same decades that Kandinsky and Brancusi turned abstract painting and sculpture into spiritual work akin to prayer, a parallel movement unfolded in the embryonic art of photography. In a sense every camera is a contemplative instrument, for it looks at the world dispassionately. Cognizant of this, Edward Weston, Ansel Adams, and others photographed barns, peppers, shorelines, torsos — whatever held artistic promise — to disclose the spiritual realities that lay hidden within an object or exposed on its surface, resident in texture, shape, or color, awaiting the eye of the photographer to make it manifest.

The principal exponent of contemplative photography was Minor White (1908–1976), cofounder and editor of the influential photography magazine *Aperture* and professor of creative photography at the Massachusetts Institute of Technology. White loved to issue oracular epigrams about art and spirituality; one of his more famous, which prefaces a retrospective study of his work published soon after his death, reads: "No matter what role we are in — photographer, beholder, critic — inducing silence for seeing in ourselves, we are given to see from a sacred place. From that place the sacredness of everything may be seen."[18] As this proclamation reveals, White was an awkward writer and a true contemplative. While still in his twenties, he affirmed his vocation, writing in his journal that "the contemplation of deity in all its manifestations is the true work of the soul," a work he soon undertook with a 35mm Argus camera purchased for $12.50. Soon after, he became a Catholic, declaring that "praying used the same energies that creativeness did."[19] Excerpts from his early journals suggest that he enjoyed an active prayer life, a blend of petition, adoration, and lamentations over his repeated struggles with chastity, somewhat reminiscent of Samuel Johnson's battles with indolence. Meanwhile, his photographic work matured under the influence of Alfred Stieglitz's theory of equivalence, which asserts that a photograph can produce in its beholder mental, emotional, and even spiritual responses. In theory, a photograph could induce a state of prayer.

White addressed photography's relation to prayer most directly in one of his last publications, *Octave of Prayer,* the catalogue of a photographic exhibition by the same name that he assembled and exhibited in 1972 at MIT. White proposes an old-fashioned hierarchy of prayer, ascending in eight stages from petition to "deifying union." No doubt to the chagrin of most of the photographers reading his catalogue, White assigns their work a rather low spot on the ladder, placing it on the rung occupied by meditation, only three steps from the bottom. In this form of prayer, he writes, "we make union with some manifestation of Father or Son, for example, a flower or a photograph of one." Taking and viewing a photograph have equal religious value; either act may bring union with the subject of the photograph and thus with an aspect of God, for God resides in all things. Photography is therefore God's work, a modern *opus Dei* for discovering spiritual truth. Once again, White affirms that the "energies" entailed in prayer — in particular, he says, reciting the Lord's Prayer — "were the same as I had brought to making photographs."[20]

What of the upper rungs on White's ladder of prayer? Here White hurls down the gauntlet, suggesting that photographers with experience of higher modes of prayer (identified as "prayer of quiet," "naked orison," "union with the all," "ecstasy," and "beatific union") should consider abandoning their cameras for a finer form of life. "At this 'y' in the road," he writes, "they either turn down the path of the artist or start the search for Reality."[21] He envisions these ex-photographers, now pledged to a deeper life, spending their lives in "orison, meditation, and mystic prayer." This astonishing declaration appears at first to be a summons to vocational mass suicide, consigning the photographer either to spiritual darkness or the rejection of his or her calling. But White offers a way out. A few artists, having attained superior wisdom, may condescend to resume their work, not for their own satisfaction but to guide and inspire others.

Did White plan to follow his own prescription and abandon photography for higher pursuits? We will never know, for he died just a few years after curating the MIT exhibition. During his last years, however, he became a disciple of the Russian spiritual teacher G. I. Gurdjieff, who described the cosmos as a set of interlocking, hierarchically ordered octaves (thus the title of the exhibition) and championed what he called "objective art," based on universal cosmic laws. White's photographs testify to the seriousness with which he undertook camera work as prayer. One of his most celebrated images depicts a landscape in the vicinity of Danville, New York, in 1955. Two farm buildings stand beneath a mackerel sky in a field of dry grass bisected by the long shadow of a telephone pole. Is the shadow a black scar, or is it a cross, the sign of Christ? In any event, what matters is the light. The sun sits low in the sky, its rays nearly horizontal, and a limpid radiance splashes across field, barn, and darkening distance. Every object juts forward in high relief, and it seems that White has uncloaked the essence of things, stripped bare of pretense or explanation, naked before God. One could meditate for days on this extraordinary image.

The same may be said of a handful of films directed by Robert Bresson, Carl Dreyer, Ingmar Bergman, Andrey Tarkovsky, and a few others — a small group, but it remains a minor miracle that the movie industry, with its love of glitter and gold, has produced anything of worth dealing with prayer. Perhaps the most inventive effort is Tarkovsky's *Andrei Rublev* (1966), an epic biography of the great Russian iconographer. Next to nothing is known about Rublev's life, so the bulk of this long film, which runs over three and a half hours in the director's cut, consists of fictional episodes with little or no historical foundation. Tarkovsky's fifteenth-century Russia is brutish and gray, populated by louts, jesters, and paranoid bureaucrats — a medieval variation on Soviet culture. The film is an anti-icon, filled not with the redeemed light of Christ but with the darkness of fallen humanity. Through this landscape wanders Rublev, with hollow cheeks and deep-set eyes, muttering "only by prayer can the soul transcend the flesh." Transcendence eludes him, at least in the world of action. He even kills a man, and as the film winds down, the viewer suspects that Tarkovsky's black vision will leave no room for the possibility of transcendent grace.

So it goes until the last ten minutes, when Tarkovsky plays his trump card. The stark black and white imagery bursts into brilliant, almost garish color as the camera pores lovingly over a montage of Rublev's most famous icons. The color comes as a revelation; instantly we enter a new world in which beauty usurps ugliness, and hope overcomes despair. Tarkovsky presents this redeemed cosmos in a distinctly modern idiom. At first he films Rublev's icons in gigantic close-up, as swirls and streaks and blocks of pigment that resemble for all the world canvases by Mondrian or Pollock. Icon paintings were never meant to be, and *could* not have been, seen like this before the advent of technology. These are icons for the postmodern age. The effect might have been idolatrous but instead is radiantly beautiful. As the camera pulls back, recognizable objects appear: a tree, a church, the face of Christ. Finally Rublev's images emerge in their entirety. Even now a discordant note sounds — literally, from a Sturm und Drang soundtrack that violates the silence and stillness of these holy images. Tarkovsky seems to suggest that icons will never entirely escape the dank, ugly, sin-soaked earth, yet nonetheless they offer a vision of supernal beauty and transcendent truth, a glimpse of God's good kingdom. So may it fare for all traditional art in the modern age.

Poetry

The place of prayer in poetry, no less than in the visual arts, has changed dramatically since the dawn of the Renaissance. Traditional prayer poetry may startle with its experimental theology (Akhenaton's *Great Hymn to the Aton*), intense sexuality (The Song of Solomon), personal pathos (Job's lamentations), and eagerness to plumb the darkest regions of the heart (Psalm 130), but for the most part it has been conservative in form, orthodox in content, and anonymous in authorship.

Not so with the work of the past four centuries. The most unexpected aspect of modern prayer poetry is its abundance; if, while examining the history of painting, we needed to tease out traces of prayer embedded or even encoded within the canvas, in scrutinizing the history of poetry we find prayer bounding into sight at every turn. Prayer, it seems, is a preoccupation of many poets, as if daily association with words leads ineluctably to speculation about and adoration of the ineffable source of words. The results defy easy classification. Prayer poems, as well as poems about prayer, may be playful or serious, ecstatic or melancholy, tuneful or discordant, cast in prose or verse; they may address God or ignore God entirely. They come to us not as the anonymous voice of tradition but rather as expressions of individual temperament, as the signature of an artist working within a particular school or shaped by the literary conventions of a given era. Their dual aim as aesthetic inventions and acts of devotion gives them a distinctly modern flavor.

A case in point is the work of John Donne (1572–1631), Anglican divine and dean of Saint Paul's Cathedral, London. Donne's prayers, both in poetry and prose, appeal to believer and atheist alike; even when his devotion fails to win the heart, his wit delights the mind. When Donne was young, wit dominated, expending itself in sparkling displays of jest, aperçus, and wordplay, mostly concerning the battle of the sexes, in such lighthearted essays as "A defence of Women's Inconstancy" and "Why do women delight much in Feathers?" (because, Donne tells us, they are by nature flighty). A series of tragedies intervened to deepen Donne's outlook. His marriage to Anne More, against her father's wishes, led to imprisonment and a decade of poverty and suffering, alleviated only when Donne was ordained a priest in the Anglican Church in 1615. In 1617 his wife died after delivering a stillborn child, an event that he witnessed from afar in a vision. His first biographer, Izaak Walton, describes in *The Life and Death of Dr. Donne* (1640, rev. 1658) the uncanny event:

> Two days after their arrival [in Paris], Mr. Donne was left alone in that room in which Sir Robert [Drewrey, a benefactor of Donne's], and he, and some other friends had dined together. To this place Sir Robert returned within half an hour; and as he left, so he found, Mr. Donne alone; but in such an ecstasy, and so altered as to his looks, as amazed Sir Robert to behold him; insomuch as he earnestly desired Mr. Donne to declare what had befallen him in the short time of his absence. To which Mr. Donne was not able to make a present answer; but, after a long and perplexed pause, did at last say, "I have seen a dreadful vision since I saw you: I have seen my dear wife pass twice by me through this room, with her hair hanging about her shoulders, and a dead child in her arms: this I have seen since I saw you."

Investigation confirmed that the apparition had appeared at the hour of the stillbirth. This paranormal episode suggests a distant spiritual kinship with visionaries such as Ramakrishna or Teresa of Ávila, but in most regards Donne's spiritual life was strictly conventional, if profoundly felt, and directed toward moral improvement and churchly devotions. His singular brilliance emerged only when he put pen to paper. He reveled in paradox and pun, in probing analysis, the play of ideas, and extravagant similitudes. In 1623, at the age of fifty-four, he suffered a crippling illness (perhaps typhus) and responded by writing his prose masterpiece, *Devotions upon Emergent Occasions. Devotions* consists of twenty-three sections; each contains a meditation describing a phase of his illness, an expostulation drawing out its moral and spiritual meaning, and a prayer directed to God for guidance and succor. These prayers explore Donne's lifelong preoccupations — suffering, sin, mercy, damnation, and salvation — in scintillating literary conceits:

> I [open] my *soule* to thee, O my *God,* in a humble confession, That there is no *veine* in mee, that is not full of the bloud of thy *Son,* whom I haue crucified, and Crucified againe, by multiplying many, and often repeating the same sinnes: that there is no *Artery* in me, that hath not the *spirit of error, the spirit of lust, the spirit of giddines in it;* no *bone* in me that is not hardned with the custome of *sin* and nourished, and soupled with the *marrow* of *sinn;* no *sinews,* no *ligaments,* that do not tie, and chain sin and sin together.[22]

This elaborate metaphor represents the literary pyrotechnics that cemented Donne's high reputation among modern critics (and that led to his dismissal by Samuel Johnson, who characterized Donne's figures of speech as "heterogeneous ideas . . . yoked by violence together"). It is also a valuable, if not original, spiritual observation on the visceral nature of sin. Like most of Donne's mature writing, it bristles with analogies (hard bone and the moral hardening wrought by sin; elastic sinew and the moral flaccidity that links one sin to the next). As God is the father of all similitude ("Then God said, 'Let us make man in our image, after our likeness . . .'"; Genesis 1:26), so the religious writer, by drawing comparisons, continues or echoes the work of God in the aesthetic sphere. The poet becomes a priest, an agent of sacred mysteries.

Donne championed the special mission of the wordsmith and the special power of the word. We ourselves are naught but sound, he declares in one of his sermons: "Man is but a voice, but a sound, but a noise, he begins the noise himselfe, when he comes crying into the world; and when he goes out, perchance friends celebrate, perchance enemies calumniate him, with a diverse voice, a diverse noise. A melancholique man, is but a groaning; a sportfull man, but a song; an active man, but a Trumpet; a mighty man, but a thunderclap." "An artistic man, but a poem," he might have added. As creatures of sound, our tongues must trumpet God's praise. "To declare Gods goodness, that hath enabled us to speak, we are bound to speak: speech is the Glue, the Cyment, the soul of Conversation, and of Religion too."[23] Donne singles out Elihu, the friend of Job, as the type of the poet whose words have become scripture, the very word of God; even more radically, and skirting the bounds of orthodox theology, he argues that our own prayers "make God," for through them "we make up the mysticall body of Christ Jesus." Thaumaturgic powers aside, our prayers serve God:

> God came to us *in verbo,* In the word; for Christ is, The word that was made flesh. Let us, that are Christians, go to God so, too, That *the words of our mouth,* as well as *the Meditations of our heart,* may *be acceptable to him.* Surely God loves the service of Prayer, or he would never have built a house for Prayer; And therefore we justly call Publique prayer, the Liturgy, *Service:* Love that place, and love that service in that place, *Prayer.*[24]

In sum, prayer alone is the unique human calling: "They will needs make us believe that *S. Francis* preached to Birds, and Beasts, and Stones joyned with *S. Francis* in Prayer. God can speak to all things; that's the office of Preaching, to speak to others: But, of all, onely Man can speak to God; and that's the office of Prayer."[25]

Donne's devotion to that office flowers most fully in his holy sonnets, which combine startling imagery with explosive rhythms; Sonnet XIV is typical:

Batter my heart, three-person'd God, for you
As yet but knock, breathe, shine, and seek to mend;
That I may rise and stand, o'erthrow me, and bend
Your force to break, blow, burn, and make me new.
I, like an usurp'd town to'another due,
Labor to'admit you, but oh, to no end;
Reason, your viceroy in me, me should defend,
But is captiv'd, and proves weak or untrue.
Yet dearely'I love you, and would be lov'd fain,
But am betroth'd unto your enemy;
Divorce me,'untie or break that knot again,
Take me to you, imprison me, for I,
Except you'enthrall me, never shall be free,
Nor ever chaste, except you ravish me.

Donne yearns for God and yet spurns him for the allurements of Satan. Even reason, God's viceroy, has been enslaved by "the enemy." The poet suffers the eternal conundrum of the backsliding sinner, pithily described by Saint Paul: "For the good that I would I do not: but the evil that I would not, that I do" (Romans 7:15). Where to turn? Donne's answer is to implore God to take him by force. No more can the weak solution — favored, no doubt, by refined Anglican clergy in their evangelizing rounds — of "knock, breathe, shine, and seek to mend" prevail. Something brutal, nasty, and irresistible is required. Donne pleads that God batter, break, blow, burn, imprison him, a crescendo of violence culminating in the terrible paradox that only chains will set him free, only rape will make him chaste. Where, in two thousand years of Christian verse, do we find a more remarkable inversion of orthodox imagery for the sake of orthodoxy? Yet the poem is impeccable in its High Church Trinitarianism. Not only is God specified as "three-person'd," but the deity's overtures toward Donne are described as triads leading to unity (A,B,C, → D): "knock, breathe, shine, and seek to mend," "break, blow, burn, and make me new." The very rhythm is trinitarian. This is Donne at his most inventive and devout, opening up new poetic territory in the service of prayer.

In the centuries after Donne, Europe witnessed revolutions in both poetry and faith. Metaphysical conceit gave way to the acid satire of Pope, the visions of Blake, and the dreamy introspections of Wordsworth. Meanwhile, the gates of Christendom, battered by Reformation schism and Enlightenment skepticism, burst asunder under the inexorable discoveries of modern science. By the time that Emily Dickinson (1830–1886) sat down in the study of her family's brick house in Amherst,

Massachusetts, to write her eighteen hundred or so poems, the hectic intellectual and spiritual climate of the mid–nineteenth century — ranging from Swedenborgianism to spiritualism, Darwinism to Mesmerism — was in full swing. Experimentation and heterodoxy had become the order of the day, and Dickinson fit perfectly into the ruling Zeitgeist. In her angst, agoraphobia, and religious doubts, her chaste dresses and her wanton syntax, her refusal to publish and her longing for immortality, she was made for modern poetry.

Dickinson's prayer poems and poems about prayer are riddled with idiosyncratic religious views. Some of her ideas may be traced to Emerson, whom she read avidly, and who in his celebrated essay "Self-Reliance" heaps scorn upon ordinary prayer, declaring that "prayer as a means to effect a private end is meanness and theft" and that "as man's prayers are a disease of the will, so are his creeds a disease of the intellect." Dickinson matched Emerson's skepticism with her own jaundiced view:

> Prayer is the little implement
> Through which Men reach
> Where Presence — is denied them —
> They fling their Speech
>
> By means of it — in God's Ear —
> If then He hear —
> This sums the Apparatus
> Comprised in Prayer — [26]

Prayer, contra tradition, is neither organic impulse or supernatural gift, but a utensil, a spiritual megaphone for amplifying speech so that it may reach God's ear — if God exists and deigns to listen. As she aged, Dickinson harbored growing doubts about whether prayer worked at all. In a late letter to a friend she writes, "You are like God. We pray to Him and He answers 'No.' Then we pray to Him to rescind the 'no,' and He doesn't answer at all . . ." Responsibility for her skepticism, she suggests, may rest with God rather than herself. In the poem "I meant to have but modest needs," God smirks at her naive trust in the value of prayer. Stung, she throws prayer away and learns to doubt, to "scan the Skies / With a suspicious Air —"[27] In a brief, undated poem, this distrust deepens into something approaching bitterness:

> There comes an hour when begging stops,
> When the long interceding lips
> Perceive their prayer is vain.

"Thou shalt not" is a kinder sword
Than from a disappointing God
"Disciple, call again."[28]

Nonetheless, Dickinson never abandoned her interest in religion, including prayer. One senses in her a battle between two views of the universe. Familiar with Darwin and with the works of many freethinkers, she scorned the starched pieties of Amherst society, ridiculed Christian dogma, refused to join a church, and liked to call herself a pagan. At the same time, she read the Bible avidly, calling it "infinitely wise & . . . merry,"[29] was fascinated by the religious faith of others, and wrote many verses on the prospect of immortality. Her rejection of conventional belief is sometimes playful rather than pointed, as when, parodying the Lord's Prayer, she refers to God as "Papa Above!" In a poem from her last decade, she makes clear her priorities:

I reckon — when I count at all —
First — Poets — then the Sun —
Then Summer — Then the Heaven of God —
And then — the List is done — [30]

Why does the poet rank so high? In an echo of Donne's doctrine, the potency of language is the reason:

Could mortal lip divine
The undeveloped Freight
Of a delivered syllable
'Twould crumble with the weight[31]

In Dickinson as in Donne, the poet wields a power analogous to that of God. The difference is that for Donne, a poem at its highest becomes a mode of prayer, while for Dickinson, any poem trumps any prayer. Poetry, like love, is a divine force: "A word that breathes distinctly / Has not the power to die." Poetry dispenses, like Holy Communion, eternal life: "He ate and drank the precious Words — / His Spirit grew robust."[32]

Poetry, then, rather than churchgoing, served as Dickinson's royal road to truth. But it may not have been her only means of ingress. Many of her poems drop tantalizing hints of private raptures, akin in some respects to those experienced in ecstatic prayer. "He fumbles at your Soul," a work from her middle years (c. 1862), speaks of a God who "stuns you by degrees" and then "Deals — One — imperial — Thunderbolt — That scalps your naked soul —"[33] "Exhilaration is the Breeze," composed five or six years later, describes a similar process in happier terms:

Exhilaration is the Breeze
That lifts us from the Ground
And leaves us in another place
Whose statement is not found —

Returns us not, but after time
We soberly descend
A Little newer for the term
Upon Enchanted Ground —[34]

This joyous experience whirls us into the air and induces a type of *metanoia* (Dickinson, who knew her Bible, may be drawing a parallel to Saint Paul's heavenly ascension in 2 Corinthians 12:4). True, she couches the transforming rapture in the first-person plural, a distancing device, but in "I Heard, as if I had No Ear," she drops the veil, describing a religious transport in which "a Vital Word" taught her to hear, "Light" allowed her to see, "Might" brought her to herself, and "Time . . . met Eternity."[35] It is difficult to know what to make of these intimations of rapture. The experiences may be mere literary inventions, and their indefinite nature invites a variety of interpretations. They may, on the other hand, be poetic representations of authentic mystical experiences.

These mysterious poems add to Dickinson's multifaceted portrait and fortify the sense that she harbored within her frail body and vigorous mind many of the contradictory forces of contemporary life. She was at once a skeptic longing for faith and a believer assailed by doubts. Her prayer poems veer from hope to despair, passion to coldness, longing to disdain, all in bewildering excess. Her tight, spare style seems thoroughly modern, no less than her enigmatic relationship to prayer, to faith, to God, and to her own poetry, which survived, in great measure, on the backs of envelopes or advertisements. In her small perfections and vast contradictions, in her doubts and affirmations, in her beautiful language that points beyond beauty to a realm of austere truths that may or may not intersect absolute Truth, she seems one of us. No wonder her poems, including those for and against prayer, are so widely read today.

It's difficult to believe that Emily Dickinson and Walt Whitman (1819–1892) shared the same century and the same country (they lived, for more than a decade, less than three hundred miles apart, Dickinson in Amherst, Massachusetts, and Whitman in Camden, New Jersey), so greatly do they differ: she, the reticent maid in the tower; he, the roaring lion who championed all of creation. Yet Whitman, too, held religion dear. Unlike Dickinson, he cared little for clambering over the still smoking ruins of Christendom; he aimed instead to erect a new faith, a post-

Christian paganism worthy of the age of engines and empire, preaching a creed of vitality, democracy, and universal love. In concert with Dickinson and Donne, he too celebrated the role of the poet, who would be seer, prophet, and divine incarnation of this new American cult, as revealed in "Passage to India":

> After the seas are all cross'd, (as they seem already cross'd,)
> After the great captains and engineers have accomplish'd their
> work,
> After the noble inventors, after the scientists, the chemist, the
> geologist, ethnologist,
> Finally shall come the poet worthy that name,
> The true son of God shall come singing his songs.[36]

Whitman famously celebrated the self in some of the most enthusiastic lines in world literature: "I celebrate myself and sing myself"; "I know I am solid and sound. . . . I know I am deathless. . . . I know I am august"; "I am the poet of the Body and I am the poet of the Soul."[37] This self-approbation is not so much an exaltation of Whitman's own personality but rather of all human beings and, by extension, the cosmos. All life is divine; Whitman, as bard, proclaims his revelation with unabashed joy. Nonetheless, to declare oneself divine creates a problem for traditional prayer. To whom does a god pray? Whitman properly asks, therefore, "Why should I pray? Why should I venerate and be ceremonious?" Why indeed, if, as he exclaims in a comparison of prodigious audacity, "Divine am I inside and out, and I make holy whatever I touch or am touch'd from, / The scent of these arm-pits aroma finer than prayer"?[38]

The answer for Whitman, and for many modern writers and artists, is that if the self is divine and the artist a kind of demiurge, then self-exploration becomes an analogue to prayer, a revelation of spiritual truth. Whitman's apparent egoism should be read as a form of mystical iconoclasm, perhaps not too distant from that of Angelus Silesius, the fifteenth-century Catholic poet who said, "I am as large as God; he is as small as I," or of Sarāhā, the ninth-century Tantric Buddhist who announced that "I have seen no shrine as blissful as my own body."

Whitman spoke in a multitude of voices, however, and in "Prayer of Columbus" (1874) he assumes the persona of the famous mariner and produced a prayer that sustains, until just before its end, an orthodox tone. As the poem begins, Columbus recites the woes of his final voyage, during which he faces mutiny, native uprisings, and the shipwreck of all hope:

A batter'd, wreck'd old man,
Thrown on this savage shore, far, far from home,
Pent by the sea and dark rebellious brows, twelve dreary months,
Sore, stiff with many toils, sicken'd, and nigh to death,
I take my way along the island's edge,
Venting a heavy heart.[39]

This portrait of despair depicts not only Columbus but Whitman as well, who wrote "Prayer of Columbus" while his life lay in apparent ruin. Death had snatched away his mother and sister-in-law, a paralytic stroke threatened his health, and *Leaves of Grass* languished in obscurity. Whitman laments his sorrows ("I am too full of woe!") and justifies himself to God, proclaiming, in what amounts to a compressed compendium of the entire arsenal of prayer, his undying faith:

Thou knowest the prayers and vigils of my youth;
Thou knowest my manhood's solemn and visionary
    meditations;
Thou knowest how, before I commenced I devoted all to come
    to Thee,
Thou knowest I have in age ratified all those vows and strictly
    kept them;
Thou knowest I have not once lost nor faith nor ecstasy in
    Thee.[40]

Petition, devotion, vision, meditation — all play a part in the chorus. By all accounts, Whitman rarely or never prayed in any conventional sense, but he devoured the literature of prayer, including Christian and Hindu scripture (and he intended *Leaves of Grass* to be the scripture of the Whitmanesque dispensation). Thanks to his erudition and genius, "Prayer of Columbus" convinces as a portrait of the explorer on his knees amid the burdens of old age and the despair that followed the failure of his dreams. This being a prayer poem by Whitman, however, one is scarcely surprised when it turns into a paean to the self. In the last stanza, the poet turns the traditional protocol of prayer upside down; instead of addressing God, Columbus prophesies glory to himself:

And these things I see suddenly, what mean they?
As if some miracle, some hand divine unseal'd my eyes,
Shadowy vast shapes smile through the air and sky,
And on the distant waves sail countless ships,
And anthems in new tongues I hear saluting me.[41]

The "hand divine" unseals Columbus's eyes only in Whitman's imagination. In truth the mariner's final years, following his return to Spain from the disastrous fourth voyage, were marred by sickness, financial difficulty, and bitterness over lack of recognition. Whitman's vision of countless ships and unfamiliar anthems saluting the explorer project, of course, his most ardent wish for his own great bardic enterprise. That this wish came true and that Whitman's cosmic enthusiasm has achieved a secure place in world literature may be reason enough for any lover of poetry to celebrate. His new idiom of praise and thanksgiving has proved remarkably fecund, inspiring the work of Carl Sandburg, Allen Ginsburg, and many others. It epitomizes a radical alternative to the gentle humility and denial of self that stand at the heart of traditional prayer; for Whitman, the world of tradition is dead and buried.

Across the Atlantic, however, a new generation of poets prepared to exhume and revitalize the corpse. The two principal champions of this artistic resurrection happened to be also the two leading English-language poets of the new century, William Butler Yeats (1865–1939) and Thomas Stearns Eliot (1888–1965).

Even as a young aesthete in Dublin and London, Yeats had rejected the staid Anglo-Protestantism of his ancestors. He sought a wilder, more esoteric tradition, one that might connect him directly to the profound spiritual currents that he was certain existed outside church walls. "Could I not found," he wrote, "an Eleusinian Rite, which would bind into a common symbolism, a common meditation, a school of poets and men of letters, so that poetry and drama would find the religious weight they have lacked since the middle ages, perhaps since ancient Greece?"[42] His quest led him into the Theosophical Society, the Hermetic Order of the Golden Dawn (a magical society where he rubbed shoulders with other occult-minded literati including Algernon Blackwood, A. E. Waite, Arthur Machen, and Aleister Crowley), and the study of Celtic folklore, pagan mythology, alchemy, reincarnation, Plato, Blake, and Swedenborg. Yeats wove these disparate strands into a tapestry of symbol, legend, oracle, and doctrine that influenced his poetry, plays, and above all, *A Vision,* a dense, enigmatic work of cosmology, anthropology, and history based on automatic writings produced by his wife soon after their marriage in 1917.

Yeats inhabited, in sum, a post-Christian world. For him, as for Whitman and, to a lesser degree, Dickinson, the long-standing verities of Christianity no longer commanded respect, much less belief. It might be more accurate, however, to describe Yeats's world as pre-Christian, for it teemed with chthonic forces, invisible elementals, mysterious correspondences, and the magic of ancient Irish folklore. Ruling over this idiosyncratic pagan cosmos was an idiosyncratic God, more a distillation of the powers of the imagination than a transcendent personal creator. Yeats refers to God in metaphors, as "the Supreme Enchanter" or "the Thirteenth Cone," and as Yeats's biographer Richard Ellmann points out, when God appears in a poem, such as "He Remembers Forgotten Beauty," the sole reason for the expressed monotheism is that it helps the rhythm in a crucial line. "Far from being a God-intoxicated man," Ellmann writes, "Yeats had only to think of God to become sober and extremely wary."[43]

Nevertheless, Yeats wrote a number of brilliant poems that qualify as prayers and helped bring prayer poetry back into the public eye. Perhaps the most intriguing, although not the most accomplished, is "Aedh Pleads with the Elemental Powers," a prayer addressed not to God or the saints but to the pagan forces that trouble and guide the cosmos:

> The Powers whose name and shape no living creature knows
> Have pulled the Immortal Rose;
> And though the Seven Lights bowed in their dance and wept,
> The Polar Dragon slept,
> His heavy rings uncoiled from glimmering deep to deep;
> When will he wake from sleep?
>
> Great Powers of falling wave and wind and windy fire,
> With your harmonious choir
> Encircle her I love and sing her into peace,
> That my old care may cease;
> Unfold your flaming wings and cover out of sight
> The nets of day and night.
>
> Dim Powers of drowsy thought, let her no longer be
> Like the pale cup of the sea,
> When winds have gathered and sun and moon burned dim
> Above its cloudy rim;
> But let a gentle silence wrought with music flow
> Whither her footsteps go.[44]

Like many of Yeats's early works, this prayer's residual Christian imagery — the "Immortal Rose," the "flaming wings" and "harmonious choirs" of the angelic powers, and the organizing image of the beloved female — reveals the influence of the Pre-Raphaelites, whom Yeats had studied and befriended during his youthful years in London. The abiding atmosphere is not, however, the lush medievalism of Dante Gabriel Rossetti or William Morris, but something more ancient and robust: the Powers that ruled the folkways of ancient Eire. To these mysterious energies, linked to wind, wave, and flame, Aedh (Irish for "fire," and here representing Yeats himself) lifts his petitions. He asks them to guide and protect "her I love," almost certainly a reference to the Irish actress and revolutionary Maud Gonne, long the object of Yeats's unrequited love. Gonne is the "Immortal Rose," a title that suggests also, as Yeats explains in his commentary on the poem, "the Rose of Ideal Beauty" that grows on the Tree of Life "in certain old mythologies."[45] Yeats begs the Powers — great powers, dim powers, powers of unknown name and shape — to protect his beloved, the incarnation of ideal beauty. This is the prayer song of a post-Christian troubadour petitioning pre-Christian deities: a prayer in a thoroughly modern idiom.

In a number of other poems Yeats sustains this note of spiritual lyricism in the service of the hermetic mysteries. "The Secret Rose" implores protection from the "Far-off, most secret, and inviolate Rose," which seems to be a compendium of Christ, the intellect, the essence of pagan deities, and perhaps a dash of Maud Gonne. "A Faery Song" presents the wee folk praying that the legendary lovers Diarmuid and Grania, sleeping beneath a cromlech, be granted "Silence and love; / And the long-dew-dropping hours of the night, / And the stars above." Somewhat more conventional, although usually with a twist, are the four poems specifically identified as prayers. In "A Prayer for my Daughter," Yeats prays — to whom, we are never told — that his newborn daughter (Anne Butler Yeats) be endowed with beauty, courtesy, and a marriage ruled by custom and ceremony, heartfelt pleas that serve as pretext for complaints about his own "dried up" mind, his failed romance with Maud Gonne, and his disapproval of women who hold political opinions. "A Prayer on Going into My House" passes as a traditional blessing, a return to the simple beseechings of the *Carmina Gadelica* ("God grant a blessing on this tower and cottage") until the concluding curse, in which Yeats begs God to blast anyone who wrecks his home's scenic view by erecting a cottage or chopping down a tree. "A Prayer for My Son," a minor effort echoing the earlier prayer for Yeats's daughter, petitions for the welfare of his son, Michael Butler Yeats. Most fascinating, perhaps, is the poet's last prayer poem, "A Prayer for Old Age." In simple, blunt verse, composed when he was nearly seventy, Yeats begs God — to all appearances the Anglo-Protestant God that he spurned in youth — to keep him from arid intellectuality, from "those thoughts men think / In the mind alone." He desires instead "to sing a lasting song," to "think in a marrow-bone." Old age is second childhood, and in Yeats's search for passion, the conventional prayers of youth once again find their place: ". . . word is out / and prayer comes round again." This is the aged Yeats willing himself young again, turning to prayer as the elixir of life.[46]

T. S. Eliot (1888–1965) was in many ways the anti-Yeats: studious and withdrawn, champion of the mainstream European literary lineage (Homer, Dante, Shakespeare, Donne), a man whose earliest verses reveal a touch of weariness or serene resignation, as if he had been born old. This is especially evident in *The Waste Land,* a poetic evocation of the spiritual desolation that afflicted the West after World War I, replete with multiple allusions to the quest for the holy grail. Five years after writing *The Waste Land,* Eliot found his grail; he was baptized and received into the Anglican Church and would write henceforth as a professed Christian. A devout convert, he regularly attended church services, studied scripture and church history, and prayed daily. According to the poet Stephen Spender, on one memorable occasion Eliot tried to explain to Virginia Woolf the essence of prayer: "to concentrate, to forget self, to attain union with God." The succinct formula fell on deaf ears, as Woolf was largely devoid of religious sensibilities.[47]

One year after his conversion, Eliot produced the first of his great prayer-poems, "A Song for Simeon," a reworking of the Nunc Dimittis, or Canticle of Simeon from the Gospel of Luke. In this celebrated hymn, recited daily as part of the Divine Office, the aged Simeon, "just and devout, waiting for the consolation of Israel," enters the temple in Jerusalem, where he spies the newborn Jesus awaiting circumcision. Simeon sweeps the babe into his arms and gives rhapsodic thanks to God, who has allowed him, before his death, this glimpse of the promised Messiah: "Lord, now lettest thou thy servant depart in peace, according to thy word. For mine eyes have seen thy salvation, which thou hast prepared before the face of all people, a light to lighten the Gentiles, and the glory of thy people Israel" (Luke 2:25, 29–32). Eliot's poem, a reverential gloss on the biblical canticle, repeats many of its famous lines but injects, in place of the original's jubilation, a somber, even ominous tone. Simeon looks far into the future, forecasting Christ's tribulations and crucifixion and the martyrdoms of the Christian saints. The bleak prospect reflects Simeon's fear of impending death rather than the joy of Christian salvation, although one of the old man's prayers, "Grant us thy peace," its words taken from the Mass, not from the biblical text of the canticle, suggests the final triumph of hope. "A Song for Simeon" is the prayer-poem of a Christian still wandering in the wasteland.

The same mood pervades "Ash Wednesday," another effort from the late 1920s. By means of this work, as he explained in a letter to his religious confessor, Eliot hoped to portray "the experience of man in search of God . . . trying to explain to himself his intenser human feelings in terms of the divine goal."[48] Those in search of God are often torn by desire and guilt, and "Ash Wednesday" echoes this state with its fractured structure and stuttering expectations. The theme is familiar — *metanoia,* the about-face toward God, the putting on of the Pauline "new man" that demands repentance, faith, and grace — and "Ash Wednesday" may be understood as Eliot's variation on the *de profundis* prayers of Chapter 4, but this poem offers no heartwarming tales of escape from the abyss through the grace of God. The tone is modern, edgy, uncertain. The poet, like the era, seems exhausted; he sings a litany of failures, unable to think, know, or act; the prospect of turning fades to nothingness. Why? Because, like all of us, he is trapped by time and space; the limitations imposed by flesh and blood, the inescapability of gravity, and the inexorability of time pin him down. Prayer is the only hope in this distressed world, and Eliot falls to his knees throughout the poem, uttering bits and pieces from the Hail Mary, the Mass, the Salve Regina, the Psalter, the Book of Micah, and other treasures drawn from the ancient reserve of the Church, as well as his own composed prayers. He prays for the redemption of time, for universal salvation; he imagines a woman walking in a garden, robed in white and blue like the Virgin, and wonders if she will pray for sinners, for children unable to pray, for those caught like him in the chains of modernity. He prays that God may hear his prayers, concluding the poem with a plea from Psalm 102, "And let my cry come unto Thee" (Psalm 102:1).

But what if the cry is itself insufficient? What if prayer fails to stir the Almighty? Eliot's last great composition, *Four Quartets,* has much to say about the failure of words, beset by imprecision and, because they exist in time, subject to death. Nonetheless, prayer is incumbent upon us, and the third quartet, "The Dry Salvages" (an outcropping of rocks off coastal Massachusetts), offers a lovely prayer to the Virgin, beseeching her to intervene on behalf of sailors, fishermen, and their grieving wives and mothers. Eliot addresses Mary by a variety of titles; the last, "daughter of your son," is most telling, for he borrows it from the last canto of the *Paradiso,* and it thus links Eliot's own prayers to those of the Italian master. "No poet, no artist of any art, has his complete meaning alone," Eliot writes in *The Sacred Wood* (1922). "His significance, his appreciation is the appreciation of his relation to the dead poets and artists."[49] Just as "A Song for Simeon" retools a biblical canticle for modern sensibilities, so does *Four Quartets* reshape the *Divine Comedy.* The same themes — the search for meaning, the mysterious relation of time to eternity, the understanding of life as a journey toward God, the urgency of self-examination — emerge in colder, more splintered and angst-ridden form. Prayer permeates both works, but while Dante, inhabiting a medieval universe of eternal hierarchies, never questions its necessity, Eliot is compelled to explain its nature and purpose.

This explanation, one of the most celebrated of poetic statements about prayer, appears in "Little Gidding," the last of the *Quartets.* The title refers to a milestone in the history of English prayer, for it was in the hamlet of Little Gidding that in 1626 Nicholas Ferrar, an Anglican cleric, established a community devoted to devotional practice, manual craft, and the contemplative life, the first monastery in England since Henry VIII's ransacking of the Catholic ecclesiastical system a century earlier. Little Gidding perished during the English Civil War, but it influenced innumerable generations of English Christians, in particular, devout converts such as Eliot, who visited the grounds in 1936.

There exist, Eliot suggests, places where stillness reigns and heaven draws near. Little Gidding is just such a locale. Pilgrims to its holy precincts have but one task, to kneel and pray. And what is prayer? More than a sequence of words that can fail so miserably; more than thoughts flitting ghostlike through the mind; more than the sound of voices reciting hymns or litanies. Prayer, as the dead know, is aflame with the Holy Spirit. Prayer partakes of that ecstatic eschatological instant when space-time will collapse into eternity and bliss conquers all; Eliot signals this final, joyful resolution by repeating (in modern orthography) the famed words of the fourteenth-century mystic Dame Julian of Norwich (1342–c. 1416), "al shal be wel, and al manner of thyng shal be wele."[50] The will of God will be accomplished and, in the *Four Quartets*' final image, two traditional Christian symbols, the fire and the rose — the former signifying the descent of the Holy Spirit into the world of matter, the latter employed by Dante in *Paradiso* XXXIII to describe the shape of the heavenly hosts when arrayed in ranks before the Celestial Throne — become one. Prayer, then, is child of silence, taste of eternity, entrance into the holy flame, and the one necessary act of all who visit Little Gidding, indeed of all who seek God. The obscure imagery, broken lines, and abundant literary allusions may place *Four Quartets* in the vanguard of experimental poetry, but Eliot's essential message regarding prayer, its urgency and incumbency, differs not a jot from that of his Anglican predecessor, John Donne, or from that of his poetic master, Dante. In Eliot, as in Yeats, the tradition of prayer-poetry continues to flourish, albeit in ever new, surprising forms.

The tradition thrives too, although in a lesser key, in a host of other poets around the globe. Two bear special mention. Rainer Maria Rilke (1875–1926) wrote a number of delicate prayer poems, most notably in *The Book of Hours,* that detail the modulations of the human soul with consummate intelligence and grace. Sometimes, however, one struggles to discern when Rilke is addressing God and when he is addressing himself, for like Whitman, he casts the long shadow of his own self-absorption over his prayers ("How, though, into myself I keep inclining!").[51] For Rilke, self-examination is a spiritual duty and an artistic act. Art comes before religion, he argues, for "religion is the art of the non-artistic. They become productive in prayer . . . they free themselves in this way." Artists, by contrast, even when deep in prayer, have "only one faith and one religious conviction burned in them: the longing search for themselves."[52] This hierarchy of values allows Rilke to produce works of beauty, but they seem more poem than prayer.

Rabindranath Tagore (1861–1941) inverts Rilke's scale of values. For Tagore, the sole purpose of art is prayer. "In Art the person in us is sending its answers to the Supreme Person, who reveals Himself to us in a world of endless beauty across the lightless world of facts." A Bengali poet and composer of songs, locally revered but unknown outside the Indian subcontinent, Tagore burst onto the international stage when a collection of his prayers, which he had laboriously translated into English despite little familiarity with the language, fell into the hands of William Butler Yeats. In his introduction to the first British edition (1913) of *Gitanjali (Song Offerings),* Yeats declares that in Tagore he had found "a world I had dreamed of all my life long," a literature "where poetry and religion are the same thing."[53] Thanks in large measure to Yeats's patronage, Tagore was lionized throughout Europe and received the 1913 Nobel Prize in Literature, the only time this august award has been bestowed on a book of prayers. Alas, Tagore's poems have not stood the test of time. A century later, his writing seems overwrought and clichéd, a counterfeit of spirituality rather than the real coin: "The light of thy music illumines the world. The life breath of thy music runs from sky to sky. The holy stream of thy music breaks through all stony obstacles and rushes on." Tagore's importance as the first modern Indian writer to conquer the West remains, but his present influence as a poet is nil. He proves that although art may not trump religion, bad art can poison fine religious sentiments.[54]

The courtship of prayer and art has been celebrated in realms beyond those of poetry and painting. Bach's cantatas consist, in large measure, of prayers set to music, and anyone who has listened closely to these sublime compositions can attest that music is itself a form of prayer. The same can be said of Beethoven's late quartets, Elgar's *Dream of Gerontius*, Ralph Vaughan Williams's *Dona Nobis Pacem*, and other classical and neoclassical works, as well as the great parallel tradition of hymns and religious songs, from the works of Charles Wesley to the anonymous spirituals of generations of African American slaves. Meanwhile, the art of sacred architecture — buildings that not only invite prayer but seem themselves to pray, exemplified by Chartres Cathedral — has continued through the centuries, championed in more recent years by Antonio Gaudí, whose Church of the Holy Family in Barcelona is a triumph of devotional excess. The novel, too, has contributed its share of memorable prayers, such as the febrile ecstasies of Alyosha Karamazov and the beatnik devotions of Jack Kerouac. This litany of prayerful art could be extended indefinitely, but piling treasure upon treasure exhausts the spirit. Let us turn to the prayers of childhood, then, and leave this chapter with the words of a small boy whose best friend, a stuffed bear, is beloved around the world. Here, then, is "Vespers," the bedtime prayer of Christopher Robin:

Little Boy kneels at the foot of the bed,
Droops on the little hands little gold head.
Hush! Hush! Whisper who dares!
Christopher Robin is saying his prayers.

God bless Mummy. I know that's right.
Wasn't it fun in the bath tonight?
The cold's so cold, and the hot's so hot,
Oh! *God bless Daddy* — I quite forgot.

If I open my fingers a little bit more,
I can see Nanny's dressing-gown on the door.
It's a beautiful blue, but it hasn't a hood.
Oh! *God bless Nanny and make her good.*

Mine has a hood, and I lie in bed,
And pull the hood right over my head,
And I shut my eyes, and I curl up small,
And nobody knows that I'm there at all.

Oh! *Thank you, God, for a lovely day.*
And what was the other I had to say?

I said "Bless Daddy," so what can it be?
Oh! Now I remember, *God bless Me.*

Little Boy kneels at the foot of the bed,
Droops on the little hands little gold head.
Hush! Hush! Whisper who dares!
Christopher Robin is saying his prayers.[55]

CHAPTER 10

Prayer and the Public Square

VISITORS TO UNION SQUARE PARK in New York City, once the stomping ground of Wobblies, Communists, and the political hacks of Tammany Hall, will discover, if they wander into the thinly shaded southwest corner, an unexpected resident of a very different sort: Mohandas Gandhi, in the form of a life-size bronze statue, staff in hand, often adorned with a garland of flowers. According to several guidebooks, New York City erected the statue in 1986 as a "symbol of peace." Perhaps so — the Mahatma, after all, was the father of twentieth-century nonviolent protest — but this monument also declares the presence of a man of prayer in the public square. Gandhi always placed prayer first on his daily agenda, declaring that "prayer is the very soul and essence of religion, and, therefore, prayer must be the very core of the life of man."[1] His writings and teachings on ahimsa (nonviolence), satyagraha (devotion to truth), cottage industry, chastity, and personal sacrifice all depend on prayer for inspiration and guidance, and it is this intense, unflagging focus that makes the appearance of a statue of Gandhi in Union Square so astonishing. Liberal democracies rarely erect statues to men and women who put prayer first. How many likenesses of Jonathan Edwards or Mary Baker Eddy, Billy Sunday or Black Elk, Mother Ann Lee or Elizabeth Ann Seton adorn public parks in America? Their absence looms especially large when one realizes that these men and women have wielded a far greater influence on American life than many of the politicians, bureaucrats, and generals who are celebrated in our civic spaces.

As we saw in the previous chapter, this separation of prayer and public life is a recent development on the world stage. When Ramses II, confronting the Hittites at the Battle of Kadesh (c. 1285 B.C.E.), prays to the great deity Amun as his father, boasting of his own triumphs of state and expecting reward for the monumental tributes he has lavished on the god, the conflation of political and sacerdotal realms is complete. Ramses prays as the embodiment of the state *and* as a divine manifestation. Two thousand years later, not much had changed; Pope Innocent III (1160–1216), although in theory acknowledging the spiritual source of his sovereignty, in practice wielded unprecedented temporal as well as religious authority throughout much of Europe. To trace the collapse of theocracy, and thus of prayer's privileged place in the public square, is to recount the rise of the modern mind and the modern world — the centuries of friction between ecclesiastical and monarchical powers that resulted in their definitive divorce; the gradual development of a new portrait of the human being, shaped by the Renaissance, the Enlightenment, and the revolutions of Darwin, Marx, and Freud; and the cyclical exhaustion and revitalization of Christianity and the parallel rise of religious pluralism, perhaps most notable in America and Europe but influential across the globe.

One upshot of these converging forces, as we enter the twenty-first century, is widespread confusion about the legitimacy of public prayer. Does prayer belong on municipal football fields and military bases, in county courtrooms and the halls of Congress? The debate is often acrimonious; typically, each side claims the moral high ground, shouting magnificent slogans — Freedom of Speech! Freedom of Worship! Rights of Minorities! — on its own behalf while hurling vitriol at its opponents. Caustic, even apocalyptic language prevails; more than one advocate of school prayer has discerned satanic manipulations behind recent Supreme Court decisions, and more than one opponent of prayer at government functions has insisted that the very future of human liberty is at stake.

Two recent events indicate the gulf that separates the disputants. In 2001 George W. Bush invited the Reverend Franklin Graham, son of famed evangelist Billy Graham, to deliver the invocation at his presidential inauguration. Graham delivered a prayer laden with tactfully generic references to God but ending with an explicit declaration of Christian belief: "We pray this in the name of the Father, the Son the Lord Jesus Christ, and the Holy Spirit. Amen." Most evangelicals applauded Graham's choice of words, seeing it as a legitimate expression of his (and the new president's) faith, but to others it smacked of intolerance or worse; the fiery lawyer Alan M. Dershowitz denounced it as "un-American" and accused Bush of consigning millions of people to "status as a tolerated minority rather than as fully equal citizens."[2]

Just a few years earlier, by contrast, many evangelicals had felt betrayed: in 1997, U.S. Army officials granted Wiccans permission to conduct classes and rituals, including witches' sabbaths, on the grounds of Fort Hood, Texas. To Wiccans, this decision was a matter of constitutionally protected religious practice, but to many Christians it amounted to a desecration of military tradition and a cultural debacle. Congressman Robert L. Barr wondered, "What's next? Will armored divisions be forced to travel with sacrificial animals for Satanic rituals?"[3] The bizarre outcome of this brouhaha was a boycott by thirteen conservative Christian groups against the army, insisting that no Christian enlist, reenlist, or allow his or her children to enlist until the military banned all Wiccan practices. The protest soon collapsed because of a lack of support.

One may take these examples as skirmishes in a war between conservatives and liberals, but in fact the situation is more complex, as demonstrated by the contrasting experiences of President Bush and British prime minister Tony Blair, by all accounts both deeply religious men. President Bush makes a point of praying in the limelight and delights in the annual National Prayer Breakfast, a lavish, highly publicized gathering established half a century ago by Dwight Eisenhower (who, in typical folksy fashion, defined prayer as "one of the simple necessities of life"), at which hundreds of America's political and social elite join in an ostentatious display of public devotion. But across the Atlantic, Prime Minister Blair can scarcely hint at prayer for fear of a public outcry. When a journalist recently quizzed him about his religious belief and practice, Blair's director of communications blocked a potentially embarrassing response by interrupting with the memorable statement "We don't do God." No doubt these anecdotes reflect differing national attitudes about self-revelation — Americans being famously more open than the tight-lipped English — but they also reflect a pan-Atlantic cultural ambivalence about the place of faith, and prayer in particular, in the civic arena. We don't really know where prayer belongs, when to broadcast it and when to muffle it, or how to pray without stepping on our neighbor's toes. Nowhere is this uncertainty more evident than in the debate about prayer in the public schools.

The Classroom as Prayer Room

The battleground for school prayer, like that of most legal debates involving religion, is the First Amendment to the U.S. Constitution, which declares, in its celebrated Establishment Clause, that "Congress shall make no law respecting an establishment of religion." Across two centu-

The first prayer in the Continental Congress, September 1774. Wood engraving, nineteenth century.

ries, these ten words, with the added mortar of numerous Supreme Court decisions, have grown into a redoubtable if not impregnable wall of separation between church and state. To understand the theoretical backdrop of the Establishment Clause, we can do no better than to consult James Madison's 1784 broadside *Memorial and Remonstrance Against Religious Assessments,* a document quoted at length by Justice Hugo Black in the majority opinion in *Engel v. Vitale,* the 1962 landmark Supreme Court decision that banned prayer in public schools. Railing against state support for Christian educators, Madison declared that "in matters of religion no man's right is abridged by the institution of civil society; and that religion is wholly exempt from its cognizance." The design of the coming "wall of separation" (Thomas Jefferson's phrase) is clearly laid out in this declaration, which states that civil society does not even acknowledge the existence of religion. What is most intriguing about Madison's *Memorial,* however, is not its fierce views on church-state separation, which have since become common coin, but the presence in the document of a heartfelt prayer — not the sort of thing one expects in a manifesto that has taken on iconic significance among those adamantly opposed to any public religious observance. Madison wrapped up his argument by "earnestly praying, as we are in duty bound, that the Supreme Lawgiver of the Universe . . . may guide [lawmakers] into every measure that may be worthy of His blessing, may redound to their own praise, and may establish more firmly the liberties of the people, and the prosperity and happiness of the commonwealth."[4] To a political scientist, the *Memorial* stands as a milestone in the advancement of church-state separation; to a psychologist, it reveals Madison's complex and ambivalent relationship to prayer; and to a historian of religion, it underscores prayer's enormous influence, so pervasive that it exercises authority even in documents devoted to the sequestering of religious practice.

Two centuries later, the same ambivalences reign. In the 1960s, the Supreme Court ruled that communal prayer cannot be conducted in public schools. *Engel v. Vitale* focused on the following brief prayer, approved for use in the New York State school system: "Almighty God, we acknowledge our dependence upon Thee, and we beg Thy blessings upon us, our parents, our teachers and our Country."[5] It would be hard to come up with a more unoffensive declaration, and in fact school officials and others composed the text with the explicit aim of producing a prayer that would pass constitutional muster with the courts and meet general public approval. Instead, this uninspired petition triggered one of the greatest firestorms in the history of American jurisprudence. Cries for the impeachment of Chief Justice Earl Warren resounded across the land. Proposed constitutional amendments defending school prayer proliferated in Congress. Many public schools ignored the ruling and continued daily prayers. Richard Cardinal Spellman declared himself "shocked and frightened" by the ruling; Billy Graham, Norman Vincent Peale, and other conservative Protestant ministers added their dissent; and even liberal Episcopal bishop James Pike announced that the Court had "deconsecrated the nation."[6] A year later, in *Abington v. Schempp* and *Murray v. Curlett* (the latter case brought by atheist Madalyn Murray, celebrated in the media as "the most hated woman in America"), the Court banned voluntary Bible readings in public school. In 1968, a prayer that achieved dizzying heights of saccharine charm and never even mentions God was similarly disallowed:

> We thank you for the flowers so sweet
> We thank you for the food we eat

We thank you for the birds that sing
We thank you for everything[7]

The immediate response to these rulings failed to match the fury following *Engel v. Vitale,* perhaps due to battle weariness on both sides, although many religious leaders again decried the decision. The Court's defense of the Establishment Clause has continued unabated in recent years; in *Wallace v. Jaffree* (1985), it struck down an Alabama law permitting a moment of silence for "meditation or voluntary prayer." The Sixth Circuit Court of Appeals in 1999 similarly banned prayer before school board meetings.

All this suggests a shift toward secularism in American public life, but such may not be the case. Sentiment in favor of school prayer remains high. According to recent Gallup/CNN/USA Today polls, 70 percent of Americans favor daily spoken prayers in public schools, and 83 percent favor prayer in graduating ceremonies. Two thirds of Americans support a constitutional amendment allowing school prayer. One may point out, as the Supreme Court did in its landmark decisions of the 1960s, that the wishes of the majority cannot infringe on the rights of the minority. Nonetheless, the Court itself has sent mixed signals about the exact height and thickness of the constitutional wall of separation, and there appears to be considerable wiggle room for constitutionally sanctioned prayer in the public square. In *Marsh v. Chambers* (1983), the Court affirmed that prayers may be said during state legislative sessions, declaring that "to invoke Divine guidance on a public body entrusted with making the laws . . . is simply a tolerable acknowledgment of beliefs widely held among people of this country."[8] How this differs from a prayer invoking divine guidance on a school and its members — also a public body — remains elusive. The Court has also given public prayer a boost by shrugging its shoulders at some flagrant instances of federal religious sentiment, including "In God We Trust" as a numismatic motto, the blessings and invocations — often homilies in disguise — prominently featured at presidential inaugurations, and the prayers that bless the Court's own sessions.

This judicial confusion reflects a complex situation that lacks a clearcut solution. One wonders at the overwhelming public support for vocal prayer in the schools, given that such prayers — to be said, one must remember, by children — may ostracize, embarrass, harass, or confuse those of differing views. A daily moment of silence may be, from the standpoint of common sense as well as constitutional law, a viable alternative; silence, after all, can be spent rehearsing yesterday's baseball game or tomorrow's exam as readily as reciting the Lord's Prayer or the Shahadah. Several justices in the 1985 *Wallace v. Jaffree* decision appeared to affirm the inviolable liberty of the mind during silence. The Alabama statute establishing a moment of silence proved unconstitutional, these justices suggested, because it explicitly endorsed prayer as a reason for the law; left undefined, the moment of silence might have met constitutional safeguards. At the very least, a moment of silence would introduce some students to the virtues of quiet in lives otherwise dominated by television, computer games, and the clamor of the mall. But this solution is flawed as well, for who can doubt that for the majority, silence would be a code term for prayer, and that the minority who do not pray would feel out of place, if not ostracized — the last impression one wants to create in a public classroom.

At the same time, a school without prayer harbors its own dangers. If prayer is indeed a fundamental human impulse, a profound and fruitful act, and an essential bridge between ourselves and God, then what have we wrought by banishing it from our children's public education? We may teach prayer at home and in church, but the hard message nonetheless resounds that religion cannot pervade the whole of life and must be abandoned at the classroom door. Such a teaching will surely affect our understanding of ourselves and our culture. That the portcullis must be lowered against prayer in public schools seems incontrovertible, but it remains a sad and painful decision, a measure of the price we pay for our pluralistic democracy.

Debate about school prayer has ebbed in recent years, despite periodic efforts by members of Congress to pass constitutional amendments to countermand *Engel v. Vitale.* When put to a vote, the amendments invariably fail, for the public — or at least their legislators — is apparently unwilling to transform the yearning for school devotions into a legal edict that carries intimations of misplaced nostalgia if not religious coercion. The fading of school prayer as a front-page issue does not mean, however, that the place of prayer in the public square finally has been settled. A new flashpoint has erupted, one that promises to be at least as volatile: interfaith prayer.

Elbow to Elbow in Prayer: The Hamtramck Case

Almost everyone agrees that prayer is, or should be, an irenic action, a gentle, generous, solicitous reaching out to others — to God, to the heavenly court of angels and saints, to our fellow creatures, to the world. "He prayeth best who loveth best / All things both great and small," wrote

Coleridge, underscoring the specific virtue that animates, at the best of times, our petitions, adorations, and thanksgivings. But we humans traffic in vice as well as virtue, and prayer can be an occasion for discord, enmity, even drawn swords. Conflicts erupt, most often, when different religions collide. The modern world has no monopoly on interfaith friction; religious pluralism and its attendant problems have been with us since ancient trade routes brought Romans to Luxor and Buddhists to Beijing. In recent years, however, religious mixing has become the order of the day. Who would have guessed, fifty years ago, that Muslim mosques and Hindu ashrams today would sit side by side with Christian churches in many American communities? We are, as historian Jon Butler puts it, "awash in a sea of faith" — a turbulent sea of manifold currents and tides. Shipwrecks are cropping up everywhere, epitomized by the recent civic crisis in Hamtramck, Michigan.

By most accounts, Hamtramck is a pleasant town of twenty-three thousand souls, a blue-collar square on the Detroit urban checkerboard built by and populated by immigrants: first German Protestants, then Polish Catholics, and most recently, Bosnian, Yemeni, and Bengali Muslims. One couldn't ask for a friendlier, more well balanced polis — at least until the local Bengali mosque, the al-Islah Islamic Center, petitioned the city council for the right to broadcast on loudspeakers, five times a day, the Islamic *adhān* (call to prayer). This practice, widespread in Europe and Asia, remains almost unknown in North America, and a segment of the non-Muslim population of Hamtramck reacted with outrage. "I don't want to be told that Allah is the true and only God five times a day, 365 days a year," protested one resident. "It's against my constitutional rights to have to listen to another religion proselytize in my ear."[9] This Hamtramckian's scholarship may get failing grades — the Constitution nowhere forbids a religion from announcing its beliefs, even if electronically amplified — but her sense of invaded privacy was shared by many. Protestors poured into Hamtramck; one man unveiled, at a city council meeting called to debate the petition, an "Allah Is No God" T-shirt while robed Muslims prayed in the hallway.

When the city council unanimously approved the Islamic Center's request to broadcast, the debate accelerated. Why, several citizens wondered, would the government ban prayer in schools and the Ten Commandments in courtrooms and yet allow a Muslim prayer to fill the public airwaves? Muslims countered by noting the torrent of Christian messages that pour their way. "When Muslims go out during the Christmas season, we hear Christian religious songs in the malls and other gathering places," wrote Shahab Ahmed, a Muslim member of the city council, in the *Detroit News.*[10] More to the point, Ahmed and others noted that church bells have pealed in Hamtramck for decades. Opponents responded that church bells "have no religious significance," a measure of spiritual amnesia rather than a serious counterargument. In any event, forces against the call to prayer remained unswayed. A petition to block the broadcast garnered 630 signatures, enough to force the city council either to rescind its decision or put the matter to a citywide referendum. The council voted unanimously to let the public decide; on July 20, 2004, the right to *adhān* was narrowly upheld, by a vote of 1,462 to 1,200, and Muslim prayers resounded through the city.

The Hamtramck brouhaha captures, in miniature, what befalls a society when prayers collide. The aggrieved parties seethe with righteous indignation; feel trampled, abused, and woefully misunderstood; assure their opponents and the world that they operate from the best of motives; and continue to press their case. In Hamtramck each side had, as it happens, a legitimate point of view. Clearly, Muslims have as much right as Christians to practice their religion, and Islam traditionally includes a vocal call to prayer. For centuries Christians did the same, through the recitation of the Angelus. And yet one can't help but sympathize with the affronted Christians, especially old-timers who watch their traditions decay (who in Hamtramck prays the Angelus today?). The answer, we believe — for Hamtramck and for all interreligious disputes of this sort — is for people to invigorate their own faith and let their neighbors do the same. Let the muezzin sound the call to prayer, and let the church bells ring out the Angelus. Let Muslims rejoice when they hear the bells, and Christians rejoice when they hear the muezzin. Let each take the other's summons as a neighborly invitation to prayer. Always, as the early morning *adhān* proclaims, "Prayer is better than sleep!"

In Hamtramck, at least, prayer still rules the day. The final outcome is anyone's guess; one can imagine, as in an Ealing Studios comedy, church bells and *adhān* sounding simultaneously, each faith frantically vying to outdo the other by daily ratcheting up the volume. Let us hope that cooler heads prevail. Hamtramck will not, we pray, become a microcosm of the Christian-Islamic culture war that exploded on September 11, 2001, but rather a model for interfaith respect and cooperation. Religious pluralism is here to stay; the Hamtramck clash will be repeated in a thousand other communities in the years to come, as different beliefs jostle for public space and battle for converts. Some nations have responded with suppression — witness the aforementioned French ban on Muslim head coverings in public schools — but such intolerance would be, in America, intolerable. Prayer, the thirteenth-century Christian mystic Mechtild of Magdeburg reminds us, "brings together two lovers, God and the soul, in a wondrous place where they speak much of love."[11] May Hamtramck, and all neighborhoods, be that wondrous place.

The case of Hamtramck reveals some of the immediate dangers and delayed benefits that can arise when the prayers of different religions collide in the public square. But what happens when such prayers join hands? Strangely, the outcome may prove yet more volatile, confusing, and disruptive, leading even to the undermining of religious belief. Or so one might surmise from the extraordinary case of Dr. David Benke and the interfaith prayer service of September 23, 2001.

Elbow to Elbow in Prayer: The Benke Case

After the terrorist attacks of September 11, 2001, the American public fell to their knees in prayer. Polls indicated that nearly three out of four Americans — 74 percent — "prayed more" to deal with the anguish, fear, and rage unleashed by the event. Elaborate commemorative events and impromptu prayer gatherings sprang up across the nation; the most prominent and publicized was the "Prayer for America" assembly held at Yankee Stadium twelve days after the catastrophe. Tens of thousands of people crammed the grandstand, and a clerical rainbow of priests, ministers, rabbis, and imams filled the stage. The event had its embarrassing moments — Oprah Winfrey turned theology on its head by proclaiming that when you die, you become an angel, and that "over 6,000, and counting, angels [had been] added to the spiritual roster these last two weeks"; Bette Midler, after crooning a sentimental song, dashed across the stage, shouting, "I love you, New York!" and blowing kisses to the mourning families — but for the most part the event did befit the occasion.[12] When David Benke, president of the Atlantic District of the Lutheran Church–Missouri Synod (LCMS), rose to deliver a brief meditation, few noticed anything out of the ordinary. His words may have transgressed the limits of formal English — "O Heavenly Father, unbind, unfear, unscorch, unsear our souls" — but the emotional exhaustion of the day excused such diction. To judge by the vigorous applause, Benke's campfire feel-good tone ("take the hand of one next to you now and join me in prayer on this 'field of dreams'") and positive thinking ("Oh, we're stronger now than we were an hour ago") were just what the audience wanted to hear.[13]

Not everyone, however, was pleased. By sharing the stage with Muslims, Hindus, and other non-Christian clergy, Benke raised the hackles of many of the 2.6 million members of his conservative synod. Shortly after the event, nearly two dozen LCMS pastors and churches accused him of syncretism, unionism (worshiping with members of other Christian denominations), defending false doctrine, and a number of other serious charges. The faculty of Concordia Theological Seminary, entrusted with training ministers for the LCMS, passed with near unanimity (one professor dissented) a "pastoral response" sharply criticizing Benke's actions. This document argued that the Yankee Stadium event was not just a civic gathering but also a worship service, one that suggested that "the gods of all religions were equal," and "participating in joint services involving false gods does not give a faithful witness to Jesus Christ."[14]

These charges struck at the heart of the synod's concerns about retaining its distinctive Christian nature, and Benke soon found himself in hot water. Wallace Schulz, second vice president of the LCMS and host of *The Lutheran Hour,* a gospel radio program carried by one thousand two hundred stations, investigated the claims against Benke, and on June 25, 2002, suspended the minister as president of the Atlantic district. Schulz's action sent shock waves throughout the LCMS, for Benke was a well-liked and respected pastor. What Benke had done, moreover, many other LCMS ministers would be glad to do. Battle lines hardened between liberal and conservative factions within the synod. To bolster their case, conservatives noted that this was not the first time that Benke had run into doctrinal quicksand. In 1998 he had taken part in an interfaith prayer service at Saint Patrick's Cathedral in New York City, hosted by John Cardinal O'Connor and featuring Muslim and Jewish clergy; Benke had later signed a *mea culpa,* admitting that his participation had been a "direct violation of the Holy Scriptures and the Lutheran Confessions."[15]

This time, however, Benke came out swinging. At a gathering at his Brooklyn church, he defiantly declared that he would never surrender the moral high ground. His dramatic appearance triggered a three-minute ovation, punctuated by chants of "Benke, Benke," after which the overflow crowd repeated, verbatim, the entire text of the notorious Yankee Stadium prayer. Congressman Gary Ackerman, overcome by the moment, raised the ante by comparing Benke to Martin Niemoeller, a German Lutheran pastor who had confronted the Nazis and had spent seven years in concentration camps. Benke argued his case on PBS's *Frontline;* "It's Okay to Pray" bumper stickers, hats, T-shirts, and coffee mugs proliferated; a Benke defense fund gathered donations from across the nation. This outpouring of support proved too much for the executive board of Lutheran Hours Ministry, which removed Schulz — now the villain in the case — as host of *The Lutheran Hour* (the suspension was lifted a few weeks later). Finally, the LCMS summoned a panel to adjudicate what was becoming a highly embarrassing situation. On April 11, 2003, the panel dismissed all charges against Benke, citing an obscure LCMS regulation that allowed ministers to participate in a "once in a lifetime" event such as the Yankee Stadium affair. Schulz declined to appeal the decision, pointing out, with evident frustration, that the panel had ignored the substance of his decision to suspend Benke, which had been based not on LCMS bylaws but on scriptural texts. Benke returned to his many posts, now a lionized hero of interfaith prayer.

To the curious outsider, the Benke case, with its squabbling ministers, doctrinal spats, and focus on ecclesiastical purity, may seem like something out of an eccentric and outdated Victorian novel. When one official statement about the case closes with the phrase "Sincerely submitted in our Lord's name, the Name above every name," we have left the world of ordinary civic debate far behind.[16] For all its quirks, however, the Benke case brings to the foreground important issues about interfaith prayer and leads, we believe, to some surprising conclusions.

The fundamental question raised by the Benke case and similar controversies boils down to this: when is it safe to pray with those of other faiths? Many people would immediately respond, "Always," but reflection may qualify this answer. Praying with others may oblige you to pray to a being that you do not believe in; by praying alongside others, you may in effect be participating, albeit passively, in the prayers uttered within your presence. These are serious concerns with serious consequences. Many people skirt the issue by drawing a firm line between prayer and worship: prayer with those of other faiths is acceptable, but worship is not. This explains the intense efforts of LCMS members to ascertain whether the Yankee Stadium event was a prayer or worship service; to this day, anti-Benke websites carry the transcript of Mayor Giuliani's press release of September 20, 2001, which describes the gathering as an opportunity to "worship together."

We believe, however, that efforts to distinguish prayer from worship must inevitably fail. All prayer involves an element of worship, for it always entails the lower addressing the higher, and this higher assumes, in the mind of the believer, a particular form conforming to a particular faith. The "Letter to the Bishops of the Catholic Church on Some Aspects of Christian Meditation," a particularly insightful 1989 Vatican document addressing interfaith prayer, notes that "Christian prayer is always determined by the structure of the Christian faith."[17] So, too, with prayers of other faiths; thus Hindu prayer to a god of the Hindu pantheon reflects Hindu theology, Hindu devotional history, and Hindu ideas about the methodology of prayer. The same principle applies to icons, candles, incense, flowers, and other aspects of the material culture of prayer. Each object is a symbol, containing a rich cargo of meaning specific to the religion that created and molded it. Thus, to burn incense or pray to an image is always an act of worship, although the import of this act differs from one faith to the next. Even silence comes under this rule: the silence of a Buddhist temple is not the silence of a Christian church, for the silence of each enclosure swarms with the spiritual gestalt of each tradition. With this understanding, the borders between prayer and worship become permeable or evaporate altogether.

It seems to us, too, that assuming it is "always" safe to pray with others ignores another significant problem: interfaith prayer may atomize rather than unite. Imagine a Jew, a Muslim, and a Buddhist praying side by side, either in silence or by saying a generic prayer such as "God have mercy." We have already pointed out that *God* and *mercy* will possess different meanings for each participant; but the problem is practical as well as semantic. The Jew, in order to pray as a Jew (and not as a Muslim or Buddhist), may need to shut out what his neighbor is doing; and so too may the others in the group. It is rather akin to the need to close your ears to nearby English conversation if you are trying to compose a sentence in Spanish. This is, needless to say, scarcely a prayerful attitude, for it violates both the instinct for community and the solicitude toward strangers that characterize the faiths of the participants. Alternatively, of course, each person may choose to surrender the specifics of his or her religion, aim for the common denominator, and pray to a generic god in an artificial context — again, a posture hardly conducive to serious interfaith prayer. Religion, like cuisine, finds greatness in particularity. Each religion has its own specific genius, and to lump them together is to risk a tasteless, unnourishing pudding of faith.

This does not mean that interfaith gatherings like the Yankee Stadium "Prayer for America" should not take place or that Wallace Schulz was right to suspend David Benke. Sometimes the course of events overrides all objection; even a man who considers lying a grave sin might well lie to save an innocent life. In the kingdom of God — including that portion of the kingdom occupied by the LCMS — love trumps scruples. As Benke himself asked, in his PBS appearance, "If religion leads people to make these kinds of accusations at exactly the worst moment in American history, then what's underneath religion? Is religion . . . a desire for absolute security so strong that people cannot see the need to reach out and help?

If that's true, then I've got a lot of wrestling to do with my own religion."[18] And so do we all.

Not every interfaith prayer service mourns the death of three thousand people. Other gatherings, some international in scale, have been convened to combat hunger or protect the environment, and it was to promote world peace that Pope John Paul II sponsored in 1986, in Assisi, Italy, the most important and influential interfaith prayer meeting of modern times. More than one hundred religious leaders, including Christians, Muslims, Jews, Buddhists, Sikhs, Hindus, and Zoroastrians, assembled in the hill town famous as the home of Saint Francis in order to pray for an end to violence and war. The event was a success, triggering ceasefires (temporary, alas) around the world and leading to a number of other interfaith prayer gatherings, including additional papal assemblies at Assisi in 1993 and 2002. The pope, knowing the difficulties inherent in his enterprise, emphasized in his addresses to the delegates that "the form and content of our prayers are very different," that "there can be no question of reducing them to a kind of common denominator," and "that we have come here does not imply any intention of seeking a religious consensus among ourselves or of negotiating our faith convictions." Peace, however, is too important a project to leave to politicians, for, as the pope reminded the delegates, its "source and realization is to be sought in that Reality beyond all of us. That is why each of us prays for peace."[19]

This was uncontroversial and just vague enough to fit the widely differing theologies of the Assisi participants. What struck a new note was the plan of the conference. The assembly, after the opening session, broke into smaller groups, with members of each religion retiring to a separate room to pray. In these isolated chambers, the pope explained, each community would have "the time and opportunity to express itself in its own traditional rite." Afterward, the delegates gathered to pray en masse, but they prayed sequentially, one religion following another. By the 2002 conference, the theological hazards of even this minimal sharing had become evident, the practice was dropped, and mutual activity centered on a meal and the reading of a "common commitment to peace." The next Assisi gathering will likely sustain this note of caution. The approach leaves much to be desired — how much better it would be if we could pray as one in the light of unveiled truth! — but such a consummation is reserved for messianic dreams; in this world of shadows, as John Paul rightly said, even if "we have a single goal and a shared intention, we will pray in different ways," for only thus can we protect the integrity of each religion and those who pray within it.[20]

The Future of Prayer in the Public Square

The public square, as we have seen, both smiles and frowns on prayer. Many of the political, social, and religious tensions described in this chapter arise because we enjoy the freedoms and accept the burdens of a pluralistic democracy, a form of government that very few of us would willingly surrender. We may assume, therefore, barring unforeseen catastrophe that may transform our society in unimaginable ways, that our present ambivalent attitude toward prayer in civic life will continue apace. In recent years, however, a number of important social developments are opening new doors for public prayer — and shutting old ones. These include the following:

• *Internet prayer.* The World Wide Web has become a fertile seedbed for prayer, as "prayer warriors," "prayer rescues," "prayer chains," and "prayer circles" proliferate. Internet prayer groups now number in the thousands and enroll millions of participants, mostly evangelical Christians but also representatives of just about every imaginable religion. The prayers of these ardent masses are largely conventional in style and substance, tending toward petitions for health or safety for oneself or others and thanksgivings when prayers are answered; what stands out is the unifying power of the sponsoring organizations, capable of gathering, as if in a giant cybernetic cathedral, countless people who would otherwise remain ignorant of one another's existence. Internet prayers enjoy an unprecedented life span, for they dwell like dream wraiths in the limbo-like land of cyberspace, where they may — who can say? — address God without pause and burst into visible form only when someone logs on to a prayer website. There multitudes may read them; they may span the globe in an instant; they may be downloaded into any number of new forms — private journals, church hymnals, college syllabuses. Internet prayer inspires both hope and fear, for whenever people come together in a common cause, the result may be a cultural breakthrough or a cultural breakdown. In any event, the Internet, blessing or curse, will undoubtedly play a major role in the future of prayer.

• *Pluralism and separatism.* The recent events in Hamtramck and elsewhere suggest that in the future the public square will resound with a medley, if not a cacophony, of differing religious voices. The long-term effect of this marketplace of faiths on prayer and other religious practices remains uncertain; it may lead to an upswing in syncretism, a rebirth of orthodoxy, or both. It is also difficult to predict its effect on America's traditional identity as a Christian nation — approximately 80 percent of the population identified itself as Christian in recent polls —

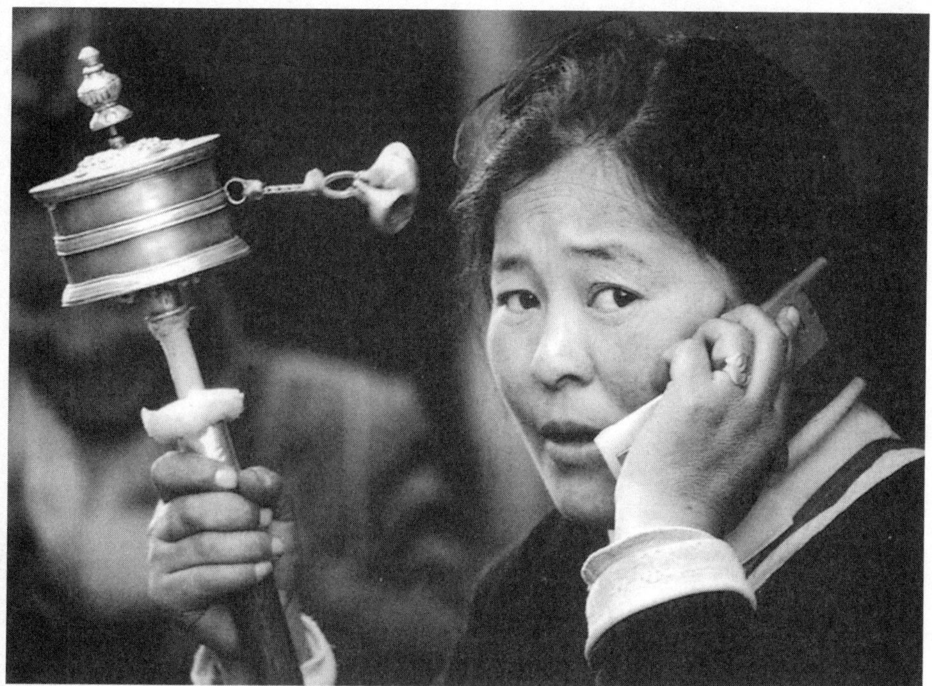

A woman swings a prayer wheel while speaking on a mobile phone in Lhasa, the capital of Tibet. Associated Press, November 10, 2003.

and whether a new national religious identity is slowly being forged. One striking aspect of pluralism has been the increased vigor of separatist religious enclaves. Not everyone is interested in mingling or melting in the public pot; groups such as the Ḥabad Ḥasidim have carved out their own niche, with well-marked geographical borders, in several American cities, and evangelical conservatives, especially in the South, boast their own neighborhoods, schools, community centers, and the like, in a deliberate attempt to avoid contamination by the larger secular society. These separatist communities nurture cultures suffused by prayer, whose influence seeps into the mainstream, if only as a reminder of the road not taken.

• *Religious migration.* Christianity is shifting its demographic center from Europe to Africa and South America; Islam has spread from the Middle East throughout Asia and Africa and is making incursions in Europe; Buddhism and Hinduism have entered the Americas and Europe. These worldwide migrations, with the accompanying cross-pollination of beliefs and practices as different religions mingle, will inevitably trigger changes in the way people pray. New forms of prayer of extraordinary beauty and power may develop; just as likely, misunderstanding and even violence will ensue as extremists of different faiths collide. Increasingly, prayer will become a weapon of propaganda, perhaps even of terrorism and war. We face, in this regard, a dark horizon, but here as everywhere, prayer, if offered with goodwill, may thwart the danger—even the danger that arises from prayer itself—melt hardened hearts, summon grace, and usher in a reign of peace.

PART IV

Something Understood

In Part IV we look at endeavors to understand prayer in the laboratories of empirical science and the laboratory of the human heart. We explore the relationship between prayer and healing, examine the efficacy of prayer as it has been questioned, measured, denied, or proclaimed by religious and secular voices, and return to some of the questions with which we began this book: How and why do we pray? What is prayer's place in human life and the cosmos? Is prayer, as the final line of George Herbert's poem obscurely suggests, "something understood"?

CHAPTER 11

Prayer and Healing

"HAVE MERCY UPON ME, O LORD; for I am weak: O LORD, heal me; for my bones are vexed," prays the psalmist. Within each of the modes of prayer that we have considered, healing is a leitmotif if not an overriding concern. The magician prays to expel the demons or ghosts that cause disease and to call forth the hidden virtues in plants, stones, or animals; the priest offers sacrifice in exchange for healing; the intercessor lifts up the afflicted into an all-embracing fellowship; the refugee and devotee find protection in the arms of grace; the ecstatic and the contemplative experience suffering transformed into bliss; confessional prayer heals sin; lamentation assuages grief; meditation restores psychic balance; sacrificial prayer makes illness itself a means of overcoming the greater illness of estrangement from God. Even prayer for a happy death has an ultimate healing in view. The world's first shrines were houses of healing, the world's first medical books were manuals of prayer, and it is not outlandish to imagine that the world's last patients in the last hospitals on earth will spend their final hours praying ardently for respite or cure.

The greatest healers of legend and history have been gods, such as Asklepios, or god-possessed, such as the twentieth-century Hindu ecstatic Anandamayi Ma. A rung below them are the priests, prophets, shamans, exorcists, or saints whose prayers have healing power. In traditional societies it often falls to the mother, grandmother, or maiden aunt to undertake long prayer vigils for the healing of family members, make arduous pilgrimages to healing shrines, or offer herself in sacrifice as a substitute victim. Yet healing prayer is a universal human prerogative, and it touches our deepest need — to feel our fragile existence supported and upheld by a wider and stronger reality.

We love to hear stories of illness overcome by prayer. It strengthens our hope that with God all things truly are possible, that prayer is something more than the pursuit of unseen, unfelt, untasted ideals, and that in prayer, as William James puts it, "something is transacting" and work is really being done. But what kind of work? One view holds that healing prayer is a matter of prescribing supernatural tonics for natural ills. A more traditional view, however, holds that sickness is itself a supernatural affair, a negative miracle, so to speak, an act of uncreation that rips a hole in the fabric of society and cosmos. "Any man's death diminishes me," says Donne, and so does any man's dysentery or pneumonia. Every sickness is a sickness unto death, and every healing a sign that God intends to rob the grave of its spoils. "O LORD," prays the psalmist in gratitude for recovery, "Thou hast brought up my soul from Sheol, restored me to life from among those gone down to the Pit" (Psalm 30:3 RSV). Life and death are engaged in a prodigious battle; and though God may sometimes send death to punish or illness to chasten, as creator, God is on the side of life.

The Hebrew Bible offers numerous examples of God's predilection for life. When the prophetess Miriam was stricken with leprosy, her brother Moses prayed, "Heal her now, O God, I beseech thee" (Numbers 12:13), and the petition was granted. "I am the LORD that healeth thee," God told Moses (Exodus 15:26), though all mortal physicians fail. When Hezekiah, king of Judah and hero of the Assyrian invasion, became "sick unto death," he turned his face to the wall and wept, praying for a change of fortune: "I beseech thee, O LORD, remember now how I have walked before thee in truth and with a perfect heart, and have done that which is good in thy sight" (2 Kings 20:3). God answered Hezekiah, "I have heard thy prayer, I have seen thy tears: behold, I will heal thee."

"I am the LORD that healeth thee" is the message of the New Testament as well. The Gospels report that Jesus radiated healing wherever he went. The afflicted, drawn by his healing charisma, prayed to him with brief, urgent petitions ("Lord, have mercy" . . . "Lord, heal me") and with the universal language of gesture and touch. When they scrambled through the crowds to catch hold of his garments, this, too, was an act of prayer. "Who was it that touched me?" Jesus asked, when the woman who had a discharge of blood for twelve years laid her hand on the fringe of his robes; "Someone touched me, for I perceive that power has gone forth from me" (Luke 8:45–46 RSV). The woman was healed by entering into personal contact with the divine physician, which for Christians is the essence of healing prayer. The first Christians prayed incessantly over the ailing members of their fellowship. "Is any among you afflicted?" asks

Christ heals a man possessed. Carved ivory tablet from Milan, Italy, c. 970.

James. "Let him pray. . . . Is any sick among you? let him call for the elders of the church; and let them pray over him. . . . Confess your faults one to another, and pray one for another, that ye may be healed. The effectual fervent prayer of a righteous man availeth much" (James 5:13–16).

Whether prayer does in fact avail much is the focus of our next chapter. Here, however, the underlying dynamism of healing prayer — whether magical or sacrificial, psychological or spiritual — is our main concern.

Healing prayer, we submit, is a work of repair, reknitting the social fabric that is frayed by illness or ruptured by death. It is a divine work, but its natural medium is a flourishing religious culture with a robust sense of communion between self and society, between society and the transcendent. Failing that sense of communion, healing prayer often takes on the appearance of a strange embellishment or an oddball obsession.

The American situation is particularly instructive. The American Southwest has played host to what may be the world's most intricate and deep-rooted system of healing prayer: the Navajo ceremonial chant ways. The American Northeast, on the other hand, has fostered, with the rise of Christian Science, New Thought, and kindred nineteenth-century sects, an individualistic, deracinated approach to healing prayer. The idea that prayer is a kind of therapy, an instrument from the divine tool kit that "works" and is valued for its results, is a legacy of this nineteenth-century metaphysical healing movement, as is the deep ambivalence, the strange mix of skepticism and credulity, that marks modern attitudes toward petitionary prayer. To gain historical perspective, we will consider these two cases in turn.

Navajo Healing Prayer

Of all the practices of healing prayer indigenous to the Americas, none is more dauntingly intricate or more comprehensively intertwined in the arts, sciences, and material culture of a people than the Navajo ceremonial tradition. Scholars who study it speak with awe and exasperation of its grandeur and "stupendous complexity."[1] Taxonomies of Navajo prayer, from its galaxy of twenty-four ceremonial systems to its hundreds of subsidiary chants, rites, and legends, are always unfinished, for the landscape of Navajo prayer is as vast as the several underworlds from which the Navajo trace their origin and as difficult to map as their migrations, some thousand years ago, from the northern lands to the high desert of the American Southwest.

The formal study of Navajo healing prayer began in the 1880s with the work of army surgeon Washington Matthews, a self-taught ethnologist.[2] It continued into the twentieth century with the work of Franciscan missionaries, in particular the admirable Father Berard Haile, who produced the first Navajo dictionary and grammar and left behind, after his death in 1961, a wealth of documents on Navajo life, lore, and medicine. Father Haile was a veritable recording angel, patient and exact in his labors, seeking to preserve an endangered oral tradition against the depredations of modernity by translating its diverse practices and compositions into a library of texts and field notes. He was joined in this work by indigenous experts and younger scholars who immersed themselves in Navajo life.[3] Thanks to their labors, Navajo healing prayer now lives a double life, as a body of sacred literature and as the evolving craft of native healers who find ways to coexist with Western medicine, Christian prayer, and the peyote practices of the Native American Church. It is some measure of success that in 1997 the U.S. Indian Health Service employed its first Navajo healer.[4]

Not all illnesses are suitable subjects for Navajo healing prayer. First a shaman, or "hand-trembler," must make a trance diagnosis of the underlying pathology. Perhaps the patient contracted the illness through contact with a snake or corpse; perhaps he or she is the victim of a sorcerer or ghost; or perhaps by some impropriety the patient has offended the *yéi* (Holy People, or gods). Only intransigent or mysterious cases require the employment of a *hataałii* (chanter) proficient in the specific prayer ceremonies that attack the root causes of disease. The patient and his or her family make a pilgrimage to the home of the chanter to beg his services in exchange for goods or cash.

The ceremony is essentially the reenactment of the beginning times when the Holy People lived closer to earth. The hogan where the healing ceremony takes place represents the first dwelling place of the ancestors, the patient is a kind of Everyman, and the chanter — part shaman, part priest — works in league with the gods to reestablish order against the chaos that perpetually assails it. The patient is like a ship that has come unmoored and is floating out to the open sea; the ceremony pulls him back and yokes him, together with his family and clan, to the world-founding events of the past. The prayers remind the Holy People of their goodwill in times past, and together with sacrificial gifts, induce them to return and restore *hózhó* (blessing, harmony, beauty, health) to the patient.

A typical healing ceremony in what is known as the Holyway tradition unfolds for as many as nine nights and days according to a prescribed sequence, with some ten or twelve distinct ritual stages.[5] It begins at sunset, with the consecration of the hogan. As night falls, the chanter spreads out the contents of his medicine bundle and makes ready the various talismans. The patient enters and sits, facing east. Dancers impersonating the principal gods enter and approach the patient, applying the talismans to the patient's body while the chanter sings and continues to work. At dawn the participants purify themselves by the heat of a sacred fire, sweating copiously and drinking a concoction to induce vomiting. After breakfast, they make sacrificial offerings of painted reeds filled with tobacco, feathers, bright mineral powders, and pollen, and they accompany the sacrifice with prayers to summon the presence of the Holy People, such as this Nightway chant:

Owl!
I have made your sacrifice.
I have prepared a smoke for you.
My feet restore for me.
My legs restore for me.
My body restore for me.
My mind restore for me.
My voice restore for me.[6]

The Holy People may have caused the illness in the first place, by placing a bad spell on the patient. If so, they are now obliged to remove it. The laws of cosmic justice are binding; therefore the healing is deemed accomplished almost in the act of praying for it:

Happily I recover.
Happily my interior becomes cool.
Happily my eyes regain their power.
Happily my head becomes cool.
Happily my limbs regain their power.
Happily I hear again.
Happily for me (the spell) is taken off.[7]

On the last day, after a bath in yucca root suds, a sand-painting ceremony may begin; it is the work of several helpers over several hours under the chanter's supervision. Once the sand painting is completed, the patient sits upon it to receive the full effect of the healing prayer. The chanter frequently touches the patient, applying various substances from his medicine bundle and anointing the patient from the feet to the top of the head with the bright pigments of the sand painting, in order to unite the patient with the Holy People there depicted. The prayers reach their crescendo with a long litany of blessing, which in its complete form is a classic instance of the 360-degree prayer:

With beauty before me, I walk.
With beauty behind me, I walk.
With beauty below me, I walk.
With beauty above me, I walk.
With beauty all around me, I walk.
It is finished (again) in beauty,

It is finished in beauty,
It is finished in beauty,
It is finished in beauty.[8]

The force of the prayer intensifies with repetition, releasing cascades of vowel sounds *(Óhohohó héya heáhi ehéyeyíyayéa),* reminiscent of Greco-Roman *voces magicae,* and spreading its healing influence from feet to legs to body to mind to voice like a potent drug. Yet the prayer is sacrificial as well as magical. One bargains with the Holy People, offering them precious gifts; one does not coerce them. The Navajo gods are, as Washington Matthews observes, too kindly to demand "smoking hearts," but they do appreciate a fragrant cigarette: "After [the cigarette] has been prayed over it is taken out and left for — *i.e.,* sacrificed to — the god for whom it is intended. The god, they say, recognizes it by its symbolic painting and by the place where it is sacrificed. He picks it up, smells and examines it. If he is satisfied that it is properly made and that it is for him, he takes it and bestows on the supplicant the favors asked."[9]

More to the point, the gods appreciate the gift of one's self. The prayer ceremony is a sacrificial ordeal — expensive, elaborate, time consuming, giddy, and cathartic. The core participants submit to sweating, vomiting, and all-night vigils to make amends for transgressions and draw down divine favor on the patient's behalf. Moreover, the individual patient is a living cell of his or her family and clan; hence the sacrifice and its effects radiate outward in ever-widening circles, not only healing the patient but also bringing blessings for the participants, family, clan, and nation. The final stage is a blowout party: an all-night sing and public dance exhibition for which signs are posted far and wide. Whether or not the patient improves, the ceremony has overcome isolation and reaffirmed the coherence and meaning underlying Navajo culture.

Navajo healing prayer is therefore not an oversized aspirin pill or a private regimen of self-enhancement. It is a highly disciplined communal work of cosmic repair. Its practitioners belong to a sacred tradition, receive training within it, and are answerable to it. It supports the total Navajo way of life, and its viability stands or falls with that way of life. It requires tribal affiliation, deep identification with one's family and nation, respect for elders, genuine belief in the powers to whom one prays, willingness to submit to what may be a long and trying apprenticeship, and docility toward the received tradition. The renowned Navajo medicine man Hosteen Klah (1867–1937) studied the Nightway for twenty-six years before he was fully qualified as its master, and he always submitted to the criticism of other experts, considering himself but one in a long line of custodians of the healing art.[10]

But what becomes of healing prayer where there is no unifying tradition, no intimate communion between self and society? Often it becomes a self-help technique; modern American culture has been inclined to understand healing prayer in this way. This prayer-soaked land is the birthplace of a novel idea that claims with bumptious confidence that health and well-being belong to us by right and that the business of prayer is to restore them to us. Prayer relaxes us, it is said, and in relieving our anxious striving reveals that the universe is on our side, and nothing is impossible. Prayer resets our spiritual clock, taps our inner plenitude, releases spiritual endorphins, and harmonizes our waking consciousness with the divinity who slumbers within. Prayer is the panacea that will outlast every elixir and snake-oil remedy on the market. Prayer heals, not just by God's grace but by its intrinsic power. No idea has a single source, but this idea has left enough footprints in American popular culture to be traceable back to the metaphysical healing movement, chiefly represented by Christian Science and New Thought, which began in the salons, clinics, and lyceums of nineteenth-century New England.[11]

Metaphysical Healers

In his Gifford Lectures on Natural Religion, later published as *The Varieties of Religious Experience,* William James observed that the metaphysical healing movement — he called it "mind–cure" — was America's "only decidedly original contribution to the systematic philosophy of life." Mind–cure could only have grown on American soil, nurtured by the peculiar American blend of revivalism, pietism, individualism, and faith in the wonders to be achieved by science. It was practical, focusing on the healing power of affirmative prayer. It was experimental, open to ingenious Yankee tinkerers and self-taught metaphysicians. It was optimistic, in keeping with the mood of a young and expanding nation. It aligned itself with progressive movements — abolition, labor and prison reform, and women's rights — that were galvanizing the American conscience. Like revivalism, it offered experiential salvation — from sickness, if not from sin. Like American Transcendentalism, it offered prayer outside the established church: a nondogmatic, noninstitutional, freethinking, and forward-looking approach to spiritual practice. Best of all, it seemed to work; it had what James called "cash value" and impressive regenerative "fruits for life":

> The blind have been made to see, the halt to walk; life-long invalids have had their health restored. The moral fruits have been no less remarkable. The deliberate adoption of a healthy-minded attitude has proved possible to many who never supposed they had it in them; regeneration of character has gone on an extensive scale; and cheerfulness has been restored to countless homes. The indirect influence of this has been great. The mind-cure principles are beginning so to pervade the air that one catches their spirit at second-hand. One hears of the "Gospel of Relaxation," of the "Don't Worry Movement," of people who repeat to themselves, "Youth, health, vigor!" when dressing in the morning, as their motto for the day.[12]

That thoughts are forces, whether for good or ill, is the central tenet of mind–cure. According to this view, prayer is simply a matter of harnessing thought forces to serve one's deepest desires. Would you pray for health? Pray like this:

> "I am wise with the wisdom of infinite Mind and I have knowledge of all things. I know that I am pure intelligence and I hereby claim my divine right to light, life, and liberty in all goodness, wisdom, love, and purity."
>
> "I affirm that I am unlimited in my power and I have increasing health, strength, life, love, wisdom, boldness, freedom, charity, and meekness now and forever. I am now in harmony with the Father and stronger than any mortal law. I know my birthright in pure Being and I boldly assert my perfect freedom. In this knowledge I am enduring, pure, peaceful, and happy."[13]

I know, I claim, I affirm! Mind–cure seizes its spiritual inheritance with all the chutzpah of Jacob robbing Esau of his primogeniture.

Two remarkable figures who seemed to possess a high degree of spiritual chutzpah can be considered the originating geniuses of the metaphysical healing movement: Phineas Parkhurst Quimby (1802–1866), one-time Mesmerist, and Mary Baker Eddy (1821–1910), founder of Christian Science. The son of a blacksmith, Quimby grew up, without great prospects, in the small town of Belfast, Maine. Clock making was his chief trade, which he learned by the old system of apprenticeship; he was also one of the first daguerreotypists in America and a prolific inventor of useful contrivances (an early combination lock, a steering device for boats, a prototype of the band saw). Ever the zealous autodidact, he soaked up the lectures of visiting pundits and tested the latest theories with ingenious household experiments. After successfully healing himself of consumption, he picked up, from a visiting expert on "animal magnetism," the rudiments of Mesmeric healing.

Quimby embraced Franz Anton Mesmer's theory of an invisible energy fluid that pervades the cosmos and the human body, responds to planets and tides, transmits influences from person to person, and obeys the laws of electricity and magnetism. Health depends, according to this theory, on the harmonious circulation of the subtle electrical fluid throughout the body; illness, caused by blockages in the flow, could be cured by inducing magnetic trance. Quimby quickly mastered the new trade, succeeding brilliantly in private demonstrations of Mesmeric healing and training a particularly susceptible subject, one Lucius C. Burkmar, to diagnose ills and prescribe remedies from a trance state. From 1843 to 1847, Quimby and Burkmar stumped the lucrative traveling-Mesmerist circuit throughout Maine and New Brunswick. Eventually Quimby realized that he could achieve equally good results without Mesmeric tricks. If he sat with his patients and concentrated, perhaps holding their hands, a vivid perception of their feelings would imprint itself, like a daguerreotype, upon his mind. He would describe their symptoms, which he never dismissed as imaginary, while daguerreotyping into their minds the knowledge that their true condition was health. For patients unable to travel, he provided "absent treatment," attending to them, clairvoyantly, from a distance. Most of Quimby's patients were chronic invalids who had suffered for long years without hope. No doubt it was deeply impressive for them to feel the full force of Quimby's sympathetic attention and assurance.

It seemed to Quimby that he was on to something tremendous. He had rediscovered the scientific basis for prayer, the principle by which Jesus Christ healed. "Disease is an error the only remedy for which is the truth," Quimby writes, and prayer is the conscious affirmation of that truth, realized within oneself and communicated telepathically to others. As mystical as this may seem to our ears, Quimby continued to be, as in his Mesmerist days, an avowed materialist. Mind is dilute matter, Quimby reasoned, and matter is condensed mind. A false belief in illness poisons the entire solution, body and mind together. Correcting the false belief causes a "chemical change" in the "fluids of the system" to effect a cure. True prayer, Quimby insists, is a rational affair, concerned with objective principles and forces rather than subjective wants. Ordinary petitionary prayer, on the other hand, is ignoble and superstitious: "No man prays but he who expects to get a favor or be rewarded for more than he deserves or perhaps has more of this world's goods than his neighbor. Witness the effects of the prayers on this world, those who pray to the earthly man. They belong to the begging, hypocritical, lowest class of mankind. No man of character will beg or pray for the sake of gain."[14]

As for himself, Quimby says, "I have no account with God. He pays me as soon as my work is done, and I do not ask favors of Him apart from His principles."[15] To his religiously minded disciples — most important, to Mary Baker Eddy and the leaders of New Thought — Quimby bequeathed the doctrine that true prayer is the conscious realization of our intrinsic well-being.

Like Quimby, Mary Baker Eddy began her career as a metaphysical healer with a dramatic self-cure. Her young adult life was marked by hardship and illness; she suffered from indigestion, kidney trouble, and spinal ailments, among other complaints. Her first husband, George W. Glover, father of her only child, died a year after their marriage. Her son, Georgie, was sent away by her family when he was four years old. Her second husband, Daniel Patterson, a dentist and Union soldier, was a philanderer and often out of town; eventually their marriage would end in divorce. Turning her back on these domestic upheavals, she set out on a quest for physical and mental healing. Water cures, homeopathy, all the standard nostrums of the day failed her until she arrived at the clinic of Phineas Quimby. There at last she found relief, and a new world opened up for her. She took to the lyceum halls, giving lectures with titles such as "P. P. Quimby's spiritual science healing disease as opposed to deism or Rochester-Rapping Spiritualism."

Soon enough, however, she learned that she could not depend on Quimby alone. Sometimes, when she was away from his influence, her symptoms would return. Two weeks after his death in 1866, she slipped on ice, injured her back, and was immobilized for three days. She was told her condition was hopeless; but when she read the Bible and chanced to light upon the healing miracles in Matthew 9, she was instantly cured. From then on she developed her own vision of Christian Science as a comprehensive spiritual path. She married one of her students, Asa G. Eddy, in 1877; announced the creation of the First Church of Christ, Scientist, in 1879; opened the Massachusetts Metaphysical College in 1881; and built the Mother Church in Boston in 1895.

It remains unclear how much of Eddy's teaching was her own and how much she owed to Phineas Quimby. There are striking resemblances between early drafts of *Science and Health* and Quimby's own voluminous writings; and in the 1890s two of Quimby's disciples sued Eddy for stealing the master's ideas. Nonetheless, there is much in Eddy's metaphysics undreamed of in Quimby's. Eddy was less the Enlightenment savant and more the Christian mystic. Though she rejected her Calvinist upbringing, she remained grateful for the love of prayer, spiritual discipline, and lively conviction of the need for regeneration that it had given her. Though she left off speaking of Satan, she suffered another form of hellish attack, "malicious animal magnetism," which had never troubled Quimby even in his Mesmerist days. Whereas Quimby was a materialist, Eddy was a thoroughgoing spiritualist, maintaining that mind alone was real and matter an illusion: "Life in matter is a dream: sin, sickness, and death are this dream. Life is Spirit; and when we waken from the dream of life in matter, we shall learn this grand truth of being."[16] Perhaps this amounts to the same thing. Whether all is matter or spirit, the implication is the same: all is undivided unity, and in that undivided unity there is little scope for petitionary prayer.

Accordingly, in the first chapter of *Science and Health with Key to the Scriptures,* Eddy insists that one must pass beyond ordinary petitionary prayer to prayer of a transcendent, spiritual, and thoroughly scientific kind. God is not swayed by praise and petitions: "God is Love. Can we ask Him to be more? God is intelligence. Can we inform the infinite Mind of anything He does not already comprehend? Do we expect to change perfection? Shall we plead for more at the open fount, which is pouring forth more than we accept?" The purpose of prayer is to change the person who prays: "Prayer cannot change the Science of being, but it tends to bring us into harmony with it."[17]

When Christian Scientists say that their prayers have been answered and their health restored, this means, according to Eddy, that through prayer they have been brought into communion with God. In communion with God, all is well. Christian Scientists do not look for future favors, but rather for greater awareness of the favors that from all eternity are poured out upon them. Dissatisfied with the petitionary approach of the Lord's Prayer, Eddy composed a new version, short on art, long on adjectives, that begins by praying for what already sublimely *is,* rather than asking for blessings still to come:

> Our Father-Mother God, all-harmonious,
> Adorable One.
> Thy kingdom is come; Thou art ever-present.[18]

True prayer, thus understood, was the foundation of Mary Baker Eddy's spiritual empire, the unifying theme of her worldwide church, publishing house, and newspaper, and the basis for a number of spin-off movements, including those loosely categorized as New Thought.

From Christian Science to New Thought

New Thought owes much to Christian Science, yet where Christian Science became a distinct sect notorious for its rejection of medical science, New Thought was and is far more diffuse, traveling under a hundred guises and known by a hundred names (Mind–cure, Mental Science, Divine Science, Unity, Religious Science, and so on), making fewer headlines than Christian Science but leaving a wider mark on mainstream prayer and contributing significantly to the modern religious gestalt.

The first generation of New Thought teachers included several of Mary Baker Eddy's students who departed from orthodox Christian Science — an apostasy that Eddy regarded as personal betrayal — to develop their own programs for metaphysical healing. Preeminent among them was the "Teacher's Teacher," Emma Curtis Hopkins (1849–1925), who has been called the "forgotten founder of New Thought," an eclectic mystic with such charisma that hopeless invalids were reportedly healed in the classroom by her lectures alone. Hopkins taught Malinda Cramer and Nona Brooks, founders of Divine Science; Ernest Holmes of Religious Science; his brother Fenwich Holmes, who inspired the Japanese New Thought movement, Seicho-No-Ie; and most important, Charles and Myrtle Fillmore, creators of Unity, foremost among the New Thought groups still flourishing in the twenty-first century.

Charles Fillmore (1854–1948) was a Quimby-like character, the home-schooled son of a Minnesota Indian trader and a seamstress. He supported himself, never comfortably, by working as a printer's helper, grocery worker, bank assistant, and railroad clerk, and he tried unsuccessfully to make a go of mining and real estate. His wife Myrtle (née Mary Caroline Page, 1845–1931), who was thirty when they married, came from a well-to-do Ohio Methodist family and had taken the yearlong "Literary Course for Ladies" at Oberlin College in Ohio. In 1884 Myrtle came down with tuberculosis and was pronounced incurable. But a lecture on the thought of Emma Curtis Hopkins introduced her to affirmative prayer. On her way home, she kept repeating to herself, "I am a child of God, and therefore I do not inherit sickness." Within two years she was completely healed.

Charles studied the matter further, taking a course with Hopkins in Chicago, and was won over sufficiently to bail out of his failing real estate business and launch the magazine *Modern Thought,* a monthly potpourri of occult metaphysics, spiritualism, and affirmative prayer. As an outreach to readers, Myrtle created the Society of Silent Help to provide a twenty-four-hour circle of healing prayer at a distance. In 1891 Charles christened the movement Unity, renaming the magazine *Unity Magazine* and the prayer group Silent Unity. His interest in esoteric subjects such as reincarnation and "spiritual ethers" gave way to a more accessible generic Christianity, with the power of affirmative prayer as the central theme; together, the Fillmores fashioned a worldwide prayer ministry. Myrtle, "the Mother of Unity" and founder of *Wee Wisdom* magazine for Unity's children, died in 1931 at age eighty-six; but Charles remarried, and with his second wife, Cora, carried on the work. Just before he died at age ninety-four, he was able to look back at the long litany of affirmations that had been his life and exclaim with Whitmanesque exuberance: "I fairly sizzle with zeal and enthusiasm and spring forth with a mighty faith to do the things that ought to be done by me."[19]

To this day the affiliated churches, schools, retreat centers, and publishing enterprises that make up Unity continue to sizzle, adapting themselves to the present technological environment. Silent Unity, a year-round, twenty-four-hour prayer vigil, perhaps the oldest of its kind, is a going concern on the Internet, logging millions of prayer requests. At the Unityonline website, one can download daily affirmative prayers for healing ("In the stillness of Your presence, God, I feel Your healing life flowing through me now, bringing peace to my mind and energy to my body"), prosperity ("I am one with the all-providing love of God that assures me of abundance"), and inner peace ("I relax, release any anxious thought, and peacefully rest in the presence of God"). With such upbeat maxims and broad outreach, Unity successfully weathered the transition to the New Age era, unencumbered by dogma or other fixed structures. Herein lies the chief difference between Christian Science and New Thought. Whereas Christian Science is a centrally organized church, for the most part New Thought has been content to drift, only occasionally settling into voluntary associations such as the International New Thought Alliance. Christian Science has an authoritative founder — a prophet whose stature is just short of divine and whose oracular writings constitute required reading alongside the Bible at every religious service. New Thought has produced a great many inspirational teachers and entrepreneurs, but no single commanding figure.

Moreover, dedicated Christian Scientists embrace a spiritual discipline almost as arduous as that of monastic life, including daily prayer, study of the Bible and the founder's writings, moral self-scrutiny, and service to others. Christian Science practitioners, and the faithful whom they serve, are bound in a union of prayer — a communion of saints — that they believe is undiminished by death. They conspire together, as it were, to deny the reality of sickness, matter, and death, and (except *in extremis*, if the person so desires) they refuse the medical treatment that reinforces "mortal mind." New Thought, which has remained porous to other systems of thought, makes no such strong or controversial demands. Perhaps that is why, without much notice taken, New Thought was able to infiltrate the larger culture, contributing to the rise, after World War II, of a roster of immensely successful teachers of positive thinking (Norman Vincent Peale, Fulton Sheen, and Robert Schuller among them) and related ministries, such as Dial-a-Prayer. Robert Schuller's "self-esteem reformation" and Norman Vincent Peale's recipe for spiritual abundance ("Picturize, Prayerize, Actualize!") may seem extreme; but milder versions of affirmative self-healing prayer now ring down the corridors of mainstream churches.

The literary style of the metaphysical healing movements is spun sugar, as grandiose and insubstantial as the cotton candy at a country fair. The spirit soars upward on italics and exclamation marks, and barely a noun escapes the pen without being capitalized and raised to a Higher Plane. The exalted diction is endemic, for a religion devoted to Forces and Principles must hypostatize them in order to compensate for their vaporous abstractness.

Only a small change of idiom takes us from nineteenth-century New Thought to the trance-dictated idealism of *A Course in Miracles* and the self-help spirituality of Louise Hay, Marianne Williamson, Wayne Dyer, Eckhart Tolle, or Neale Walsch. Prayer for good things such as health, happiness, prosperity, and love is their stock-in-trade, and yet they share with New Thought a discomfiture with the idea of petition — not because we have no right to ask, but because everything we want is already on offer. As Nona Brooks put it a century ago, "The great lesson of prayer today is that God and man are one; the high purpose of prayer is to establish this relationship in men's thinking. Instead of the old conception of a God who is reluctantly withholding his favors from the lives of men, and who, therefore, must be appeased and besought in order that he may grant favors, there is a new concept — Infinite Spirit sharing its all."[20] This new concept of God calls for a new, more enlightened way of praying, Brooks maintains, which makes no primitive attempts to change God's mind but instead centers on the self-realization of God within. The inner God always has our best interests in view; always takes the side of reason, progress, and personal growth; and never makes arbitrary or inconvenient demands.

Countless sicknesses have been cured, lives made whole, and despairing hearts mended; yet in this optimistic program of do-it-yourself redemption there is something that seems, paradoxically, to vitiate prayer. All too easily, prayers that are pure *alleluia* and no *miserere* collapse into a dull monotone. All too easily, the dialogue between I and Thou becomes a monologue between I and Me. All too easily, the spirituality of thoughts as forces shrinks down to a psychology of self-hypnosis. The God within, who is always on call, is not nearly as evocative as the God without, whose face is sometimes hidden. Even great mystics such as Ramana Maharshi and Sri Ramakrishna experienced, in the midst of their union with the divine, the mystery of God's awful and wonderful otherness. Healing prayer is an inestimable gift; but prayer that is therapeutized surely lacks the resources to sustain a flourishing religious culture like that of the Navajo or the crofters of the *Carmina Gadelica.*

Eventually one tires of oneself, even of one's higher Self. It avails much to pray, but when it becomes no more than a self-help technique, the adventure of prayer is over.

CHAPTER 12

The Efficacy of Prayer

THE HISTORY OF SAILING abounds in reckless adventures, but few as madcap as that of a middle-aged Latvian known to the world by the portentous pseudonym of Fred Rebell (1886–?). As a young man, Rebell lived up to his chosen name, rejecting home and a steady job in favor of trans-European wanderings that ended when he stowed away on a ship bound for Australia. There he found romance and heartbreak and resolved to push on toward America. He bought a small cabinless sailboat, nineteen feet long with a seven-foot beam, cobbled together a sextant from a hacksaw blade and a Boy Scout's magnifying glass, copied some out-of-date navigational charts, and on New Year's Eve, 1931, lifted anchor and aimed for the high Pacific. He had never sailed before in his life.

Rebell made it to America, barely. His craft leaked, his centerboard fell apart, he lost his sea anchor while blundering through a cyclone. His nautical misadventures, recorded in *Escape to the Sea* (1939), make for lively reading, but what matters to us are his spiritual adventures. His mysterious inner life manifested itself first in relation to dreams: spying some unknown islands, he suspected that his boat was off course until, dozing, he heard "a kindly but authoritative male voice" declare in English: "Trust your instruments! There are islands in the Fiji group farther south than those shown on your chart."[1] This disembodied intelligence proved to speak the truth. Other mantic visions, equally mysterious, ensued.

Until this event, Rebell had considered himself a metaphysical skeptic — for twenty years or more he had never thought of God — but now his incredulity wavered: "Ever since my student days, I had prided myself on having that rational mind then fashionable among the intelligentsia; and all my life I had been guided by it. But looking back over my life, I could not see that it had guided me very well, neither into great achievement, nor pleasant courses. Indeed, few lives can have been so disastrous and futile as mine had hitherto been." He decided it was time for an experiment. Wind and thunderstorms threatened; cloudy skies prevented a sextant reading; he was lost in mid-Pacific. Swallowing his pride — and his faith in a mechanistic cosmos — he turned, for the first time as an adult, to prayer. *"God Almighty, Who hearest every prayer, please let me see the sun at noon, so that I can take a sight."*[2] Instantly he realized the difficulty of his request, for a double bank of clouds obscured the sun, and both would have to disperse for his petition to be answered. His heart sank, and he prepared for the worst. But just then he spied a brightening on the boat's hood. Soon the sun appeared, Rebell seized his sextant, took a reading, and checked the time. It was, as his prayer had stipulated, exactly high noon.

This first answered prayer shook the foundations of Rebell's worldview; he now allowed that "perhaps, after all, the billions of people who have prayed in the past, the millions who are praying today, have not entirely deluded themselves." He decided a second test was in order and petitioned God to send his boat, by sunrise, to the coast of Fiji. Sure enough, at the appointed hour the island's tallest mountain hove into view. This event permanently reset Rebell's religious compass; henceforth he would believe in God, come what may. But would God answer *any* prayer, however extravagant? When battling gale-force winds northeast of Hawaii, he asked God to quell the storm. "I know that most people will laugh at the idea of anyone trying to stop a tempest by prayer," he later remembered, "yet the words were hardly out of my mouth when the gale began to ease off."[3] Three times now he had prayed to God, and three times God had responded. Nonetheless, the worm of doubt still gnawed — one does not easily shed a lifetime of ingrained agnosticism. What if he had experienced a series of coincidences? "Disbelief," he remarked, "is elastic as India-rubber: once the pressure of evidence is released, back it springs to its former position." When another storm struck, Rebell again prayed for release, and again God responded. Four days later, when the winds picked up, he "settled down contentedly" to make his familiar request, by now fully expecting his petition to be answered. Again the winds abated. Prayer, he concluded, never failed.[4]

Rebell finally reached the United States on January 7, 1933, making landfall at San Nicholas Island, eighty miles south of Los Angeles. The press adored him, and he made the rounds in Hollywood. In order to better understand his discoveries, he set sail again, this time into the ocean of theology, canvassing Buddhism and theosophy, Swedenborg and Taoism, before finally dropping anchor in fundamentalist Christianity. He continued to pray, and God never failed to heed his prayers. His favorite story, recounted with great relish in his memoirs, involves the acquisition of an automobile. Even a Model T cost too much, so he turned to the Lord. "The very next day," he reports, "I saw a car for sale and the price, incredible though this may seem, was *three* dollars! Less than the cost of a new tire."[5] The car may have been only a Model T, but truly this was prayer on automatic overdrive.

The value of this curious tale is that it throws the problem of the efficacy of prayer into high relief. What do we make of Rebell's claims? That he believed them there can be no doubt; he writes with a directness and conviction that is difficult to simulate, and no marine historians have questioned the veracity of his ocean voyage. Well, was he mad? Was he dreaming? Did he mistake coincidence for cause and effect? Rebell's story is sui generis, but the questions it raises are universal. What kind of efficacy do we suppose prayer to have, and by what means or standards do we test it?

In societies endowed with an active sense of the supernatural, such as those of medieval Europe or preconquest Tibet, the efficacy of prayer is almost axiomatic, for it is an integral part of the accepted worldview. Yet it would be naive to suppose that our ancestors were invulnerable to doubt. They may not have questioned the ability of God to hear prayers, but they did sometimes doubt his willingness to listen. "O LORD, how long shall I cry, and thou wilt not hear!" (Habakkuk 1:2) is not an uncommon sentiment; and the sheer abundance of devout tracts exhorting the faithful to pray often, pray fervently, and pray with confidence in achieving desired results suggests that belief in the efficacy of prayer has always needed some degree of shoring up. Hence we encounter, in the legends of desert monks and medieval saints, countless *exempla* (didactic exemplary tales) of religious heroes and heroines overcoming demons through prayer. The virgin martyr Saint Margaret is remembered in medieval legend for vanquishing a dragon with the power of this unambiguous prayer: "Invisible God, full of every good thing, whose wrath is so fierce that the inhabitants of hell and heaven and all living things quake before it; help me Lord, against this terrible creature, so that it not harm me." Some versions of the legend say that the dragon swallowed Margaret, only to split asunder and release her unharmed.[6]

There are cautionary *exempla* as well, warning of the harm caused by prayers left unsaid. Writing in the seventeenth century, the Benedictine mystical theologian Augustine Baker relates "a fearful example of the mischief following the neglect of internal prayer" on the part of a certain zealous preacher named Bernardine Ochinus, who persuaded himself that he could substitute good works for prayer and as a result ended up "a wretched Antitrinitarian apostate." Baker owed his own faith and monastic profession to an incident of answered prayer that became in seventeenth-century letters a famous *exemplum* against the skepticism of the Age of Reason. One day while he, an aristocrat and proud atheist in the full swagger of youth, was out riding, a moment's distraction left him stranded on a narrow bridge high above a deep and violent river. Despairing of any natural recourse, he made a hasty prayer, as his biographer recounts: "'If I escape this danger I will believe there is a God who hath more care of my life and safety than I have heed of his love and worship.' Thus he thought, and in a moment without his perceiving how it was done, he found his horse's head was turned the other way and himself and horse out of all danger." Though Baker's prayer may be an unspiritual "if, then" proposition, he felt sure that his deliverance had been miraculous, and he stayed the course to which providence had turned him.[7]

Yet another way of instilling confidence in the efficacy of prayer is the encomium, extolling prayer's benefits to body and soul. The fourth-century mystical theologian and bishop Saint Gregory of Nyssa introduces his sermons on the Lord's Prayer with an impressive list of such benefits, beginning with "physical well-being, a happy home, and a strong and well-ordered society," "a good harvest for the farmer and a safe port for the sailor," and going on to wonders greater still:

> Prayer is your advocate in lawsuits. If you are in prison, it will obtain your release; it will refresh you when you are weary and comfort you when you are sorrowful. . . . Prayer turned the whale into a home for Jonas; it brought Ezechias back to life from the very gates of death; it transformed the flames into a moist wind for the Three Children. Through prayer the Israelites triumphed over the Amalecites, and 185,000 Assyrians were slain in one night by the invisible sword. Past history furnishes thousands of other examples beside these which make it clear that of all the things valued in this life nothing is more precious than prayer.[8]

Thus do the masters of prayer defend the efficacy of prayer in all traditions; by furnishing encomiums in praise of prayer, enumerating prayer's benefits (often in numbered lists designed for memorization), and citing *exempla* to add color and increase conviction. They make bold claims — not just that prayers are miraculously answered, but that the very act of praying has a transforming effect. The wandering Russian saint of *The Way of a Pilgrim* received through prayer, as we saw in Chapter 5, a radiant suffusion of grace that brought warmth to his limbs, understanding to his mind, and an almost prelapsarian ability to communicate not only with God but also with animals and men. Prayer delights the joyful and comforts the afflicted, Gregory of Nyssa writes, and if that is not enough, he continues, consider that it assuages all our yearnings and elevates us to equality with the angels.

Similarly comprehensive claims are made for the contemplative disciplines of classical Hinduism, Buddhism, and Taoism. The fifth-century Indian Buddhist monk Buddhaghosa (his name means "speech of Buddha"), whose commentaries and synthetic expositions gave Theravāda Buddhism its definitive classical form, presents in the *Visuddhimagga (Path of Purity)* an exhaustive account of the benefits of Buddhist meditation. Meditation, as Buddhaghosa sees it, is a kind of *imitatio Buddha.* Those who persevere on the Buddhist path may taste, on a lower level, what the Buddha attained in his famous vigil under the bodhi tree: mastery of the "four trances" and "four formless states," insight into the transience of composite things, and invincible awakening, accompanied by supernormal powers, including the ability to perceive the mental states of other beings, the all-hearing divine ear, the all-seeing divine eye, and the recollection of past lives.

Buddhaghosa recounts *exempla* of experienced practitioners whose depth of meditative concentration rendered them immune to harm: an elder, absorbed in meditation, unaffected by a shattering blow to his head from an evil spirit; another whose clothing would not catch fire even when a group of local cowherds (thinking him dead) poured dung over him and set it ablaze; another whose serenity made him invisible to a band of robbers; a laywoman whose singleness of mind kept her safe when an envious harlot dumped a basin of hot oil over her head; a queen, unjustly accused of treachery, who disarmed the wrathful king by the power of her meditation on lovingkindness:

> Intending to kill her, [the king] took his bow and aimed a poisoned arrow. Sāmāvatī with her retinue pervaded the king with lovingkindness. The king stood trembling, unable either to shoot the arrow or to put it away. Then the queen said to him, "What is it Sire, are you tired?" — "Yes, I am tired." — "Then put down the bow." The arrow fell at the king's feet. Then the queen advised him, "Sire, one should not hate one who has no hate." So the king's not daring to release the arrow was success by intervention of concentration in the laywoman Sāmāvatī.[9]

Such are the fruits of *śamatha* (the state of tranquility or "calm abiding") attained by withdrawal into deep concentration *(samādhi).* Accompanying *śamatha,* though in principle distinct from it, is the cultivation of "right mindfulness" — an open, expansive, nongrasping attention to whatever appears before one's consciousness, which enables one to see things as they are, uncomplicated by second-order judgments and reactions: "In what is seen there must be only the seen; in what is heard there must be only the heard; in what is sensed (as smell, taste or touch) there must be only what is sensed; in what is thought there must be only what is thought." Even if a doubt should cross one's mind as to the efficacy of meditation, mindful recognition of the doubt removes its sting: "When *doubt* is present in him, the monk knows, 'There is doubt in me,' or when doubt is absent, he knows, 'There is no doubt in me.'"[10]

The monk has seen his doubt come and go and is no longer at its mercy. "This is the sole way," the Buddha tells his disciples in the "Greater Discourse on the Setting Up of Mindfulness," "for the purification of beings, for the overcoming of sorrow and lamentation, for the destroying of pain and grief, for reaching the right path, for the realization of Nibbāna."[11] The modern Buddhist scholar Nyanaponika Thera offers a gloss on the Buddha's encomium:

> Right Mindfulness recovers for man the lost pearl of his freedom, snatching it from the jaws of the dragon Time. Right Mindfulness cuts man loose from the fetters of the past which he foolishly tries even to reinforce by looking back to it too frequently, with eyes of longing, resentment or regret. Right Mindfulness stops man from chaining himself even now, through the imaginations of his fears and hopes, to anticipated events of the future. Thus Right Mindfulness restores to man a freedom that is to be found only in the present.[12]

There is compelling psychological wisdom in such observations, for the way we employ our attention greatly influences overall well-being, as we have seen in the lives of Thomas Kelly and Brother Lawrence. We are happiest, it seems, when attention is absorbed in *samādhi*-like concentration or expanded beyond its habitual range. The psychologist Mihaly Csikszentmihalyi, among others, has shown that such deeply satisfying alterations of attention are most likely to occur not when we are passively "relaxing" before a television, but rather when we are fully engaged in a complex task that matters to us and challenges us, like the piano player whose seemingly effortless grace is the fruit of much rehearsing or the athlete who by dint of arduous training finds herself, for a time, "in the zone."[13] On the other hand, when attention is restless, inert, or contracted without being stilled, we are easily bored; and like children we cast about for some mischief to distract us. Boredom, Kierkegaard tells us, is the root of all evil.

The attainment of "flow," as Csikszentmihalyi calls it, is therefore no mean thing. Even the subjective benefits of prayer and meditation, which are manifold, have objective value for the world. Peace instilled in the mind and heart spills over into the surroundings to the benefit of all. The good, to say the same thing more metaphysically, is self-diffusing. There can be no better cure for the diseases of attention, for boredom, anxiety, alienation, and anomie, than those disciplines of prayer and meditation that focus the soul on the highest good without neglecting the needs of others. "To contemplate, and pass on to others the fruits of one's contemplation," as the Dominican motto has it, is surely a boon to humankind.

Yet the efficacy of such disciplines, insofar as they involve unmeasurable spiritual or even supernatural events, resists impartial scientific assessment. What can the psychologist who studies prayer tell us of its success in achieving its own transcendent goals? As the Buddhist convert and scholar Edward Conze has observed, psychologists "differ profoundly" from practitioners of traditional meditation "in their definitions of mental health, in their theoretical assumptions about the structure of the mind and the purpose of human existence, and in the methods which they prescribe for the attainment of mental health." He wrote these words in 1956, when the psychological study of meditation was in its infancy; but there is no reason to think he would qualify them today. Conze (1904–1979) was a brilliant and cantankerous scholar, a former Marxist disillusioned by the clashing ideologies of the West who converted to Buddhism at the beginning of World War II under the influence of D. T. Suzuki, learned to meditate from Buddhaghosa's formidable *Visuddhimagga,* and became one of the preeminent modern translators of Mahayānā Buddhist texts. It was his intention to encounter Buddhism whole, not as a fashionable therapy but as a race for the ultimate prize of salvation. Buddhist meditation, he insists, is for people whose aim, incomprehensible to secular psychology, is not to adapt to the stresses of modern life, but "to get out of the world altogether." The classical meditation practices, Conze maintains, "thrive only in the climate of a living spiritual tradition, which to some extent guarantees their basic assumptions and success."[14]

Conze overstates his case at the expense of ordinary believers whose aspirations are more worldly and humble, but he does have a point. Prayer is never efficacious in a vacuum; it is efficacious in the context and along the lines of a particular religious worldview. Navajo healing prayer works, as we saw in the previous chapter, by reaffirming the Navajo cosmos and community; it works, in a sense, even though the patient who is prayed over may die. Prayer sets to flight the forces of chaos and grounds one in a coherent worldview. The masters of prayer in every tradition sing its praises to the heavens, but its concrete benefits are as varied and as difficult to track as are all other objects of human aspiration. This greatly complicates the enterprise of scientifically investigating the claims made for prayer. Nonetheless, the scientific study of prayer has a story of its own to tell, and to that story we now turn.

Prayer in the Laboratory: The Early Years

The scientific study of prayer finds its origins not among the beakers and retorts of a primitive early laboratory, but in the documentation and disputation that marks the canonization procedures of the Catholic Church. From the first days of the Christian community, the faithful prayed to the deceased to intercede with God on their behalf; answered prayers — especially when a miracle was involved — were considered signs of holiness, echoes of the miracles performed by Jesus, and reports of supernatural intervention loomed large in the dossiers of candidates for sainthood. As early as the fifth century, local bishops required that such miracle accounts be written down and, if possible, be accompanied by eyewitness testimony or other concrete evidence. The methodology was crude but helped to eliminate egregious fraud; over the centuries the system grew more sophisticated and rigorous. Canonization hearings turned into judicial trials, with a postulator for the saint's cause pitted against a devil's advocate who attempted to debunk the evidence. By the nineteenth century, in response to the many healing miracles reported at the Marian pilgrimage site at Lourdes in France, an official Vatican committee arose whose sole responsibility was to sift the medical evidence surrounding answered prayers.

In the twentieth century this work has fallen to the Consulta Medica, a group of physicians, mostly hospital directors or medical school professors, who examine eyewitness testimony, laboratory reports, historical precedents, and the like, and pass judgment on claims of miraculous intervention. The doctors are inclined toward skepticism, debunking most cases that come their way, but occasionally they encounter events that evade all natural explanation. As one panel member, a heart and liver specialist, confessed to journalist Kenneth Woodward: "I myself, if I did not do these consultations, would never believe what I read. You don't understand how fantastic, how incredible — and how well-documented — these cases are. They are more incredible than historical romances. Science fiction is nothing by comparison."[15]

But science fiction, or rather fictional science, is precisely the charge that skeptics have launched most often toward these Vatican-appointed physicians. This seems too harsh: the doctors of the Consulta Medica pore over the data with admirable precision, and the cases deemed miraculous do defy simple explanation. At the same time, it remains true that today's miracle is sometimes tomorrow's science, that the Consulta Medica has been assembled by a church convinced of the reality of medical miracles, and that each physician's deliberations entail, necessarily, a degree of subjective judgment. Is there any way around these objections?

Enter the statistician. The quantitative approach to the study of prayer began in the nineteenth century, with the work of the Victorian polymath Sir Francis Galton (1822–1911), a cousin of Charles Darwin who attained fame as an African explorer, anatomist, inventor of the first system for classifying fingerprints, and popular proponent of eugenics. Galton once issued a *Beauty Map of the British Isles,* charting female pulchritude city by city; London came in first; Aberdeen dead last. One can only speculate on the map's effect on early eugenic experiments, but it does indicate his passion for applying statistical analysis to practical matters and thus anticipates another line of research more germane to our interests: in 1872, Galton decided to examine, through statistics, the power of prayer.

"The efficacy of prayer," Galton writes in his seminal article in the *Fortnightly Review,* "seems to me a simple, as it is a perfectly appropriate and legitimate subject of scientific inquiry." In fact Galton had already been nudged toward religious skepticism by his cousin's *On the Origin of Species* (1859), and one suspects that he set out, as so many researchers do, with conclusions already in hand. In any event, with characteristic ingenuity Galton hit upon the idea of measuring prayer's effectiveness by examining the longevity of various social classes and professional groups. The health of the royal family was in the nineteenth century a constant motif of British prayer, so one would expect, if such prayers were answered, that the queen and her relatives would enjoy long, vigorous lives. The evidence proved otherwise; the royals possessed the lowest life expectancy of any group that Galton studied. Similar dismal results turned up for clergy, who also should benefit, if prayers are efficacious, from the petitions for good health offered on their behalf by devoted congregations. Nor did prayer improve the lot of any other group that Galton studied, including missionaries, businessmen, and sailors. Prayer,

Sir Francis Galton, *by Charles Wellington Furse. Oil on canvas, 1903.*

Galton concludes, is all smoke and mirrors. He credits it nonetheless with strengthening those who pray in the face of adversity and calming those on the brink of death. In his 1883 *Inquiries into Human Faculty and Its Development,* a collection of essays upon subjects such as the capriciousness of females and the benefits of racial manipulation, Galton reprinted his prayer study but dropped the faint praise, leaving only the cold assessment that "the civilized world has already yielded an enormous amount of honest conviction to the inexorable requirements of solid fact; and it seems to me clear that all belief in the efficacy of prayer, in the sense in which I have been considering it, must be yielded also."[16]

The subsequent history of scientific research on prayer has been, in a sense, nothing but a reaction to Galton's devastating conclusions. Scores of experiments have been undertaken, many if not most by scientists wishing to vindicate the legitimacy of prayer. The first well-publicized study, cited to this day in many books lauding prayer's curative powers, unfolded at the University of Redlands (California) in 1951–52. Forty-five volunteers, suffering from psychological ailments ranging from depression to unreasonable fears, were divided into three groups by the project director, William F. Parker. Group I received conventional, nonreligious psychotherapy; Group II, which consisted entirely of Christians, prayed to be healed; and Group III undertook a combination of prayer and psychotherapy. The outcome, based on a battery of tests, revealed a 65 percent improvement in Group I, no improvement at all in Group II, and a 72 percent improvement in Group III. These results might dismay many pro-prayer researchers — after all, the dedicated prayers of Group II failed entirely, and Group III showed only minuscule improvement when it added prayers to the psychotherapy of Group I — but Parker was elated. In *Prayer Can Change Your Life* (1957), he jubilantly announces that prayer "properly understood might be the single most important tool in the reconstruction of man's personality" and that it "can heal your diseases, renew your mind and body, [and] calm the storms of daily living." As for the failure of the Christian Group II to improve, Parker remarks only that they "asked [God] amiss" — a slap at ordinary Christian prayer that still crops up in New Age prayer literature.[17]

Parker's study suffers from many drawbacks and defects, not least the difficulty of judging psychological well-being, heavy emphasis on anecdotal evidence, and a failure to develop objective measures of improved health. Even Larry Dossey, physician and author of several bestsellers advocating the medical benefits of prayer, panned the Redlands study as "simply not good science." Its sloppiness, as it happens, was par for the age. Inadequate prayer studies continued for years to come. Another example, notable for the investigator's admirable but perhaps quixotic desire to avoid altogether the quagmire of human psychology, was the Reverend Franklin Loehr's study of the power of prayer on plants. One of those odd souls who enjoy both occult and scientific research, Loehr earned a college degree in chemistry but acquired fame as the channel for a disembodied spirit guide who specialized in past-life readings. In the early 1950s, just as Parker was wrapping up the Redlands experiments, Loehr began his own research into prayer. The experiments — designed, he claimed, with the "very helpful" advice of Aldous Huxley — involved sweet peas, corn, wheat, lima beans, ivy, and other vegetation. Loehr's method was simplicity itself. He separated seeds into two groups and then prayed over one and ignored the other. The results, captured in a series of black and white photographs, speak for themselves. Lima beans with "the extra prayer boost" tower over their paltry brethren; the prayed-over ivy positively foams with chlorophyllic exuberance, its leaves large and luxuriant. Other plants had been heaped with scorn or had received "negative" prayers; these specimens withered or failed to grow.

Loehr's report on his experiments teems with delightful curiosities, for instance, his discovery that prayed-over water loses its spiritual potency over time — he speculates that this might be the case with Catholic holy water as well — and that wheat is "harder to negate" than corn, and his description of chats with Vice President Richard Nixon on the value of fighting Communism. The experiments themselves, for all their homespun charm, fail as rigorous science. They lack reliable controls, and it is impossible to determine which extraneous factors — type of soil, amount of sunshine, presence of chemical additives, and so on — might have influenced the results. A similar study, conducted under more exacting conditions at Duke University by celebrated parapsychologist J. B. Rhine, failed to detect any influence of prayer on plants.

Prayer in the Laboratory: Today

A half century later, the scientific study of prayer has blossomed beyond Parker's and Loehr's wildest dreams. The past two decades alone have seen more than a score of carefully monitored investigations reported in influential medical journals such as the *American Journal of Public Health* and the *American Journal of Psychiatry.* At first glance, these new experiments tend to bear out the optimism of Parker and Loehr; almost all conclude that prayer helps fight disease. The general public holds similar views; one recent survey found that 40 percent of Americans believe they have experienced a cure or significant improvement in health thanks to prayer, while another discovered that 99 percent of family physicians consider prayer and related religious practices to be efficacious in promoting health. Prayer, the united chorus of scientists, physicians, and public agree, results in fewer heart attacks, lower blood pressure, less anxiety, stronger immune systems, and longer, happier, healthier lives.

If the definition of prayer is expanded to include meditation, then this chorus is further amplified: a vast body of clinical and experimental literature demonstrates that the various methodical spiritual practices lumped together under this name, or their secular surrogates (such as Herbert Benson's all-purpose mantra, Patricia Carrington's "clinically standardized meditation," or Jon Kabat-Zinn's "mindfulness-based stress reduction" programs), elicit positive changes in respiration, circulation and heart rate, and neural and hormonal activity. The result is sharpened perception, enhanced memory, improved performance, reduced chronic pain, and well-regulated sleep patterns, suggesting that meditation can be a helpful adjunct to therapy for addiction, anxiety, depression, and a host of other affective and behavioral disorders.[18]

One might reasonably conclude from such highly touted studies that Galton's objections to the efficacy of prayer have been answered — that the case is closed and prayer now stands alongside penicillin as a magic bullet in our arsenal against disease. But this is far from certain. Although a case can be made that regular prayer and meditation offer health benefits (such as lower blood pressure and the like), it is quite another thing to claim that the efficacy of prayer to achieve its own stated objectives has been irrefutably demonstrated. Most people pray not as a supplement to workouts at the gym, but because they long for a specific end and ask God's help to achieve it: recession of cancer for a relative, recovery of a lost object, relief from drought or famine. Research that claims to prove this kind of efficacy has received scorching criticism, often from eminent scientific authorities who insist that these studies suffer from faulty methodology, biased interpretation, and a pervasive lack of intellectual rigor. To understand the arguments of the detractors, let us look at the two most celebrated studies in the medical literature.

The first, a study designed by cardiologist Randolph Byrd and published in 1988 in the *Southern Medical Journal,* is generally considered the most significant experiment to date in the scientific study of prayer. At San Francisco General Hospital, 393 patients in the coronary care unit were divided into two groups. One group of 192 patients was the object of daily prayer offered by born-again Christians, whereas the other group of 201 patients received no prayers. The assignment of participants was random and double-blind, done by computer, and neither doctors nor patients knew which participants were receiving prayers. After ten months, the medical data were collated; results showed that the prayed-over patients needed less antibiotic medication and fewer artificial breathing aids, suffered less pulmonary edema, and enjoyed a lower rate of death and a higher rate of "good" as opposed to "bad" outcomes. The experiment appeared to succeed admirably, producing scientifically sound testimony to the benefits of prayer for cardiac health.

But skeptics, poring over the details of the tests, disagree. The experiment, they say, failed the double-blind criterion because the test coordinator — a woman who punched patient names into the computer — knew to which group each patient had been assigned and kept records throughout the study. More important, those conducting the experiment placed no controls on the nature or duration of prayer; they also failed to gauge the relative expertise of the doctors assigned to each patient, raising the possibility that the prayed-over group may simply have received more competent medical care. In addition, no one could guarantee that patients in the control group (those supposedly free of prayer) did not pray for themselves or have relatives pray for them. Larry Dossey makes the interesting observation that "for all we know the control group may have been prayed for *more* than the formal prayer group. If so . . . the entire study might be interpreted as evidence not that prayer works, but that it is actually harmful."[19] One must conclude that Byrd's study was irredeemably flawed.

Ten years later, a second study involving cardiac patients took place at St. Luke's Hospital in Kansas City, Missouri. The aim of the project, according to William S. Harris, the doctor in charge, was "to replicate Byrd's findings." The research met its goal. The 990 participants were divided into two groups, one of which received daily doses of Christian prayer. As anticipated, this group exhibited significantly better medical outcomes than the control group did, according to thirty-four standard criteria (use of antibiotics, catheterization, diuretics, and so on). The happy news was trumpeted around the world, even occasioning a notice in the orthodox scientific journal *New Scientist.* In addition, Harris's study appeared in the *Archives of Internal Medicine,* a publication of the American Medical Association, thus receiving the imprimatur of this influential organization.

It didn't take long for critics to swoop down on the St. Luke's Hospital study. Harris's methodology received, for the most part, passing grades. Several of the flaws in Byrd's test had been addressed; the St. Luke investigation was truly double-blind, as neither doctors nor patients even knew that a test was being conducted. Of course, this in turn raises troubling ethical questions: what right have we to experiment on unwitting patients, even if the test can do no harm? Harris, in his report, justified the practice by observing that "there was no known risk associated with receiving remote, intercessory prayer" and with the perhaps over-subtle excuse that asking for consent might have triggered anxiety among religious believers placed in the control group, and thus cut off from prayer, as well as among atheists who found themselves the unwilling recipients of fervid prayer. In other words, in order to protect the patients' sensibilities, they had to be unwitting guinea pigs.

Most criticism of the Harris study took aim at its conclusions. The weight of the evidence, critics insisted, actually argued *against* the efficacy of prayer. While it was true, for example, that the results, according to the criteria employed by Harris, indicated significant medical improvement among the prayed-for group, applying different criteria — such as those used by Byrd — revealed no such advantage. Speed of recovery, another standard indication of success, also showed no improvement; in fact, the length of hospital stay increased by 9 percent among those who had received prayers. Nicholas Humphrey, a professor of psychology at the Graduate Faculty of New School University in New York, uncovered yet another peculiarity of the Harris study that further challenged its validity. Twenty-three patients were removed from the study because their stay in the Coronary Care Unit lasted fewer than twenty-four hours, too short a time for the home prayer groups to swing into action. Of these twenty-three patients, eighteen had been assigned to the group scheduled to receive prayers and only five to the regular-care group. These numbers are statistically significant and lead to two possible conclusions: either the mere promise of future prayer triggered a medical improvement — a result so far-fetched that no one takes it seriously — or else the test contained a hidden flaw, perhaps that healthier patients were inadvertently assigned to the prayer-receiving group. Humphrey brought this problem to the attention of Harris, who could only suggest that perhaps those patients who had left the CCU early had done so not because they had recovered but because they had died. To this Humphrey responded, "If it should turn out that patients who were assigned to the to-be-prayed-for group were actually significantly more likely to die within twenty-four hours, the implications of this study would surely be more interesting still!"[20]

Behind these scientific objections loom serious theological criticisms. The studies undertaken by Byrd and Harris involved Christian prayer — that is, petitions directed to a personal God who would presumably respond or not in accordance with divine justice and love. The nature of the divine response cannot be anticipated, not least because God transcends human understanding, a precept well-attested by the Bible: "For my thoughts are not your thoughts, neither are your ways my ways, saith the Lord" (Isaiah 55:8). But these hospital studies implicitly assume that God will play along with the experiment and obligingly cure only those for whom prayers have been said, while turning his divine back on the rest; or, if the control group inadvertently receives some prayer, perhaps from family or friends, these few petitions will be outweighed by the larger number received by the officially prayed-for group. In other words, God will bestow blessings on a strictly quantitative basis, like a machine dispensing cures in proportion to the number of coins put in the slot. Surely this is a shallow understanding of divine mercy.

There is, however, a way to approach the medicinal value of prayer that avoids these theological tangles. It simply leaves God out of the equation. According to this view, even if prayer happens to come from religious believers, its efficacy depends not on a transcendent being but rather on some power inherent in prayer itself; prayer is not an exchange between creature and Creator but an impersonal force that possesses healing qualities. Loehr anticipated this perspective with the somewhat vulgar suggestion that "prayer can produce on its own, and not just because someone who loves us plays Santa Claus to us. Our prayer research with plants has taken prayer out of dependence on Santa Claus."[21] With Santa out of the picture, we are free to describe prayer as an undetected natural power akin to electromagnetism, a form of astral energy or subtle matter (as Phineas Quimby proposed), or perhaps a type of pure consciousness that in some mysterious way affects the material world. Larry Dossey inclines to this latter theory; in his best-known work, *Healing Words,* he enumerates the changes that will ensue when this view becomes widespread. Physicians that leave prayer out of their prescriptions will be guilty of medical malpractice, belief in an immortal and omniscient soul will become scientific orthodoxy, and we will realize that the immortal spark within is a "Radical Cure" for the "Big Disease, physical death."

Admittedly, when compared to Dossey's intoxicating zeal, the sober assessment of the skeptics is off-putting. Only a curmudgeon would wish laboratory studies to fail to establish the efficacy of prayer; only a biased observer would say that they have failed entirely. At the same time, it is hard to demonstrate that they have succeeded beyond a reasonable doubt. Too many variables need to be pinned down, too many loopholes remain. While admiring the courage of scientists who study prayer, sometimes in the face of considerable ridicule from colleagues, we are forced to conclude that the studies so far devised have proved inadequate to the task, not least because they depend on an unsophisticated understanding of both God and prayer. The most judicious assessment of the situation remains that enunciated in 1999 by Britain's leading medical journal, the *Lancet:* "Even in the best studies, the evidence of an association between religion, spirituality, and health is weak and inconsistent."[22] Any other conclusion tends toward wish fulfillment rather than fact finding by glossing over the medical and theological complexities involved.

CHAPTER 13

The Mystery of Prayer

ARTHUR SCHOPENHAUER, in a typically pessimistic mood, once remarked that "the more unintelligent a man is, the less mysterious existence seems to him." We may question his choice of words — isn't *unperceptive,* rather than *unintelligent,* closer to the mark? — but the observation rings true, almost to the point of truism. Inverting the premise draws out its implications: the more a person weighs and measures, absorbs and ponders his or her own life and that of others, as well as the nature and end of the cosmos, the more unfathomable it all grows; one's immediate neighborhood becomes terra incognita, while creation as a whole becomes a shimmering web of irrefrangible mystery.

This conviction of the strangeness of things, of the world as an unsolved puzzle or veiled truth, provokes a range of reactions, from fear and anger to despair and world-rejection (the last being Schopenhauer's). It may, on the other hand, call forth the one fructifying, vivifying response, which is *wonder.* "In wonder all philosophy began, in wonder it ends," observes Coleridge, Schopenhauer's contemporary and in some ways his philosophical antitype, adding that "admiration fills up the interspace; but the first wonder is the offspring of ignorance; the last is the parent of adoration."[1] Wonder is the way out; wonder awakens us to the numinous; wonder points to the meaning within the mystery; wonder leads us to God. It is unclear what Coleridge meant by *admiration,* but we may understand it as the collective and individual response to the astonishing fact of being alive; face to face with the mystery of the cosmos, the human being is galvanized and a subsidiary cosmos — that of art, science, language, business, of culture in all its manifestations — pours forth in profusion. Finally, however (and we should understand this sequence not as historical but as repeating itself in the life of every human being), wonder issues in prayer: in adoration, as Coleridge specifies, but also in devotion, thanksgiving, petition, ecstasy, and mystical union. Prayer crowns mystery, for through prayer we approach the Source of all mystery. To paraphrase Saint Augustine: Thou hast made us for thyself, O Lord, and our hearts are restless until we abide, through prayer, in Thee.

For the English metaphysical poet George Herbert (1593–1633), this great truth — that prayer is the zenith of civilization and the high road to God — inspired and guided his many vocations, as writer, pastor, preacher, husband, and friend. We have enjoyed Herbert's company in the introduction to this book; his poem "Prayer" lends its lines to the titles of our main sections and provides the overall structure of our study. Let us turn to him again, now in his role as the poet laureate of prayer, to receive our parting instruction.

Most of our information about Herbert derives from the short *Life* published in 1670 by Izaak Walton, author of that delightful piscatory classic *The Compleat Angler.* Herbert and Walton reportedly fished together, a ritual act that may explain the warm, almost hagiographical tone of the biography. Herbert's life, seen through Walton's eyes, was a series of artful casts by a nimble angler in the placid, slow-moving stream of existence, bringing up spiritual riches for the nourishment of all. Always, God was foremost in Herbert's mind. Even as a seventeen-year-old undergraduate at Cambridge University, the young poet resolved "that my poor Abilities in *Poetry* shall be all, and ever consecrated to Gods glory." An outstanding student, fluent in Latin, Greek, Spanish, Italian, and French, he became in 1619 public orator for the university. This post promised a brilliant career, likely culminating in high public office, but when Herbert's patrons unexpectedly died, he reversed course, donned the white collar and black cap of an Anglican priest, and settled in the sleepy hamlet of Bemerton, on Salisbury Plain. There he remained until his death, exhorting his congregation to greater faith and himself to absolute purity of life. An engraved portrait, first published in Walton's *Life,* shows a long face framed by shoulder-length, wavy black hair, a large sharp nose — reminiscent of Newman — and an intelligent, tranquil gaze. The eyes are large, black, and luminous. It is the face, one might say, of a poet or a dreamer. At Bemerton he wrote hundreds of poems, collected in a manuscript that he called *The Temple,* and also a prose work, *The Country Parson,* detailing the character and comportment of the ideal priest.

By all accounts, Herbert enjoyed a blissful marriage and, in the little church of St. Andrews, a devoted country congregation. It was during his final years, before he succumbed to tuberculosis at the age of forty, that Herbert's goodness ripened into sanctity; neighbors took to calling him "Holy Mr. Herbert," and stories circulated of his generosity, courage, humility, and unflagging goodness. The following anecdote, set down by Walton and repeated by T. S. Eliot in his enthusiastic monograph on Herbert, bears retelling:

> In another walk to *Salisbury*, he saw a poor man, with a poorer horse, that was fall'n under his Load; they were both in distress, and needed present help; which Mr. *Herbert* perceiving, put off his Canonical Coat, and help'd the poor man to unload, and after, to lead his horse: The poor man blest him for it: and he blest the poor man; and was so like the *good Samaritan* that he gave him money to refresh both himself and his horse; and told him, *That if he lov'd himself, he should be merciful to his Beast.* Thus he left the poor man, and at his coming to his musical friends at *Salisbury*, they began to wonder that Mr. *George Herbert* which us'd to be so trim and clean, came into the company so soyl'd and discompos'd; but he told them the occasion: And when one of the company told him, *He had disparag'd himself by so dirty an employment;* his answer was, *That the thought of what he had done, would prove Musick to him at Midnight; and that the omission of it would have upbraided and made discord in his Conscience, whensoever he should pass by that place; for, if I be bound to pray for all that be in distress, I am sure that I am bound so far as it is in my power to practise what I pray for. And though I do not wish for the like occasion every day, yet let me tell you, I would not willingly pass one day of my life without comforting a sad soul, or shewing mercy; and I praise God* for this *occasion:* And now let's tune our instruments.[2]

All who encountered Herbert revered him; Walton declared that "he liv'd and . . . he dy'd like a Saint, unspotted of the World, full of Alms-deeds, full of Humility" and proposed that "he may, and ought to be a pattern of vertue to all posterity." Among Herbert's fellow poets, Henry Vaughan recalled "that blessed man, Mr. *George Herbert*, whose holy *life* and *verse* gained many pious *Converts* (of whom I am the least)," while Richard Crashaw found in Herbert's words "divinest love." Such encomiums continue to the present day; few read Herbert without being changed; he burrows into a reader's soul and there works a wondrous transformation. As a result, generations have celebrated his character as fully as his writings. Of how many other major poets can this be said? Coleridge avows that "I find more substantial comfort, now, in pious George Herbert's 'Temple' . . . than in all the poetry since the poems of Milton." For John Ruskin, "Whatever has been wisest in thought or happiest in the course of my following life was founded at this time on the teaching of Herbert"; George MacDonald exclaims, "Thank God for George Herbert," and declares, in anticipation of the afterlife, that "I [will] look for the face of George Herbert, with whom to talk humbly would be in bliss a higher bliss"; Auden simply says, "Oh, how I would like to have been an intimate friend of his!"[3]

What was the source of Herbert's goodness? Character is always an enigma; in Herbert's case we can say, at least, that virtue did not descend unbidden but was earned through bitter sacrifice. Eliot takes aim, rightly, at a 1907 edition of Herbert's verse whose fantastical introduction situates the poet within that mythical species, the "benign, white-haired parson" who "as the cattle wind homeward in the evening light . . . stands at his gate to greet the cowherd," a tranquil figure in an ideal pastoral. In fact, Herbert spent his years in pitched battle against sin — both his own and that of his congregation — with faith his armor and prayer his arsenal. He preened himself, as a young man, upon his aristocratic blood and high social standing; he was hot-headed and fond of finery; in sum he was a bit of a peacock. These defects and others he conquered through self-discipline inspired and guided by prayer. A few weeks before his death, he referred to his history of spiritual combat, handing a visitor a sheaf of unpublished writings, with instructions that

> I pray deliver this little Book [*The Temple*] to my dear brother Ferrar and tell him, he shall find in it a picture of the many spiritual Conflicts that have passed betwixt God and my Soul, before I could subject mine to the will of Jesus my Master; in whose service I have now found perfect freedom; desire him to read it: and then, if he can think it may turn to the advantage of any dejected poor Soul, let it be made publick: if not, let him burn it: for I and it, are less than the least of God's mercies.[4]

Ferrar did not burn the poems but published them within the year; they may serve even now to comfort the dejected poor Soul. Read as a whole, they comprise a compendium of prayer in almost all its guises, written with hot intensity and a sense of mission ("Awake my lute, and struggle for thy part with all thy art"), encompassing every state of the soul and every stage of life — and thus, incidentally, serving as a compendium of many of the themes addressed in this book. Herbert wrote laments that speak of paradise lost:

> At first thou gav'st me milk and sweetnesses;
> I had my wish and way:
> My days were straw'd with flow'rs and happiness;
> There was no month but May.

But with my years sorrow did twist and grow,
And made a party unawares for woe.
(from "Affliction [I]")

He confesses to God his sins and failings:

Lord, I confess my sin is great;
Great is my sin. Oh! gently treat
With thy quick flow'r, thy momentary bloom;
    Whose life still pressing
    Is one undressing,
A steady aiming at a tomb.
(from "Repentance")

He cries from the depths:

    Oh do not use me
After my sins! look not on my desert,
But on thy glory! then thou wilt reform
And not refuse me: for thou only art
The mighty God, but I a silly worm;
    Oh do not bruise me!
(from "Sighs and Groans")

He exults in new life (Eliot calls this stanza "a miracle of phrasing"):

    And now in age I bud again,
After so many deaths I live and write;
    I once more smell the dew and rain,
And relish versing: Oh my only light,
        It cannot be
        That I am he
    On whom thy tempests fell all night.
(from "The Flower")

He praises and adores:

Lord, I will mean and speak thy praise,
        Thy praise alone.
My busy heart shall spin it all my days:
    And when it stops for want of store,
Then will I wring it with a sigh or groan,
    That thou mayst yet have more.
(from "Praise [III]")

He describes experiences that suggest ecstasy:

It cannot be. Where is that mighty joy,
Which just now took up all my heart?
(from "The Temper [II]")

and mystical union:

Whether I fly with angels, fall with dust,
Thy hands made both, and I am there:
Thy power and love, my love and trust
Make one place ev'rywhere.
(from "The Temper [I]")

In the alembic of prayer, Herbert recast his soul. He never dated his poems, so we must take *The Temple* not as a chronological account of one man's ascent to God but as a treasure chest or memory box in which are piled helter-skelter the seasons of a soul. Nonetheless, a clear upward movement is present in almost every poem — from darkness to light, from self to selflessness, from earth to heaven. Herbert's deathbed avowal of worthlessness, delivered to his literary executor — "My dear Friend, I am sorry I have nothing to present to my merciful God but sin and misery" — reveals both realism and humility, the latter the surest sign of sanctity. The measure of the man may be taken by his valuation of communal prayer, with its implicit love of neighbor, over the sometimes selfish demands of personal prayer:

Though private prayer be a brave design,
Yet public hath more promises, more love:
And love's a weight to hearts, to eyes a sign.
We all are but cold suitors; let us move
Where it is warmest. Leave thy six and seven;
Pray with the most: for where most pray, is heaven.
(from "Perirrhanterium")

Herbert's prose writings, published nineteen years after his death, reveal how hard he struggled to perfect his prayer life as the apex of his priestly duties. A priest, Herbert believed, must be all in all, "not only a Pastor, but a Lawyer also, and a Physician." The key to attaining such a catholicity of roles, such fullness of being, lies in prayer. When praying, the parson should lift up heart, hands, and eyes "as being truly touched and amazed with the Majesty of God." He must speak to inspire reverence and devotion: "his voice is humble, his words treatable, and slow." Herbert counsels his congregation (and we can be certain he addresses himself as well) to pray gently and attentively, "not in a huddling, or slubbering fashion, or scratching the head, or spitting." He spends considerable time dilating on the physical details of prayer, tolerating no idle talk, wandering eyes, slouching, or sleeping, but rather insisting on "a straight, and steady posture." Prayer is not one act among many; it is the one essential act.[5]

This intense vigilance about the methodology of prayer may give the impression that Herbert was a bit of a prig, if not a spiritual martinet. Happily, not only the testimony of his contemporaries but Herbert's own writings belie such a conclusion. He had a playful, inventive streak and relished wordplay:

MARY
Ana — ARMY — gram
How well her name an Army doth present,
In whom the Lord of Hosts did pitch his tent!

He succumbed, now and then, to the temptation of bad puns:

J E S U is in my heart, his sacred name
Is deeply carved there . . .
to my broken heart he was *I ease you,*
And to my whole is J E S U.

He composed maxims that foreshadow *Poor Richard's Almanac:*

Who goes to bed and doth not pray
Maketh two nights to ev'ry day
(from "Charms and Knots")

And he shaped "Easter Wings" to mimic lepidopteral form, the first and last lines of each stanza spreading out as if in flight, and "The Altar" to resemble a table, thus helping to pioneer concrete poetry three centuries before it became a fad. He was, in short, a man of imagination, courage, ingenuity, and art, whose many talents, through the alchemy of prayer, turned to gold.

This gold Herbert dispenses freely to all who read him. He tells us as much about prayer as any man. He demonstrates that prayer is offering, and thus sacrifice, and that prayer is power, and thus magic; that prayer is both subjective and objective, an expression of self and an encounter with the Other; that prayer is father of art and mother of morality; that prayer is sorrow distilled and joy unbounded; that prayer possesses a multiplicity of forms that may be catalogued by metaphor ("Churches banquet, Angels age / God's breath in man returning to his birth" and so on) or, as we have done in this book, by archetype and era. He records his thoughts, feelings, and sensations while on his knees; he reveals what occasions prayer and what results from it; he presents prayer's vertiginous height and depth; he may be called the consummate spokesman for prayer.

But there is one thing that Herbert does not do. He does not describe the actual movement of the soul during prayer, its tidal ebb and flow in relationship to God. This master of prayer would seem perfectly positioned to open the innermost chamber of being, as a veteran watchmaker does a timepiece, and describe the whirrings and tickings within. This he refuses to do. It may be a matter of discretion, a belief that such things are not to be spoken of. We suspect that it is more, that Herbert, like the great company who prayed before him, alongside him, and after him, realized that there is in prayer a certain mystery that cannot be breached.

Recently, physicists have reconstructed the sound of the big bang (imagine the sound of a jet engine six inches from your ear) and no doubt will succeed one day in showing us its appearance. These admirable theatrics reveal nothing regarding the essence of the big bang — its inner workings, its meaning, its place in God's plan and humankind's dreams. So it is with prayer. We can describe the visible world of prayer in sumptuous detail, and a resplendent and fascinating world it is; but the most intimate dance between God and the soul occurs at a level beyond human perception. This is the real terra incognita referred to at the beginning of this chapter. Schopenhauer came close to the mark: not only does the universe appear mysterious; it *is* mysterious. At the heart of this mystery is prayer; an exchange, as Newman put it, *cor ad cor*, heart to heart, person to Person. In a way that surpasses understanding, it may even be that person and Person pray as one; Saint Paul in his Letter to the Romans confesses that "the Spirit helps us in our weakness; for we do not know how to pray as we ought, but the Spirit himself intercedes for us with sighs too deep for words." All this is beyond our ken. We know its effects, sometimes so intense that all motions become genuflection, all speech confession and praise. In time even this passes away. To the person who prays, however, the value of prayer remains ever burning, as it did for Herbert:

> . . . I value prayer so
> That were I to leave all but one,
> Wealth, fame, endowments, virtues, all should go;
> I and dear prayer would together dwell,
> And quickly gain, for each inch lost, an ell.

Noah leaving the ark, praying. Detail from a marble sarcophagus, fourth century C.E.

Works Cited

Ackroyd, Peter. *T. S. Eliot: A Life.* New York: Simon and Schuster, 1984.

Alcoholics Anonymous Comes of Age: A Brief History of AA. New York: Alcoholics Anonymous World Services, 1957.

Alcoholics Anonymous: The Story of How Many Thousands of Men and Women Have Recovered from Alcoholism. 3rd ed. New York: Alcoholics Anonymous World Services, 1976.

Allanson, Athanasius, O.S.B. *Biography of the English Benedictines.* Composed and collected at the direction of the General Chapter of the English Benedictines 1842. Edited by Anselm Cramer, O.S.B., and Sue Goodwill. *Saint Laurence Papers IV.* Ampleforth, UK: Ampleforth Abbey Press, 1999.

Alley, Robert S. *School Prayer: The Court, the Congress, and the First Amendment.* Buffalo, NY: Prometheus Books, 1994.

Alper, Harvey P., ed. *Understanding Mantras.* Albany: State University of New York Press, 1989.

Amos, Dan Ben, and Jerome R. Mintz, trans. and eds. *In Praise of the Ba'al Shem Tov [Shivhei ha-Besht]: The Earliest Collection of Legends About the Founder of Hasidism.* Bloomington and London: Indiana University Press, 1970.

Andrewes, Lancelot. *The Private Devotions of Lancelot Andrewes.* Translated by F. E. Brightman. New York: Meridian Books, 1961.

Anker, Roy M. *Self-Help and Popular Religion in Early American Culture: An Interpretive Guide.* Westport, CT: Greenwood Press, 1999.

———. *Self-Help and Popular Religion in Modern American Culture: An Interpretive Guide.* Westport, CT: Greenwood Press, 1999.

Appleton, George, ed. *The Oxford Book of Prayer.* New York: Oxford University Press, 1985.

Artscroll Siddur. Translated by Rabbi Nosson Scherman. Brooklyn, NY: Mesorah Publications, 2001.

Athanasius. *The Life of Antony.* Edited by Archibald Robertson. In *A Selected Library of Nicene and Post-Nicene Fathers of the Christian Church,* series 2. New York: The Christian Literature Company, 1892.

——. *The Life of Antony and the Letter to Marcellinus.* Translated and introduced by Robert C. Gregg. New York: Paulist Press, 1980.

Augustine. "On the Lord's Sermon on the Mount." In *A Select Library of Nicene and Post-Nicene Fathers,* edited by Philip Schaff. New York: Christian Literature, 1886–1890.

B., Dick. *The Good Book and the Big Book: A.A.'s Roots in the Bible.* Kihei, HI: Paradise Research Publications, 1995.

The Babylonian Talmud: Seder Mo'ed: Ta'anith. Translated by J. Rabbinowitz. Edited by Isadore Epstein. London: Soncino Press, 1938.

Baker, Augustine. *Holy Wisdom: or, Directions for the prayer of contemplation: extracted out of more than forty treatises by the Ven. F. Augustine Baker/methodically digested by Serenus Cressy; and now edited from the Douay ed. of 1657 by Abbot Sweeney.* London: Burns & Oates; New York: Benziger, 1911 (?).

Barker, Jane. *Poetical Recreations.* London: Benjamin Crayle, 1688.

Barnstone, Willis, ed. *Borges at Eighty.* Bloomington: Indiana University Press, 1982.

Bartleman, Frank. *How Pentecost Came to Los Angeles.* Los Angeles: Frank Bartleman, 1925.

Baudelaire, Charles. *Les fleurs du mal: Ouvres complètes.* Édition définitive I. Paris: Calmann-Levy, 1913.

Behr-Sigel, Elisabeth. *The Place of the Heart: An Introduction to Orthodox Spirituality.* Translated by Fr. Stephen Bigham. Torrance, CA: Oakwood Publications, 1992.

Benedict. *RB 1980: The Rule of St. Benedict in Latin and English with Notes.* Edited by Timothy Fry, O.S.B. Collegeville, MN: The Liturgical Press, 1981.

Benson, Herbert. *Beyond the Relaxation Response.* New York: Times Books, 1984.

——. *The Relaxation Response.* New York: William Morrow, 1975.

Betz, Hans Dieter, ed. *The Greek Magical Papyri in Translation, Including the Demotic Spells.* 2nd ed. 2 vols. Chicago and London: University of Chicago Press, 1992.

The Bhagavad-gita: Krishna's Counsel in Time of War. Translated by Barbara Stoler Miller. Toronto and New York: Bantam Books, 1986.

Bhave, Vinoba. *Talks on the Gita.* In *Modern Indian Interpreters of the Bhagavadgita,* edited by Robert N. Minor. Albany: State University of New York Press, 1986.

Bierhorst, John, ed. *In the Trail of the Wind: American Indian Poems and Ritual Orations.* New York: Farrar, Straus, Giroux, 1971.

Birnbaum, Philip, trans. *Daily Prayer Book.* New York: Hebrew Publishing Company, 1977.

Black Elk. *The Sacred Pipe: Black Elk's Account of the Seven Rites of the Oglala Sioux.* Compiled and edited by Joseph Epes Brown. Norman: University of Oklahoma Press, 1953.

Bonaventure. *Life of St. Francis.* In *Bonaventure,* translated by Ewert Cousins. New York: Paulist Press, 1978.

The Book of Daily Prayers for Every Day in the Year: According to the Custom of the German and Polish Jews. Edited by Isaac Leeser. Philadelphia: C. Sherman, 1848.

Breasted, James Henry. *A History of the Ancient Egyptians.* London: Smith, Elder, 1912.

Breuil, Henri. *Beyond the Bounds of History: Scenes from the Old Stone Age.* Translated by Mary E. Boyle. Introduction by J. C. Smuts. New York: AMS Press, 1979.

——. *Five Hundred Centuries of Cave Art.* Translated by Mary E. Boyle. Realized by

Fernand Windels. Montignac, France: Centre d'études et de documentations préhistoriques, n.d.

Brianchaninov, Ignatius. *On the Prayer of Jesus.* Translated by Father Lazarus. Shaftesbury, UK: Element Books, 1987.

Brooks, Nona L. *Mysteries.* St. Louis, MO: Divine Science Federation, 1924.

Brunton, Paul. *A Search in Secret India.* New York: Dutton, 1935.

Buddhaghosa. *The Path of Purification.* Translated by Bhikku Ñyānamoli. Berkeley, CA, and London: Shambhala, 1976.

Burgess, Stanley M., and Gary B. McPhee, eds. *Dictionary of Pentecostal and Charismatic Movements.* Grand Rapids, MI: Regency Reference Library, 1989.

Carmichael, Alexander. *Carmina Gadelica: Hymns and Incantations.* Edinburgh: Oliver and Boyd, 1928–.

Carrington, Patricia. *Freedom in Meditation.* 2nd ed. Kendall Park, NJ: Pace Educational Systems, 1984.

Cassian, John. *Conferences.* Translated by Colm Luibheid. New York: Paulist Press, 1985.

Cathey, James E. *The Heliand: Text and Commentary.* Morgantown: West Virginia University Press, 2002.

Caussade, Jean-Pierre de. *Abandonment to Divine Providence.* Translated by John Beevers. Garden City, NY: Image, 1975.

Chariton, Igumen, comp. *The Art of Prayer: An Orthodox Anthology.* Translated by E. Kadloubovsky and E. M. Palmer. Edited by Timothy Ware. London: Faber and Faber, 1966.

Christopher, Rev. Joseph P., Rt. Rev. Charles E. Spence, and Rt. Rev. John F. Rowan, eds. *The Raccolta.* New York: Benzinger Brothers, 1952.

Clark, Veve A., Millicent Hodman, and Catrina Neiman. *The Legend of Maya Deren: A Documentary Biography and Collected Works.* Director of photography Francine Bailey Price. General editor Hollis Melton. New York: Anthology Film Archives/Film Culture, 1984.

Cleanthes. "Hymn to Zeus." In *The Teaching of Epictetus: Being the "Encheiridion of Epictetus," with Selections from the "Dissertations" and "Fragments,"* translated by T. W. Rolleston. London: Walter Scott, 1888.

Clément, Olivier. *The Roots of Christian Mysticism: Texts and Commentary.* New York: New City Press, 1995.

The Cloud of Unknowing and Other Works. Translated with an introduction by Clifton Wolters. Harmondsworth, UK, and New York: Penguin, 1978.

Coleridge, Samuel Taylor. *Aids to Reflection.* Edited by Thomas Fenby. Edinburgh: John Grant, 1905.

Conze, Edward. *Buddhist Meditation.* London: George Allen & Unwin, 1956.

Cornplanter, Edward. "The Revelation of Handsome Lake." In *Native American Traditions: Sources and Interpretations,* edited by Sam B. Gill. Belmont, CA: Wadsworth, 1983.

Crampton, Georgia Ronan, ed. *The Shewings of Julian of Norwich.* Kalamazoo, MI: Medieval Institute Publications, 1994.

Csikszentmihalyi, Mihaly. *Flow: The Psychology of Optimal Experience.* New York: Harper & Row, 1990.

Dali, Salvador. *The Collected Writings of Salvador Dali.* Edited and translated by Haim Finkelstein. Cambridge and New York: Cambridge University Press, 1998.

Dante Alighieri. *La divina commedia.* 3 vols. Edited and annotated by C. H. Grandgent. Boston: D. C. Heath, 1909–c. 13.

Davies, Wade. *Healing Ways: Navajo Health Care in the Twentieth Century.* Albuquerque: University of New Mexico Press, 2001.

Day, Dorothy. *Thérèse.* Springfield, IL: Templegate, 1979.

Defoe, Daniel. *The Life and Strange Surprizing Adventures of Robinson Crusoe, of York, Mariner.* 4th ed. 2 vols. London: Printed for W. Taylor, 1719.

Deren, Maya. *Divine Horsemen: The Living Gods of Haiti.* New Paltz, NY: McPherson, 1983 [c. 1953].

Dickie, Matthew W. *Magic and Magicians in the Greco-Roman World.* London and New York: Routledge, 2001.

Dickinson, Emily. *The Complete Poems of Emily Dickinson.* Edited by Thomas H. Johnson. Boston: Little, Brown, 1960.

Di Nola, Alfonso M., comp. *The Prayers of Man: From Primitive Peoples to the Present.* Edited by Patrick O'Connor. New York: Ivan Obolensky, 1961.

Dionysios of Fourna. *The Painter's Manual of Dionysios of Fourna.* Translated by Paul Hetherington. Torrance, CA: Oakwood Publications, 1989.

Donne, John. *John Donne and the Theology of Language.* Edited by P. G. Stanwood and Heather Ross Asala. Columbia: University of Missouri Press, 1986.

———. *The Works of John Donne.* 6 vols. London: John W. Parker, 1839.

Dossey, Larry. *Healing Words: The Power of Prayer and the Practice of Medicine.* San Francisco: HarperSanFrancisco, 1993.

Doyle, Arthur Conan. *The Memoirs of Sherlock Holmes.* Edited by Christopher Roden. Oxford: Oxford University Press, 2000.

Dresser, Horatio, ed. *The Quimby Manuscripts.* New York: Crowell, 1921.

Eberwein, Jane Donahue, ed. *An Emily Dickinson Encyclopedia.* Westport, CT: Greenwood Press, 1998.

Eck, Diana L. *Darśan: Seeing the Divine Image in India.* Chambersburg, PA: Anima Books, 1981.

Eddy, Mary Baker. *Christian Healing: A Sermon Delivered at Boston.* Boston: The First Church of Christ, Scientist, 1914.

———. *Science and Health with Key to the Scriptures.* Boston: The First Church of Christ, Scientist, 1875, 1906; copyright renewed 1934.

Eliot, T. S. *Christianity and Culture: The Idea of a Christian Society and Notes Towards the Definition of Culture.* New York: Harcourt, Brace, 1968.

———. *Collected Poems, 1909–1935.* New York: Harcourt, Brace, 1936.

———. *Four Quartets.* New York: Harcourt, Brace, 1943.

———. *The Sacred Wood: Essays on Poetry and Criticism.* 2nd ed. London: Methuen, 1928.

Ellmann, Richard. *The Identity of Yeats.* New York: Oxford University Press, 1954.

The Epic of Gilgamesh. Translated by R. Campbell Thompson. London: Luzac, 1928.

Faraone, Christopher A., and Dirk Obbink, eds. *Magika Hiera: Ancient Greek Magic and Religion.* New York and Oxford: Oxford University Press, 1991.

Faris, James C. *The Nightway: A History and a History of Documentation of a Navajo Ceremonial.* Albuquerque: University of New Mexico Press, 1990.

Fillmore, Charles. *Atom-Smashing Power of Mind.* Unity Village, MO: Unity Books, 1949.

———. *Teach Us to Pray.* Kansas City, MO: Unity School of Christianity, 1941.

Florensky, Pavel. *Iconostasis.* Translated by Donald Sheehan and Olga Andrejev. Crestwood, NJ: St. Vladimir's Seminary Press, 1996.

Forst, Rabbi Binyomin. *The Laws of B'rachos.* With Rabbi Aaron D. Twerski. New York: Mesorah Publications, 1990.

Freud, Sigmund. *The Future of an Illusion.* Translated by W. D. Robson-Scott, edited by James Strachey. Garden City, NY: Doubleday Anchor, 1964.

Frisbie, Charlotte J., ed. *Southwestern Indian Ritual Drama.* Albuquerque: University of New Mexico Press, 1980.

Galton, Sir Francis. *Inquiries into Human Faculty and Its Development.* London: Macmillan, 1883.

Gandhi, Mohandas K. *Prayer.* Edited by John Strohmeier. Berkeley, CA: Berkeley Hills Books, 2000.

Gauchet, Guy. *The Story of a Life: St. Thérèse of Lisieux.* San Francisco: HarperSanFrancisco, 1987.

Gill, Sam D. *Sacred Words: A Study of Navajo Religion and Prayer.* Westport, CT, and London: Greenwood Press, 1981.

Gillet, Lev (A Monk of the Eastern Church). *The Jesus Prayer.* 2nd ed. Crestwood, NY: St. Vladimir's Seminary Press, 1987.

Godman, David, ed. *Be as You Are: The Teachings of Sri Ramana Maharshi.* London: Arkana, 1985.

Goff, James R. *Fields White unto Harvest: Charles F. Parham and the Missionary Origins of Pentecostalism.* Fayetteville: University of Arkansas Press, 1988.

Goodman, Philip, ed. *The Yom Kippur Anthology.* Philadelphia: Jewish Publication Society, 1992.

Graf, Fritz. *Magic in the Ancient World.* Translated by Franklin Philip. Cambridge, MA, and London: Harvard University Press, 1997.

Gregory of Nyssa. *The Lord's Prayer.* Translated by Hilda C. Graef. *Ancient Christian Writers 18.* Westminster, MD: The Newman Press; London: Longmans, Green, 1954.

Hadot, Pierre. *Philosophy as a Way of Life: Spiritual Exercises from Socrates to Foucault.* Edited by Arnold I. Davidson. Translated by Michael Chase. Oxford and New York: Blackwell, 1995.

Halpern, Katherine Spencer, and Susan Brown McGreevy. *Washington Matthews: Studies of Navajo Culture, 1880–1894.* Albuquerque: University of New Mexico Press, 1997.

Hebrew-English Edition of the Babylonian Talmud: Berakoth. Translated by Maurice Simon. Edited by Isadore Epstein. London: Soncino Press, 1960.

Heiler, Friedrich. *Prayer: A Study in the History and Psychology of Religion.* Translated by Samuel McComb. London: Oxford University Press, 1932.

Helminski, Kabir. *The Knowing Heart: A Sufi Path of Transformation.* Boston and London: Shambhala Publications, 1999.

Herbert, George. *The Country Parson; The Temple.* Edited by John N. Wall, Jr. New York: Paulist Press, 1981.

———. *George Herbert.* Selected by W. H. Auden. Harmondsworth, UK: Penguin, 1973.

Heschel, Abraham J. *The Circle of the Baal Shem Tov: Studies in Hasidism.* Chicago and London: The University of Chicago Press, 1985.

Hixon, Lex. *Great Swan: Meetings with Ramakrishna.* Boston: Shambhala, 1992.

Homer. *The Iliad.* Translated by Andrew Lang, Walter Leaf, and Ernest Myers. London: Macmillan, 1882.

Hopkins, Gerard Manley. *The Journals and Papers of Gerard Manley Hopkins.* Edited by Humphrey House and Graham Storey. Oxford: Oxford University Press, 1959.

——. *Sermons and Devotional Writings.* Edited by Christopher Devlin. London and New York: Oxford University Press, 1959.

Hulten, Pontus, Natalia Dumitresco, and Alexandre Istrati. *Brancusi.* New York: Abrams, 1987.

Hume, Robert Ernest, trans. *The Thirteen Principal Upanishads.* 2nd ed. London and New York: Oxford University Press, 1931.

Isherwood, Christopher. *Ramakrishna and His Disciples.* New York: Simon & Schuster, 1959.

James, William. *The Varieties of Religious Experience.* New York: Longmans, Green, 1902.

Jasper, R.C.D., and G. J. Cuming, eds. *Prayers of the Eucharist: Early and Reformed.* New York: Oxford University Press, 1970.

Jeffares, Norman A. *A Commentary on the Collected Poems of W. B. Yeats.* Stanford, CA: Stanford University Press, 1968.

Johnson, Samuel. *Johnsonian Miscellanies.* Compiled and edited by George Birkbeck Hill. Oxford: Clarendon Press, 1897.

Jones, Ernest. *The Life and Work of Sigmund Freud.* New York: Basic Books, 1957.

Joyce, James. *Finnegan's Wake.* New York: Viking Press, 1939.

Jung, Carl Gustav. *Collected Works.* Princeton, NJ: Princeton University Press, 1953.

Justin Martyr. *The First and Second Apologies.* Translated and edited by Leslie William Barnard. New York: Paulist Press, 1997.

Kabat-Zinn, Jon. *Full Catastrophe Living: Using the Wisdom of Your Body and Mind to Face Stress, Pain, and Illness.* New York: Delacorte Press, 1990.

——. *Wherever You Go, There You Are: Mindfulness Meditation in Everyday Life.* New York: Hyperion, 1994.

Kadloubovsky, E., and G.E.H. Palmer, trans. *Writings from the Philokalia on Prayer of the Heart.* London: Faber and Faber, 1973.

Kandinsky, Wassily. "Reminiscences." In *Modern Arts on Art: Ten Unabridged Essays,* edited by Robert L. Herbert. Englewood Cliffs, NJ: Prentice-Hall, 1965.

Kant, Immanuel. *Lectures on Ethics.* Translated by Louis Infield. London: Methuen, 1930.

——. *Religion Within the Limits of Reason Alone.* Translated by T. M. Greene and Hoyt H. Hudson. New York: Harper & Row, 1960.

Kee, Howard Clark. "Magic and Messiah." In *Religion, Science, and Magic: In Concert and in Conflict,* edited by Jacob Neusner, Ernest S. Frerichs, and Paul Virgil McCracken Flesher. New York: Oxford University Press, 1989.

——. *Medicine, Miracle, and Magic in New Testament Times.* Cambridge: Cambridge University Press, 1986.

Kelly, Thomas R. *A Testament of Devotion, with a Biographical Memoir by Douglas V. Steere.* New York and London: Harper & Brothers, 1941.

Keynes, Edward. *The Courts vs. Congress: Prayer, Busing, and Abortion.* With Randall I. Miller. Durham, NC, and London: Duke University Press, 1989.

Kliebard, Herbert M., ed. *Religion and Education in America: A Documentary History.* Scranton, PA: International Textbook Company, 1969.

Kluckhohn, Clyde, and Leland C. Wyman. *An Introduction to Navaho Chant Practices with an Account of the Behaviors Observed in Four Chants. Memoirs of the American Museum of Natural History 53;* supplement to *American Anthropologist* 42:2.2. Menasha, WI: American Anthropological Association, 1940.

Kurtz, Ernest. *Not-God: A History of Alcoholics Anonymous.* Center City, MN: Hazelden Educational Services, 1979.

The Language of the Heart: Bill W.'s Grapevine Writings. New York: The A.A. Grapevine, 1988.

Lawrence, D. H. *The Rainbow.* Harmondsworth, UK: Penguin, 1949 [1915].

Lawrence of the Resurrection, O.C.D. *Writings and Conversations on the Practice of the Presence of God.* Edited by Conrad De Meester, O.C.D. Translated by Salvatore Sciurba, O.C.D. Washington, DC: ICS Publications, 1994.

Leclercq, Jean. *The Love of Learning and the Desire for God: A Study of Monastic Culture.* Translated by Catherine Misrahi. New York: Fordham University Press, 1961, 1974.

Levenson, Jon D. *The Death and Resurrection of the Beloved Son: The Transformation of Child Sacrifice in Judaism and Christianity.* New Haven, CT, and New York: Yale University Press, 1993.

Lewis, C. S. *God in the Dock: Essays on Theology and Ethics.* Edited by Walter Hooper. Grand Rapids, MI: Eerdmans, 1970.

——. *The Lion, the Witch, and the Wardrobe.* London: Geoffrey Bles, 1950; New York, Macmillan, 1950; rpt. New York: HarperCollins, 1994.

——. *Perelandra.* New York: Macmillan, 1944.

Liberman, Alexander. *The Artist in His Studio.* New York: The Viking Press, 1960.

Lings, Martin. *A Moslem Saint of the Twentieth Century: Shaikh Ahmad al-'Alawi, His Spiritual Heritage and Legacy.* London: Allen & Unwin, 1961.

Lipsey, Roger. *An Art of Our Own: The Spiritual in Twentieth-Century Art.* Boston and Shaftesbury, UK: Shambhala, 1988.

Loehr, Franklin. *The Power of Prayer on Plants.* Garden City, NY: Doubleday, 1959.

Lois Remembers: Memoirs of the Co-Founder of Al-Anon and Wife of the Co-Founder of Alcoholics Anonymous. New York: Al-Anon Family Group Headquarters, 1979.

Madison, James. *Memorial and Remonstrance Against Religious Assessments.* In *A Nation Dedicated to Religious Liberty: The Constitutional Heritage of the Religion Clauses,* by Arlin M. Adams, Charles J. Emmerich, and Warren E. Burger. Philadelphia: University of Pennsylvania Press, 1990.

Mahadevan, T.M.P. *Ramana Maharshi: The Sage of Arunchala.* London: George Allen & Unwin, 1977.

Mails, Thomas E. *Sundancing at Rosebud and Pine Ridge.* Sioux Falls, SD: Center for Western Studies, 1978.

Malcolm X. *The Autobiography of Malcolm X.* With Alex Haley. New York: Ballantine, 1992.

Marshack, Alexander. *The Roots of Civilization: The Cognitive Beginnings of Man's First Art, Symbol, and Notation.* Rev. expanded ed. New York: Moyer Bell, 1991.

Matthews, Washington. *Navajo Legends.* Boston: Houghton Mifflin, 1897.

——. *The Night Chant: A Navaho Ceremony.* Publications of the Hyde Southwestern Expedition, May 1902. *Memoirs of the American Museum of Natural History,* Whole Series vol. 6. Anthropology Series vol. 5. New York: Knickerbocker Press, 1902.

Maugham, W. Somerset. *The Razor's Edge.* Harmondsworth, UK: Penguin, 1984.

McDaniel, June. *The Madness of the Saints: Ecstatic Religion in Bengal.* Chicago: University of Chicago Press, 1989.

Mechtild of Magdeburg. *The Revelations of Mechtild of Magdeburg, or, The Flowing Light of the Godhead.* Translated by Lucy Menzies. London: Longmans, Green, 1953.

Merton, Thomas. *The Seven Storey Mountain.* New York: Harcourt, Brace, 1948.

Meyer, Kuno, trans. *Ancient Irish Poetry.* London: Constable, 1913.

Michon, Jean-Louis. "The Spiritual Practices of Islam." In *Islamic Spirituality: Foundations,* edited by Seyyed Hossein Nasr. New York: Crossroad, 1987.

Millgram, Abraham. *Jewish Worship.* Philadelphia: Jewish Publication Society, 1971.

Milne, A. A. *When We Were Very Young.* London: Methuen, 1924.

Mitchell, Frank. *Navajo Blessingway Singer: The Autobiography of Frank Mitchell, 1881–1967.* Edited by Charlotte J. Frisbie and David P. McAllester. Albuquerque: University of New Mexico Press, 1978.

Mookerjee, Nanda, ed. *Sri Ramakrishna in the Eyes of Brahma and Christian Admirers.* Calcutta: Firma KLM Private Ltd., 1976.

Murphy, G. Ronald, S.J. *The Heliand: The Saxon Gospel.* New York: Oxford University Press, 1992.

——. *The Saxon Savior.* New York: Oxford University Press, 1989.

Murphy, Gerard, ed. and trans. *Early Irish Lyrics: Eighth to Twelfth Century.* Oxford: Clarendon Press, 1956.

Murphy, Michael, and Steven Donovan. *The Physical and Psychological Effects of Meditation: A Review of Contemporary Research with a Comprehensive Bibliography, 1931–1996.* 2nd ed. Edited by Eugene Taylor. Sausalito, CA: The Institute of Noetic Sciences, 1999.

Musil, Robert. *The Man Without Qualities.* Translated by Eithne Wilkins and Ernst Kaiser. London: Secker & Warburg, 1960.

Newcomb, Franc Johnson. *Hosteen Klah: Navaho Medicine Man and Sand Painter.* Norman, OK, and London: University of Oklahoma Press, 1964.

Newman, John Henry. *The Idea of a University.* London: Longmans, Green, 1907.

Nicholson, Reynold. *The Mystics of Islam.* London: Routledge and Kegan Paul, 1966 [1914].

Niles, John D. "The Æcerbot Ritual in Context." In *Old English Literature in Context.* Cambridge: D. S. Brewer, 1980; Totowa, NJ: Rowman and Littlefield, 1980.

Nyanaponika Thera. *The Heart of Buddhist Meditation.* New York: Samuel Weiser, 1969.

Ouspensky, Leonid, and Vladimir Lossky. *The Meaning of Icons.* Translated by G. E. H. Palmer and E. Kadloubovsky. Crestwood, NY: St. Vladimir's Seminary Press, 1989.

O'Flaherty, Wendy Doniger, trans. *The Rig Veda.* Harmondsworth, UK: Penguin, 1981.

Olivelle, Patrick, trans. *Upanisads.* Oxford and New York: Oxford University Press, 1996.

O'Rahilly, Alfred. *Father William Doyle S. J.: A Spiritual Study.* London: Longmans, Greene, 1932.

Padwick, Constance. *Muslim Devotions: A Study of Prayer-Manuals in Common Use.* London: SPCK, 1961.

Parker, William F. *Prayer Can Change Your Life: Experiments and Techniques in Prayer Therapy.* Englewood, NJ: Prentice-Hall, 1957.

Pass It On: The Story of Bill Wilson and How the A.A. Message Reached the World. New York: Alcoholics Anonymous World Services, 1984.

Patrul Rinpoche. *The Words of My Perfect Teacher.* Translated by the Padmakara Translation Group. Foreword by the Dalai Lama. San Francisco: HarperCollins, 1994.

Patton, George S., Jr. *War as I Knew It.* Annotated by Col. Paul D. Hawkins. Boston: Houghton Mifflin, 1947.

Pennington, M. Basil, O.C.S.O. *Centered Prayer: The Way of Centering Prayer.* Garden City, NY: Image, 1988.

———. *Centering Prayer: Renewing an Ancient Christian Prayer Form.* Garden City, NY: Image, 1982.

Perry, Whitall N., ed. *A Treasury of Traditional Wisdom.* Cambridge: Quinta Essentia, 1971.

Pierce, Charles E., Jr. *The Religious Life of Samuel Johnson.* Hamden, CT: Archon Books, 1983.

Plato. *The Collected Dialogues of Plato.* Edited by Edith Hamilton and Huntington Cairns. New York: Pantheon Books, 1963.

Plotinus. *The Six Enneads.* Translated by Stephen MacKenna and B. S. Page. London and Boston: The Medici Society, 1926–1930.

Pseudo-Dionysius. *The Complete Works.* Translated by Colm Luibheid with Paul Rorem. New York: Paulist Press, 1987.

Pulleyn, Simon. *Prayer in Greek Religion.* Oxford: Clarendon Press, 1997.

Quarrick, Gene. *Our Sweetest Hours: Recreation and the Mental State of Absorption.* Jefferson, NC: McFarland, 1989.

Raine, Kathleen. Introduction to *The Fairy Faith in Celtic Countries,* by W. Y. Evans-Wentz. Gerards Cross, UK: Colin Symthe, 1977.

Ramakrishna. *The Gospel of Sri Ramakrishna.* Translated by Swami Nikhilananda. New York: Ramakrishna-Vivekananda Center, 1942.

———. *The Gospel of Sri Ramakrishna.* Abridged version. Translated by Swami Nikhilananda. New York: Ramakrishna-Vivekananda Center, 1980.

Ramana Maharshi. *The Spiritual Teaching of Ramana Maharshi.* Foreword by C. G. Jung. Boston: Shambhala, 1988.

Rebell, Fred [pseud.]. *Escape to the Sea: The Log of a Homemade Sailor.* New York: Dodd, Mead, 1939.

Reichard, Gladys. *Navajo Religion: A Study of Symbolism.* 2 vols. New York: Pantheon Books, 1950.

———. *Prayer: The Compulsive Word.* New York: J. J. Augustin, 1944.

Ridington, Robin. "Beaver Dreaming and Singing." In *Native American Traditions: Sources and Interpretations,* edited by Sam D. Gill. Belmont, CA: Wadsworth, 1983.

Rilke, Rainer Maria. *The Book of Hours: Prayers to a Lowly God.* Translated by Annemarie S. Kidder. Evanston, IL: Northwestern University Press, 2001.

———. *Rainer Maria Rilke: Selected Works.* Translated by J. B. Leishman. New York: New Directions, 1967.

Rodd, Laurel Rasplica. *Nichiren: A Biography.* Tempe: Arizona State University, 1978.

Rohrbach, P. T. "St. Thérèse of Lisieux." In *The New Catholic Encyclopedia.* 2nd ed. New York: Thomson Gale, 2003.

Rosman, Moshe. *The Founder of Hasidism: A Quest for the Historical Ba'al Shem Tov.* Berkeley: University of California Press, 1966.

Rubenson, Samuel. *The Letters of St. Antony: Monasticism and the Making of a Saint.* Minneapolis, MN: Fortress Press, 1995.

Rubenstein, Jeffrey L., trans. *Rabbinic Stories.* New York and Mahwah, NJ: Paulist Press, 2002.

Sackville-West, Vita. *The Eagle and the Dove: A Study in Contrasts: St. Teresa of Ávila, St. Thérèse of Lisieux.* London: M. Joseph, 1943.

Salinger, J. D. *Franny and Zooey.* Boston: Little, Brown, 1955.

Sanders, Cheryl Jeanne. *Saints in Exile: The Holiness-Pentecostal Experience in African American Religion and Culture.* New York: Oxford University Press, 1996.

Śāntideva. *Bodhicāryavatāra.* Translated by Vesna A. Wallace and B. Alan Wallace. Ithaca, NY: Snow Lion Publications, 1997.

Saradananda, Swami. *Sri Ramakrishna, the Great Master.* 4th ed. Translated by Swami Jagadananda. Madras: Sri Ramakrishna Math, 1970 [c. 1952].

Schimmel, Annemarie. *Mystical Dimensions of Islam.* Chapel Hill: University of North Carolina Press, 1975.

Sears, David. *The Path of the Baal Shem Tov.* Northvale, NJ: Jason Aronson, 1997.

Segal, Alan F. *The Other Judaisms of Late Antiquity.* Atlanta, GA: Scholars Press, 1987.

Sewall, Richard. *The Life of Emily Dickinson.* New York: Farrar, Straus, Giroux, 1974.

The Shepherd of Hermas. In *The Apostolic Fathers: Greek Texts and English Translations of Their Writings.* 2nd ed. Translated by J. B. Lightfoot and J. R. Harner. Edited and revised by Michael W. Holmes. Grand Rapids, MI: Baker Book House, 1992.

Sherrill, John L. *They Speak with Other Tongues.* New York: McGraw-Hill, 1964.

Shinagel, Michael, ed. *Robinson Crusoe: An Authoritative Text; Backgrounds and Sources; Criticism.* New York and London: Norton, 1975.

Simpson, Evelyn M. *A Study of the Prose Works of John Donne.* Oxford: Clarendon Press, 1924.

Simson, Otto Georg von. *The Gothic Cathedral: Origins of the Gothic Architecture and the Medieval Concept of Order.* 3rd ed. Princeton, NJ: Princeton University Press, 1988.

Six, Jean-François. *Light of the Night: The Last Eighteen Months in the Life of Thérèse of Lisieux.* Notre Dame, IN: University of Notre Dame Press, 1998.

Smith, Morton. *Jesus the Magician.* San Francisco: Harper & Row, 1981.

Smith, William Cantwell. *The Faith of Other Men.* New York: Harper & Row, 1972.

Solecki, Ralph S. *Shanidar: The First Flower People.* New York: Knopf, 1971.

Southam, B. C. *A Guide to the Selected Poems of T. S. Eliot.* San Diego: Harcourt, Brace, 1996.

Staal, Frits, with C. V. Somayajipad and M. Itti Ravi Nambudiri. *Agni: The Vedic Ritual of the Fire Altar.* Berkeley, CA: Asian Humanities Press, 1983.

Steinsaltz, Adin. *A Guide to Jewish Prayer.* New York: Schocken Books, 2000.

Stevenson, James. *Ceremonial of Hasjelti Dailijis and Mythical Sand Painting of the Navajo Indians.* Bureau of American Ethnology Eighth Annual Report, 1886–1887. Washington, DC: U.S. Government Printing Office, 1891.

Stevenson, Mrs. Sinclair. *The Rites of the Twice-Born.* London: H. Milford, Oxford University Press, 1920.

Storms, Godfrid. *Anglo-Saxon Magic.* The Hague: M. Nijhoff, 1948.

Suzuki, Daisetz Teitaro. *Zen and Japanese Culture.* Princeton, NJ: Princeton University Press, 1970.

Synan, Vinson. *Century of the Holy Spirit: 100 Years of Pentecostal and Charismatic Renewal, 1901–2001.* Nashville, TN: Thomas Nelson Publishers, 2001.

Tagore, Rabindranath. *Lectures and Addresses.* Compiled by Anthony X. Soares. Calcutta: Macmillan, 1970.

Teresa of Ávila. *Obras completas.* 3 vols. Edited by Efrén de la Madre de Dios, Otilio de Niño Jesus, and Otger Steggink. Madrid: Editorial Católica, 1951–59.

Tertullian. *Quinti Septimii Florentis Tertulliani quae supersunt omnia.* Edited by F. Oehler. Leipzig: T. O. Weigel, 1851–1854.

Thérèse of Lisieux. *Story of a Soul: The Autobiography of St. Thérèse of Lisieux.* 3rd ed. Translated by John Clarke, O.C.D. Washington, DC: ICS Publications, 1976.

Thomas Aquinas. *Summa Theologiae.* Blackfriar; New York: McGraw-Hill; London: Eyre & Spottiswode, 1964.

Tolkien, J.R.R. *The Letters of J.R.R. Tolkien.* Edited by Humphrey Carpenter, with Christopher Tolkien. London: George Allen & Unwin, 1981; Boston: Houghton Mifflin, 2000.

Tolkien, J.R.R. *The Return of the King: Being the Third Part of the Lord of the Rings.* Rev. 2nd ed. London: George Allen & Unwin, 1966.

Tomlinson, A. J. *The Last Great Conflict.* New York: Garland Publishing, 1985 [1913].

Trinkhaus, Erik, and Pat Shipman. *The Neandertals: Changing the Image of Man.* New York: Knopf, 1993.

Tylor, Edward Burnett. *Primitive Culture.* Vol. 1, *The Origins of Culture.* Vol. 2, *Religion in Primitive Culture.* London: John Murray, 1871.

Underhill, Ruth Murray. *Papago Indian Religion.* New York: Columbia University Press, 1946.

———. *Papago Woman.* Prospect Heights, IL: Waveland Press, 1985.

Vasari, Giorgio. *Lives of the Artists: A Selection.* Translated by George Bull. Harmondsworth, UK: Penguin, 1965.

Wacker, Grant. *Heaven Below: Early Pentecostals and American Culture.* Cambridge, MA: Harvard University Press, 2001.

Wallace, Dewey D., Jr. "Theocracy." In *The Encyclopedia of Religion,* editor-in-chief Mircea Eliade. New York: Macmillan, 1987.

Walton, Izaak. *Walton's Lives of Dr. John Donne, Sir Henry Wotton, Mr. Richard Hooker, Mr. George Herbert, and Dr. Robert Sanderson.* New rev. ed. Edited by A. H. Bullen. London: G. Bell, 1884.

The Way of a Pilgrim. Translated by R. M. French. New York: Ballantine, 1974.

Weil, Simone. *Waiting for God.* Translated by Emma Craufurd. Introduction by Leslie A. Fieldler. New York: Putnam, 1951.

White, Minor. *Octave of Prayer.* New York: Aperture, 1972.

———. *Rites and Passages: His Photographs Accompanied by Excerpts from His Letters and Diaries.* Millerton, NY: Aperture, 1978.

Whitehead, Alfred North. *Process and Reality: An Essay in Cosmology.* Cambridge: Cambridge University Press, 1929.

Whitman, Walt. *Complete Poetry and Selected Prose.* Edited by James E. Miller Jr. Boston: Houghton Mifflin, 1959.

Wilde, Oscar. *De Profundis.* New York and London: Putnam, 1905.

Wilkinson, Bruce. *The Prayer of Jabez: Breaking Through to the Blessed Life.* Sisters, OR: Multnomah, 2000.

Williams, Charles. *Charles Williams: Essential Writings in Spirituality and Theology.* Edited by Charles Hefling. Cambridge, MA, and Boston: Cowley Publications, 1993.

Winstead, Karen, ed. and trans. *Chaste Passions: Medieval English Virgin Martyr Legends.* Ithaca, NY, and London: Cornell University Press, 2000.

Wittgenstein, Ludwig. *Remarks on Frazer's Golden Bough.* Edited by Rush Rhees. Translated by A. C. Miles. Revised by Rush Rhees. Atlantic Highlands, NJ: Humanities Press, 1979.

Wolfe, Michael. *The Hadj: An American's Pilgrimage to Mecca.* New York: Atlantic Monthly Press, 1993.

Woodward, Kenneth. *Making Saints: How the Catholic Church Determines Who Becomes a Saint, Who Doesn't, and Why.* New York: Simon & Schuster, 1990.

Wyman, Leland, ed. *Beautyway: A Navaho Ceremonial.* New York: Pantheon Books, 1957.

———. "Navajo Ceremonial System." In *Handbook of North American Indians,* edited by Alfonso Ortiz. Washington, DC: Smithsonian Institution, 1983.

Yeats, William Butler. *The Collected Poems of W. B. Yeats.* New York: Macmillan, 1933.

———. Introduction to *Gitanjali,* by Rabindranath Tagore. London: Macmillan, 1913.

———. *The Poems.* Edited by Richard J. Finneran. New York: Macmillan, 1989.

———. *The Wind Among the Reeds.* London: E. Mathews, 1899.

Zapeda, Ofelia. Foreword to *Singing for Power: The Song Magic of the Papago Indians of Southern Arizona,* by Ruth Murray Underhill. Tucson: University of Arizona Press, 1993.

Zibawi, Mahmoud. *The Icon: Its Meaning and History.* Collegeville, MN: Liturgical Press, 1993.

The Zohar. Translated by Harry Simon and Maurice Sperling. London: The Soncino Press, 1934.

Zundel, Veronica, comp. *Eerdmans Book of Famous Prayers.* Grand Rapids, MI: Eerdmans, 1984.

Notes

All biblical quotations are from the authorized (King James) version unless otherwise noted.

1. THE FOUNDATIONS OF PRAYER

1. Mechtild of Magdeburg, *The Revelations of Mechtild of Magdeburg, or, The Flowing Light of the Godhead,* trans. Lucy Menzies (London: Longmans, Green, 1953), 136.

2. Ruth Murray Underhill, *Papago Woman* (Prospect Heights, IL: Waveland Press, 1985), x.

3. Ruth Murray Underhill, *Papago Indian Religion* (New York: Columbia University Press, 1946), 45–46.

4. Ibid., 43.

5. Ibid., 46.

6. Underhill, *Papago Woman,* 17; Ofelia Zepeda, foreword to *Singing for Power: The Song Magic of the Papago Indians of Southern Arizona,* by Ruth Murray Underhill (Tucson: University of Arizona Press, 1993), vi.

7. George S. Patton Jr., *War as I Knew It,* annotated by Col. Paul D. Hawkins (Boston: Houghton Mifflin, 1947), 184–85.

8. Ibid., 185.

9. James H. O'Neill, "The True Story of the Patton Prayer," *The New American,* January 12, 2004 (repr. from *The Review of the News,* October 6, 1971). In 1950 Chaplain O'Neill wrote an account of the Patton prayer that differs in some details from the one presented in Patton's war memoir. According to O'Neill, a phone call rather than a face-to-face meeting initiated the writing of the prayer; he also mentions Patton's belief — completely characteristic of the general — that prayer is "power" and that if people don't pray, sooner or later they will "crack up."

10. Patton, *War as I Knew It,* 185.

11. Ludwig Wittgenstein, *Remarks on Frazer's Golden Bough,* ed. Rush Rhees, trans. A. C. Miles, rev. Rush Rhees (Atlantic Highlands, NJ: Humanities Press, 1979), 12e.

12. Underhill, *Papago Woman,* 25.

13. Simone Weil, *Waiting for God,* trans. Emma Craufurd (New York: Putnam, 1951), 26.

14. Wilfred Cantwell Smith, *The Faith of Other Men* (New York: Harper & Row, 1972), 56–57.

15. Malcolm X, *The Autobiography of Malcolm X.* With Alex Haley (New York: Ballantine, 1992), 390–91.

16. Ralph S. Solecki, *Shanidar: The First Flower People* (New York: Knopf, 1971), 250.

17. Erik Trinkaus and Pat Shipman, *The Neandertals: Changing the Image of Man* (New York: Knopf, 1993), 186–87.

18. Henri Breuil, *Beyond the Bounds of History: Scenes from the Old Stone Age,* trans. Mary E. Boyle, introduction by J. C. Smuts (New York: AMS Press, 1979), 31.

19. Henri Breuil, *Four Hundred Centuries of Cave Art,* trans. Mary E. Boyle, realized by Fernand Windels (Montignac, France: Centre d'études et de documentation préhistoriques, n.d.), 15.

20. Breuil, *Beyond the Bounds of History,* 82.

21. Ibid., 79.

22. Alexander Marshack, *The Roots of Civilization: The Cognitive Beginnings of Man's First Art, Symbol, and Notation,* rev. expanded ed. (New York: Moyer Bell, 1991), 274.

23. Ibid., 321–22.

24. Robin Ridington, "Beaver Dreaming and Singing," in *Native American Traditions: Sources and Interpretations,* ed. Sam Gill (Belmont, CA: Wadsworth, 1983), 24.

25. Edward Burnett Tylor, *Primitive Culture,* vol. 1, *The Origins of Culture* (London: John Murray, 1871), 37.

26. Ibid., vol. 2, *Religion in Primitive Culture,* 12.

27. Ernest Jones, *The Life and Work of Sigmund Freud* (New York: Basic Books, 1957), 3:351.

28. Sigmund Freud, *The Future of an Illusion,* trans. W. D. Robson-Scott, ed. James Strachey (Garden City, NY: Doubleday Anchor, 1964), 72.

29. William James, "Other Characteristics," in *The Varieties of Religious Experience* (New York: Longmans, Green, 1902), lecture 19, 454–55.

30. Ibid., 456.

31. Friedrich Heiler, *Prayer: A Study in the History and Psychology of Religion,* trans. Samuel McComb (London: Oxford University Press, 1932), 65.

32. Ibid., iv.

33. Arthur Conan Doyle, *The Memoirs of Sherlock Holmes,* ed. Christopher Roden (Oxford: Oxford University Press, 2000), 227.

2. MAGIC

1. Hans Dieter Betz, ed., *The Greek Magical Papyri in Translation, Including the Demotic Spells,* 2nd ed., 2 vols. (Chicago and London: University of Chicago Press, 1992). The translation is from *Papyri Graecae Magicae,* 2nd ed. (Stuttgart: Teubner, 1973–74), commonly abbreviated *PGM.* The prayers cited in this paragraph are from *PGM* VII:149–54 and *PGM* XVIIIb:1–4, *The Greek Magical Papyri,* 119 and 255. See also line drawings, p. 134.

2. Ibid., *PGM* CXXX, 323.

3. Ibid., *PGM* IV:475–829, 48–54. All quotations from the Mithras Liturgy are from these pages.

4. "Cleanthes' Hymn to Zeus," trans. T. W. Rolleston, in *The Teaching of Epictetus: Being the "Encheiridion of Epictetus," with Selections from the "Dissertations" and "Fragments"* (London: Walter Scott, 1888), 1.

5. See Fritz Graf, *Magic in the Ancient World,* trans. Franklin Philip (Cambridge, MA, and London: Harvard University Press, 1997), for an extensive discussion of Greek and Roman attitudes toward magic; Aristotle, *De mundo* 400a16, in *Prayer in Greek Religion,* by Simon Pulleyn (Oxford: Clarendon Press, 1997), 189; see discussions in Matthew W. Dickie, *Magic and Magicians in the Greco-Roman World* (London and New York: Routledge, 2001); Pulleyn, *Prayer in Greek Religion,* 184–88; *Magika Hiera: Ancient Greek Magic and Religion,* ed. Christopher A. Faraone and Dirk Obbink (New York and Oxford: Oxford University Press, 1991); and Pieter W. van der Horst, "Silent Prayer in Antiquity," *Numen,* January 1994, 1–25.

6. Simon Pulleyn, *Prayer in Greek Religion,* 94, n. 73.

7. Plato, *Republic,* trans. Paul Shorey (Cambridge, MA: Harvard University Press, 1930), 2:364bc.

8. Plotinus, *The Six Enneads,* trans. Stephen MacKenna and B. S. Page (London and Boston: The Medici Society, 1926–1930), fourth ennead, tractate 4, section 26.

9. Apuleius, *Apology and Florida,* trans. H. E. Butler, in *The Other Judaisms of Late Antiquity,* by Alan F. Segal (Atlanta, GA: Scholars Press, 1987), 93.

10. See Godfrid Storms, *Anglo-Saxon Magic* (The Hague: M. Nijhoff, 1948), 174–75; Stopford A. Brooke, *The History of Early English Literature* (New York and London: Macmillan, 1892); Thomas D. Hill, "The Æcerbot Charm and Its Christian User," *Anglo-Saxon England* 6 (Cambridge: Cambridge University Press, 1977), 213–221; and John D. Niles, "The Æcerbot Ritual in Context," in *Old English Literature in Context* (Cambridge: D. S. Brewer, 1980; Totowa, NJ: Rowman and Littlefield, 1980), 44–56.

11. *The Babylonian Talmud: Seder Mo'ed: Ta'anith,* trans. J. Rabbinowitz, ed. Isadore Epstein (London: Soncino Press, 1938), Ta'anith 23a, 115–17. See *Rabbinic Stories,* trans. Jeffrey L. Rubenstein (New York and Mahwah, NJ: Paulist Press, 2002), 128–32.

12. *The Babylonian Talmud: Seder Mo'ed: Ta'anith* 23a, 116–17.

13. Ibid., 117.

14. See Kedushah, *Artscroll Siddur,* trans. Rabbi Nosson Scherman (Brooklyn, NY: Mesorah Publications, 2001), 465.

15. *Bereshith* 23b–24b, in *The Zohar,* trans. Harry Simon and Maurice Sperling (London: The Soncino Press, 1934), 1:97.

16. "From a Denunciation of the Hasidim by Traditional Eastern Europe Rabbinic Authorities, Circa 1772," on the website for the PBS documentary *A Life Apart: Hasidism in America,* http://www.pbs.org/alifeapart/intro.html/.

17. Moshe Rosman, *The Founder of Hasidism: A Quest for the Historical Ba'al Shem Tov* (Berkeley: University of California Press, 1996), 168–69.

18. Dan Ben-Amos and Jerome R. Mintz, trans. and ed., *In Praise of the Baal Shem Tov [Shivhei ha-Besht]: The Earliest Collection of Legends About the Founder of Hasidism* (Bloomington and London: Indiana University Press, 1970), 161–63.

19. Abraham J. Heschel, *The Circle of the Baal Shem Tov: Studies in Hasidism* (Chicago and London: The University of Chicago Press, 1985), 30.

20. David Sears, *The Path of the Baal Shem Tov* (Northvale, NJ: Jason Aronson, 1997), xv.

21. Ben-Amos and Mintz, *In Praise of the Baal Shem Tov,* 24–26.

22. Ibid., 86–87.

23. "Hasidic Tales and Teachings," in *The Yom Kippur Anthology,* ed. Philip Goodman (Philadelphia: Jewish Publication Society, 1992), 118.

24. Abraham J. Heschel, address to the annual convention of American reform rabbis, 1952, quoted in introduction by Samuel H. Dresner to Heschel's, *The Circle of the Baal Shem Tov,* xxi–xxii.

25. Ibid., 28.

26. G. Ronald Murphy, S.J., *The Heliand: The Saxon Gospel* (New York: Oxford University Press, 1992), 153. See also G. Ronald Murphy, S.J., *The Saxon Savior* (New York: Oxford University Press, 1989) and James E. Cathey, *The Heliand: Text and Commentary* (Morgantown: West Virginia University Press, 2002).

27. Murphy, *The Heliand,* p. 54.

28. Ibid., 55–56.

29. Ibid., 55, n. 91.

30. See also Mark 6:46, 14:32–40.

31. See Romans 6:3–10 and 1 Corinthians 1:10–16, 8:1–11, 11:17–24.

32. Howard Clark Kee, "Magic and Messiah," in *Religion, Science, and Magic: In Concert and in Conflict,* ed. Jacob Neusner, Ernest S. Frerichs, and Paul Virgil McCracken Flesher (New York: Oxford University Press, 1989), 121–141; Howard Clark Kee, *Medicine, Miracle, and Magic in New Testament Times* (Cambridge: Cambridge University Press, 1986).

33. Morton Smith, *Jesus the Magician* (San Francisco: Harper & Row, 1981).

34. Formerly attributed to Saint Bernard of Clairvaux but popularized in its present form by the French priest Claude Bernard, the Memorare is prayer number 339 in the *Raccolta,* the book of Roman Catholic prayers to which indulgences (remission of the temporal punishment due to sin) have been attached. The *Raccolta* first appeared in Rome in 1807; its earliest English translation, by Ambrose St. John, John Henry Newman's friend, appeared in 1857. Perhaps because of waning interest in the system of indulgences, the *Raccolta* is no longer being reissued in English, but in its most recent English version, edited by the Rev. Joseph P. Christopher, the Rt. Rev. Charles E. Spence, and the Rt. Rev. John F. Rowan (New York: Benziger Brothers, 1952), the Memorare carries an indulgence of three years.

35. Lancelot Andrewes, *Preces Private, The Private Devotions of Lancelot Andrewes,* trans. F. E. Brightman (London: Methuen, 1903), 79. "Christ's Cross," in *Early Irish Lyrics: Eighth to Twelfth Century,* ed. and trans. Gerard Murphy (Oxford: Clarendon Press, 1956), 33.

36. "The Deer's Cry," in *Ancient Irish Poetry,* trans. Kuno Meyer (London: Constable, 1913), 26–27.

37. Constance Padwick, *Muslim Devotions: A Study of Prayer-Manuals in Common Use* (London: SPCK, 1961), 212.

38. De corona Militis (On the military garland), 3, in *Quinti Septimii Florentis Tertulliani quae supersunt omnia,* ed. F. Oehler (Leipzig: T. O. Weigel, 1851), vol. 1, 415. Translated by Carol Zaleski.

39. Justin Martyr, First Apology, 55. *The First and Second Apologies,* trans. and ed. Leslie William Barnard (New York: Paulist Press, 1977), First Apology, chap. 55.

3. DEEPER MAGIC

1. C. S. Lewis, *The Lion, the Witch, and the Wardrobe* (London: Geoffrey Bles, 1950; New York: Macmillan, 1950; rpt. New York: HarperCollins, 1994), 178.

2. J. R. R. Tolkien, *The Return of the King: Being the Third Part of the Lord of the Rings* (London: George Allen & Unwin), 309.

3. *The Letters of J. R. R. Tolkien,* ed. Humphrey Carpenter, with Christopher Tolkien (London: George Allen & Unwin, 1981; Boston: Houghton Mifflin, 2000), 53–54.

4. William James, "Circumscription of the Topic," in *The Varieties of Religious Experience* (New York: Longmans, Green, 1902), lecture 2, 47.

5. Edward Burnett Tylor, *Primitive Culture,* vol. 2, *Religion in Primitive Culture* (London: John Murray, 1871), 461.

6. Hebrews 13:15; cf. "sacrifice of thanksgiving" (Psalms 50:14, 116:17).

7. Ṛgveda 1.1, *The Rig Veda,* trans. Wendy Doniger O'Flaherty (Harmondsworth, UK: Penguin, 1981), 99.

8. Ṛgveda 1.26.8, ibid., 100.

9. Ṛgveda 8.48.1, ibid., 134; Ṛgveda 7.23.5, trans. Ellison Banks Findly, in *Understanding Mantras,* ed. Harvey P. Alper (Albany: State University of New York Press, 1989), Ṛgveda 10.119.4, 5, *The Rig Veda,* trans. Wendy Doniger O'Flaherty, 131.

10. Ṛgveda 10.90.16, *The Rig Veda,* trans. Wendy Doniger O'Flaherty, 31.

11. Ṛgveda 10.130.3, ibid., 33.

12. Frits Staal, *Agni: The Vedic Ritual of the Fire Altar.* With C. V. Somayajipad and M. Itti Ravi Nambudiri (Berkeley, CA: Asian Humanities Press, 1983), 1:xxxiii.

13. Ibid., 2:464–65.

14. Ibid., 2:469.

15. Ibid., 2:474.

16. Bṛhad-Āranyaka Upaniṣad, trans. Robert Ernest Hume, *The Thirteen Principal Upanishads,* 2nd ed. (London and New York: Oxford University Press, 1931), 1.3.28.

17. Maitri Upaniṣad, ibid., 6.23; Katha Upaniṣad, ibid., 1.2.18.

18. *The Bhagavad-gita: Krishna's Counsel in Time of War,* trans. Barbara Stoler Miller (Toronto and New York: Bantam, 1986), book 3, 44.

19. Ibid., book 18, 144.

20. Ibid., book 10, 92, 95.

21. Diana Eck, *Darśan: Seeing the Divine Image in India* (Chambersburg, PA: Anima Books, 1981), 35. Eck quotes Pillai Lokācārya, a Vaisnavite theologian from South India.

22. Mohandas K. Gandhi, *Prayer,* ed. John Strohmeier (Berkeley, CA: Berkeley Hills Books, 2000), 77.

23. Vinoba Bhave, *Talks on the Gita,* in *Modern Indian Interpreters of the Bhagavadgita,* ed. Robert N. Minor (Albany: State University of New York Press, 1986), 126.

24. Jon D. Levenson, *The Death and Resurrection of the Beloved Son: The Transformation of Child Sacrifice in Judaism and Christianity* (New Haven and London: Yale University Press, 1993).

25. Tractate Megillah 31b, in *Jewish Worship,* by Abraham Millgram (Philadelphia: Jewish Publication Society, 1971), 85.

26. Cf. Hosea 14:3. Philip Birnbaum, trans., *Daily Prayer Book* (New York: Hebrew Publishing Company, 1977), 36.

27. *Prayers of the Eucharist: Early and Reformed,* ed. R. C. D. Jasper and G. J. Cuming (New York: Oxford University Press, 1970), 121–22.

28. Similarly, 1 Peter affirms that Christians are called to be the "kingdom of priests" spoken of in Exodus through a life of sacrificial prayer and self-giving: "Ye also, as lively stones, are built up a spiritual house, an holy priesthood, to offer up spiritual sacrifices, acceptable to God by Jesus Christ" (2:5).

29. Śāntideva, *Bodhicaryāvatāra,* trans. Vesna A. Wallace and B. Alan Wallace (Ithaca, NY: Snow Lion Publications, 1997), 34–35. John Donne, *Devotions Upon Emergent Occasions* (1645), 17.

30. Charles Williams, *He Came Down from Heaven,* chap. 6, quoted in *Charles Williams: Essential Writings in Spirituality and Theology,* ed. Charles Hefling (Cambridge, MA, and Boston: Cowley Publications, 1993), 230.

31. Dante Alighieri, *Purgatorio,* canto XI, 1–24. Translated by Carol Zaleski.

32. Christopher Bamford, "Badaliya," *Parabola* 28:1 (Spring 2003), 32–42.

33. Jane Barker, "*To My Friend* Exillus, *on his persuading me to Marry Old Damon*" in *Poetical Recreations* (London: Benjamin Crayle, 1688), part 1, 14.

34. Rose Mary Sheldon, "The Sator Rebus: An Unsolved Cryptogram?" *Cryptologia* 27:3 (July 2003).

4. THE REFUGEE

Quotations on pp. 95–97 from Bruce Wilkinson, *The Prayer of Jabez: Breaking Through to the Blessed Life* (Sisters, OR: Multnomah, 2000).

1. *The Cloud of Unknowing and Other Works,* trans. with an introduction by Clifton Wolters (Harmondsworth, UK, and New York: Penguin, 1978), 108.

2. Constance E. Padwick, *Muslim Devotions: A Study of Prayer Manuals in Common Use* (London: SPCK, 1961), 187–88.

3. *The Epic of Gilgamesh,* trans. R. Campbell Thompson (London: Luzac, 1928), 10.

4. Homer, *The Iliad,* book 15, trans. Andrew Lang, Walter Leaf, and Ernest Myers (London: Macmillan, 1882).

5. Patrul Rinpoche, *The Words of My Perfect Teacher,* trans. the Padmakara Translation Group (San Francisco: HarperCollins, 1994), 171.

6. John Bierhorst, ed., *In the Trail of the Wind: American Indian Poems and Ritual Orations* (New York: Farrar, Straus, Giroux, 1971), 29.

7. Robert Louis Stevenson, "Evening Prayer," in *Eerdmans Book of Famous Prayers,* comp. Veronica Zundel (Grand Rapids, MI: Eerdmans, 1984), 83.

8. Saint Augustine, "On the Lord's Sermon on the Mount," in *A Select Library of Nicene and Post-Nicene Fathers,* ed. Philip Schaff (New York: Christian Literature, 1886–1890), 6:38.

9. Thomas Aquinas, *Summa Theologiae,* 2a2ae83.2 (Blackfriars; New York: McGraw-Hill; London: Eyre & Spottiswoode, 1964), 53.

10. Immanuel Kant, *Religion Within the Limits of Reason Alone,* trans. T. M. Greene and Hoyt H. Hudson (New York: Harper & Row, 1960), 182–83.

11. Immanuel Kant, *Lectures on Ethics,* trans. Louis Infield (London: Methuen, 1930), 99.

12. C. S. Lewis, "Work and Prayer," in *God in the Dock: Essays on Theology and Ethics,* ed. Walter Hooper (Grand Rapids, MI: Eerdmans, 1970), 105.

13. Samuel Taylor Coleridge, in *Robinson Crusoe: An Authoritative Text; Backgrounds and Sources; Criticism,* ed. Michael Shinagel (New York and London: Norton, 1975), 289. Coleridge's text was originally published in *Literary Remains,* 1830.

14. Samuel Johnson, *Johnsonian Miscellanies,* comp. and ed. George Birkbeck Hill (Oxford: Clarendon Press, 1897), 1:vii.

15. Charles E. Pierce Jr., *The Religious Life of Samuel Johnson* (Hamden, CT: Archon Books, 1983), 9, 64.

16. Johnson, *Johnsonian Miscellanies,* 1:5.

17. Ibid., 1:7.

18. Ibid., 1:26.

19. Ibid., 1:28.

20. Ibid., 1:25–26.

21. Ibid., 1:36, 91.

22. Ibid., 1:31, 71.

23. Ibid., 1:14; Paul Johnson, *Samuel Johnson and the Life of Writing* (New York: Harcourt, Brace, Jovanovich, 1971), 112.

24. Samuel Johnson, *Johnsonian Miscellanies,* 1:20.

25. Padwick, *Muslim Devotions,* 81.

26. *The Oxford Book of Prayer,* ed. George Appleton (New York: Oxford University Press, 1985), 351–52.

27. Edward Cornplanter, "The Revelation of Handsome Lake," in *Native American Traditions: Sources and Interpretations,* ed. Sam B. Gill (Belmont, CA: Wadsworth, 1983), 146–47.

28. Ibid.

29. Translation by Philip Zaleski.

30. Oscar Wilde, *De Profundis* (New York and London: Putnam, 1905), 43, 56, 57.

31. *Alcoholics Anonymous Comes of Age: A Brief History of AA* (New York: Alcoholics Anonymous World Services, 1957), 54.

32. *Lois Remembers: Memoirs of the Co-Founder of Al-Anon and Wife of the Co-Founder of Alcoholics Anonymous* (New York: Al-Anon Family Group Headquarters, 1979), 31; *Pass It On: The Story of Bill Wilson and How the A.A. Message Reached the World* (New York: Alcoholics Anonymous World Services, 1984), 108.

33. *The Language of the Heart: Bill W.'s Grapevine Writings* (New York: The A.A. Grapevine, 1988), 277.

34. Carl Gustav Jung, letter to Père Lachat, in *Collected Works* (Princeton, NJ: Princeton University Press, 1953–), 18:683.

35. *Alcoholics Anonymous Comes of Age,* 59.

36. Ibid., 63.

37. *Pass It On,* 125.

38. Ernest Kurtz, *Not-God: A History of Alcoholics Anonymous* (Center City, MN: Hazelden Educational Services, 1979), 26.

39. *Alcoholics Anonymous: The Story of How Many Thousands of Men and Women Have Recovered from Alcoholism,* 3rd ed. (New York: Alcoholics Anonymous World Services, 1976), 68.

40. *The Language of the Heart,* 241–42.

41. *Alcoholics Anonymous Comes of Age,* 167.

42. Dick B., *The Good Book and The Big Book: A.A.'s Roots in the Bible* (Kihei, HI: Paradise Research Publications, 1995), 114.

5. THE DEVOTEE

1. David Steindl-Rast, "Praying the Great Dance," *Praying Magazine* (November–December 1996).

2. *The Rule of St. Benedict in Latin and English with Notes,* ed. Timothy Fry, O.S.B. (Collegeville, MN: The Liturgical Press, 1981), 243.

3. Thomas Merton, *The Seven Storey Mountain* (New York: Harcourt, Brace, 1948), 368.

4. Ibid., 379.

5. Jean Leclercq, *The Love of Learning and the Desire for God: A Study of Monastic Culture,* trans. Catherine Misrahi (New York: Fordham University Press, 1961, 1974), 288.

6. Adin Steinsaltz, *A Guide to Jewish Prayer* (New York: Schocken Books, 2000), 91.

7. James Joyce, *Finnegan's Wake* (New York: Viking Press, 1939), 593.

8. Michael Wolfe, *The Hadj: An American's Pilgrimage to Mecca* (New York: Atlantic Monthly Press, 1993), 64.

9. Annemarie Schimmel, *Mystical Dimensions of Islam* (Chapel Hill: University of North Carolina Press), 150.

10. Martin Lings, *A Moslem Saint of the Twentieth Century: Shaikh Ahmad al-'Alawi, His Spiritual Heritage and Legacy* (London: Allen & Unwin, 1961), 37.

11. Schimmel, *Mystical Dimensions of Islam,* 149.

12. Kabir Helminski, *The Knowing Heart: A Sufi Path of Transformation* (Boston and London: Shambhala Publications, 1999), 185–86.

13. Merton, *The Seven Storey Mountain,* 302–3.

14. Salvador Dali, "The Tragic Myth of Millet's *L'Angelus:* Paranoiac-Critical Interpretation," in *The Collected Writings of Salvador Dali,* ed. and trans. Haim Finkelstein (Cambridge and New York: Cambridge University Press, 1998), 283.

15. Ibid., 290, 294.

16. Salvador Dali, "Mystical Manifesto," in *The Collected Writings of Salvador Dali,* 364.

17. J. D. Salinger, *Franny and Zooey* (Boston: Little, Brown, 1955), 38.

18. *The Way of a Pilgrim,* trans. R. M. French (New York: Ballantine, 1974), 6.

19. Ibid., 31.

20. Ibid., 32.

21. "The Shepherd of Hermas," in *The Apostolic Fathers: Greek Texts and English Translations of Their Writings,* 2nd ed., trans. J. B. Lightfoot and J. R. Harner, ed. and rev. Michael W. Holmes (Grand Rapids, MI: Baker Book House, 1992), 491.

22. John Cassian, *Conferences,* trans. Colm Luibheid (New York: Paulist Press, 1985), 135–36.

23. Elisabeth Behr-Sigel, *The Place of the Heart: An Introduction to Orthodox Spirituality,* trans. Fr. Stephen Bigham (Torrance, CA: Oakwood Publications, 1992), 86.

24. Lev Gillet (A Monk of the Eastern Church), *The Jesus Prayer,* 2nd ed. (Crestwood, NY: St. Vladimir's Seminary Press, 1987), 46.

25. Constance E. Padwick, *Muslim Devotions: A Study of Prayer-Manuals in Common Use* (London: SPCK, 1961), 15.

26. Ignatius Brianchaninov, *On the Prayer of Jesus,* trans. Father Lazarus (Shaftesbury, UK: Element Books, 1987), 65.

27. Alfred O'Rahilly, *Father William Doyle, S.J.: A Spiritual Study* (London: Longmans, Greene, 1932), 212.

28. Ibid., 200.

29. Ibid., 202–3.

30. Salinger, *Franny and Zooey,* 37–39.

31. Padwick, *Muslim Devotions,* 94–95.

32. Ibid., 95.

33. Schimmel, *Mystical Dimensions of Islam,* 168.

34. Lings, *A Moslem Saint of the Twentieth Century,* 113.

35. Jean-Louis Michon, "The Spiritual Practices of Islam," in *Islamic Spirituality: Foundations,* ed. Seyyed Hossein Nasr (New York: Crossroad, 1987), 282.

36. Reynold Nicholson, *The Mystics of Islam* (London: Routledge and Kegan Paul, 1966 [1914]), 168.

37. *The Way of a Pilgrim,* 11; Laurel Rasplica Rodd, *Nichiren: A Biography* (Tempe: Arizona State University, 1978), 11.

38. Nikodemus of the Holy Mountain, *The Life of St. Gregory of Palamas, Archbishop of Thessalonica, the Wonderworker,* trans. St. Gregory Palamas Monastery, Hayesville, OH, http://www.orthodoxinfo.com/praxis/continualprayer.aspx.

39. Olivier Clément, *The Roots of Christian Mysticism: Text and Commentary* (New York: New City Press, 1995), 209.

40. *The Art of Prayer: An Orthodox Anthology,* comp. Igumen Chariton of Valamo, trans. Kadloubovsky and E. M. Palmer, ed. Timothy Ware (London: Faber and Faber, 1966), 83.

41. Thomas R. Kelly, *A Testament of Devotion, with a Biographical Memoir by Douglas V. Steere* (New York and London: Harper & Brothers, 1941), 3.

42. Ibid., 29–32.

43. Ibid., 36–37.

44. Ibid., 61.

45. Ibid., 38–43.

46. Brother Lawrence of the Resurrection, O.C.D., *Writings and Conversations on the Practice of the Presence of God,* ed. Conrad De Meester, O.C.D., trans. Salvatore Sciurba, O.C.D. (Washington DC: ICS Publications, 1994), 116.

47. Ibid., 53, 60.

6. THE ECSTATIC

1. Christopher Isherwood, *Ramakrishna and His Disciples* (New York: Simon & Schuster, 1959), 2.

2. *Borges at Eighty,* ed. Willis Barnstone (Bloomington: Indiana University Press, 1982), 11.

3. Ibid., 168.

4. C. S. Lewis, *Perelandra* (New York: Macmillan, 1944), 28.

5. *Sri Ramakrishna in the Eyes of Brahma and Christian Admirers,* ed. Nanda Mookerjee (Calcutta: Firma KLM Private Ltd., 1976), 1, 110, n.p.

6. Ramakrishna, *The Gospel of Sri Ramakrishna,* abridged version, trans. Swami Nikhilananda (New York: Ramakrishna-Vivekananda Center, 1980), 119, 121.

7. Ibid., 3–4.

8. Ibid., 5.

9. Ibid., 7.

10. Richard Schiffman, *Sri Ramakrisna: A Prophet for the New Age* (New York: Paragon House, 1989), 37.
11. Ibid., 38.
12. Ramakrishna, *The Gospel of Sri Ramakrishna,* 20.
13. Ibid., 22.
14. Ibid., 29.
15. Ibid., 35.
16. Ibid., 43.
17. Ibid., 48.
18. Ibid., 49–50.
19. Ibid., 59.
20. Lex Hixon, *Great Swan: Meetings with Ramakrishna* (Boston: Shambhala, 1992), viii.
21. Ramakrishna, *The Gospel of Sri Ramakrishna,* 176, 282, 378.
22. Ibid., 260, 282, 396, 419, 733.
23. Ibid., 93, 231, 373, 487.
24. Ibid., 364, 365.
25. Ibid., 505, 725.
26. Swami Saradananda, *Sri Ramakrishna, the Great Master,* 4th ed., trans. Swami Jagadananda (Madras: Sri Ramakrishna Math, 1970 [c. 1952]), 651–22.
27. June McDaniel, *The Madness of the Saints: Ecstatic Religion in Bengal* (Chicago: University of Chicago Press, 1989), 1.
28. Teresa of Ávila, *Obras completas* (Madrid: Editorial Católica, 1951–1959), *Libro de la Vida,* 4:4, 5:9, translation by Carol Zaleski.
29. Jean Leclercq, *The Love of Learning and the Desire for God: A Study of Monastic Culture,* trans. Catherine Misrahi (New York: Fordham University Press, 1961, 1974), 21–22.
30. *Libro de la Vida,* 4:9.
31. Ibid., 7:6.
32. Ibid., 28:7.
33. Ibid., 10:1.
34. Ibid., 27:2.
35. Ibid., 7:26, 29:7.
36. Ibid., 29:13.
37. Ibid., 16:1.
38. Ibid., 18:10.
39. *Castillo Interior o Las Moradas,* Moradas Sextas, V: 1, 7, translation by Carol Zaleski.
40. Vita Sackville-West, *The Eagle and the Dove: A Study in Contrasts: St. Teresa of Ávila, St. Thérèse of Lisieux* (London: M. Joseph, 1943), 48.
41. *Castillo Interior o Las Moradas,* Quartas Moradas III:11.
42. *Libro de la Vida,* 25:2.
43. Translation by Carol Zaleski.
44. Vinson Synan, *Century of the Holy Spirit: 100 Years of Pentecostal and Charismatic Renewal, 1901–2001* (Nashville: Thomas Nelson Publishers, 2001), 44.
45. James R. Goff, *Fields White unto Harvest: Charles F. Parham and the Missionary Origins of Pentecostalism* (Fayetteville: University of Arkansas Press, 1988), 67–68.
46. Ibid.

47. Synan, *Century of the Holy Spirit,* 49.

48. *Dictionary of Pentecostal and Charismatic Movements,* ed. Stanley M. Burgess and Gary B. McPhee (Grand Rapids, MI: Regency Reference Library, 1989), 781; Grant Wacker, *Heaven Below: Early Pentecostals and American Culture* (Cambridge: Harvard University Press, 2001), 231, 342, 343.

49. Goff, *Fields White unto Harvest,* 132.

50. Synan, *Century of the Holy Spirit,* 51.

51. Ibid., 55.

52. Frank Bartleman, *How Pentecost Came to Los Angeles* (Los Angeles: Frank Bartleman, 1925), 58–60.

53. A. J. Tomlinson, *The Last Great Conflict* (New York: Garland Publishing, 1985 [1913]), 211–14.

54. Synan, *Century of the Holy Spirit,* 174.

55. John L. Sherrill, *They Speak with Other Tongues* (New York: McGraw Hill, 1964), 141.

56. Cheryl Jeanne Sanders, *Saints in Exile: The Holiness-Pentecostal Experience in African American Religion and Culture* (New York: Oxford University Press, 1996), 49.

57. Veve A. Clark, Millicent Hodman, and Catrina Neiman, *The Legend of Maya Deren: A Documentary Biography and Collected Works,* dir. of photography Francine Bailey Price, general ed. Hollis Melton (New York: Anthology Film Archives/Film Culture, 1984), ix.

58. Maya Deren, *Divine Horsemen: The Living Gods of Haiti* (New Paltz, NY: McPherson, 1983, [c. 1953]), 141, 145.

59. Ibid., 253.

60. Ibid., 259.

61. Ibid., 260.

62. Ibid., 320.

63. Ibid., 248, 323.

64. Robert Musil, *The Man Without Qualities,* trans. Eithne Wilkins and Ernst Kaiser (London: Secker & Warburg, 1960), 3:112f.

65. Ibid.

66. D. H. Lawrence, *The Rainbow* (Harmondsworth, UK: Penguin, 1949 [1915]), 204–5.

67. Musil, *The Man Without Qualities,* 3:112f.

7. THE CONTEMPLATIVE

1. Richard of St. Victor, *Benjamin Major,* book 1, chap. 3, trans. Clare Kirchberger, in *Richard of Saint-Victor: Selected Writings on Contemplation* (London: Faber and Faber, 1957), 136–37.

2. *The Complete Poems of Emily Dickinson,* ed. Thomas H. Johnson (Boston: Little, Brown, 1960), 327.

3. Saint Athanasius, *The Life of Antony,* ed. Archibald Robertson, in *A Select Library of Nicene and Post-Nicene Fathers of the Christian Church,* series 2 (New York: The Christian Literature Company, 1892), 4:196.

4. Ibid.

5. Ibid.

6. Ibid., 198.
7. Ibid., 199.
8. Ibid., 200.
9. Ibid.
10. Samuel Rubenson, *The Letters of St. Antony: Monasticism and the Making of a Saint* (Minneapolis, MN: Fortress Press, 1995), 199.
11. Plato, *Phaedo* 69a, trans. Hugh Tredennick, in *The Collected Dialogues of Plato,* ed. Edith Hamilton and Huntington Cairns (New York: Pantheon Books, 1963), 51–52; Athanasius, *The Life of Antony and the Letter to Marcellinus,* trans. Robert C. Gregg (New York: Paulist Press, 1980), 7; Plato, *Phaedo* 69a, 51–52.
12. *The Cloud of Unknowing and Other Works,* trans. Clifton Wolters (Harmondsworth, UK: Penguin, 1978), 105.
13. Pseudo-Dionysius, *The Complete Works,* trans. Colm Luibheid with Paul Rorem; (New York: Paulist Press, 1987), 140–41.
14. Ibid., 135, 137.
15. *The Cloud of Unknowing,* 63.
16. Ibid., 51.
17. Ibid., 52.
18. Ibid., 60.
19. Ibid., 73.
20. Ibid., 98.
21. Ibid., 10; *The Cloud of Unknowing,* trans. Ira Progoff (New York: The Julian Press, 1957), 24.
22. M. Basil Pennington, O.C.S.O., *Centering Prayer: Renewing an Ancient Christian Prayer Form* (Garden City, NY: Image Books, 1982), 65.
23. M. Basil Pennington, O.C.S.O., *Centered Prayer: The Way of Centering Prayer* (Garden City, NY: Image, 1988), 92.
24. Guy Gauchet, *The Story of a Life: St. Thérèse of Lisieux* (San Francisco: HarperSanFrancisco, 1987), 18.
25. P. T. Rohrbach, "St. Thérèse of Lisieux," in *The New Catholic Encyclopedia,* 2nd ed. (New York: Thomson Gale, 2003), 13:938.
26. Gaucher, *The Story of a Life,* 67.
27. Dorothy Day, *Thérèse* (Springfield, IL: Templegate, 1979), 110.
28. Saint Thérèse of Lisieux, *Story of a Soul: The Autobiography of St. Thérèse of Lisieux,* trans. John Clarke, O.C.D., 3rd ed. (Washington, DC: ICS Publications, 1976), 277.
29. Ibid., 194.
30. Gauchet, *The Story of a Life,* 51; Saint Thérèse of Lisieux, *Story of a Soul,* 276.
31. Ibid., 195–96.
32. Ibid., 196.
33. Jean-François Six, *Light of the Night: The Last Eighteen Months in the Life of Thérèse of Lisieux* (Notre Dame, IN: University of Notre Dame Press, 1998), 104.
34. Plato, *Meno* 86b., trans. W. K. C. Guthrie, in *The Collected Dialogues of Plato,* 371; Plato, *Phaedo* 79d, trans. Hugh Tredennick, 62–63, 64.
35. Pierre Hadot, *Philosophy as a Way of Life: Spiritual Exercises from Socrates to Foucault,* ed. Arnold I. Davidson, trans. Michael Chase (Oxford and New York: Blackwell, 1995), 84.
36. Ibid., 130.

37. Ibid., 131, 133.

38. Saint Nicephorus the Solitary, "A Most Profitable Discourse on Sobriety and the Guarding of the Heart," in *Writings from the Philokalia on Prayer of the Heart,* trans. E. Kabloubovsky and G. E. H. Palmer (London: Faber and Faber, 1973), 31.

39. Jean-Pierre de Caussade, *Abandonment to Divine Providence,* trans. John Beevers (Garden City, NY: Image, 1975), 30, 50–51.

40. Ibid., 28.

41. Ibid., 50–51, 112.

42. T. M. P. Mahadevan, *Ramana Maharshi: The Sage of Arunacala* (London: George Allen & Unwin, 1977), 17.

43. Ramana Maharshi, *The Spiritual Teaching of Ramana Maharshi,* foreword by C. G. Jung (Boston: Shambhala, 1988), xiii–xiv.

44. W. Somerset Maugham, *The Razor's Edge* (Harmondsworth, UK: Penguin, 1984, [c. 1943, 1944]), 273–74.

45. *Be as You Are: The Teachings of Sri Ramana Maharshi,* ed. David Godman (London: Arkana, 1985), 107.

46. Ibid., 54.

47. Paul Brunton, *A Search in Secret India* (New York: Dutton, 1935), 140–41.

48. Ibid., 159–60.

49. Ibid., 161.

50. Saint Athanasius, *The Life of Antony,* 200; Mahadevan, *Ramana Maharshi: The Sage of Arunacala,* 76.

51. Alfred North Whitehead, *Process and Reality: An Essay in Cosmology* (Cambridge: Cambridge University Press, 1929), 450.

52. Daisetz Teitaro Suzuki, *Zen and Japanese Culture* (Princeton, NJ: Princeton University Press, 1970 [c. 1959]), 220.

53. Bashō haikus are translated by Philip Zaleski.

54. Suzuki, *Zen and Japanese Culture,* 228–29.

55. Gerard Manley Hopkins, *Sermons and Devotional Writings,* ed. Christopher Devlin (London and New York: Oxford University Press, 1959), 239.

56. Ibid.

57. Gerard Manley Hopkins, *The Journals and Papers of Gerard Manley Hopkins,* ed. Humphrey House and Graham Storey (Oxford: Oxford University Press, 1959), 289.

58. Hopkins, *Sermons and Devotional Writings,* 129.

Part III. The Land of Spices

T. S. Eliot, "Tradition and the Individual Talent," in *Selected Prose of T. S. Eliot,* ed. Frank Kermode (New York: Harcourt, Brace, Jovanovich; Farrar, Straus, Giroux, 1975), 38.

8. PRAYER AND TRADITION

1. Alexander Carmichael, *Carmina Gadelica: Hymns and Incantations* (Edinburgh: Oliver and Boyd, 1928–), 4:xxx–xxxi.

2. Ibid., 1:xxxiii.

3. Ibid., 1:xxi.
4. Ibid., 1:231.
5. Ibid., 2:15.
6. Ibid., 3:291.
7. Ibid., 3:274.
8. Ibid., 1:272.
9. Mrs. Sinclair Stevenson, *The Rites of the Twice-Born* (London: H. Milford, Oxford University Press, 1920), 227.
10. *The Book of Daily Prayers for Every Day in the Year: According to the Custom of the German and Polish Jews,* ed. Isaac Leeser (Philadelphia: C. Sherman, 1848), 158.
11. *Hebrew-English Edition of the Babylonian Talmud: Berakoth,* trans. Maurice Simon, ed. Isadore Epstein (London: Soncino Press, 1960), Tractate Berakoth, 35a.
12. *The Book of Daily Prayers for Every Day in the Year,* 219.
13. Rabbi Binyomin Forst, *The Laws of B'rachos.* With Rabbi Aaron D. Twerski (New York: Mesorah Publications, 1990), 276.
14. Thomas Merton, *The Seven Storey Mountain,* 36–37.
15. T. S. Eliot, *Christianity and Culture: The Idea of a Christian Society and Notes Towards the Definition of Culture* (New York: Harcourt, Brace, 1968), 101.
16. Otto Georg von Simson, *The Gothic Cathedral: Origins of the Gothic Architecture and the Medieval Concept of Order,* 3rd ed. (Princeton, NJ: Princeton University Press, 1988), 15.
17. Black Elk, *The Sacred Pipe: Black Elk's Account of the Seven Rites of the Oglala Sioux,* comp. and ed. Joseph Epes Brown (Norman: University of Oklahoma Press, 1953), 75.
18. Thomas E. Mails, *Sundancing at Rosebud and Pine Ridge* (Sioux Falls, SD: Center for Western Studies, 1978), 13.
19. Black Elk, *The Sacred Pipe,* 69–70.
20. Ibid.
21. Ibid., 85, 87, 91.
22. Leonid Ouspensky and Vladimir Lossky, *The Meaning of Icons,* trans. G. E. H. Palmer and E. Kadloubovsky (Crestwood, NY: St. Vladimir's Seminary Press, 1989), 72.
23. Mahmoud Zibawi, *The Icon: Its Meaning and History* (Collegeville, MN: Liturgical Press, 1993), 19.
24. Pavel Florensky, *Iconostasis,* trans. Donald Sheehan and Olga Andrejev (Crestwood, NY: St. Vladimir's Seminary Press, 1996), 71–72.
25. Ibid., 92.
26. Dionysios of Fourna, *The Painter's Manual of Dionysios of Fourna,* trans. Paul Hetherington (Torrance, CA: Oakwood Publications, 1989), 1–2.
27. Florensky, *Iconostasis,* 97.
28. *The Prayers of Man: From Primitive Peoples to the Present,* comp. Alfonso M. di Nola, ed. Patrick O'Connor (New York: Ivan Obolensky, 1961), 78.
29. John Henry Newman, "University Preaching," in *The Idea of a University* (London: Longmans, Green, 1907), 406–7.
30. Robert Alter, "The Poetry of the Bible: The Vision Behind the Verse," *The New Republic* 193 (September 30, 1985): 29.
31. See Dewey D. Wallace Jr., "Theocracy," in *The Encyclopedia of Religion,* Mircea

Eliade, editor-in-chief (New York: Macmillan, 1987). Wallace adds to this typology a fourth category, "eschatological theocracy," which strikes us as better subsumed under the theocracy of the law.

32. James Henry Breasted, *A History of the Ancient Egyptians* (London: Smith, Elder, 1912), 273–77.

9. PRAYER AND THE MODERN ARTS

1. Alexander Carmichael, *Carmina Gadelica: Hymns and Incantations* (Edinburgh: Oliver and Boyd, 1928–), 3:274, 4:xxxi.

2. Kathleen Raine, introduction to *The Fairy-Faith in Celtic Countries,* by W. Y. Evans-Wentz (Gerards Cross, UK: Colin Smythe, 1977), xviii.

3. Translation by Carol Zaleski.

4. Giorgio Vasari, *Lives of the Artists: A Selection,* trans. George Bull (Harmondsworth, UK: Penguin, 1965), 58.

5. Ibid., 205–6.

6. Ibid., 204.

7. Saint Bonaventure, *Life of Francis,* in *Bonaventure,* trans. Ewert Cousins (New York: Paulist Press, 1978), 189.

8. Roger Lipsey, *An Art of Our Own: The Spiritual in Twentieth-Century Art* (Boston and Shaftesbury, UK: Shambhala, 1988), 60. Our discussion of modern art owes much to this pioneering work.

9. Alexander Liberman, *The Artist in His Studio* (New York: Viking Press, 1960), 44.

10. Wassily Kandinsky, "Reminiscences," in *Modern Artists on Art: Ten Unabridged Essays,* ed. Robert L. Herbert (Englewood Cliffs, NJ: Prentice-Hall, 1965), 30.

11. Ibid., 32.

12. Ibid., 32, 33, 41, 42.

13. Ibid., 35.

14. Pontus Hulten, Natalia Dumitresco, and Alexandre Istrati, *Brancusi* (New York: Abrams, 1987), 68; Liberman, *The Artist in His Studio,* 48.

15. Lipsey, *An Art of Our Own,* 228.

16. Ibid., 236.

17. Ibid., 246.

18. Minor White, *Rites and Passages: His Photographs Accompanied by Excerpts from His Letters and Diaries* (Millerton, NY: Aperture, 1978), 5.

19. Ibid., 20–21.

20. Minor White, *Octave of Prayer* (New York: Aperture, 1972), 18, 20.

21. Ibid., 22.

22. Evelyn M. Simpson, *A Study of the Prose Works of John Donne* (Oxford: Clarendon Press, 1924), 232.

23. John Donne, *John Donne and the Theology of Language,* ed. P. G. Stanwood and Heather Ross Asala (Columbia: University of Missouri Press, 1986), 26, 47.

24. Ibid., 26.

25. Ibid., 27.

26. Emily Dickinson, *The Complete Poems of Emily Dickinson,* ed. Thomas H. Johnson (Boston: Little, Brown, 1960), 210.

27. *An Emily Dickinson Encyclopedia,* ed. Jane Donahue Eberwein (Westport, CT: Greenwood Press, 1998), 237; Dickinson, *The Complete Poems,* 230.

28. Ibid., 709.

29. Richard Sewall, *The Life of Emily Dickinson* (New York: Farrar, Straus, Giroux, 1974), 600.

30. Dickinson, *The Complete Poems,* 277.

31. Ibid., 602.

32. Ibid., 616, 658.

33. Ibid., 148.

34. Ibid., 503.

35. Ibid., 475–76.

36. Walt Whitman, *Complete Poetry and Selected Prose,* ed. James E. Miller Jr. (Boston: Houghton Mifflin, 1959), 290–91.

37. Ibid., 25ff.

38. Ibid., 42.

39. Ibid., 295–96.

40. Ibid.

41. Ibid.

42. Richard Ellmann, *The Identity of Yeats* (New York: Oxford University Press, 1954), 305.

43. Ibid., 55.

44. William Butler Yeats, *The Wind Among the Reeds* (London: E. Mathews, 1899), 57.

45. Norman A. Jeffares, *A Commentary on the Collected Poems of W. B. Yeats* (Stanford, CA: Stanford University Press, 1968), 82.

46. William Butler Yeats, *The Collected Poems of W. B. Yeats* (New York: Macmillan, 1933,) 43–44, 78–79; William Butler Yeats, *The Poems,* ed. Richard J. Finneran (New York: Macmillan, 1989), 282.

47. Peter Ackroyd, *T. S. Eliot: A Life* (New York: Simon & Schuster, 1984), 161.

48. B. C. Southam, *A Guide to the Selected Poems of T. S. Eliot* (San Diego: Harcourt Brace, 1996), 219.

49. T. S. Eliot, *The Sacred Wood: Essays on Poetry and Criticism,* 2nd ed. (London: Methuen, 1928), 49.

50. Georgia Ronan Crampton, ed., *The Shewings of Julian of Norwich* (Kalamazoo, MI: Medieval Institute Publications, 1994), 72.

51. Rainer Maria Rilke, *The Book of Hours,* in *Rainer Maria Rilke: Selected Works,* trans. J. B. Leishman (New York: New Directions, 1967), 2:28.

52. *Tagebücher aus der Frühzeit (1899–1902),* eds. Ruth Rilke Sieber and Carl Sieber (Leipzig: Insel Verlag, 1942), quoted in translator's introduction, Rainer Maria Rilke, *The Book of Hours: Prayers to a Lowly God,* trans. Annemarie S. Kidder (Evanston, IL: Northwestern University Press, 2001), x.

53. Rabindranath Tagore, *Lectures and Addresses,* comp. Anthony X. Soares (Calcutta: Macmillan, 1970), 100; William Butler Yeats, introduction to *Gitanjali,* by Rabindranath Tagore (London: Macmillan, 1913), xiii–xiv.

54. Tagore, *Gitanjali,* 3.

55. A. A. Milne, *When We Were Very Young* (London: Methuen, 1924), 99–100.

10. PRAYER AND THE PUBLIC SQUARE

1. Mohandas K. Gandhi in *Young India* (January 23, 1930), quoted in Mohandas K. Gandhi, *Prayer,* ed. John Strohmeier (Berkeley, CA: Berkeley Hills Books, 2000), 23.

2. Franklin Graham, "2001 Inaugural Invocation," http://www.wheaton.edu/bgc/archives/inaugural07.htm; Alan M. Dershowitz, "Bush Starts Off by Defying the Constitution," *Los Angeles Times* (January 24, 2001): B9.

3. Robert M. Barr, press release, May 18, 1999, www.religioustolerance.org/boy_arm3.htm.

4. James Madison, *Memorial and Remonstrance Against Religious Assessments* (1785), in Arlin M. Adams, Charles J. Emmerich, and Warren E. Burger, *A Nation Dedicated to Religious Liberty: The Constitutional Heritage of the Religion Clauses* (Philadelphia: University of Pennsylvania Press, 1990), 104.

5. "Engel et al. v. Vitale et al.," in *Religion and Education in America: A Documentary History,* ed. Herbert M. Kliebard (Scranton, PA: International Textbook Company, 1969), 198.

6. Robert S. Alley, *School Prayer: The Court, the Congress, and the First Amendment* (Buffalo: Prometheus Books, 1994), 109–10.

7. Edward Keynes, *The Courts vs. Congress: Prayer, Busing, and Abortion.* With Randall K. Miller (Durham, NC, and London: Duke University Press, 1989), 184.

8. See www.law.umkc.edu/faculty/projects/ftrials/conlaw/marsh.html/.

9. John Leland, "Tension in a Michigan City over Muslims' Call to Prayer," *New York Times,* May 5, 2004.

10. Shahab Ahmed, "Cities Should Treat All Religions the Same; Muslim Broadcasts Are Just Like Church Bells," *Detroit News,* May 2, 2004.

11. Mechtild of Magdeburg, *The Revelations of Mechtild of Magdeburg, or, The Flowing Light of the Godhead,* trans. Lucy Menzies (London: Longmans, Green, 1953), 136.

12. LaTonya Taylor, "The Church of O," *Christianity Today* 46:4 (April 1, 2002): 38.

13. From transcript of Yankee Stadium "Prayer for America," http://www.cat41.org/News/Archives/BenkeResources/YSTranscript.txt.

14. Concordia Theological Seminary–Fort Wayne Pastoral Statement December 14, 2001, http://crisisinthelcms.org/ctsresponse.htm.

15. LCMS News #98–87. November 20, 1998, quoted in http://www.crisisinthelcms.org/lcmsnews11.20.98.htm.

16. Rev. Wallace Schulz, letter to Dr. Raymond L. Hartwig, http://crisisinthelcms.org/lettertohartwig.htm.

17. Congregation for the Doctrine of the Faith, "Letter to the Bishops of the Catholic Church on Some Aspects of Christian Meditation," http://www.ewtn.com/library/CURIA/CDFMED.HTM.

18. Transcript of Benke segment from PBS *Frontline,* September 3, 2002, http://crisisinthelcms.org/frontline.htm.

19. Pope John Paul II, Address in Basilica of St. Francis, October 27, 1986, http://www.vatican.va/holy_father/john_paul_ii/speeches/1986/october/documents/hf_jp-ii_spe_19861027_prayer-peace-assisi-final_en.html; Pope John Paul II, Address in Basilica of St. Mary of the Angels, http://www.vatican.va/holy_father/john_paul_ii/speeches/1986/october/documents/hf_jp-ii_spe_19861027_prayer-peace-assisi_en.html.

20. Ibid.

11. PRAYER AND HEALING

1. Clyde Kluckhohn and Leland C. Wyman, *An Introduction to Navaho Chant Practice with an Account of the Behaviors Observed in Four Chants. Memoirs of the American Museum of Natural History* 53; supplement to *American Anthropologist* 42:2, 2 (Menasha, WI: American Anthropological Association, 1940), 13.

2. Washington Matthews, *The Night Chant: A Navaho Ceremony.* Publications of the Hyde Southwestern Expedition, May 1902. *Memoirs of the American Museum of Natural History,* Whole Series vol. 6, Anthropology Series vol. 5 (New York: Knickerbocker Press, 1902). Another early ethnological study is that of James Stevenson, *Ceremonial of Hasjelti Dailijis and Mythical Sand Painting of the Navajo Indians.* Bureau of American Ethnology Eighth Annual Report, 1886–1887 (Washington, DC: U.S. Government Printing Office, 1891).

3. In addition to the works already mentioned, see Gladys Reichard, *Prayer: The Compulsive Word* (New York: J. J. Augustin, 1944) and *Navajo Religion,* 2 vols. (New York: Pantheon Books, 1950); Leland C. Wyman, ed., *Beautyway: A Navaho Ceremonial* (New York: Pantheon Books, 1957); Charlotte J. Frisbie, ed., *Southwestern Indian Ritual Drama* (Albuquerque: University of New Mexico Press, 1980); Sam D. Gill, *Sacred Words: A Study of Navajo Religion and Prayer* (Westport, CT, and London: Greenwood Press, 1981); Katherine Spencer Halpern and Susan Brown McGreevy, *Washington Matthews: Studies of Navajo Culture, 1880–1894* (Albuquerque: University of New Mexico Press, 1997); James C. Faris, *The Nightway: A History and a History of Documentation of a Navajo Ceremonial* (Albuquerque: University of New Mexico Press, 1990); *Navajo Blessingway Singer: The Autobiography of Frank Mitchell, 1881–1967,* ed. Charlotte J. Frisbie and David P. McAllester (Albuquerque: University of New Mexico Press, 1978).

4. Wade Davies, *Healing Ways: Navajo Health Care in the Twentieth Century* (Albuquerque: University of New Mexico Press, 2001), x.

5. This summary follows the account of Holyway ceremonials provided by Leland C. Wyman in *Beautyway,* 1–39; and Leland C. Wyman, "Navajo Ceremonial System," in *Handbook of North American Indians,* ed. Alfonso Ortiz (Washington, DC: Smithsonian Institution, 1983), 10:536–57.

6. Matthews, *The Night Chant,* 73.

7. Ibid., 144.

8. Ibid., 143–45.

9. Washington Matthews, *Navaho Legends* (Boston: Houghton Mifflin, 1897), 42.

10. Franc Johnson Newcomb, *Hosteen Klah: Navaho Medicine Man and Sand Painter* (Norman, OK, and London: University of Oklahoma Press, 1964).

11. For an introduction to sources and scholarship on the metaphysical healing movement, see Roy M. Anker, *Self-Help and Popular Religion in Early American Culture: An Interpretive Guide* (Westport, CT: Greenwood Press, 1999) and *Self-Help and Popular Religion in Modern American Culture: An Interpretive Guide* (Westport, CT: Greenwood Press, 1999).

12. William James, "The Religion of Healthy-Mindedness," in *The Varieties of Religious Experience* (New York: Longmans, Green, 1902), lecture 4, 95.

13. Charles Fillmore, *Teach Us to Pray* (Kansas City, MO: Unity School of Christianity, 1941), 184, 188.

14. "Prayer, I," *The Quimby Manuscripts,* ed. Horatio Dresser (New York: Crowell, 1921), 205.

15. Ibid., 206.

16. Mary Baker Eddy, *Christian Healing: A Sermon Delivered at Boston* (Boston: The First Church of Christ, Scientist, 1914), 9.

17. Mary Baker G. Eddy, *Science and Health with Key to the Scriptures* (Boston: The First Church of Christ, Scientist, 1875, 1906; copyright renewed 1934), 2.

18. Ibid., 16–17.

19. Charles Fillmore, *Atom-Smashing Power of Mind* (Unity Village, MO: Unity Books, 1949), 26.

20. Nona L. Brooks, *Mysteries* (St. Louis, MO: Divine Science Federation, 1924), 126.

12. THE EFFICACY OF PRAYER

1. Fred Rebell [pseud.], *Escape to the Sea: The Log of a Homemade Sailor* (New York: Dodd, Mead, 1939), 55.

2. Ibid., 50.

3. Ibid., 52, 170.

4. Ibid., 174–75.

5. Ibid., 212.

6. Elesha Coffman, "Maggie, the Dragon Slayer?" *Christian History* 20:4 (Nov 2001): 25; Karen A. Winstead, ed. and trans., *Chaste Passions: Medieval English Virgin Martyr Legends* (Ithaca, NY, and London: Cornell University Press, 2000), 93.

7. Augustine Baker, *Holy wisdom: or, Directions for the prayer of contemplation: extracted out of more than forty treatises by the Ven. F. Augustine Baker/methodically digested by Serenus Cressy; and now edited from the Douay ed. of 1657 by Abbot Sweeney* (London: Burns & Oates; New York: Benziger, 1911[?]), 176–77; Athanasius Allanson, O.S.B., *Biography of the English Benedictines,* comp. General Chapter of the English Benedictines 1842, ed. Anselm Cramer, O.S.B., and Sue Goodwill. Saint Laurence Papers IV (Ampleforth, UK: Ampleforth Abbey Press, 1999), 33.

8. Saint Gregory of Nyssa, *The Lord's Prayer,* trans. Hilda C. Graef. Ancient Christian Writers 18 (Westminster, MD: Newman Press; London: Longmans, Green, 1954), 24–25.

9. Bhadantācariya Buddhaghosa, *The Path of Purification,* trans. Bhikkhu Ñyānamoli (Berkeley, CA, and London: Shambhala, 1976), 1:417.

10. "Udāna," in *The Heart of Buddhist Meditation,* by Nyanaponika Thera (New York: Samuel Weiser, 1969), 152; Dīgha Nikāya 22, the "Mahā-Sattipatthāna-Sutta" (Greater Discourse on the Setting Up of Mindfulness), ibid., 124.

11. Ibid., 117.

12. Ibid., 40–41.

13. Mihaly Csikszentmihalyi, *Flow: The Psychology of Optimal Experience* (New York: Harper & Row, 1990). See also Gene Quarrick, *Our Sweetest Hours: Recreation and the Mental State of Absorption* (Jefferson, NC: McFarland, 1989).

14. Edward Conze, *Buddhist Meditation* (London: George Allen & Unwin, 1956), 38–39.

15. Kenneth L. Woodward, *Making Saints: How the Catholic Church Determines Who Becomes a Saint, Who Doesn't, and Why* (New York: Simon & Schuster, 1990), 200.

16. Sir Francis Galton, *Inquiries into Human Faculty and Its Development* (London: Macmillan, 1883), 294.

17. William F. Parker, *Prayer Can Change Your Life: Experiments and Techniques in Prayer Therapy* (Englewood, NJ: Prentice-Hall, 1957), ix, 34–35.

18. Herbert Benson, *The Relaxation Response* (New York: William Morrow, 1975) and *Beyond the Relaxation Response* (New York: Times Books, 1984); Patricia Carrington, *Freedom in Meditation,* 2nd ed. (Kendall Park, NJ: Pace Educational Systems, 1984); Jon Kabat-Zinn, *Wherever You Go, There You Are: Mindfulness Meditation in Everyday Life* (New York: Hyperion, 1994) and *Full Catastrophe Living: Using the Wisdom of Your Body and Mind to Face Stress, Pain, and Illness* (New York: Delacorte Press, 1990); for a detailed overview of meditation studies, see Michael Murphy and Steven Donovan, *The Physical and Psychological Effects of Meditation: A Review of Contemporary Research with a Comprehensive Bibliography 1931–1996,* 2nd ed., ed. Eugene Taylor (Sausalito, CA: The Institute of Noetic Sciences, 1999).

19. Larry Dossey, *Healing Words: The Power of Prayer and the Practice of Medicine* (San Francisco: HarperSanFrancisco, 1993), 184.

20. Nicholas Humphrey, "The Power of Prayer," *The Skeptical Inquirer* 24, 3 (May 2000): 61.

21. Franklin Loehr, *The Power of Prayer on Plants* (Garden City, NY: Doubleday, 1959), 139–140.

22. R. P. Sloan, E. Bagiella, and T. Powell, "Religion, Spirituality, and Medicine," *The Lancet* 353, 9153 (February 20, 1999): 664–67.

13. THE MYSTERY OF PRAYER

1. Samuel Taylor Coleridge, *Aids to Reflection,* Aphorism IX.

2. Izaak Walton, *The Life of Mr. George Herbert* (1670).

3. W. H. Auden, *George Herbert,* comp. W. H. Auden (Harmondsworth, UK: Penguin, 1973), 7.

4. Ibid.

5. George Herbert, *The Country Parson; The Temple,* ed. John N. Wall, Jr. (New York: Paulist Press, 1981), 60–61, 87.

Index

Note: Page numbers in italics refer to illustrations.